Cities Back from the Edge

Cities Back from the Edge

New Life for Downtown

ROBERTA BRANDES GRATZ

WITH

NORMAN MINTZ

PRESERVATION
PRESS

JOHN WILEY & SONS, INC.

New York • Chichester • Weinheim • Brisbane • Singapore • Toronto

Published by John Wiley & Sons, Inc.

Published simultaneously in Canada.

This publication is designed to provide accurate and authoritative information in
regard to the subject matter covered. It is sold with the understanding that the
publisher is not engaged in rendering professional services. If professional advice or
other expert assistance is required, the services of a competent professional person
should be sought.

Book design by Tenth Avenue Editions, Inc.
for John Wiley & Sons, Inc.

Library of Congress Cataloging-in-Publication Data:
Gratz, Roberta Brandes.
    Cities back from the edge : new life for downtown / Roberta
Brandes Gratz with Norman Mintz.
        p.   cm.
    Includes index.
    ISBN 0-471-14417-7 (cloth : alk. paper)
    1. Urban renewal–United States.   2. Central business districts-
-United States.   3. Urban policy–United States.   I. Mintz, Norman.
II. Title.
HT175.G67   1998
307.3'416'9973–dc21   97-45916

Printed in the United States of America.

10 9 8 7 6 5 4 3

For Rebecca, Corey, Laura, Jon, and Halina.
If all future generations are like them,
the world will be in good shape.

CONTENTS

ACKNOWLEDGMENTS

The ideas of many people have been incorporated into this book. Throughout this effort, I have tested assumptions, sought different opinions, and used challenges to rethink, modify, or sharpen the conclusions contained herein.

I am particularly indebted to Ron Shiffman, Richard Rabinowitz, Donovan Rypkema, Constance Beaumont, Kennedy Smith, and Margot Wellington. Their understanding of the issues and insights into complex dilemmas has had an enormous impact on my thinking. They have never said "no" to my endless requests to brainstorm and have given generously of their time to help think through problems and issues. Without them this book would be considerably diminished.

Since I was first introduced to her when I began work on *The Living City* more than 20 years ago, Jane Jacobs has been my most valuable resource, inspiration, and mentor. She has encouraged and challenged me, giving me new insights in every conversation. Time and the continuing mistakes that undermine our cities underscore the wisdom of her teaching. The numbers of people fighting for the principles she teaches grows daily. That bodes well for the future of our cities. Her courage to stand firm outside the mainstream is a constant source of strength.

An important assist for this endeavor was provided by Joan Davidson and her Furthermore Foundation, a rare but valuable support for publications that might otherwise not be realized. A grant from the Surdna Foundation provided early support for research on transportation issues, and a grant from the Corning Foundation provided support for travel research.

I am particularly grateful to have a conducive, phoneless work-space in The Writers Room, an urban writers' colony in Greenwich Village that is unique to New York. My friends and room buddies, Nancy Milford, Shelby White, and Lois Gould, have provided critical moral support, warm friendship, and unquestioning confidence. Only other writers can understand the ups and downs of the book writing process.

Special thanks are due to Joan Tally, Nina Rappaport, and Susan DeVries for research and administrative assistance at various times. Louis Facundo has done a masterful job illustrating each chapter and Ignacio Ciocchini has saved us from a technological meltdown on many occasions. Norman's colleagues at the Grand Central Partnership, especially Dan Biederman and Dan Pisark, have been supportive throughout. All photographs not specifically credited were taken by Norman Mintz.

A number of people have read and commented on sections of this manuscript, providing invaluable criticism and encouragement. Longtime friend and former *New York Post* colleague Anthony Mancini deserves a special thanks for help above and beyond the call of friendship. I am particularly grateful to readers Thomas J. Schwarz, Steve Davies, William Josephson, Hooper Brooks, Eliot Asinof, Don Forst, and Victor Navasky. This manuscript has been through the hands of three helpful editors: Buckley Jepson, Jan Cigliano, and Amanda Miller. Each has added a new dimension.

Scores of people to whom we are grateful are quoted throughout so their names to do not appear here. We wish to thank the following people who, in ways small and large, have been helpful but are not quoted: Nancy Cooperstein Charney, Laurie Beckelman, Alexia Lalli, Lynda Kaplan, Amy Waterman, Carol Biderman, Burt Biderman, Hannah Evans, Petr Stepanek, William Moody, Kevin Milstead, Larry Lund, Aaron Rose, Margot Gayle, Ken Narva, Dan Corman, Frank Addio, Ken Greenberg, Judith Corbett, Rick Cole, Judith Salomon, Jerry Weiss, Laura Skaggs, Robert Ganz, Rich Ganz, John Shapiro, Sarah King Reinecker, David Sweeney, Judy Owens, Valecia Crisafulli, Margaret Saliske, Carole Clark, Ted Marks, Patricia Seiter, Jody Boese, Mary Jukuri, Kathleen Wendler, Mathew Bauer, Bill Purcell, Josh Bloom, Eliot Sklar, Kim Richards, Helise Benjamin, Karen Sawyer, Jim Stillwell, Barbara Swanda, Paul Levy, Martin McDermitt, Betty Stoltz, Tom Carrol, William Mosher, Alan Boss, Philip Morris, Henry Beuhl, Gwen Howard, Randy Harris, Jane Thompson, George Williams, Rosemary Doute, Hilary Baum, Ted Spitzer, Marsha Morgan, Carol Clark, Antonia Mitman, Rich Bradley, Brian Williams, Amanda West, Ronald T. Bailey, Eldon Scott, Elise Johnson-Schmidt, Arnold Chase, Kevin Geoghan, Chris Lincoln, David Sampson, Ed McMahon, Evan Janovic, Nancy Bisignani, Kim Stahlman, Kathy Kahng, Steve Facey, Tony Wood, and Judy Coyne Becker.

Above all, unending gratitude goes to Donald Gratz and Melanie Mintz for sharing our passionate interest in all that is in these pages, for enjoying the exploration of new places critical to understanding what works and what doesn't work, and for offering observations and insights that found their way onto the pages of this book.

March 1998

*I feel the hints, the clues, the
whisper of a new time coming.*
—Norman Mailer, l956 column, *The Village Voice*

INTRODUCTION

Is downtown dead? Can it live again? Most accepted rules of thumb about downtown are wrong. About why it died—and how to bring it back. About why retail and manufacturing left—and how to bring them back. About what constitutes rebirth—and how to make it happen. Zoning, building and fire codes, traffic, parking, signage standards, market strategies, financial formulas, and economic development strategies tend to discourage or prevent the right things from happening and guarantee that the wrong things will. Doing it right today and tomorrow means shattering the rules of yesterday—especially the rules of city planning and transportation—that persist today.

This does not mean breaking or eliminating rules for the sake of it. High-level-official advocacy of eliminating rules usually means making it easier for more of the wrong things to happen in a bigger way. Instead, institutionalized thinking must be dislodged.

Positive change and sustainable growth are occurring in many American downtowns, neighborhood commercial streets, Main Streets, and big city business districts. From New York's Corning, to Michigan's Holland, to California's Pasadena, and beyond, rebirth is clear. The list is extensive, but this good news is not acknowledged as significant in official circles of influ-

*Opposite left: Corning, New York:
Market Street streetscape.*

*Opposite right: Holland, Michigan:
Eighth Street streetscape.*

*Above: Pasadena, California: Colorado
Boulevard streetscape. Photo: John Andrews.*

ence. Worse, the new, positive downtown life identified in this book is often dismissed by experts as, at best, singular or unique and, at worst, meaningless. We disagree. The public values the innovative change spotlighted in this book. People defying conventional practice are invariably the catalysts. In fact, where citizen initiatives or resistance to official oversized plans occur are precisely the places where positive rebirth takes place. Positive public response fuels gradual expansion. Experts miss it entirely, diagnose it wrongly, or acknowledge it belatedly...and reluctantly. The lessons are lost or purposely ignored.

Some downtowns have, in their own ways, grown more exciting, from Miami Beach to Denver, from Portland, Oregon, to Portland, Maine, from Boston to Savannah. Others have just been rebuilt, but not reborn, from Indianapolis to Charlotte, North Carolina, from St. Louis to Little Rock, from Cleveland to Scranton, from Detroit to Atlanta. This book illustrates the difference between those rebuilt and reborn, between what we identify as Project Planning and Urban Husbandry.

The ones rebuilt, but not reborn, have done so according to expensive plans, bankers' plans, planners' plans, politicians' plans, developers' plans—all Project Plans. The result is a collection of expensive, big activity places—tourist attractions—connected to each other and the suburbs by a massive auto-based network. When the elusive goal is merely tourism, efficiency, and big copycat civic projects, little real energy and downtown life follows, just single-activity places. The complex, multidimensional urban fabric has been effectively replaced. A collection of visitor attractions does not add up to a city.

The places that have become more exciting have done so, most often, despite conventional plans, with modest public investment and through the catalytic efforts of creative citizens. We call this Urban Husbandry. When the rules of the excessive visions and overblown plans have been broken or ignored, new life, excitement, and the out-of-the-ordinary occur. New life spreads to adjacent areas where the cycle can repeat itself organically. The urban fabric is renewed.

MAIN STREET RULES, NOT MAINSTREAM RULES

Some city planners and elected officials erroneously insist that anything happening is better than nothing. Headline-grabbing civic projects, from big cultural centers to new stadiums, always requiring huge capital investments that cost taxpayers dearly, detract attention from complicated, fundamental difficulties. *Convention centers, stadiums, aquariums, cultural centers, enclosed malls—these are about politics and development profitable for a few, not about developing local economies, enlivening downtowns, or stimulating revitalization. Downtowns compete for these headline-grabbing, budget-straining projects but overlook the actual, complex cities in which they sit.*

The list is always familiar, although some schemes drop out of favor as their exaggerated promise fades (remember the rush on festival market-places?) and new ones are hyped. Aquariums are recent favorites. Stadiums are a current craze. Convention centers are long-standing ones. Gambling casinos are the most deceptive recent attraction. Entertainment complexes are a current magic bullet. Enclosed downtown malls, endless-ly popular, are a poor urban application of a suburban formula or a seman-tic replacement for festival marketplaces. Easily, all of these Project Plans still add up to No Place. No economic diversification and growth. No expan-sion of the local economy. No meaningful opportunity. No excitement. No sidewalk bustle. No serendipity. No intermingling. No street theater. No people contact. No added residential population. No informal gathering or people-watching. No complexity that should distinguish a downtown. No life, except during scheduled events or at a limited site. The authentic character of place is forgotten. This book values the essences that enliven. Project Plans don't solve problems. We offer Urban Husbandry as an alter-native, a proven rejuvenation approach.

Enduring, positive change evolves...slowly. No big ideas will be offered here. No big new government programs will be proposed. Just the opposite. So much time, money, energy, and attention are focused in directions and on projects that are big, visible, simplistic, and wrong that few notice or heed the breakthrough.[1] Few learn lessons from unpredicted successes and few revise their attitudes to reflect reality.

As H. L. Mencken wrote, "For every complex, difficult problem, there is a simple, easy solution...and it is wrong."

Between the two of us, we have visited, explored, examined, and studied hundreds of downtowns around the United States. We have con-sulted in some, lectured in others. We have talked to residents, mer-chants, city officials, planners, designers, preservationists, civic activists, journalists, architects, educators, students, business people, developers, builders, engineers, visitors, shoppers. Seldom do we find opinions, conditions, myths, or rules that are unique. There is a same-ness and sadness to all the deadened downtowns and a variety and excitement to all the revived ones.

Although the past and present are significant, this is not an exercise in nostalgia. The present points to what the future may hold. But there is nothing more relevant than the past as a building block for that future. The past offers lessons on which future alternatives can be based, alternatives to Project Planning. Often, the innovations presented here are located in a familiar building type and may inspire other places to initiate a similarly catalytic project. Each innovation generated spinoff businesses and stim-ulated the local economy. Each success offers one answer to the questions posed to us in so many communities: "What can we do with...?" "How do we make use of...?" "How can we bring back...?"

Innovation is the common thread. An innovative view of transit stops. An innovative view of farmers' markets. An innovative business type exhibiting the unlimited new potential of any locality. An innovative program to encourage new entrepreneurs. An innovative use of existing resources, whether an old building or open space. An innovative entertainment use that stimulates new businesses. An innovative economic activity that is location-neutral but helpful to downtown momentum. An innovative corporation enhancing a downtown effort. An innovative handling of public uses. An innovative developer who prefers rebuilding the existing fabric to replacing it. An innovative planner or architect creatively breaking with the conventional views of his or her profession.

MAKING IT RIGHT BY DOING IT WRONG

The chapters that follow reveal different approaches to correcting the mistakes of the past several decades. The direction from which a community attacks the issues and the problems does not matter. Everything is connected. Any one piece of the puzzle leads to the next. A farmers' market or a traffic problem may be the first piece. A battle to keep open a library or an effort to revive an open space may start things going. A fight against a proposed superstore can be the catalyst for renewing downtown. A struggle to retain a post office. An effort to stop a highway. All the threads of the downtown fabric are connected.

A downtown is *only* the synergy of its parts. The pieces cannot be isolated. The whole is enhanced by each of its parts, but those parts must relate and connect to make a complex whole.

Defying convention or breaking rules begins the process of unraveling the mess we have created. Bad rules and destructive guidelines have accrued during 50 years of automobile-oriented planning. Professions have grown up to perpetuate them. Urban planners. Architects and engineers. Traffic engineers. Retail consultants. Real estate developers. These professionals have a stake in keeping the public believing in their expertise. But the so-called experts too often ignore or deny the legitimacy of local citizen instincts, common sense, and accumulated wisdom. They are so often focused on their own area of expertise that they overlook, ignore, or misjudge the web of interrelated impacts. Experts too often want to "educate" people instead of "learn from" *and* be "educated by" them. These experts ignore the mistakes of their profession's earlier "expertise." These experts write and uphold the rules, rules that have produced a dysfunctional form. They are the rules that keep us here. They must be broken.

Downtown *can* be brought back to life again. In some places it's actually happening. This book celebrates those examples. They are offered as lessons to learn from, not to be replicated.

1. Unless it is a large-scale breakthrough, of course. When Boston's Faneuil Hall Marketplace opened in 1976, everyone noticed and copied its success badly.

WHERE ARE WE?

Mansfield, Ohio—Richland County Carousel.

CHAPTER ONE

MANSFIELD, OHIO
GETTING OFF THE BIG PROJECT
MERRY-GO-ROUND

The first thing one sees driving into Mansfield, Ohio (population 54,000), is a colorful, handpainted sign, "Welcome to Mansfield—A Reason for All Seasons." With its whimsical and colorful seasonal images of a daisy, sun, red maple leaf, and snowflake above the lettering, this well-designed sign is understated but eye-catching. Already, this distinguishes Mansfield from the majority of American downtowns. *Most have only the cookie-cutter Department of Transportation name sign and little else on the commercial strip leading into downtown to indicate a center exists.* Yards past the welcome sign is the more familiar framework of the insignias of Mansfield's service clubs and fraternal organizations. This hard-to-read, trelliswork of 10 images is topped by a faded "Welcome" and once-colorful images depicting Mansfield characteristics, symbolizing the lack of attention and caring once evident downtown, as well. Then comes the most familiar blue-and-white "H" which, at least, indicates that this place is big or important enough to warrant a hospital.

Shortly past these signs, downtown's center is visible from atop a hill down which the four-lane road continues. A few ten- to twelve-story office or bank buildings, the variety favored in commercial centers in the 1920s, are visible from afar. Beyond lie red brick factory complexes, grain elevators, smokestacks, and railyards, reflecting the dual personality of this once self-sufficient agricultural center that evolved into a significant industrial city.

More of the strip combination of drive-in businesses and spacious parking lots continues along the downtown approach. Gradually, however, appear remnants of compact, sidewalk neighborhoods once connected to down-

A nice touch to tell you're entering a special place.

town by trolley. "A matted carpet of housetops, interwoven with green strands of tree-lined streets," was how the 1940 WPA Guide described these flourishing enclaves. *Residential areas that developed along trolley or rail lines (see Chapter 4) exhibit distinct streetscapes recognizable today, even without the tracks and trolleys, in every town and city where they have not been totally replaced.* They are another signal that the community's original center is approaching.

Then comes the all-too-familiar interruption, the glaring red "Do Not Enter," the clear indication that, at some point since the 1950s, traffic engineers reconfigured downtown into a maze of one-way thoroughfares meant to speed up traffic, smooth the vehicular flow, and remake downtown into a model of vehicular transportation efficiency. One is now rerouted onto this system, *designed as much to carry the driver **through** as **into** Mansfield.*

The familiar assortment of parking lots and pre-auto streetfront and post-auto setback buildings lines the remainder of the route, which ends at a nice, sizable, lush green Central Park, about two blocks square, divided down the middle by an east-west four-lane road created in the 1960s. A classic tiered cast-iron fountain with cascading water was the centerpiece until it was moved to make way for the road. Mansfield is one of the lucky downtowns, whose public lawn was merely bifurcated and the fountain moved instead of wiped out entirely by an auto route. Nevertheless, this central incision is a stark reminder of what has been the downtown priority since the 1950s. Mansfield's

An immediate interruption imposed by traffic engineers.

Mansfield's Central Park—beautiful and well-maintained resting place for shoppers, an ideal public place for community events.

upbeat, colorful initial "welcome" greeting and its downbeat, drab, and lifeless center reflect the pulls of two downtown directions that are evident in America today.

Central Park is still Mansfield's primary center. The strengths and scars exhibited here parallel conditions elsewhere in the city. A banal, 1960s county courthouse sits on one side of the park. Its continued downtown location is the good news. Its replacement of what the 1940 WPA Guide[1] called a "venerable red brick" Victorian is the bad news. On another corner is another modern banality, a deadening stone building with small windows housing county social services. This replaced a 1940s Sears, Roebuck & Co., the kind of appealing and flexible structure being creatively converted for varied uses today. An oversized garage stands nearby (adjustable in the future).

Two local banks in 12-story office buildings still anchor key corners of the square (very good news), one a classic Beaux-Arts Revival and the other, Art Deco, both built for their pre-merger predecessors. Long-established businesses and good street-level retail buildings remain facing the park (good news). "Smart shops embellish the square," the WPA Guide noted. The former locally-owned downtown department store, H. L. Reed (1864), in a three-story painted beige brick building, is shuttered (bad news), comparable to many around the country (one of many chal-

The former H. L. Reed's Department Store.

lenges), but at least standing (good news), awaiting a smart reuse idea. And a former hardware store in a three-story building with a classic and rare 1950s façade completely sheathed in stainless steel is similarly closed (bad news) but poised for a well-thought-out new idea (good news). On the other side of the square, a sizable three-story building with four ground-floor stores beautifully restored (good news) with city funding sits empty and has for years (bad news) because its owner stubbornly insists on further public subsidy (greedy) and the city has not sought legal recourse.

The dilemma of the absentee landlord dampening downtown regeneration is troublesome and often serves as a rationale for why nothing positive is happening. Until something happens to that *building, people often believe, nothing else will. The idea that nothing can happen until one specific thing does establishes an artificial and unimaginative threshhold for success. This merely avoids the hassle of risk. That defeatist attitude is more the cause of no action than the stubborn property owners with unreasonable expectations. The target empty building is usually sizable. It may even be the biggest in the vicinity, which will be the last to which anything would happen anyway. This is a small-scale version of the "big fix" approach to rejuvenation. Surely, strict code enforcement is important, as is making sure the building does not appear worse than it is. Beyond that, getting something started elsewhere is the best route to making something happen to the larger building.*

Widened sidewalks, gracious trees, and street lighting improvements are attractive Mansfield amenities. Planters are full of colorful flowers. Local garden clubs tend them well. *Such physical upgrades—*

popular everywhere in the 1970s and 1980s—are a visual asset but were never sufficient to generate a new growth momentum. They were the easiest, high-visual impact improvement. Superficial but of great immediate appeal, physical upgrades never got at the essence of downtown problems.

Central Park has a small, attractive amphitheater. Midday entertainment occasionally occurs, but there is nothing to draw evening activity. A Victorian gazebo, Civil War monument, benches, and the fountain are additional amenities (all good news). Few pedestrians are evident (explainable bad news). A county bus stop is located on one corner (good news). Angled parking spaces are provided around the park (good news) and are full most working days. *Angled parking provides more convenient spots than parallel spaces, helps narrow streets to make pedestrians feel more comfortable, and inhibits speeding vehicles. Angled parking is anathema to traffic experts concerned with "traffic flows."*

Too many empty spaces where buildings once stood are scattered around. Blatantly ugly one-story rebuilds minimize pedestrian appeal with windowless, blank walls guaranteed to perpetuate the absence of street life. Even a renovated (good news) Victorian commercial building with five window bays separated by cast-iron columns a block from the park reinforces the hostile street feeling with partially bricked-in street-level display windows (bad news). Next door is another elegantly restored (good news) Victorian mansion with two floors of retail kept empty (bad news) by a stubborn and unimaginative owner.

Underused but desirable buildings are scattered around the downtown. Several are quite appropriate for residential use (good news). Factory and warehouse buildings remain, a few unoccupied, others home to long-standing businesses and more recent start-ups (good news). Ten blocks from the center, the sprawling former Westinghouse factory, which closed in 1990, was bought in 1991 by a group of investors, revived, and is partially tenanted by Commerce Center, which includes a business incubator, low-rent space for light manufacturers, and small offices (excellent news). The former Ohio Brass Building was refurbished for a technical college. Freight service on one rail line continues (good news), where three lines once brought passengers and freight. The newspaper is still downtown and shows genuine interest in and commitment to downtown (good news). The magnificently restored 1400-seat Renaissance Theater, a 1928 movie palace in the grand Baroque style, contains five meeting rooms, banquet facilities, and a serviceable motel next door (good news). The Renaissance is the kind of activity generator many downtowns could also have. Many similar theaters stand empty. Despite its diversified meeting spaces here, at the Westinghouse plant, and in other theaters, some Mansfield leaders think a "new" convention center is needed (bad news and foolhardy). The Mansfield Playhouse exists in a former church a block off the square. An Andrew Carnegie limestone public library, its original Beaux Arts building well preserved and expanded admirably by Mansfield architect, Dan Seckel, remains well used (good news).

In 1984, when the *New York Times* Sunday Magazine wanted an all-American place "to test the political waters" during the Walter Mondale/Geraldine Ferraro challenge to the Ronald Reagan/George Bush re-election, it sent the late Pulitzer Prize-winning journalist Anthony Lukas to Mansfield. Mansfield is "heavily industrial, but hemmed in by the stoutly conservative farm belt of north central Ohio," Lukas reported, a good political bellwether. Now, as then, Mansfield reflects the worst of past mistakes and the best of new initiatives of rebirth in downtowns across America. It is as good a representative downtown today as it was a mirror of American politics in 1984.

"Mansfield has all the complexity of a truly American community," Lukas wrote. Mansfield was home to Johnny Appleseed, the pioneer nurseryman, Sen. John Sherman of antitrust fame, novelist-conservationist Louis Bromfield, and Marabel Morgan, author of *The Total Woman*, best known for suggesting that women greet their husbands in the evening, dressed in pink baby-doll pajamas and white boots.

Mansfield's substantial home-grown industries weathered the Depression well and brought Mansfield through the Depression in surprisingly good shape. But in 1984, Mansfield was suffering from crippling trends undermining many American commercial centers. Local companies, like the giant Mansfield Tire & Rubber Company and Martin Steel Products, closed. Others, like the Ohio Brass and Tappan Stove companies, sold all or major divisions to conglomerates. Distant directors were now making decisions and Mansfield was losing out. Few American communities escaped this experience. More recently, an acceleration of the trend has erased as many local small businesses as it had earlier the bigger, more industrial ones.

"We're like a lot of manufacturing towns," Tom Brennan, editor of the *Mansfield News Journal*, told *Chicago Tribune* columnist Bob Greene in 1994. "Towns where grandfathers and fathers and sons all grew up and worked in the same plants. The troubles in cities are going all over the country. It has more to do with the times than with the towns themselves. But if you've never lived anywhere else and if things begin to go wrong in your town, you tend to think there's something wrong with you."

Of Mansfield in that condition, Greene wrote: "You've been in dozens of downtowns in dozens of aged, medium-sized Midwestern cities, and they all feel like this one. The big department stores are gone, the manufacturing plants have moved away, and there is a dim sense of something having been lost....This is the sort of downtown seemingly ripe for an easy obituary."

MANSFIELD'S OBITUARY IS FORESTALLED

Today, Mansfield is a good example of an old style of death and a new style of rebirth, the story of which we will examine shortly. It is unclear yet which will prevail. The new energy derives from recent changes two blocks from the center. In short, a grass-roots effort started with a risky but innovative idea initiated by a downtown business group and championed by one quiet, determined businessman, John Fernyak. Momentum accelerated when Fernyak, that necessary singular leader, started buying empty buildings and restoring them because he refused to see his hometown continue to deteriorate and because he wanted to give back something to his community. More than expected subsequently evolved under the savvy direction of the useful outsider, Katherine Glover, an untrained urbanist who instinctively combined common sense and retailing experience to market Fernyak's fixed-up buildings. Glover found tenants for the renovated buildings with techniques she figured out herself, after learning directly from potential customers what businesses they wanted.

Elements of downtown Mansfield are familiar across the country. Only the combinations of features change. But, no matter how many useful assets are in place, they remain only separate pieces of a complex puzzle until someone or something puts it together. Many recipes don't work without the one ingredient called for that blends and binds all the others into one dish. Breads require yeast to make them rise. So, too, with failing downtowns. The catalyst, the small but dramatic change, the persistent or passionate individual(s)—these are the required binders and yeast equivalents.

As we will see throughout this book, the rebirth catalyst is often the untrained citizen user of the Fernyak mold, whose attachment to and feeling for the community has a deeper wisdom than most professionals possess. If, in addition, these citizens either have the means or develop access to the means to make it happen, an authentic rejuvenation often begins. But it is never more than a beginning which needs *all* elements of the locality as participants to continue, deepen, and spread with enduring potential.

THE UNLIKELY CATALYST

In Mansfield, it started with a carousel. Actually, it started with Bill Cosby. In 1984, Cosby performed at the Renaissance Theater. Before the show, he walked down North Main Street. "There were no cars, no people, and all the buildings were boarded up," he was quoted in the local newspaper as observing. "I wonder why North Main Street exists." Cosby was saying the obvious, but coming from such a national celebrity, the words stung.

These were the hemorrhaging years of the early 1980s, with Mansfield's biggest plants closing and no new jobs coming in. Public money, scarce as it was, was going into industrial retention. "For downtown," then-mayor Ed Meehan recalls, "we had to piecemeal only small projects that we could afford to maintain. We needed to do something to show attention when nothing else was happening." Admirable street plantings and sidewalk widening were accomplished—cosmetic at best, Meehan acknowledges.

But Cosby's words were like a cattle prod. North Main was the entryway into the city from the highway, a route traveled by many between Columbus and Cleveland. This route passes through the industrial side of town, coming from the north, the opposite route described in the opening of this chapter. The Chamber of Commerce met to think of new ways to bring people downtown. "The idea of a carousel came out of one of those meetings, and I did the homework," recalls John Fernyak. Fernyak, low-key, modest, a third-generation Mansfielder, emerged as the persistent, passionate, committed person who carried the ball and took most of the heat but insists on downplaying his role. "At first we laughed and chuckled at the idea," Fernyak recalls, "but the more we talked about alternatives, the more it made sense." A prime North Main corner was chosen, smack in the middle of the most abandoned, unpopular, and seedy area, the center of prostitution and bars, two blocks from the square but directly on the heavily-used through-traffic street. The public went nuts.

"So they are going to put a merry-go-round uptown," one irate citizen wrote. "Some taxpayers believe they are already on one." "Instead of carved horses to decorate the carousel," wrote another, "why don't we use a ring of little white elephants?" A new bumper sticker was seen around town: "Last one out of town, please turn out the lights at the carousel."

The business group stood firm and raised $1.2 million in private money from dozens of citizens for the carousel and the pavilion to enclose it. They commissioned a new carousel, which became the first all-wooden hand-carved carousel to be built in America since the 1930s. Then-mayor Meehan shared the heat and committed city condemnation powers to acquire the site, demolish the few remaining buildings, and relocate seven businesses. "Wooden-like figures that go up and down and around in circles, but never get anywhere," wrote another dumbfounded Mansfielder, referring now to the partnership of businessmen and the mayor. Meehan stood firm. But he lost his subsequent bid for re-election.

Another published poison-pen letter reflects the sentiments of many local residents everywhere when the unconventional new idea emerges, especially from within the community. Prevailing public sentiment often accepts widespread, conventional assumptions. A demolition/startover approach, many believed, would make way for the "world-class hotel," "four-star restaurant," and "convention center" combination, perfectly in keeping with the quick-fix, big-project thinking of the day that would have produced an imitation of projects found in scores of downtowns. One Mansfield resident wrote:

> I think (the carousel) is great! With Mansfield facing high unemployment, a full landfill, and needing the new city tax so badly, the carousel is a great solution to those problems. And its location is simply brilliant. I mean, look at all the shops close by: a magazine store with *Playboy* and *Penthouse* and who knows what other pornography, a pool hall that Minnesota Fats would be afraid to go into, and beer joints and prostitutes all around it. What a great place for my wife and kids to go and so safe an area of town, too!

Long-time residents are often die-hard skeptics. They see things as they are without fresh vision of what can be. They remember what things were and think nothing as good can replace that. They long ago gave up on downtown, took their loyalties elsewhere, and view suspiciously anyone who refuses to give up on downtown. In big cities and small, this crippling phenomenon is widespread. Only the most committed believers can sustain the darts and arrows and inevitable discouragement that stand perilously in the path of innovation.

A carousel is an old-fashioned entertainment vehicle too easily dismissed as a nostalgic folly, ignoring its potential as a tool for future growth. When it opened on Labor Day weekend 1991, enthusiasts thought if they got 30,000 riders the first year, that would be an impressive start. They did that the opening Labor Day weekend, and counted 200,000 riders the first year.

Ironically, one of those letter-writing skeptics' words took on a reverse meaning. "Things got so bad on North Main, they called in the cavalry and here's what they got: Thirty horses, four bears, four ostriches, four cats, four rabbits, two goats, two chariots, a lion, a zebra, a tiger. Oh my!" And it worked.

To visit the Richland County Carousel Park, to ride one of its smile-provoking creatures and hear its authentic military waltzes from the Stinson band organ, is to wonder why anyone would ever doubt its power. Housed in a handsomely designed all-weather pavilion, all 53 carousel figures and two chariots were designed, carved, and painted by Carousel Works of Bristol, Connecticut, whose owners moved their company to Mansfield to do the job and stayed. This striking work of art in the style of G. A. Dentzel, one of the most revered carousel carvers of the early 1900s, is the same magnet for the young and old it always was.

Who can resist strutting ostriches, strolling zebras, roaring tigers, along with a charming giraffe with a monkey hanging on its back, and assorted horses? Even the finely carved chariots with historic Mansfield scenes painted on them are a joy to ride. Locals, tourists, riders, and watchers never stop coming. The elderly sit on the side and watch from the new old-fashioned porch rocking chairs purchased with money raised by the employees of the local phone company. School children come from a broad Ohio region. Grandparents and parents come with kids. Teen-age couples come for romance. Birthday celebrations are regularly scheduled. The appeal is endless. Could there be a better way to draw people, especially when one considers the big corporate business that "entertainment malls" have become? Twenty-two new businesses with 100 employees have begun since the opening of the carousel and the subsequent upgrading and occupancy of Fernyak's nearby buildings.

One could quibble with the pavilion's siting. One could question the need to demolish some of the buildings that were torn down. One could debate the need of the surrounding, larger-than-necessary "all-

Above: A happy rider.

Below: The Richland County Carousel.

purpose park," lovingly planted and cared for by the Men's Garden Club but essentially unused. But these are quibbles and do not diminish the strength of the result one bit. The spinoffs have been many but, as shall be seen, the carousel was one component of an ongoing process that has not stopped, should not stop, and will continue to generate new things if nothing is taken for granted. But the full value of the carousel is already being misunderstood, as communities all over the country seek to follow in Mansfield's footsteps.

The carousel's magic is not reserved for Mansfield. Many European small towns still have a local carousel, attracting neighbors, passersby, young and old, serving as a center of community life. And many an American city child remembers the small, truck-size versions that regularly visited neighborhoods, stirring a bustle of street activity. New York's Riverbank State Park, built on top of a sewage treatment plant on the Hudson River waterfront in the mid-1990s and now one of the city's most used parks, includes an innovative new carousel with animals created by New York artist Milo Mottola, based on fantasies and designs offered by children in the community.

But the qualities associated with attracting activity, stimulating connections between people, bringing people onto the streets and into the stores—these are the attributes that make the carousel a vehicle for reinvigoration. Those qualities are not exclusive to carousels. Carousels are not an answer for every community and just any site. Carousel mania risks repeating the pattern of Boston's Quincy Market, a great success for its time, place, and unique qualities. The Festival Marketplace quickly became a formula many places latched onto, failing miserably in most of them. **Innovation can't be reduced to formula.**

For Mansfield, the carousel was the dramatic small step necessary to wake up the city to future possibilities. Mansfield is now one of the carousel centers of the country. A letter with a carousel stamp and a Mansfield postmark is a must for collectors. A second family-run carousel carving company, Carrousel Magic!, opened, having moved from Rexburg, Idaho, because Mansfield was becoming a carousel capital. Carrousel Magic! gives tours as carvers work. Two carousel magazines are now based in Mansfield. The carousel is not the salvation of Mansfield. Nor did advocates think it would be. But it surely exceeded expectations.

In so many places, the first hurdle for downtown rebirth is the feeling of hopelessness and skepticism. They seem to go hand in hand. The second hurdle is the "me too" syndrome, the assumption that to be competitive, the big ideas happening elsewhere must be imported. The third hurdle is the view that something big and quick has to be done to turn things around. Nothing could be further from the truth, as the successes highlighted in this book demonstrate. For Mansfield, the carousel was the right idea at the right time, but it was not all that was happening.

ONE INDIVIDUAL SETS A NEW COURSE

John Fernyak is president of Infoshare, formerly the Mansfield Typewriter Company, started by his father. Originally, the company sold and serviced typewriters; it now specializes in a wide assortment of office machines and technology. Fernyak is a Mansfield loyalist. He had not really thought of himself as such. In fact, he hadn't really given downtown's future too much thought. At the time of the "Cosby affair," Fernyak was vice chairman of the Chamber of Commerce. No one questioned Cosby's assessment of North Main. "We thought the solution was to change the downtown entry route and divert traffic to a street with empty land. We called on developers to consider building on this alternate street and were laughed out of their office."

Fernyak was thoroughly discouraged. He and his sister owned a building on North Main, a four-story Victorian commercial building that had once housed their grandfather's jewelry store on the ground floor. They decided to sell, and when all the costs were deducted from the laughably low price of $20,000, they netted $25. "A month later," Fernyak recalls in continued disbelief, "we had just finished installing a $250,000 job at the bank (located on North Main), when the bank offered to sell me its building (a six-story neo-Classical building) for $30,000. I told them that was an absurd price, the building was a mess, the roof leaked, and, anyway, I had just sold that piece of junk across the street. They offered to lend me the money to buy it, lowered the price, and the next thing I knew, I owned the building. My 87-year-old father really thought I was nuts. I asked myself, 'Now, what am I going to do?' That was the extent of my vision."

In the best tradition of instinctive investigation, Fernyak and his wife, Mimi, another long-time Mansfielder, spent vacations traveling to cities with successfully restored historic buildings—Larimer Square in Denver, Ghirardelli Square in San Francisco, and Harbour Place in Baltimore, along with the downtowns of Savannah, Lexington, Kentucky, and Dover and Portsmouth, New Hampshire. "Deep down," he says, "I realized that I really love old buildings and old things. I like fixing old things. I saw some great projects and learned a lot about what and what not to do."

Fernyak got excited. He decided one building would never do. He persuaded a group of Mansfielders to join him in buying and fixing up property along North Main in an effort to make something good happen in their hometown. Current owners would never do anything to improve those buildings, they realized, so the only solution was to buy them, fix them up, and then...and then. Fernyak did not know the answer to "and then?" but he started anyway. Before undertaking any major renovation work, they just bought buildings and did emergency and roof work. They were aiming for 20 storefronts and, by 1989, wound up with 35 buildings in a three-block radius.

"We just figured we could help downtown to come back," says Fernyak, "because shopping centers offer nothing of the character of downtown streets and nothing of architectural significance." They decided to be selective about tenants, to create parking on small, scattered lots without breaking up the street, to improve the street lighting, install new fixtures, make people feel safe. Beyond that, they did not have a clue what to do. They accumulated buildings, started renovations, put big "For Rent" signs in the windows, and waited for tenants. No promotion, no marketing. The buildings sat empty.

This is the critical turning point for property owners in so many places. They throw the party to which nobody comes unless, of course, the territory is already desirable. This is also the most challenging juncture. The hardest thing is to make it happen. Property acquisition is fine. Design is fine. Construction, new or renovation, is fine. Streetscape improvements are fine. All such **physical** *improvements are important and necessary.* **But they are never enough.**

FAMILIAR FORMULA OR LOCAL INNOVATION?

Where to turn next? How this question is answered determines the character and quality of the place. High-priced consultants with shopping center experience, big project credits, and flashy brochures are too frequently the conventional option chosen. This is understandable. Most communities have a residual inferiority complex, do not have faith in the strength of their local appeal, and obsess about their handicaps rather than celebrate their assets. They are vulnerable. They designate distant "experts" to shape the future and make important direction-setting decisions. Slick marketing consultants can dazzle. They deliver—for a big price—a thick report about placing stores in just the right locations to achieve the proper "merchandise mix," along with the idea of creating "clusters." The result is, perhaps, suitable for a mall where one property owner controls 100 percent of the space, with no local character, no businesses, no history, no place. But it cannot and should not be imposed on a downtown.

Clustering, the grouping of similar businesses, is a natural phenomenon of downtowns, mostly cities. Networks of interrelated businesses that work with and often depend on each other, or of similar product businesses, evolve naturally over time into urban districts. They can be encouraged once started, nurtured, and, when necessary, protected. They are vital economic elements. But they cannot be artificially created and imposed. When they are, natural, unpredicted things don't happen.

Consultants' favorite recommendations are franchises or chains. They pay the biggest rent, are easiest to find, and supposedly carry no risk because the public already knows them well. And, after all that time and money are spent, the consultant hands over a list of recommended stores to the sponsoring organization to devise a recruitment process. That process is key.

If the recruitment process succeeds, what do you wind up with? Familiar stores, often found in malls. Occasionally, a nice local restaurant opens. Certain businesses are typically local—antique shops, restaurants, video stores—and are often included. But it still adds up to no special place, with no local character created by local people and shaping a local economy. The reasons are understandable. Communities like Mansfield are desperate for something—anything—to happen. This result is not terrible, if—and this is a big "if"—the bottom line is just to "make something happen." After all, formerly empty stores will be occupied, open, alive, paying taxes, and making people feel better than before about their downtown.

But what they are getting is not nearly as significant as what they are losing. The opportunity is missed to cultivate new, local economic uses and social stability with fresh local entrepreneurial energy. People often don't see what is right under their noses, in their own backyard, special qualities, talented people, untapped resources. They are absorbed by the big-ticket items, over-covered in the press, touted by elected officials and high-visibility professionals. The alternative is unrecognized, the different course, rooted in old traditions, drawing on old patterns, using old buildings or new ones in compatible scale. Such ideas are dismissed as being nostalgic, back to the past, not where it's happening. Many people are still deceived by the propaganda developed to a high art since World War II that says: Old means old. The past is past and represents tired thinking. New is good. Bigger is better. The message is delivered every day in so many ways that it pervades the country's thinking. It is, unfortunately, the American way.

Our culture is so mesmerized and saturated with the appeal of the latest fad, the Disney of the moment, that we exist in a trancelike state, unsure of the value of anything not advertised on television or produced by Hollywood.

REINVENTING THE WHEEL IS SOMETIMES THE RIGHT IDEA

Downtown property owners or local officials ask, "Why reinvent the wheel?" and instead proceed to follow in another's path. This is the easiest, but not necessarily the most successful, approach, taking what conventional marketers recommend and relying on boilerplate thinking. *Reinventing the wheel, however, is not a waste of time. Imitation is. There is more to gain than to lose in arriving at a new solution. Decisions are not taken out of local hands. Individualized, creative, fun solutions are the potential result.* Serendipitously, this is what happened in Mansfield, when John Fernyak hired his daughter's friend, Katherine Glover. "I have this friend you ought to talk to," his daughter, Susan, told her father when they were sitting around one day, casually talking about what should happen.

Born and raised in the Washington, D.C., area, schooled at the University of Wisconsin in Madison, Glover had 11 years of varied retailing experience, as a buyer at Carson Pirie Scott in Chicago, as a manager of specialty retail, and in marketing with an apparel manufacturer in California. At that moment, she and Susan Fernyak were roommates in California.

From the start, Glover didn't do anything conventionally. She offered Fernyak some ideas about what she thought should happen. "He wanted the Gap, Williams-Sonoma, Talbots," she remembers, "and I told him that would never work, that they would never come because of the number of people but, instead, it might be possible to get stores comparable to Williams-Sonoma or Barnes & Noble that were local or regional. He was intrigued. That is what clicked for him." He caught her by surprise on a second visit when he asked if she wanted a chance to test her ideas. Before answering, she interviewed about 30 Mansfielders "to see if the necessary community support was there to pull off a retail district."

After she took the job in 1993, she spent three months meeting with key people in all corners of the community. "I talked to any organization that collected a group—the Kiwanis Club, Rotary, a women's club. I asked how they experienced downtown, what they hoped to see happen, and what kind of stores did they want." She convened panels of customers, from age 20 to 80 and with a variety of backgrounds, trying to learn how they would like to use downtown. She found the pulse of the community.

People of all ages, she learned, wanted local restaurants and pubs where ownership and management are rooted in the community and the clientele is familiar. Women, particularly, feel comfortable in a familiar place. Everyone wants a place to go where they feel part of the community. Chains make people feel like strangers in their own town. The longing expressed here is for what sociologist Ray Oldenburg, in *The Great Good Place*,[2] identified as the "third place," the informal gathering spot, removed from home and work, where one encounters people not normally part of either. These "unplanned" local places, Oldenburg points out, have been rapidly disappearing from the American landscape during decades of megadevelopment projects unconducive to such places. A "third place," Oldenburg noted, must be within walking distance from home, where one feels valued as more than a faceless consumer; where socializing, loitering, and lingering are recognized social assets, not commercial liabilities; where conversation and camaraderie prevail; and where the hot political issues and the latest football scores gain equal attention. In the rejuvenated downtowns of America, these "third places" are reappearing.

Young people, Glover found, wanted a specialty food market for gourmet food, fresh bread, and fresh ready-to-eat dishes. Old people want simpler foods they can cook for themselves. They all wanted "corn by the ear, not the package." Clearly, a farmers' market would make many people happy and bring people back to the street. Everyone, she discovered, missed having a bookstore.

So there was her first list of targets: a bookstore, a bakery, a farmers' market, a micro-brewery restaurant. You can't leave it to chance if you want to build a local customer base. How she went about obtaining them is another lesson in commonsense planning. But first, she realized she had to have something to offer potential businesses. Sure, she needed the basic statistical profile—"demographics," as they are called in the trade. More importantly, she knew, she needed something different, something to make it special, to create a new upbeat image for downtown. Of course, the district name and banners were symbols. The content made it all work. This distinction is often lost when downtowns don't get past the district name and banners.

Fernyak's bank building, now renovated and home to his Engwiller Property office, faced the carousel. The three-block, 35-building district in which he was buying buildings bordered the popular entertainment attraction. The carousel had become known statewide. So she dubbed the restored historic area "the Carousel District" and made the most of the theme with a lively logo, street banners, energetic promotions, and special events.

One event was particularly noteworthy. Soapbox derbys had been a Mansfield tradition for decades. In recent years, the annual race was held away from downtown. In 1993, *The Mansfield News Journal*, sponsor of the race, was looking for a new location. The paper had never given up on downtown, was still located there, and, when Glover suggested North Main, it responded positively and persuaded race officials to relocate. Research subsequently revealed that the race used to take place right on that very street, because of the steepness of the hill. The hill is so big, the race started midway. Great fanfare surrounded the event. A 1937 winner was a guest of honor. Film clips of his victory were shown. Hundreds of people of all ages showed up, more than had been in downtown in years.

"Do you realize where you are?" Glover inquired of a father, accompanied by his children. The father looked at her quizzically, then looked around him, smiled and replied: "Yeah, I'm downtown, just where I swore I'd never let my family go."

Step by step, the psychology of fear surrounding downtown diminished.

*Carefully restored buildings are filled with appropriate stores—
some were existing and improved, others are new.*

ATTRACTING TENANTS: A PERSONAL STYLE BREAKS THE RULES

On a midweek day now, one would hardly know that North Main had ever been a dying street. People are constantly walking to and from the carousel, some with children, some in business suits, some with cameras, all with smiles. The metered parking spaces on the street are less than half full, but cars are continuously coming and going, not just passing through. In front of North Main's storefronts, the pedestrian flow is modest but constant. Browsers mix with destination shoppers. People are pursuing all manner of missions. Within view of the carousel, signs of positive change are as evident as pre-carousel conditions. An electrical supply and lighting fixture store spruced up its façade and has a new lamp display in its window. A pawn shop remains. A hair salon, ice cream store, and hat store have opened. Several buildings remain boarded up. Four storefronts next to Fernyak's bank were handsomely renovated but sat empty for a long time, owned by a landlord who did not understand that putting a "For Lease" sign in a window is not enough in an area only at the beginning of a turnaround.

To walk down North Main with Katherine Glover is to gain a lesson in how to bring a downtown district past the physical improvement stage and into an economically functional condition. There is no "one way" to achieve this. A strategy should evolve from the personality of the local place and the needs of the local and regional customer base. The personality and style, and, to a lesser extent, the experience, of the person charged with managing this process are similarly important. Retail, not downtown, experience got her the job. Katherine Glover is the model of a smart instinctivist who applied an innovative planning process. Equally creative people exist everywhere.

Six businesses were in the district when Glover came on board, and she did not immediately recognize the value of keeping them. It did not matter. She didn't have a choice. The Coney Island Diner, for example, with its 1940s hot-dog-image neon sign outside and Formica counter and eating booths inside, had been, for decades, a hangout for steelworkers, businessmen, police, kids, and shoppers. New owners had just taken over the diner when Fernyak bought the building. Glover sensed they had good instincts. They made improvements, but were careful not to get too chic. They kept the menu, the prices, and the decor, with some modest sprucing up, so the integrity of this local landmark and its mix of people remain. Glover just gave them an assist with advertising, publicity, and general exposure. They did the rest.

City News, the next-door magazine and newspaper store, was also a long-time fixture. "Mansfield's most complete newsstand," the 1940s neon sign proclaims. Like so many stores in every downtown, the store and its offerings were unchanged and unappealing. Everyone's first instinct was to get rid of it. This is frequently the case in downtowns where long-time businesses do not convey a sense of freshness and look anything but up-to-date. Glover hung out in the store for a while, watched a cross section of the community come and go, recognized it as a significant meeting place, and realized it would be "a kiss of death" to lose it, in the same way it would have been to lose the Coney Island Diner. Instead, Glover worked with the owner, suggested new products (*New York Times*, hot coffee, cooking and fashion magazines, stationery, specialty cards) to create new customer interest and negotiated a lease that increased the rent as business improved. Business tripled. Physical improvements were made as the tenant could pay higher rent. Lottery tickets are still sold here. Local and national sports memorabilia decorate the store. A smoking room was added in the back, where cigar, pipe, and cigarette smokers can meet away from their antagonists. City News is now more of an institution than ever. "When I think of the mistake I could have made...," Glover says.

The issue of existing businesses is always a thorny one in upgrading areas. Too often, they are forced out with no attention paid to helping them stay, upgrade, and respond to new markets and changing times. "Not all existing businesses are worth helping," Glover points out. "Some merchants are apathetic, not willing to listen to new ideas, to be team players, to reconsider the hours they are open, or to make product improvements as the landlord makes physical improvements." But many other merchants have just never thought about such things, consumed as they are 18 hours a day, seven days a week with running their businesses. "Customers today are more sophisticated, have traveled and seen more than the local merchant whose business does not let him get out of town," observes Glover. "They have no idea that changing a store entrance, upgrading a window display or advertising can add to their business." And, while Glover's job description did not anticipate this role, she found it to be an important function, one not recognized as necessary in downtown management schemes.

When it came to finding new tenants for North Main, Glover was as innovative as she was dealing with existing ones. She knew that starting a farmers' market was an important early goal, but failed with her first attempt. "I learned the greatest lessons from failure," she says. "Failure should not mean giving up a good idea. If one approach doesn't work, figure out what is wrong and try another." The farmers' market is a growing success, having expanded from one to two days and from 8 farmers to 20.

A fresh bread business was on Glover's early target list. The market was the place to launch such a business and introduce it to the public. The challenge was to find one. Glover had already discovered that the Short North area of downtown Columbus, an hour away, was experiencing a renaissance similar to the vision—though larger in scale—for the Carousel District. She found a small bread shop, Pane—An Italian Bakery, hung around it on and off, got to know the owner, Dennis Howard, even participated in his cooking classes, before suggesting the idea of a Mansfield store. "You have to test out a new business and get to know their product," she says. Glover is personally very interested in cooking and used herself as a test for many things. "If it does not make sense to you, chances are it won't to many people," she notes. First, Pane opened in the farmers' market. Glover helped promote it and bring it a lot of attention. A strong customer base developed. Then, Glover arranged for Howard to open in a renovated space where steady and new customers knew where to find him.

Also in Columbus, Glover found a brewery interested in opening its first combination brewery and restaurant. Schmidts is a family-owned business going back to 1849 in German Village, a Columbus neighborhood that began the rebirth process long before Short North. Brewery restaurants have become an interesting phenomenon in the past decade, a frequent fixture of old neighborhoods on the rebound. Brew pubs, as they are frequently called, are a reincarnation of a very old tradition with important potential for becoming community gathering places. Glover recognized their universal appeal to all ages, their fresh food offering at reasonable prices, and their current trendiness. And, she noted, a big brewery had once existed in downtown Mansfield. She researched the industry. Beer had become the number-one seller. Alcohol sales were dropping. People wanted more flavor. Sales of imported beers had increased, but local brewing was gaining appeal. The idea of a local product was part of the appeal. A Mansfield couple opened the Wooden Pony, a restaurant/brewery, off North Main but near the carousel in a building not in Fernyak's portfolio. This helped set the stage for a broader brewery customer base.

The Schmidts deal fell apart. Opening a 9000-square-foot restaurant was a bigger investment and undertaking than anyone anticipated. Renovation bids came in way over the architect's budget. Schmidts and Fernyak's investment group were already sharing renovation costs, but this was bigger than either could accept. Instead, the space that was already two stores remained two stores: a 5000-square-foot antiques center and 1200-square-foot wine and cheese store, both nice additions to a diversifying downtown. This should be viewed as a failure with value. The good news is that the local investment group was in place, stayed in place, and just shifted gears, not losing confidence in downtown. North Main gained two new businesses it did not have, and the momentum did not cease.

Interesting, individualized stories lie behind almost every new business that has opened in the Carousel District. An art gallery and frame shop's owner serendipitously discovered his renovated storefront (formerly a cigar factory) on a visit to a festival at Mansfield's Greek Orthodox church. A home decorating and furniture store owner shares the space with the art gallery, grew up in Mansfield, left to study interior design and work elsewhere in retailing, and was delighted to return to own her own business. A bookstore owner, whom Glover lured downtown from a mall, created a small balcony gathering space used for readings and hired a young manager with an instinctive knack for creating an individualized bookstore that has become a community gathering place. And then there is Farrell's Watch and Jewelry Company, in the very building that Fernyak and his sister sold just before the bank purchase and where their grandfather had his jewelry store at the turn of the century. Fernyak had repurchased the building and beautifully restored it. Merchant Patric Farrell, who had left his job as a Mansfield school employee to open a jewelry store in a mall, sold that store in 1992, did freelance antique watch repair, and embarked on the eternal search for an intact set of jewelry store showcases and a store to put them in. He found the showcases in Louisiana. He found the storefront on North Main. His outside clock sign is almost identical to the one used by Fernyak's grandfather. All North Main merchants love showing the "before" pictures of their buildings, proudly pointing out original features preserved, such as pressed metal ceilings or restored wood floors; sell or display something carousel-related; and invariably report they never expected to find the kind of positive change in downtown Mansfield that inspired them to locate there.

LOOKING FOR A DOWNTOWN LIFE

Individualized merchant stories are at the heart of many downtowns. Combinations of local merchants give a downtown its personality. Two characteristics are common among the new Mansfield entrepreneurs and found, as well, in many downtowns today. Many of the new business owners have local or regional ties and are returning after years of studying, working, and living elsewhere. Others want to be downtown after growing up "suburban mall rats," as one of them put it. They all seem to be looking for similar things: an affordable urban life style; an entrepreneurial opportunity where they can turn to personal investors among family or other people they know[3]; a place where they can be part of a community or where they already have roots; a business opportunity where the overhead is not exorbitant, where they can be independent, and where their business can develop a real identity. Many of them want to live in downtown apartments or lofts, an opportunity largely unavailable in downtown Mansfield.

People steadily call the Main Street and Carousel District offices seeking downtown residential space. State and local overly restrictive building and fire codes add prohibitive costs to conversion, thus discouraging apartment creation. They are geared to extreme safety and take nothing about downtown rebirth into account. An extra fire wall separator between ground floor retail and upper floor retail is required even if a sprinkler system is included. This can add $10,000 to the cost of each unit. Fernyak and other Mansfielders remain skeptical, especially since the cost of creating apartments is high. Few can believe an interest is possible in living where there is no grocery store, unaware that people are moving into downtown commercial areas elsewhere in the most unlikely places where there isn't even a two-day-a-week farmers' market or grocery stores a short drive away.

The positive momentum of change continues in Mansfield today. The appeal of the carousel grows. A children's museum is opening a block away in a restored 1920s retail building with a beautiful glazed terra cotta façade. Fernyak continues to restore buildings. Glover completed the marketing and development plan she was hired to do and then went out on her own as a consultant. Chris Buchanan, an Ohio native with a background in construction management and historic preservation, has replaced her. New businesses keep opening. Some existing ones are upgrading: others just wait to feel a positive impact without doing much to make it happen. Talk continues about a new convention center, a persistent negative.

A proposal to convert the Reed's Department Store building into senior housing gained serious consideration for a while and fell through only when the potential developers wanted a free building plus a $300,000 subsidy. A subsequent proposal suggests reusing Reed's for retail, a smart idea since downtown could clearly sustain more retail. Whether this proposal will prevail remains a question.

Just beyond the Carousel District, former manufacturing buildings of great architectural appeal are being reoccupied and upgraded. Mostly warehousing and service companies are occupying the converted factories, but sprinkled through are new light manufacturing companies and other new, homegrown businesses.

A young black entrepreneur, Tom Fagin, opened a new nightspot, the Da-Shiznit Night Club, for live music on the block behind Fernyak's buildings. It quickly became popular, with even the mayor being a frequent customer. A prison guard by day, Fagin had run several hotel bars and jazz spots before renting an old Masonic hall to fulfill a lifetime dream of having his own business. Financed totally out of his own savings, Fagin struggled to succeed, but was uninitiated in many entrepreneurial basics. Glover and Fernyak helped secure business advice from a local attorney for him, the "first meaningful interaction between the black and white community Mansfield has seen in a long time," one observer noted. Upon Glover's advice, Fagin planned a summer jazz night/block party that was a big success and introduced more new people to the attractions of downtown. Young blacks occasionally came in, Fagin reported, "to ask if it is true I own this place and how did I do it. Black people in this town don't think owning their own business is possible." There was no recent experience of black entrepreneurs downtown, no mentors for Fagin to learn from, and none to inspire the next generation to even try.

Unfortunately, long-term success would elude Fagin. His lack of experience and the absence of a mentor behind him interfered. Pilferage drained profits. External pressures took their toll. And then, a shooting occurred, scaring away most business. The club closed.

Fagin's story offers important lessons. This was another failure with value. Fagin's fate is not atypical. Many new, small businesses don't last. A fragile, marginal business like a nightclub is particularly vulnerable. But a lot of people with drive and ideas fail. Failure itself does not mean the idea was a bad one or the entrepreneur untalented. The criminal incident may not have occurred or the business might have even survived its occurrence, if it had been managed differently. Incidents do occur but a fragile, newly established business can't absorb external blows. This underscores the need for small training and entrepreneurial assistance programs (Chapter 12). This experience also highlights the extra bridge-building necessary in communities where minorities are effectively closed out of downtown's local economy. The black entrepreneurial tradition so strongly evident in many downtowns up until World War II did not survive integration in many areas and was totally wiped out in others by urban renewal and highway clearance programs. The riots of the 1960s were the final straw. But the Tom Fagins of many communities can be trained to renew that entrepreneurial heritage.

Only time will tell where all this will lead for Mansfield. Undoubtedly, setbacks will occur. Plateaus will be reached. Advances will be made. The important point is that a process is under way that, if nourished in modest and innovative ways, Mansfield will continue upward. At least Mansfield is on the right track, coming back to life.

1. During the Depression, a series of state guides was produced by the Works Progress Administration, using professional writers in need of work. They are excellent guides to understanding what American communities were before professional planners and transportation planners altered them.
2. New York: Paragon House, 1989.
3. A local loan program important to this success story is discussed in Chapter 12.

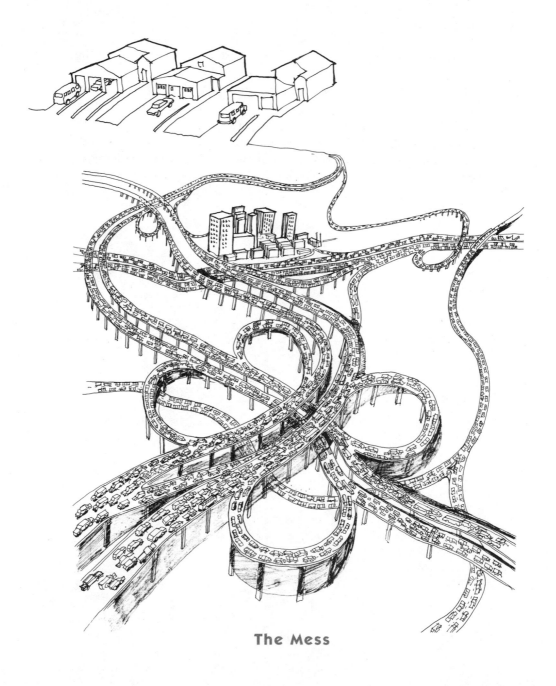

The Mess

CHAPTER TWO

THE MESS WE HAVE MADE

To understand America you have to understand the highways. In the past half century...these masochistic mar-
vels have...reshaped American culture...no one
envisioned that highways would be catalysts for huge
social disruptions...The 1950s' illusion was that government created only benign social change.
    Robert J. Samuelson, columnist
    Newsweek, June 30, 1986

Automobile madness is affecting
all of our planning.
    Dr. Vincent Scully

OUR FORM IS DYSFUNCTIONAL

We have built a physical landscape that does not function and we have done
it by design, not by chance. We have allowed the car and highway engineers
to design and shape our lives. In 50 years, America has been remade to
accommodate the car. Progress has been measured by increased vehicular
accessibility, economic health by the number of American cars produced
and sold, and social health by the numbers of families improving their standard of living by escaping cities for the suburbs and rural countryside. The
myth prevails that the car offers Americans freedom and independence.
Today, sitting in traffic and being dependent on time-consuming car trips for
essential functions and trivial errands come with that freedom. Perhaps the
current state of our manmade environment fits someone's standard of
progress, but, to achieve it, the social, economic, and political fabric of the
nation and the sustainability of the natural landscape have been seriously
undermined.

    The highways and parking lots built since the 1950s have so sepa-
rated, segregated, and isolated the American people that we have
become pockets of hostile aliens. The garage door has replaced the front
door, the parking lot the public steps to City Hall, and the underground

garage the office building lobby. The suburban majority lives in isolating communities, increasingly walled, gated, guarded, and protected by limited-access roadways.

In cities, the social interaction of the row house stoop and nearby neighborhood commercial street is giving way to the separation of the carport and the car-dependent shopping centers. Leisure has been privatized, with the backyard and swimming pool replacing the front yard and public park. Everywhere, open spaces are being privatized into exclusive enclaves instead of inclusive gathering places. We have isolated the urban poor, built projects to keep them there, given them little opportunity to reshape their environment for self-help purposes, and, in too many places, guaranteed their physical, social, and economic isolation with barrier-forming highways. We are as socially, economically, and racially divided as ever.

We do not communicate or forge connections as a people and we have few public places left to do that, even when we choose to do so. We have all but eliminated "public places" from the physical and mental geography of the country. Without the variety of common grounds on which a diverse people mix and mingle in an unplanned manner, the health of the commonweal is undermined. Genuine "public places"—whether a town square or downtown sidewalk—are where planned, chance, formal, and informal meetings occur, the opportunity for people to come together, to hear about new ideas, share concerns, understand the dilemmas of others, listen to differing opinions, debate proposals for change, and, perhaps, even resolve differences. Without a variety of true arenas for public meeting and discourse, people feel isolated, frustrated, and powerless.

De Tocqueville taught us that democracy defines itself through the connections of its diverse people. Too many of those connections—and the public places to make them—have been stolen from us. Americans feel disconnected, discontent, and angry. "A nation of soreheads," Garrison Keillor proclaimed us.

Americans feel disconnected from an economy so focused on its global connections that it ignores the value of its local economy, the foundation on which all else rests. The personality of place is expressed in a local economy. If there is no local economy to speak of and no downtown that truly reflects the personality of a community, to what place do people feel connected? Where are debate and discourse to take place? Where is our common ground to build the connections that can bind us together? Main Street, downtown, *is* the local economy. It is where the global economy begins.

HOMOGENIZED AMERICA

The nation's built landscape no longer differentiates between places. The "look of anywhere" prevails. If people don't know and feel where they are, they don't know who they are. A plastic road culture has replaced individual identity of place. The "crudscape," as environmental designer Ed McMahon calls it, has spread across the country like kudzu (the rampant Southern vine that kills everything it covers), strangling everything natural, indigenous, and historic. An enormous dissatisfaction with the character, or lack of character, of our cities and towns grows.

Identity, personality, and place are inextricably connected. Your city, your town, your community is where you come from. It has identity and character. Like the work you do, it is part of who you are. It helps define you. When strangers meet, one of the first questions they ask of each other is usually "Where do you live?"

A daughter of a friend reported this story. Two young women were sitting together on a train ride from New York City to Albany, New York. One was from New Jersey, the other from Saratoga Springs, a treasure of a place in northern New York that was saved years ago from demolition and redevelopment by ardent historic preservationists. Today, Saratoga Springs functions as a well-rounded downtown and a magnet for new growth. The New Jersey woman asked the Saratoga Springs woman where she was from. The Saratoga woman answered. The New Jersey woman had never heard of Saratoga Springs. Seeking a better description of the location, she asked, "What is your mall?" "What?" replied the Saratoga woman, not yet understanding the query. "What mall are you near?" clarified the New Jersey woman. When the Saratoga resident named a mall less than an hour from her home, the New Jersey woman knew exactly where that was. Can a mall really substitute for an identity of place?

A few years ago, the "Metropolitan Diary" column of *The New York Times* reported a conversation overheard on New York City's Fifth Avenue. One pedestrian asked another for directions to the Empire State Building. "Continue on down Fifth and you'll see it right across from McDonald's," was the reply. Can it be that the Empire State Building needs to be identified by an adjacent McDonald's?

Identity does not come franchised. Or does it? We are becoming "extensions" of corporate life, shaped by the advertising, enthralled with the product name, be it the logo or corporate image. Are we being used? At what price? We are they, not us.

The malling of America has so homogenized us, so franchised our places of work, residence, and leisure, and so separated our daily functions from each other that there are fewer and fewer places in downtown America and in the rural countryside where people can connect as individuals, as neighbors, as different people with an unchallenged capacity to develop a civic concern for each other regardless of differences. Suspicion and fear of "them" (whatever race, nationality, or minority distinction is the local "them") has replaced familiarity and comfort among neighbors. Isolated homogeneous enclaves have replaced connected or adjacent heterogeneous communities. Local stores owned by familiar members of a community have been replaced by anonymous corporate entities that drain resources from that local economy.

A public place is the physical manifestation of a democracy's need for different people *not* of like mind or like look to come together for unplanned reasons. The public and private realms are *both* vital to a democracy, not one without the other and, surely, not one at the expense of the other. The public realm is the place where divisive boundaries may be crossed, differences mediated, experiences shared, unexpected connections made, alliances forged, and conflicts mitigated. It is the place where people learn from each other, inform themselves, debate hard questions, and organize for responsible change. Yet, too much of the public realm has been erased in the physical reconfiguring of the country since World War II. What are those places one can call public today? Where can they exist if there is no downtown, no city center, no Main Street?

Amazingly, physical, manmade change is nowhere brought into discussions about the economic, social, and political reasons of the nation's current unrest.[1] Inner-city poverty, disappearing farmland, the depleted ozone, the collapse of downtowns, sprawlmarting of consumer goods, loss of community, and the undermining of democratic discourse—none of these issues, and more, can be addressed without confronting how America has been reshaped for the car. One hardly knows it to hear the political rhetoric of the day.

This is not to suggest that 40 years of reshaping the American landscape to accommodate the car explains the nation's problems. But it is most definitely a real part of the problem too commonly not recognized at all. Columnist Neal Peirce has observed:

> Our presidential campaigns have yet to produce a murmur about the scandal of sprawl as it decimates our great cities, devours our landscapes, undermines our sense of community, threatens our economic security.
>
> Republicans routinely reject restraints or guides on growth as anti-business. President Clinton comes from a lightly urbanized state. One of his early backers was the late Sam Walton, prime town killer and sprawl spreader of the age.[2]

The ramifications of autocentrism are, in fact, endless. In a thoughtful "My Turn" column in *Newsweek*,[3] entitled "Hold Your Horsepower," for example, Lyla Fox noted that teenagers are too often putting the after-school jobs needed to make car payments ahead of their education. An English teacher at Michigan's Kalamazoo Central High School, Fox noted that on too many mornings, "...my students sit with eyes glazed or heads slumped on their desks as I try to nurture a threatening-to-become-extinct interest in school." These are mostly good, "high-achieving" students, she adds. But when she initiated a classroom discussion about the student fatigue evident first thing in the morning, half the class reported "how hard it is to try to balance schoolwork, sports and jobs...My students have a desperate need to drive their own vehicles proudly into the school parking lot. The car is the teenager's symbolic club membership." The car is adult society's status symbol and transportation need. Why shouldn't it so be for society's children?

In a San Diego suburb with no sidewalks and no school buses for children living less than 3 miles from school, a resident reports, children are afraid to bike or walk to school, even when they don't live too far. Here, older kids buy cars and help pay for them by charging younger kids for a ride. Parking spaces at the school range from $400 for the closest to free for the farthest. At least the local school budget is not weighed down with *this country's most expensive, publicly subsidized single-purpose transportation system—the school bus*. School busing costs have become an incredible burden on local and state budgets. As of 1996, for example, New Jersey, with the highest school busing costs in the country, was spending slightly less than $250 million annually to transport school-children in its 618 school districts.[4]

School site requirements in many states render existing functional schools obsolete and force new ones to be built in a configuration possible only on wide-open land, a car ride away from every student and teacher. The Council of Educational Facility Planning in Scottsdale, Arizona, makes recommendations many states accept.[5] Acreage requirements, for example, are 10 acres for an elementary school, 20 for a middle school, 30 for a high school *plus*, in each case, one acre for every 100 students. Centrally-located schools are often abandoned for distant, highway-convenient locations. Parking lots are often larger than school buildings. Sprawl has taken children farther and farther from the schools to which students used to be able to walk or bike.

The car, whether a teenager's after-school job to pay for it or a bread-winner's distance traveled in it for the commute necessary to support a family, consumes inordinate time and resources that could be otherwise productively directed. There is, for another example, a widespread concern for the loss of citizen engagement. This concern is legitimate and, in fact, quite serious. "Americans are losing hold of the idea of citizen involvement in community problem-solving as the norm," syndicated columnist William Raspberry wrote in a *Washington Post* column, "Our Declining Civic Mindedness." "Worse," he continues, "we don't seem to notice the loss." Yet, he emphasizes, "...the routine involvement of neighbors in solving community problems was a very good thing—and in more ways than we imagine." Many explanations are offered. None spotlights the problem of time. Where is the time for citizen participation and civic engagement in a car-bound, long-distance commuting society?

DIMINISHMENT OF "PLACE" DOES NOT HAVE TO BE INEVITABLE

We despair at the "uglification" of the manmade environment, the loss of a sense of place, the sterility of our road culture, the repetitious "strip-scape" devouring the countryside, the repetitious "mall-scape" replacing downtowns, the frustration of our traffic congestion, the bankruptcy of our culture of commerce, and the homogenized aesthetic that passes for design. But we accept these physical changes as inevitable, allow those who benefit financially and professionally to rationalize its continuance, and don't stop to seriously examine the inherently undemocratic qualities and dysfunctional nature of a car-dependent society.

Even what are supposed to be public spaces or parks (parks should function as public places) don't work as public spaces, drawing people for many reasons at different times during a day. Too many parks, waterfronts, and open spaces serve worker populations well at lunchtime, offer leisure-time crowds organized entertainment, and serve sports audiences well for competitive events. Louisville, Pittsburgh, Cleveland, Cincinnati, St. Louis, Charlotte, North Carolina, and many other cities have lavish, expansive, and highly acclaimed waterfronts that fit this bill. Without programs to draw people from afar and too many arriving by car, they are dead. While the band is playing, the space is splendid. Lots of people. Few undesirables. Between planned events, these public places sit empty because a diverse mixture of people do not live, work, visit, or spend leisure time in the vicinity, keeping the place populated throughout the day.

A true public space in a downtown should not need to be programmed to draw people. No matter how beautiful, how "designed" a public space or park is, it will be empty of people most of the time if a user population does not live nearby. That user population must bring *on foot* the variety of humanity witnessed in such landmark parks as New York's Central Park, San Francisco's Golden Gate Park, the Boston Common, or Seattle's Pioneer Square. People who work, play, live, go to school, or just visit must be in the vicinity on a regular basis, or, at least, be an easy mass transit trip away.

BRYANT PARK—A MODEL PUBLIC SPACE

Just visit Manhattan's Bryant Park, one of the country's most celebrated public spaces today, at 42nd Street and Sixth Avenue, created in 1871. Like many parks, this one had become a haven for drug dealers. But after years of deliberation, design, debate, and considerable public involvement, this midtown oasis was transformed back into the traditional gathering place it once was, attracting an average of 8000 visitors a day since its reopening in 1992. It is now one of the crown jewels of Manhattan. Office workers, parents with baby carriages, shoppers, visitors, the homeless, strollers, sleepers, chess players, people watchers, laptop computer users, and businessmen with folding chairs arranged in a circle assemble at various times all day on or around the great green carpet of a football field-size lawn. Black, white, varied nationalities, rich, poor, blue-collar, white-collar, the assemblage is a democratic mélange. It was not always so.

In 1976, William H. Whyte, journalist, editor, and author of *City: Rediscovering the Center,*[6] among others, conducted a study to evaluate Bryant Park. Whyte, an astute observer of cities, was for years an articulate critic of the kind of Project Planning (see Chapter 3) that destroyed urban street life, edited out serendipity from public spaces, and called for large public expenditures on capital projects when modest repairs and improvements could accomplish more. Following his study, Whyte wrote a memorandum to Bill Dietle, head of the Rockefeller Brothers Fund, suggesting improvements to both the Public Library entrance and Bryant Park, which sits behind the library. Whyte wrote:

> There is a great opportunity for action. The situation is bad, yes, but so bad it's good, and from this level even modest actions can have a dramatic effect on these spaces and people's perception of them. It's not just a matter of reclamation. Both of these spaces have potentials that have never been realized and there is every reason they should be among the greatest and most enjoyable spaces.

That memo was the blueprint that transformed the six-acre park and provided the country with one of the best lessons in achieving well-used, vibrant, accessible, and appealing parks and an equally exemplary model of a well-functioning public realm. Whyte's ideas contrast sharply with conventional Project Planning.

Dope dealers dominated both spaces, Whyte observed, "but they are not the cause of the problem. The basic problem is underuse. It has been for a long time. It antedated the invasion of the dope dealers and in part induced it. Access is the nub of the matter. Psychologically, as well as physically... Relatively few people use these spaces, nor are they invited to." And how, according to Whyte, is

Bryant Park—a crown jewel and welcome resting place in the midst of midtown New York City.

access achieved? Through steps that are the antithesis of today's Project Planning and gating instinct.

On the terraces flanking the library's entrance, Whyte recommended rejecting expensive capital proposals, then under consideration, that would redesign and rebuild the terraces. "What gives one pause," Whyte wrote, "is the enormous differential in costs between many of these projects and the basics that are called for. The basics are relatively inexpensive...First things first. A few thousand dollars' worth of chairs and tables and food facilities would do more to liven up the front than hundreds of thousands worth of marble and paving. And they can be immediate." Cafés, Whyte had observed elsewhere, are the best security measures and create appealing, congenial places. What he suggested was as successful as he predicted.

For Bryant Park, the prescription was equally basic. Remove the spiked iron fence and the thick overgrown shrubbery "that block what view there is, and like the 'NO' signs posted on them, they do not invite but deflect." Create more and wider entrances, provide a feeling of easy exit, and encourage a pedestrian flow into and through the park. In other words, reverse all the things that a 1934 redesign plan provided and that made the park a walled-off sanctuary in which people would feel safe. "We now know that a healthy pedestrian flow is a great asset; it enhances the activities and acts as something of a magnet. Characteristically, the most favored places for sitting, reading, shmoozing, are apt to be athwart the main pedestrian flow, rather than isolated from it."

Whyte's suggestions were all followed, including the establishment of a privately-funded management entity in charge of security and maintenance. The Bryant Park Restoration Corporation, an organization of landlords and property owners on the surrounding blocks, fulfills this function. No detail is too small for its attention. Sidewalks and walkways are swept daily. Grass is well weeded and cut. Flower beds are immaculate. Anything broken is repaired immediately. Restrooms are spotless and even get fresh flowers daily. Whyte's ingenious idea of movable chairs is considered by many as the most successful feature, the extra magic, since it permits visitors to make an arrangement most suitable for their purposes. It is amusing to watch people move the chairs just a few inches, nothing to make a real difference except that it personalizes the space. Apparently, Bryant Park is the only public park in the country that uses such lightweight movable chairs. In 1996, 2400 were put out and 350 needed replacement at $22 each, a modest expense for a public space that draws approximately 8,000 people a day.

At the library end of the park are two splendid restaurants at different price levels. Kiosks sell takeout food at the other end. The restaurant idea, for a while, was quite controversial. After Whyte's strategy was offered, modified, and accepted, city planners enlarged the modest café idea into a 40,000-square-foot development extravaganza that included reducing the number of park entrances Whyte clearly had shown were imperative. Not surprisingly, a public controversy ensued. While the park was closed for four years to install eight floors of library stacks below grade, the restaurant project failed. Even a process so well set up to be incremental runs the risk of intervention by Project Planners. Eventually, the scale was reduced from 40,000 square feet to less than 10,000. At this scale, the public fully embraced the idea. Many improvements and modifications, of course, were made along the way by many design and public space experts. None, however, transformed Whyte's strategy into a big project.

Today, many claim credit for the park's success and, in effect, each is correct. Each consultant, architect, landscape designer, and civic organization, especially the Parks Council, New York's preeminent parks advocacy group, added to Whyte's original, simple, but brilliant strategy.

Successes are often the better, the more diverse the input. Step by step, ideas have been proposed, debated, revised, debated again, and modified since the reopening in 1992, just like a garden that gets weeded, cultivated, and fertilized over time. Today, much celebrated and much loved, Bryant Park still attracts "undesirables," an unfortunate term of varied meaning depending on who is using it. In this case, it is whomever the individuals now congregating so comfortably in Bryant Park today would stay away from if they were not part of a crowd.

Unlikely pairs easily share common space.

The drunk, the poorly dressed, the unstable, the menacing. But they are so in the minority and so unthreatening, people hardly notice...or care. The poor, the homeless, the so-called undesirables have the right to be there too, after all, and their presence forces people to be aware, to let a different reality intrude, to reflect. Without them visible, we don't think about them. Out of sight, out of mind is what too many people strive for today, a sure way to avoid difficult societal dilemmas that don't just disappear. Bryant Park, in that respect, is as democratic a space as one can find in an American city today.

Perhaps the greatest lesson of Bryant Park is that it is never "done," "finished," "complete." It is continually being modified, improved, adjusted, always fluid, never frozen. This is a defining quality of an urbanistically vibrant place. To his credit, Dan Biederman, executive director of the Bryant Park Restoration Corporation, is always prowling the park, observing how things are working, reviewing the care and attention given by staff, looking for new ideas, changing what he thinks needs changing. And while his judgment may not always be to everyone's liking, at least he is giving the care and attention a public place needs to fulfill its promise.

Bryant Park is the greatest legacy of William H. Whyte, who is one of this country's cogent urban critics. Whyte personifies the non-expert expert, the problem solver, who, like Jane Jacobs, embodies the urban wisdom many planners ignore. "In the age of specialists," architecture critic David Dillon (*Dallas Morning News*) wrote in *Preservation Magazine,*[7] "Whyte remains an inspired amateur who follows his nose rather than theories and fashions." "The premier urban gadfly," Dillon added. As fitting as Whyte's strategy was, no one anticipated—and, surely, no one planned for—the kind of splendid center of urban life it became, the very definition of spontaneity, at the heart of one of the city's most important districts. The fashion industry turned it into its front lawn, taking it over for two annual fashion shows. A summer film festival shows classics outside while viewers sprawl on the lawn. Concerts and chess tournaments are favorites too.

While Whyte focused on a specific park and building entrance, his observations can be broadly applied to parks, public spaces, town centers, and building entrances. Noting the need to redesign the park, Whyte wrote:

> There has been some concern that easier access would undercut the sanctuary and refuge quality that people cite as a reason for coming. I see no merit in this charge. In the first place, if people really wanted a walled-off sanctuary, Bryant would be a great success. It's a walled-off sanctuary. But it isn't a success and there's some fairly obvious evidence that they come, say, to enjoy the lawn because of the lawn, and not because there's a wall and iron fence around the outside. Well used places accommodate all sorts of use, all sorts of people, and in varying moods.

NOT SIMPLY A DESIGN ISSUE

We have developed one-class, one-color, one-family formation, one-age communities. They are human monocultures that not only eliminate opportunities to meet and mix with dissimilar people, but also make difficult interaction among themselves. In many recently built walled suburban enclaves, most residents have few opportunities to walk down the street or around a corner to visit a neighbor or to sit in a public park or drop in at a neighborhood hangout. More commonly, one has to get in a car and drive around winding roads even if, as the crow flies, the distance is short. A single-purpose destination cannot function as a public crossroads.

Design issues are the umbrella under which all of this customarily falls, described in such separate terms as urban design, transportation planning, city planning, architecture, park design, and historic preservation. These are viewed as frills or secondary concerns, at best on the fringe of our life, not central to it. That humankind is shaped by its environment is understood, but "environment" in this broadest context is not considered.

"We shape our buildings and then our buildings shape us," Sir Winston Churchill said. We have reshaped our environment into a form that does not function as an interconnected whole. Unavoidably, that dysfunctional form shapes us. Disconnected pieces serve separate uses: a financial center, a retail center, a sports center, a residential center, a convention center, a cultural center. These are bone fragments without any flesh, sinews, or muscle to connect them as one living organism.

Public discourse focuses every day on strengthening family values, rebuilding community, integrating people, building secure communities, and eliminating crime. The importance of "place," of downtown, of the "somewhere" that marks a community is not recognized as an appropriate starting point to address all these challenges in a multiple-benefit way. Yet, across the country, efforts abound to recreate destroyed public places, rebuild undermined downtowns, stimulate new entrepreneurial opportunities, and repopulate the stores on Main Street and their upstairs apartments. Groups diligently repairing, restoring, reweaving, and replacing those communities, Main Streets, public meeting places, small businesses, parks, cultural landmarks, and historic buildings are actually repairing democracy itself. This book identifies many of them, but there are thousands more.

CENTRAL EUROPE DOES IT BETTER

I have spent a lot of time, of late, in the Czech Republic and, to a lesser extent, in Slovakia. Not long ago, I was in an appealing city in central Slovakia called Banska Bystrica. Like most Czech and Slovak towns and cities, Banska Bystrica grew up around a medieval square that was for centuries the center of civic life. For most of this century, however, the square in Banska Bystrica became merely the crossroads for the city's extensive bus system and a through street for automobiles. The bus station sat in the middle, a dismal legacy of the Communist regime. A few years ago, all traffic was removed and the square was restored, with wonderful stonework and under-the-pavement lights.

Looking at historic photos, only minor differences are detectable. Benches, though not enough of them, were installed and most of the buildings around the square were restored. I spent hours watching life pass through that square at all hours. Classes of small schoolchildren and clusters of flirting teenagers. Elderly persons strolling with canes, mothers with baby carriages, men and women with briefcases, shoppers with full food baskets, and occasional bikers defying the rules. Chance meetings, serious conversations, romantic snuggling, and the whole assortment of street users kept passing through. There were assorted misbehavers, too, who in American cities would either appear threatening to some or seem in need of harsh police attention to others. The stream of humanity never stopped from morning to night. I could not remember when I had seen such a vibrant center. Certainly, there are few of them left on these shores.

"It is a mark of status to have a central pedestrian square, for all towns in the Czech and Slovak Republics," I was told.

Over a series of trips, I had been observing the determination of Czechs and Slovaks to put life back into their historic squares. It became their first civic mission after the revolution of 1989. Many communities are doing it in different, innovative ways. Czechs and Slovaks understand that the square is where the soul of the community is defined, among the first things the Nazis and Communists destroyed, and now so important for each place to reclaim. It is in the squares and public spaces that democracy was reborn in 1989. Cafés with chairs and tables were the first visible change after the success of the Velvet Revolution. People in conversation sitting on walls or along the base of monuments. These are the fundamental signs of true democratic civic life, the kind of life once so common in centers or on streets of American communities and now so rare. Its recapture should be as important a priority for American society as it is for the Czechs and Slovaks.

True centers can come in many forms. It is the activity, not the architecture or physical form, that defines them. The car-less civic center was translated in this country into the failed pedestrian malls of the 1970s. They work only where pedestrian density is high and a wide variety of reasons exist to draw people. They don't work in car-dependent communities. *True civic centers, genuine public squares, cannot be automobile destinations. They must be the natural crossroad of civic life, accessible to a cross section of people. Much of the same can be said about parks. Vitality of place will always be a struggle when the majority of users get there by car.*

The historic values lost, human connections broken, and personal networks severed did not happen naturally. Their destruction was carefully planned, poorly designed, and fully engineered during the heyday of pave-over Project Planning and highway-building programs since the 1950s. These lost connections were not destroyed overnight and can't be renewed any faster, but the renewal must shape itself according to the foundation that was destroyed.

Downtown, public places, neighborhood or downtown parks, historic districts, waterfronts, Main Streets, open spaces, and rail trails are all good places for the rebuilding process to begin. These achievements are commonly viewed and valued as separate and distinct elements, but together, they help connect and strengthen the whole. They are individual flowers in a potentially fertile garden and likely involve many local people, making many small decisions. Renewing neighborhoods and downtowns reconnects people, invigorates the democratic process, and is the start of rebuilding community. We deceive ourselves if we do not recognize this. In fact, we ignore it at our peril as a critical place to start.

DOWNTOWNS COME ALIVE

Downtown, struggling against enormous odds, is down but it is not out, which is a testament to its inherent value and lasting strength. Where a place remains to let it happen, where people exist to make it happen, where local economies are reborn or nurtured, and where projects of the kind described in this book occur, rebirth happens.

People may find farmers' markets (Chapter 9) quaint, but they are a growing and thriving business bringing in $1000 a square foot at Pike Place Market or $1200 a square foot at Vancouver's Granville Island. Shopping mall stores do well to produce $200 to $250 a square foot. Farmers' markets are the first and the most successful tool for economic regeneration of a community center. They do more to sustain and strengthen surrounding regional small farm economies than any government subsidy program. If done right, new local businesses spontaneously emerge around them.

Home-grown businesses (Chapter 12) seem insignificant to people who think the national and international economy is all that counts. But if the aim is to rebuild downtown America, the local economy counts the most and locally-owned businesses are the backbone of Main Street. The Vitrix Hot Glass Co. in Corning, New York, the Glass Factory in Brooklyn, New York, the Dean James Glass Works in Ybor City, Florida, the Simon Pearce glass works in Queechee, Vermont, and Flickingers Glass Works in Red Hook, Brooklyn, are all producers—yes, in fact, manufacturers—of specialty glass items, but they are growing businesses of only a few years occupying downtown buildings that were empty (a storefront, a power plant, another storefront, a hydro-powered old mill, a waterfront warehouse) and exhibiting interesting expansion potential.

Foodworks, a small business incubator in Arcata, California, the Food from the 'Hood Salad Dressing in Crenshaw, Los Angeles, and the Hudson Valley Foodworks in Dutchess County, New York, are food businesses that are significant in their local economies, important job sources, and greatly undervalued resources. Creative food enterprises seem to be a leading start-up form, showing up in many downtowns. Food is one of the fastest-growing sectors of the national economy. Many of these new food businesses are incubated in local farmers' markets. But many are founded by smart, young entrepreneurs seizing an opportunity. Nina Gianquinto, in Farmington, Maine, saw an opportunity for a specialty food store because people in the area were driving two hours to Portland to buy specialty foods, wine, cheese, and fresh baked goods. She opened Up Front & Pleasant Gourmet, "Specializing in Decadence," offered nearby delivery and special order services, and found a strong market in western Maine. A specialty doll store followed next door and a brewery up the street. Farmington already was on a slow but sure upswing, with the opening in recent years of locally-owned businesses, including two bookstores, one for new books and one for used. A J. C. Penney closed in 1996 and, a year later, the space had been divided into three stores, two already occupied. The rebirth momentum was solid.

NOT A FORMULAIC SOLUTION

The Penn Wells Hotel in Wellsboro, Pennsylvania, the Township Stores in Bonaparte, Iowa, the Brickner Woolen Mills Building in Sheboygan Falls, Wisconsin, and the Richland County Carousel in Mansfield, Ohio, all started out as community projects to which many local people contributed time and money. But they resulted in substantial economic anchors, new businesses and job creators, and rebirth catalysts for their downtowns. Bonaparte's Township Stores is an historic department store restored and converted to small stores. Sheboygan Falls' Brickner Building is a downtown factory converted to street-level retail, with offices and apartments above.

These businesses exhibit different degrees of success. Communities struggling to initiate or accelerate the rebirth of their downtowns can draw lessons from all of them. These innovations, however, are not replicable like a formula mall. Their success and particular character depend very much on their location and the people who own, operate, and patronize the businesses. They were commonplace in the fertile ground of downtowns in the past. Each project should be viewed as an idea to be built upon, one that will vary according to where it is transferred and, especially, by whom. These individual successes reflect American ingenuity at its best, the fundamentals of American entrepreneurship and knowhow. They can't be dismissed as anomalies. Distinctive successes from which to learn can be found all over.

Increasingly, large corporations are rethinking their lack of investment in repairing the fabric of downtown. But why are there not more enlightened corporations to fill the void the way the Corning Glass Works (now Corning Incorporated) did in Corning, New York, in the mid-1970s, investing in a downtown restoration program that showed what Main Street America was still capable of?[8] The Corning-sponsored Market Street Program (started in 1974) did for small town Main Streets what Boston's Quincy Market did for urban America. Market Street is the ultimate U.S. Main Street that so many had given up on. After Corning's remarkable suc-

Easton, Pennsylvania. Crayola on the ground floor, City Hall above, a building renewed, a center reborn. Photo: Antonia Mitman.

cess, however, people from downtowns across America traveled there to learn and were inspired by Corning's success. In fact, they still do.

Recently, Binney & Smith Inc.'s Crayola gave the downtown of Easton, Pennsylvania, just the boost it needed. Easton, a small gritty city at the confluence of two major waterways, is where Crayola was invented in 1903. For years, Easton struggled to gain momentum for its exceedingly slow regeneration. Local energy, interest, and citizen participation were in abundance, but sustained, directed leadership remained lacking. Then, Crayola moved its visitor center from the Crayola factory to downtown's Centre Square and opened its first and only retail store in the ground floor of an empty office building next door, enabling City Hall to move in upstairs. The visitor center is in a new building, shared with the National Canal Museum and National Heritage Corridor. Downtown Easton is on the rebound.

The nation is accustomed to corporate downsizing, outlandish executive salaries, and shrinking worker paychecks. But before all the embers were extinguished from the fire that destroyed so much of the historic Malden Mills in Lawrence, Massachusetts, owner Aaron Feuerstein stunned the country when he announced he would rebuild, protect the 2500 jobs so critical to this depressed region, continue paychecks for 30 days, and maintain medical coverage. Feuerstein is the third generation of the family to run the mill. His Hungarian-born grandfather, a classic American success story, started on a pushcart in New York. Feuerstein had long resisted moving his thriving textile business overseas and out of the community that grew up around it. He remained tightly connected to that community so he felt simply that he was doing the "natural thing by rebuilding in the same community." Local, private owners don't have to think first about their shareholders.

In Portland, Maine, a wealthy resident, Elizabeth Noyce, decided to use her wealth to improve downtown. Within five years, she started a bank to ensure the availability of local capital; bought an endangered bakery to prevent hundreds of jobs from leaving; acquired, restored, and then leased up several nearly vacant downtown buildings; and concluded that a public market could aid revitalization and benefit small food producers around the state. A seasonal, outdoor farmers' market is already a tradition in the central square, but now a new Public Market Hall stands a half-block from the square that will house some 30 independent, locally-owned food businesses.

In Wooster, Ohio, 20 residents purchased a three-generation locally-owned department store, a 110-year-old downtown anchor in danger of closing. The store was renovated and its operation upgraded and made economically viable. More investors upgraded another derelict building, donated it to the city, and then persuaded the Rubbermaid manufacturing company to locate downtown and open its first retail store, Everything Rubbermaid. Both Crayola and Rubbermaid are reaping benefits way beyond expectations and, at the same time, serving as catalysts for downtown rebirth, similar to the pattern set more than 20 years ago in Corning.

Local banks used to be the mainstays of downtown economies until, piece by piece, they were bought up or merged into national conglomerates. The small, local merchant was known to the local bank loan officer and could depend on him or her for the kind of financing so unavoidable today. Some local banks, however, were as quick as the rest of them to move their financial support on the road out of town. But that, too, is changing slowly. Local banks are renewing their downtown commitments. Many resist the temptation to move their offices out of downtown and are taking a new look at downtown investments. Now, the challenge is to get them to eschew the easy, suburban transplant, formula investment in favor of the more sidewalk- and pedestrian-friendly investment that adds real life.

INNOVATION CHANGES PERCEPTIONS

Before Quincy Market's success in Boston, experts declared cities and their commercial centers dead, places that could no longer hope to draw shoppers or visitors. When Quincy Market opened, those same experts were astounded at the response. Boston's Quincy Market, the combination of food, fun, informal public gathering, history, and pushcart entrepreneurs, illustrated the great untapped regenerative potential of downtowns. Filled at first with small, local businesses selling regionally produced goods, the public flocked there when it opened in 1976.[9] Developers rethought their lack of confidence in the future of cities. Success continued, but familiar chains moved in and now dominate. Quincy Market is a mere shadow of what it was, a model of innovation and an incubator of new local businesses. Sales are now flat. While the stores are primarily the same chains as in ordinary malls, Quincy Market remains a great pedestrian-oriented gathering place, even if it is no longer innovative. Strategies to rejuvenate the original Festival Marketplace emphasize the need to regenerate local businesses.

A key to Quincy's uniqueness and subsequent success is that it is, essentially, several busy shopping streets. A street-like aisle even runs through each building with vendors in very tight spaces. Important layout and design issues were dictated by the site and the buildings. Enclosure was never a possibility, and the car not the defining force. The street, an unequivocal urban passageway, is the defining feature. Imitations always omitted the character-forming elements of the original.

BUILDING ON RESOURCES

In Denver, preservationist Dana Crawford's rescue and restoration of a handsome block of traditional storefront buildings, renamed Larimer Square, showed that the downtown shopping experience in a big city could still have appeal, even in the 1960s.[10] Crawford, with her husband John and a group of investors, demonstrated that late-19th century commercial buildings had a 20th-century use which, by itself, was a major achievement. Demolition fever was then like a cancer spreading across the American landscape, stopping only where tenacious and farsighted citizens, like Crawford, stood their ground successfully.

In 1954, Crawford moved to Denver from Boston to work for a public relations consulting firm. Immediately, she saw the potential of renovating and reusing the wonderful old downtown buildings under the same kind of single-owner management then happening in suburban shopping centers. She did not buy any property until 1964, when she started assembling what became Larimer Square. She was aware that both sides of Larimer Street were scheduled for demolition for an urban renewal plan, which was not officially announced until 1965. But she was already moving ahead. Soon, she had a few buildings occupied with up-and-running businesses: Your Father's Mustache, a banjo night spot; four small shops; 6000 square feet of upper-floor offices; a restaurant, Café Promenade; and an ice cream parlor. "Enough," says Crawford, "to catch on, especially with our first big block party event at Christmastime. It doesn't take John Q. Public long to discover something new and wonderful." The urban renewal project was officially approved in 1967 and Crawford had to "fight it out building by building" to keep the bulldozer away from Larimer Square. But scores of downtown blocks of what Crawford describes as "gorgeous, magnificent" buildings were lost. As popular as Larimer Square and Lower Downtown are today, Crawford still believes that "most people in this city don't understand what was lost, although they do appreciate what has been saved and revitalized." Learning lessons is just not something American cities are good at.

While the Boston and Denver projects are both in big-city downtowns, they are markedly different. Quincy Market is in one big notable landmark, while Larimer Square is a block of typical Victorian storefront buildings. Larimer Square was bought building by building, never fully assembled into one operating entity, and tenanted slowly, since few believed any new business could make it in a downtown. In fact, Crawford herself opened a restaurant and the first combination fresh food market and café. One building remains an office supply store and in the same ownership as 30 years ago, the owner refusing to sell to Crawford and subsequent Larimer Square owners.

Larimer Square emulated shopping center management techniques, notably with a lease with a base rent, a percentage of profits, and assessments for joint promotions. Single ownership and control of every building was Crawford's goal, and is something considered necessary by many people. Yet the dynamic of a successful street does not require it. Two sites Crawford also never acquired, where single buildings had been demolished, now have new buildings on them, appropriately designed to fit in scale without replicating the old. And Crawford transformed two empty sites into a vest-pocket park that has become very important to the district.

Sold twice since Crawford began, Larimer Square has a comfortable mix of retail, restaurant, and upstairs uses and a balance of locally-owned and national chain stores. Nothing about this block appears unusual today. It is very much part of the larger downtown street network. The blocks around it are similarly filled with a mélange of commercial, residential, and retail uses. Pedestrians are plentiful. New things are happening in small increments. Nothing seems predictable. It is as urban as can be.

Larimer Square was indeed a pioneering enterprise in the 1960s and it still is. It was a catalyst for the rebirth of the surrounding Lower Downtown, a wonderful hodgepodge of 19th-century warehouse and factory buildings, filled with apartments, artists' lofts, offices, galleries, restaurants, and stores. SoHo West, one might call it.[11] The Lower Downtown loft conversion trend did not start until the 1980s, again with a Crawford first,[12] but the fact that Larimer Square was there and represented a win against traditional urban renewal, and a contrast to it, helped accelerate the momentum in the 1990s. Lower Downtown has already changed—and continues to change—the face and personality of Denver. Today, the rich and varied economic life of Denver is clearly much more apparent in this older section of downtown. People are everywhere, shopping, meeting, doing business, socializing. New woven into the old. The adjacent high-rise section of downtown that functions more like an office park than a city is sterile and lifeless in comparison.

The Corning, Boston, and Denver efforts all showed how downtown architectural resources can be put to good use to produce something economically viable. The answer to how most of the successful downtown rebirth efforts have started all over the country—from modest Main Streets, like Medina, Ohio; Saratoga Springs, New York; and Boulder, Colorado, to major cities, like Seattle, Boston, San Francisco, and San Antonio—is not what most project-focused developers, planners, and political leaders ever want to hear. But the evidence is clear. Most started as historic preservation projects, or, at least, renovation and reuse of existing buildings or spaces not always considered architecturally noteworthy. They exemplify Urban Husbandry, not Project Planning, the two conflicting revitalization approaches spotlighted in the next chapter. *Renewal efforts that start modestly with the reuse of existing, mostly underutilized, and often long-neglected buildings have the added, little-recognized bonus of doing more for the local economy and creating more local jobs than major new construction projects.*

As real estate economist Donovan D. Rypkema writes:

> The rehabilitation of historic structures is generally cost competitive with new construction but is much more labor intensive. The net effect of this difference is that the local economic impact of construction expenditures on older buildings is significantly greater than on new buildings. Each million dollars spent on rehabilitation will create 3.4 **more** jobs than will the same amount spent on new construction. Each $1 million spent on rehabilitation of historic buildings creates 15.6 construction jobs [and] 14.2 jobs elsewhere in the economy...[13]

PEOPLE MAKE THE DIFFERENCE

The businesses and programs that make downtown unique and, thereby, successful are those that reflect the personality of people, local people, not the formula chains. There is nothing anonymous about any of the rejuvenation efforts we will describe. No one is calling the shots in some distant corporate headquarters. The decision makers, employers, employees, primary customers, marketers, all have a personal stake in the community. And they spend their hard-earned income in the community.

An East Aurora, New York, woman takes sandwiches around town serving merchants and business people and, thereby, creates a

Karen Mayhew, of Daily's, takes sandwiches around to merchants and business people on Main Street in East Aurora, New York.

new food business. She branches out to catering, opens a retail store for baked goods and specialty foods, and contemplates opening a restaurant in the center of downtown. A pair of enterprising Ybor City (once a trolley-car neighborhood of Tampa), Florida, coffee shop owners chose not to put their business on Main Street but rather on the side street, where it was cheaper and more offbeat. Unwittingly, they helped spark expansion of the commercial district. Similarly, a new Ybor City tile business chose a side street to avoid being overwhelmed by walk-in trade and helped the rebirth spread. In scores of downtowns, property owners adapt the upper vacant floors of Main Street buildings for apartments and live/work space, reintroducing a round-the-clock residential component for the first time in decades. New, inexpensive housing is created in the process. Schoolchildren and adults—100 volunteers in all—in Corning, New York, help move a bookstore across the street, transferring 11,000 books in a half hour. The store owner contributes three cents for each book to the public library. A Blytheville, Arkansas, bookstore owner decides to restore the façade of her downtown store. She invites children and adults in the community to design tiles based on their favorite book. One thing leads to another, new community traditions are born, and a downtown store evolves into a community center. High school biology students, a stone's throw from riot-torn Crenshaw Boulevard in South Central Los Angeles, turn a class project garden into a farmers' market enterprise and then a bottled salad dressing business, Food from the 'Hood, that is funding college scholarships and giving hope to a depressed community.

The conventional spotlight on change around the country rarely focuses on the individuals who make positive change happen in small, steady, incremental doses, but they are what really makes it happen. Such catalysts for positive, enduring change are the true heroes of downtown rebirth.

One former Brooklyn policeman saw economic potential and aesthetic value for small-shop manufacturers in an empty Civil War warehouse and took a risk in rehabilitating the building in the face of disbelieving city planners. The planners assumed that such buildings lacked future use and believed erroneously that manufacturing is an enterprise in irreversible decline. Old manufacturing neighborhoods could be replaced with new uses and big projects, they reasoned. Forty businesses now occupy several revived buildings around this warehouse. In another section of Brooklyn, city planners viewed an old vacant manufacturing building as unusable. They viewed it as a site for future residential and commercial redevelopment with great views of the Manhattan skyline, the kind of project plans for which big investors would be found. Unbeknownst to city planners who don't get very familiar with the sites they plan for, small furniture manufacturers using new, computer-based state-of-the-art technology had been happily renting space in this declared surplus building, creating desperately needed blue-collar jobs. That Greenpoint Design Center is now a model being emulated around the country. New York has been losing manufacturing for decades because planners and elected officials with limited vision operate on the misguided assumption that manufacturing has no future; they are not inclined to help sustain it and don't know how to nurture its growth.

Greenpoint Manufacturing and Design Center, Brooklyn, New York. A formerly vacant manufacturing building filled with small furniture and related businesses.

Some planners are far-sighted. In the former lumber-dependent community of Arcata, California, three incubator projects were started by planners who surveyed what was already getting started by aspiring local entrepreneurs and then provided them appropriate workspace in city-owned buildings. A sleeping bag maker who was using the back of his Volkswagen van as a sewing room, an architectural wood products maker who was using his garage, and assorted specialty food producers who were using their own kitchens were all given workspace in empty manufacturing buildings owned by the city. In addition, and most importantly, they were given access to market-rate financing rarely available to new enterprises, along with marketing assistance and invaluable exposure in a mail-order catalogue created to promote locally-made goods.

These new manufacturing enterprises are providing the financial boost that economic development experts have been trying to achieve for years. The success here is based on giving birth to new businesses instead of trying to lure mature businesses from outside the local economy at great expense and without enduring success. Similar projects are sprouting up across the country. They are an untapped potential of new downtown growth. This is how cities and their vibrant economic life started.

INCREMENTAL DEVELOPMENT BUILDS ON LOCAL CHARACTER

At one time, most of downtown America had the potential for the kind of renewal illustrated in this book. The assortment of building types in every downtown reflects historic growth patterns, and economic and social uses indigenous to each town and city across the country. Variation occurs in numbers and combinations. Architectural styles are classic, with some local differences reflective of individual craftsmen and builders. But a 22-foot-wide, three- or five-story Italianate Victorian commercial building with wide storefront windows could be the same in Montana as in Vermont. A 19th-century red brick factory building on a Brooklyn pier does not look very different from one at the dam site of Sheboygan Falls, Wisconsin. A 1920s neo-Classical-styled bank in Hannibal, Missouri, now a museum, looks the same as a bank in Hudson, New York, now a city hall. A Newberry's, one of the five-and-dime chain stores of the early 20th century, on Canal Street in New Orleans, looks no different from the Newberry's in Burlington, Iowa.

Distinctively ornamented 1920s downtown office buildings, entered through majestic lobbies,[14] announced to visitors they were in a cathedral of commerce. Woolworth's and Newberry's, with their deep-red signage and gold leaf letters, the Art Deco McCrory's, the black-on-yellow-porcelain-front Kresge's, all with their almost uninterrupted glass storefronts, created displays to lure pedestrian shoppers. Movie palaces of the 1920s, 1930s, and 1940s offered fantasy to the audience even before the lights went out—styled in Baroque, Egyptian, Mediterranean, and Colonial Revival. Art Deco and Carrara glass (generically called structural pigmented glass) storefronts of the 1930s, the incorporation of neon in the 1940s, and the use of stainless steel in the 1950s reflect the economic substance and changing tastes of a community. The porcelain-enamel fronted car showrooms of the 1950s sprang up first in the very downtowns being left behind as the car culture evolved.

These building forms emerged when local growth took place. While these building types and architectural styles were generically American, they varied from place to place, often in delicate details. In fact, where enough buildings remain, an observer can "read" the community's history on its streets, tell in what era the downtown prospered, and sometimes discern the source of its prosperity. One can also determine when the Depression hit and if the economy did well during World War II.

American commercial centers had different origins—a trading post, a market town, a river crossing, a railroad stop, a manufacturing center—but they shared similar development patterns. Buildings were built to fill real needs, often by the business owners planning to occupy them. Downtown's physical growth paralleled a town's social and economic growth. Planning, as we know it today, had nothing to do with it.

Growth and change continued this historic building-by-building, block-by-block pattern until World War II and the post-war government "renewal" programs that followed. Massive highways and urban renewal projects tore through many downtowns, ripping apart the complex fabric that was a "place" and an economy, making the reweaving challenge extraordinarily difficult. Investment left town on the new highways to the new suburbs. Government-subsidized mortgage programs encouraged "new" home purchase outside of cities. An astronomically expensive, publicly-sponsored new infrastructure (financed with urban tax dollars) made regional malls a developer's dream. Existing downtown infrastructure and commercial districts were sapped of maintenance and reinvestment resources.

THE COST KEEPS MOUNTING/PAYBACK TIME

The public investment in a new and sprawling landscape was what government was about in those days, when attention was concentrated on converting a vast economic war machine to domestic service. The automobile and construction industries were the primary beneficiaries and as long as they were fueled, the thinking went, prosperity would continue. The society in which, as Jane Holtz Kay observes in *Asphalt Nation,*[15] "everything was linked by rail and available by motorcar" began to unravel slowly. The automobile became the engine that drove the economy in the put-people-back-to-work days after World War II. And the 1956 Highway Act put us firmly on the road to the current condition, where more than half the space in the downtowns of our cities is devoted to cars (two-thirds for Los Angeles), 20 percent of most family budgets is devoted to the car, more than half of the oil consumption of the country is car-related, the annual cost of owning and using a car has reached $6500, and automobile accidents cause 120 deaths a day. The environment was damaged. Democratic institutions dependent on the connections among people eroded. Investors abandoned existing communities. The consequences were ignored or dismissed.

Now, the price tag is beyond calculation. The rescue of our once-great mass transit systems, existing deteriorating infrastructure, once-thriving and still functional downtowns, and once-stable and architecturally irreplaceable historic neighborhoods of both the affluent and lower income is imperative and expensive. *Spending public dollars on such essentials as mass transit, downtown sidewalks, street lights, and water systems was once considered public investment. Today such spending is labeled public subsidy.*

Electoral power has followed the highway to suburbia and downtowns are left with a diminished tax base and fewer financial resources to make up for years of neglect and suburban-focused investment. But great resources remain, often intact and undervalued. Downtown's location, its infrastructure, the buildings, *whatever* remains is still a resource, and can be redeveloped to greater advantage than starting from scratch on undeveloped land.

Economist Donovan Rypkema affirms the value of downtown America's mature infrastructure, above- and below-ground, when he tells audiences:

A downtown that is allowed to deteriorate with buildings sitting empty wastes assets that have already been paid for. It is exactly the same as buying a new police car but only driving it on Fridays, or paying a full-time salary to an assessor who only works twice a week. Certainly taxpayers wouldn't stand for that as public policy. A community wastes taxpayers' dollars every day when downtown is being used at thirty or forty or fifty percent of its capacity. Commitment to downtown revitalization and reuse of historic buildings may be the most effective single act of fiscal responsibility a local government can take.

Kennedy Smith, director of the National Main Street Center in Washington, D.C., reports receiving a steady stream of inquiries from new or growing businesses of all kinds seeking to locate in traditional downtowns of all sizes where needed services and stores—the post office, copying services, office supply stores, government offices, the bank—are within walking distance. In this location-neutral, telecommunications era, many businesses *can* be anywhere. But they still rely on networks of other businesses, services, and *people*. Quality of life and quality of place become critical for location-neutral businesses. Downtown has what many are looking for.

The computer age has not diminished the need for human interaction. In fact, the need for interaction has intensified. Computers have not made isolation preferable to social congregation. They have, however, broadened the choices for living and working. And where are people often choosing to set up shop—in centers, in small towns and big cities, on Main Street, or in gritty urban areas like New York's Silicon Alley (see Chapter 13), the lively section of lower Manhattan where hundreds of small companies with creative young talent are creating new industries in computer-cluttered lofts.

Talk of "community-based" planning is everywhere, although few actually mean genuine community planning where the wisdom of the local users with the real experience with and knowledge of the local place is expressed foremost in plans. Renewed respect for traditional patterns of development that predate the Project Planners is clearly widespread. Historic Preservation. Transit-Oriented Design. Pedestrian-Friendly Design. Community Redevelopment. New Urbanism. The terms are flying fast. Strengthening existing downtowns, renewing community centers, reactivating public spaces, reweaving compact walkable, efficient, practical, and human scale communities is urgent. This starts downtown. Understanding this is the first step to renewal.

1. In one area, transportation, these issues did penetrate congressional debate, during consideration of the 1991 Intermodal Surface Transportation and Efficiency Act (ISTEA) and during reauthorization in 1997. ISTEA embodied a major reversal from a highway-directed federal transportation policy to a balanced policy that focuses on moving people, not vehicles.
2. *Washington Post Writers group,* March 11, 1996.
3. *Washington Post Writers group,* March 25, 1996.
4. "Mobilizing the Region," the Tri-State Transportation Campaign Newsletter. This weekly newsletter is a model bulletin of new developments relating to transportation and sprawl issues. The Tri-State Transportation Campaign is a regional transportation and mass transit advocacy group.
5. Constance E. Beaumont, *Smart States, Better Communities* (Washington, D.C.: National Trust for Historic Preservation, 1996).
6. New York: Doubleday, 1988.
7. September 1996.
8. Collaborator Norman Mintz was the creator of this program and its director for the first nine years. The Main Street Manager concept was born here. For the full story of both Corning's Market Street Project and Boston's Quincy Market, see *The Living City: Thinking Small in a Big Way* by Roberta Brandes Gratz, copyright 1994, published by the Preservation Press/John Wiley & Sons, Inc.
9. See *The Living City*, p. 285, for the full story.
10. In 1995, Dana Crawford received the Louise duPont Crowninshield Award for lifetime preservation achievement from the National Trust for Historic Preservation for her recognition of the aesthetic and economic value of commercial buildings and for being a spark for renewing vibrant life in Denver's downtown.
11. See Chapter 13, The SoHo Syndrome.
12. Crawford converted the Edbrooke Warehouse to a 44-unit condominium in 1990, before Denver real estate values recovered from the regional depression of the early 1980s. The solid, red brick structure was designed by Frank Edbrooke, the most prolific architect of 19th- century Denver, who designed some of the most notable landmarks Denver lost to demolition. He considered a warehouse worthy of equal design attention.
13. *Virginia's Economy and Historic Preservation: The Impact of Preservation on Jobs, Business and Community*, a 1995 study for the Preservation Alliance of Virginia.
14. As distinguished from the mammoth-scale lobbies today that try to do with super-scale and super-glitz what older lobbies had in class and elegance. Today's oversized lobbies tend to squelch the human spirit, instead of making it soar.
15. New York: Crown, 1997, p. 161.

Disney on 42nd Street

New York
Public Library
on 42nd
Street

Bryant Park

Mega towers
still to come

Times Square's New
Year's ball drops

CHAPTER THREE

PROJECT PLANNING OR URBAN HUSBANDRY
THE CHOICE

Two approaches invariably conflict in each story of downtown change. The first and most prevalent is the project approach to rebirth, what I call *Project Planning*. The fundamentals are always recognizable.

This approach assumes that a void exists that can be filled with a project. The planning process is designed to achieve the project, market it, sell it, and involve the public in selecting a predetermined solution—in other words, the project. The Project Planning process should not be confused with a problem-solving process. A problem-solving process may or may not involve a project. Project-based Planning does. The problem, if there was one, remains unsolved.

Under Project-based Planning, a project must be big to be meaningful. Big projects require big, experienced developers, big contractors, big government agencies, big public financial support, and lots of investment banking and legal fees. Under this Project-based Planning, the new is added at a large enough scale to overwhelm and alter what exists. What exists may be wiped out entirely, as with urban renewal. Something radically replaces it. Few clues are left as to what has been lost and what alternative strategy has been missed.

Historian Richard Rabinowitz takes an interesting view of the project approach to change. The word project, he notes, derives from the Latin for "throw forward," to throw forward into the future, to thrust into a void. For many centuries, the word in English, when used as a noun, meant a plan or design, not the activity by which the design was carried out. With the introduction of calculus into engineering in the 1860s, the term "project" took on new meanings. Construction became more and more the province of professional architects and engineers. University-trained professionals began to use more sophisticated mathematical tools like integral calculus and probability theories of one kind or another, rather than working in an improvisational manner, learning on-site or "playing it by ear." Calculus permitted making projections with less information. Designers could thus make bolder assumptions about building loads or stresses, and they could more confidently schedule work tasks, labor needs, and expenses. Gradually, more and more of the entire job was dictated by the original design or "project."

The word "project" became a part of educators' jargon around 1910, when it was decided that children would learn more by being given assignments in writing, history, or science. The schools thus fostered the notion that everything first had to be planned, that all the steps of the process had to follow what had been originally planned, and that success would come when the plan had been fulfilled, when the "project was done," rather than (as before) when a good job had been performed. *A completed project and a job well done are not the same thing.*

By the 1930s, the word had been applied, now as a plural, to the public housing built during the New Deal. After World War II, it triumphed as the choice word to describe virtually every task, activity, enterprise, endeavor, or piece of work in the social world. Businesses, government, and nonprofit organizations have since adopted "project budgeting," by which each discrete activity is the subject of an independent forecast and assessment.

Inevitably, designers working over a drawing board fall prey to an illusion: They begin to think of the world or of the future as if it were a piece of blank paper. The completed project, projected into the future, becomes the singular focus. The setting of the work, the existing conditions in the field, are often reduced to information at the margins of the paper. Everything else that might be happening at the same time is closed off from view as the engineer draws his or her finger along the project timeline.

We are all now captives of Project Planning, without recognizing the way it narrows our understanding of the world. Accountability is reduced to complete implementation of a pre-existing plan. No matter how hard we try to do "master planning," taking account of more and more variables and contingencies, using more and more complex software planning programs, we harden ourselves against an awareness of what places are really like—where people live, work, own property and businesses—and how they persist, change, and evolve around the tyranny of our plans. Project Planning is a scientific approach to change, based on data,[1] calculations, and projections.

The key word is science, a science based on calculations, projections, and formulas. Planning has become science-like, a practice based on theory, statistical data, demographics, and projections. A project gets planned, measured, calculated, projected. It gets implemented in well-planned stages. And then it is done, finished, completed, occupied, or used. Perfect for ribbon-cutting. Cities, downtowns, and active places, however, defy scientific assessments. They cannot be reduced to scientific formulas. Urbanism is an art, not a science. Urbanism, not urbanology.

When city problems are approached scientifically, the complexity that is the essence of urbanism is unrecognized, ignored, or lost. "...there is no use wishing it were a simpler problem or trying to make it a simpler problem, because in real life it is not a simpler problem," writes Jane Jacobs.[2]

Jacobs, probably the 20th century's most influential critic of urban planning, wrote in clear and enduring terms about the complex organisms that are cities in *The Death and Life of Great American Cities* and *The Economy of Cities*, among others. We must "think of cities as problems in organized complexity—organisms that are replete with unexamined, but obviously intricately interconnected, and surely understandable, relationships," she wrote. "Although the inter-relations of their many factors are complex, there is nothing accidental or irrational about the ways in which these factors affect each other."[3] Many Project Planners and the developers who cite the ideas of Jane Jacobs claim to embrace them, and then totally misapply them.

Project Planners dominate the citadels of power. Planning professionals, developers, Wall Street investors, and the like consider Project Planning the only approach worth talking about, the only one requiring complicated financial packages. Only Project Planning, of course, is dependent on *them*. Project Planners dismiss anything else as irrelevant, anything that places more confidence in the judgment of citizen users. Downtowns are pockmarked with their accomplishments. Only Project Planners, their followers, and the public persuaded by their rhetoric define these downtowns as reborn. *Rebuilt, yes; reborn, hardly.*

Opponents of Project Planning recognize and celebrate the complexity about which Jacobs writes. We call them *Urban Husbanders*. Urban Husbanders is a term I introduced and summarized in *The Living City*.[4] Urban Husbanders assume that assets are already in place to be reinvigorated and built onto in order to stimulate a place-based rejuvenation that *adds* to the long-evolving, existing strengths, instead of *replacing* them. Planning is meant to be about problem solving, relying heavily on the expertise of citizen users, the accumulated experience and wisdom of the community. Building on resources to diminish or overcome problems is the chosen route, instead of projects that obliterate those worthy resources. Urban Husbanders advocate introducing change incrementally and monitoring it carefully, providing a great opportunity to learn from each step. Urban Husbanders are the initiators of most of the downtown successes in this book.

Proponents of Urban Husbandry strengthen what exists before adding anything new. They involve many entrepreneurs of various sizes, not just one big developer. Urban Husbanders rely only on modest doses of government support, if any. Urban Husbanders are the most frequent opponents of Project Planners. They work to add a layer of organic urban growth, rather than replace what has taken decades to grow. This layer may look and feel in many ways radically different from what was there before but, fundamentally, the connection between before and after is not broken.

Urban Husbanders view any place, a downtown or a neighborhood, as a garden. Something exists with which to work, something fundamentally of value by virtue of its history of organic growth over time. Maybe the garden contains dead plants to weed out. Undoubtedly, other plants need attention, need to be nurtured, cut back, fertilized. Introducing a new and alien plant, and plowing under the remaining garden in the process, is not considered. Replacement is not only uncalled for, but it also requires a great deal more effort, money, and big machinery. The garden is rebuilt with some or most of the existing plants in place. Urban Husbanders change the proportions of the plant mix. They may add new varieties and remove some old ones. But the essential garden remains and, in the end, only requires continued, modest attention from local gardeners, Urban Husbanders, with occasional small outside help.

URBANOLOGY VERSUS URBANISM

Project Planners don't need to worry much about the people or businesses in place or the existing garden when they devise a downtown redevelopment policy. People and businesses get relocated or "plowed under." Plants are transplanted, perhaps to a garden with a different, less compatible soil. Sometimes they are torn out from their roots and discarded. The garden is replaced.

If you look at a downtown from the Project Planner's point of view, you can easily support the demolition in 1989 of Omaha's Jobber's Canyon District, seven blocks of solidly built, 19th-century red brick warehouses, for a suburban campus-style headquarters of the multinational, agri-business, ConAgra, instead of recognizing the greater intrinsic value of a SoHo-style rejuvenation that would have enhanced the entire downtown. This missed opportunity and tragedy was compounded by the demolition of 1.7 million square feet of loft space for the construction of less than 200,000 square feet of office space. Five hundred existing jobs and plenty of growth room were lost and 430 corporate headquarters jobs gained. Plus, if ConAgra moves, there will be no jobs, not to mention the impact of "downsizing."

A Project Planner would also support the Circle Centre Mall in Indianapolis, with its up-in-the-air, off-the-street park and enclosed walkways to six hotels, the convention center, and RCA Dome. With shops, nightclubs, a nine-screen theater, and a virtual reality playground, what chance does the downtown outside the walls of the mall have? Circle

Centre Mall incorporates into its exterior wall the façades of the demolished 130-year-old historic buildings. This technique is called "Façadism." Façadism provides an illusion of urbanism. *An illusion of urbanism is what many downtowns have settled for.* An Urban Husbander would have instead nurtured those Indianapolis streets and their individual assortment of buildings, celebrated and enhanced the peculiar personality of those streets, and fostered genuine urbanism that draws people to a street, not a separate and segregated single interior space.

An Urban Husbander would have found creative ways to enhance what little urban fabric is left in that downtown into a lively, diverse place that reflects the city of Indianapolis instead of the developer of the mall. Boston's Newberry Street, Pasadena's Colorado Avenue, or New York's Columbus Avenue. Denver's Lower Downtown, New York's SoHo, or San Francisco's South of Market. These are streets and districts that distinguish a place. They nurture urbanism and foster its spread. An enclosed mall does the reverse. Indianapolis and the multitude of other over-projected, becalmed cities need this kind of nurturing desperately, if they actually have any authentic urban fabric left to nurture. Too many are still going the anti-urban, anti-place route of the enclosed suburban mall. In Norfolk, Virginia, a SoHo-like district was showing signs of renewed life and slowly but naturally attracting new businesses and people. Instead of nurturing this revival, building on and adding to its momentum, the city followed the conventional Project Planning route of the enclosed mall. This pattern is all too familiar elsewhere.

Highway fights are endless. Route 710 is the Extension of the Long Beach Freeway (Pasadena Freeway). This button has become generic.

A Project Planner could advocate highways to take vehicles *through* the Bronx for the Cross-Bronx Expressway where, in one mile out of seven, 113 streets were bisected, 159 buildings containing 1530 families (5000 people) and countless small businesses in working-class neighborhoods were wiped out, creating an instant slum that would forever need more big projects to rebuild. The resulting slum, in the end, blighted hundreds of thousands of housing units and many square miles of land. This four-decade-old tale has its counterpart in the current embattled planned project of the South Pasadena Freeway Extension that would destroy 1000 homes, five historic districts, and 6000 trees. An Urban Husbander would never favor massive highways at the expense of a balanced, functioning mass transit system. Through-town highways undermine the social, economic, and physical fabric of a large swath of city with destructive impacts that continue and spread for decades. They obliterate what has been intelligently built up over time.

Similarly, a Project Planner could support a Nehemiah housing project in Brooklyn's East New York that destroyed the remnants of an authentic urban neighborhood where resources remain to rebuild on.

This is the antithesis of Pittsburgh's once-infamous Hill District being renewed as a neighborhood, not just a monocultural housing project. The lower Hill was a typical 1950s urban renewal project. The occupied homes of more than 8000 residents were demolished for an arts acropolis and new apartments that never happened. "First they took away their homes and built roads to take them out of town," says Arthur Ziegler, a model Urban Husbander who, as head of Pittsburgh History and Landmarks Foundation, has been working for two decades to reweave Pittsburgh's remaining pieces. Those vanished residents are now counted in the numbers of people who "fled" the cities instead of being properly identified as having been "demolished out" of them. The current proposal to fill that still vacant land is to build a 5000-car garage adjacent to the Civic Arena—a Project Plan—creating a further barrier between it and the historic Hill District where cleared land is being appropriately rebuilt. In renewing The Hill, existing housing has been retained, whether split-level 1950s suburban houses or scattered small turn-of-the century brick apartment houses. New two- and three-story attached and detached row houses were built with parking in the rear, side alleys, and lot lines close to the street. Small multi- and single-family units were constructed. This traditional urban variety appeals to a mix of incomes, ages, and family formations.

In East New York, by contrast, 124 buildings, mostly single-family and 10- or 12-unit apartment houses, were demolished, 102 of which were occupied by owners or tenants. A few pockets of occupied buildings were spared only because of a hard-fought battle by community residents. Entire blocks of commercial storefronts were demolished, some containing viable businesses. In place of this traditional urban neighborhood, 650 units of *only* single-family homes with carports were built, a horizontal housing project for homeowners. A low-density suburban housing project on a high-density urban infrastructure, a short walk from a subway. No traditional

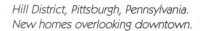

Hill District, Pittsburgh, Pennsylvania.
New homes overlooking downtown.

neighborhood shopping streets were left within walking distance. No nurturing of a corner store, a local eatery, or even barbershop as a community gathering place, social networking opportunities that strengthen a communal fabric. What a wasted opportunity to rejuvenate a place, a community, a neighborhood. Nehemiah was motivated by "lowest cost" thinking, a bottom-line only approach to housing but, in this case, was endorsed and fought for by the City Planning Commission.

Urban Husbandry considers existing life first, respects it, views it as an asset, not a problem, and determines with local users what remedies could improve things. It examines problems from the site, not from a color-coded map, looks at where people live and work, where physical and non-physical impacts will be felt. Urban Husbandry starts with a strategy or a vision that possibly, eventually, but not at first, may include projects of modest scale, projects that repair and add but don't overwhelm. The strategy is adjusted as conditions change.

PROCESS, NOT PROJECTS

Again, the garden analogy is applicable. This is the way a community, a downtown, a neighborhood, a city grows. New things get planted, grow, run out of space, move to new space, and the cycle repeats itself. Things grow at their own pace. This is what is exciting about cities, why they change, grow, evolve. Nothing is frozen in a city. Continuous change is a sign of health in a complex and vibrant downtown. People can move around, according to life requirements. A single person can start in a small apartment, move to a larger one, or even a house, after marriage. With children, larger space may be needed. Alternatives are readily available. Similarly, a business might start small in one district, expand to another with growth, and yet another with more growth, and, perhaps, leave town with maturity and expansion. In a healthy city, businesses move and leave town, but new emerging businesses take their place. Variety of opportunity—the variety within the garden—nurtures the new. This variety gives the city, the community, the neighborhood its strength.

Understanding this, Urban Husbanders fought an excessive development project on the unused railyards of downtown Santa Fe, defeated the project, and persuaded the developer to sell the land to the city. With the help of the Trust for Public Land, a genuine participatory planning process is unfolding that will produce a very localized vision for the railyards' development and a step-by-step strategy to make it happen. Participatory planning is the antithesis of Project Planning.

Urban Husbanders, in the 1970s, fought the demolition in Brooklyn of the tight-knit Northside neighborhood of small homes, local businesses, and scattered factories for the excessive expansion of one company, and assisted that community in strengthening the resources already in place. Some demolition occurred anyway. That company eventually moved to

Ireland and was replaced by a number of small companies and new replacement housing where the old was demolished. The mix of residential and small industry in one neighborhood is once again being appreciated. Only Urban Husbanders recognized its value then. Urban Husbanders understand and value the delicate connections that weave together a stable community and defend that fragile fabric in the face of Project Plans.

Urban Husbanders, in many places, fought for the future of downtown, the local economy, and community values in the face of surrounding mall proliferation. Burlington, Iowa; Holland, Michigan; Franklin, Tennessee; Sheboygan Falls, Wisconsin; and hundreds of other communities of all sizes have successfully followed this route by following the rebirth strategy developed by the National Main Street Center (of the National Trust for Historic Preserva-tion) that starts from the premise that the historic buildings, existing infrastructure, and functioning local businesses are an undervalued resource on which new growth can occur. A rebirth momentum often emerges from the Main Street approach to withstand the competition of surrounding or nearby malls. The rebirth naturally reflects the personality of its place, its local garden.

Urban Husbanders fight suburban home builders wanting to build in inner-city neighborhoods, like Pittsburgh's Manchester, and restore, instead, a splendid assortment of Victorian homes for ownership by neighborhood residents. With the help of the Pittsburgh History and Landmarks Preservation loan fund, Pittsburgh banks, and the Pittsburgh Housing Authority, decades of damaging disinvestment are being reversed. Neighborhoods once written off as "gone" have extraordinary new life. In fact, the vitality and success of these reborn neighborhoods puts to shame the experts' predictions of failure. Project Planners have difficulty recognizing existing assets to build on.

When city problems are approached mechanistically, the complexity that is the essence of urbanism is misunderstood, ignored, or lost. Most significantly, the ability of a city to renew itself without big, publicly financed interventions is lost. The public cost factor is always rationalized. *But it takes more money to damage a downtown with overwhelming Project Plans than to strengthen it and let diverse activities flourish.*

Steve Davies, a vice president of The Project for Public Spaces (PPS), an environmental design firm that helps renew communities, was working with a West Coast city to redesign its center with input from community residents and public officials. PPS was working on small streetscape and parking improvement projects along the Main Street that, years before, had been totally demolished for an enclosed mall. Small groups of local citizens were involved. One public employee from the redevelopment agency coordinated all the city agencies. Small things started happening. Momentum was building. Suddenly, the state got interested in constructing a state office building downtown that would consolidate dispersed offices.

Davies was staggered when he walked into the first meeting about the new state office building. "There was this roomful of men and one woman," he recalls. "Several architects, engineers, a traffic consultant, a cost estimator, a construction manager, parking consultant, retail consultant, several space layout programmers, landscape architects, an environmental consultant, and, of course, staff members of each agency." This is the usual network of people or teams of experts required for a big, planned project. "The cost of that meeting in staff salaries alone," Davies says, "would have paid for one of the small projects we had proposed, such as benches, flower planting, or even a mural. And this was about *consolidating* state offices now sprinkled around town, so there would not even be a net gain for downtown!"

Project Planners don't know how to respond to natural urban change. When challenged, they throw up their hands and say, "The market will take care of it." A fundamental inconsistency marks this view. For almost 30 years, for example, Manhattan's SoHo underwent gradual, evolutionary change. No public incentive or public investment was involved. SoHo had, by the mid-1990s, reached a level of success unsurpassed by any other old manufacturing neighborhood in the country. (See Chapter 13.) By the mid-1990s, however, the art center character appeared threatened. Art galleries were moving out and big retail chains, looking for opportunities in interesting urban locations, were anxious to come in. Planning and elected officials advocated increasing the size limitation of retail businesses from the current 10,000 square feet. The zoning restrictions, planners argued, had not preserved the artistic quality of the district. The market prevails anyway, they said.

Facts contradict this view. Restrictions, in fact, had, up to that point, done a good job limiting *excessive* change. The idea of "no change" was never an option, and can't be achieved anyway. But removing those restraints would surely accelerate unavoidable erosion of the arts-based community and local economic uses. Attributing future change to the "market, anyway" removes responsibility from the city for the zoning changes that would accelerate continued loss of artistic character and guarantee that loss. Inconsistently, in another part of town, the Wall Street area, planners argued on behalf of developer incentives and zoning adjustments to *spur renewal*. Zoning rules could be relied on to encourage developers and spur the market downtown, but not to discourage development and modify the market in SoHo. Zoning can—and does—work both ways. Restraints work to prevent overly large flowers, or killer weeds, from pushing out smaller flowers in a garden. Incentives work to fertilize. The issue with incentives is what is being fertilized, and to what end.

Such inconsistencies represent only one aspect of the Project Planners' approach. Project Planners are *not* trying to solve problems, although that excuse is offered. They seek to fill contrived voids with projects or to fulfill a political agenda. In the case of SoHo, the agenda is to facilitate the entrance into the neighborhood of the superstore clones restrained up until now by zoning limits. *Project Planners expedite real estate development. They do not foster rebirth. Project Planners argue the two are the same. They are not.* The Project Planning story seems to repeat itself, differing in scale and form, but not too much in substance.

42nd STREET AS METAPHOR

The premier example of this sad tale, repeated in microcosm in downtowns across America, is the slow decline and slower rebuilding of 42nd Street, a major spine of Times Square. This story epitomizes them all.

People west of the Hudson resist the notion that what happens in New York City is relevant elsewhere in the country. Similarly, New Yorkers resist the notion that anything that happens west of the Hudson is relevant to them. Holders of both views, east and west of the Hudson, are wrong. Insular thinking undermines learning lessons from other places and limits innovation. New York has a lot to learn from outside places. Those places could learn, as well, from New York City. Parallel tales unfold east and west of the Hudson, north and south of the Mason-Dixon Line, and on both sides of every arbitrary divide.

The particulars vary, but Project Planning has transformed primary streets from New York to Buffalo, Atlanta to San Francisco, and San Antonio to Chicago. Almost every step of the transformation of 42nd Street has its counterpart in other downtowns rebuilt according to big Project Plans. The problems used as the excuse for the 42nd Street Project Plan have *not been solved.* They just have been moved, primarily around the corner and up Eighth Avenue, now an excuse for more Project Plans.

For New York, 42nd Street is one of the primary Main Streets, both the symbolic and real heart of the Big Apple. Times Square, where the diagonal of Broadway crosses 42nd Street, is the crossroads of the city's vibrant life. Every tourist is drawn to this street, not despite its risqué and risky reputation but *because of it.* The aura of danger permits the tourist to report bravely on a visit there. Understandably, tourists seek an excitement and adventure not available close to home.

For decades, 42nd Street, and the entertainment district around it, contained a mix of gathering places, famous restaurants, oddball attractions, and specialty stores selling musical instruments, costumes, wigs. Times Square was the preeminent place where people converged and where anyone and everyone felt more than welcome. Endless choices drew people. This was an unparalleled pedestrian magnet, a place to "hang out," to see and be seen, where novelty was its own reward and the appeal of the place was an exaggeration of the downtown "draw" once experienced in many American downtowns in modest doses.

Decline started slowly and, although it got pretty bad and looked worse, it was never as bad as alarmists maintained, certainly never bad enough to keep people away entirely. The same can be said of downtowns across the country. Perception was always worse than reality. Cities, themselves, were losing their luster. The sense that great popular culture was centered in cities collapsed. Pornography in a permissive atmosphere filled a vacuum left by the diminishment of other "respectable" attractions. Landlords exploited public displeasure with sex-related businesses, neglected their property, and promoted the need for generous government subsidies to "clear" the area of negative uses. Landlords played the waiting game. Planners played the project game. Officials used pornography for political gain.

The rebuilding of 42nd Street was the story of the decade from the 1950s on. Mayors grabbed headlines with promises to clean it up. "Clean up" was the code word for replace with projects, called at various times, "urban renewal" and then "economic development." Expensive tax dollar giveaways followed each mayoral pronouncement, doing everything to lobotomize 42nd Street's personality and nothing to rejuvenate it. Glitzy, foolish, big Plans (with a capital P) to renew the legendary street cropped up every few years. "New Plan to Clean up Downtown" was a formula headline across the country. In the Times Square district, as elsewhere, undistinguished office towers and cookie-cutter hotels, stimulated by official planning and zoning policies and political agendas, replaced mid-size hotels, small businesses, neon, and streetlife (each a variety of flower) of the theater district that reaches north along Broadway to 52nd Street, all the variety and complexity that made the district a splendid garden.

Sex-related businesses (the weeds) survived, however. Illicit uses (varieties of weeds) changed with the times and multiplied. Flowers were rooted out. The long-appealing entertainment district of small interests, large surprises, and co-existence of the legitimate and the disreputable was traded in for the best that a formula-based culture could provide. "Cleaning up" 42nd Street is the longest-running saga in New York, just as renewing downtown is the longest ongoing drama in almost every American city and town. The variation among downtowns can be measured by what was demolished and what is left to rejuvenate.

When I was a young reporter starting in the 1960s at *The New York Post*, "Mayor Promises Cleanup of 42nd Street" could have been a headline left in permanent type. In fact, I worked on one of the investigative stories finding out which landlords were renting to sex-related businesses. Upstanding citizens were prominent among them. Sex businesses paid good rent. Purposeful neglect was rampant. Money was always being made. In every downtown, *the unspoken agenda was often radical surgery and replacement, not to really address the problem. The real problem was never defined and always changed.* This is bait-and-switch planning strategy: Substitute the problem that planning can't solve with one that it can, and for which there is big money available. The solution "to the perennial problem, cleaning up Times Square," wrote *New York Times* architecture critic Herbert Muschamp, was "stomp it to death...'the new 42nd Street' places too much emphasis on the consumption of popular culture, not enough on its production."[5]

In 1981, the city and state had unveiled the $1.6 billion plan. The proposal provided for a rezoning to permit construction of 4.1 million square feet of office space in four towers, two of which would be twice as bulky as zoning normally allows, and all of which would be among the city's largest. The plan also called for a 2.4-million-square-foot merchandise and apparel mart, a 500-room hotel/retail complex, and direct and indirect subsidies of incalculable value. The much-abused Times Tower would be torn down for open space.[6] The mart idea disappeared quickly. Times Tower still stands. Four office towers are being built, one by one. The development of the four towers was supposed to fund a mix of cultural uses on the block. Public officials and real estate experts insisted that the extraordinary scale of office development was *essential* to move forward with the rebirth of the street's soul. No such scenario was necessary.

WAITING FOR DISNEY

Now, at the close of the century, something is happening, something as close as possible to what could have happened without all the big visions and zillions of public dollars. Sadly, it is a sanitized version of the real thing, a nostalgic approximation, a make-believe configuration, the regional mall definition of urban life, a fitting place for a Disney Corporation entry into New York with a big store and a gloriously restored former premier musical house, the 1903 New Amsterdam Theater, for Disney-produced shows.[7] This is not to disparage Disney. Disney on 42nd Street excites a lot of people. This is, after all, the Disney decade. Disneyland's Main Street, still the most popular attraction at Disneyland, is better than most versions created by 20th-century city-building experts, the Project Planners. *Disney's legendary creativity is bound to do more for 42nd Street than decades of wasted public dollars and sterile planning proposals. But it still must be understood as a replacement, not a rejuvenation.* None of the individualized, quirky businesses that were always more plentiful than the porno shops and that once gave the district its unique character will have room to appear. No unusual flowers in this predictable garden. None of the expressions of individual genius that once made the district famous. "A sanitized stage set for tourists on leave from the mall," *New York Times* columnist Frank Rich called it. In other words, a theme park. The only flowers of the original garden will be the unreplicable, historic theaters, saved from destruction by persevering preservationists and theater people. Those theaters are the only attractions distinguishing the street from a mall. And what of all those sex businesses to be removed by big projects? Some left the scene, though not the city, when their buildings were condemned for redevelopment. Some died, put out of business by competition with home videos. Others just moved around the corner and up Eighth Avenue. Problem sex businesses endure. The rest of the mix, however, is gone. As stated earlier, Project Planning is not problem solving.

All the wrongheaded notions that have deadened or killed Main Streets across America played themselves out on 42nd Street, especially on the entertainment segment between Broadway and Eighth Avenues. The saga of 42nd Street's rebirth is a metaphor for downtown America, except that both the street and its city are, of course, larger than life.

Forty-Second Street was an organically formed entertainment district. Cultural- and economics-based districts naturally evolve in healthy cities, one of the many aspects of real cities neither sufficiently recognized nor appreciated. Forty-Second Street and its environs illustrates the phenomenon of great urban districts, unique to cities, in fact. They are agglomerations that have an important impact on the economy of a city, providing fertile ground for new entrepreneurs to get started, to grow to maturity, and to leave. Where that cycle is allowed to repeat itself with new agglomerations replacing old ones (e.g., Silicon Alley in Manhattan's Flatiron District, as will be discussed) and where urban downtowns remain a starting place for new economic uses, urban economies do well. Where such districts are destroyed, it becomes harder for cities to propagate new businesses or cultural institutions. They function like a monoculture, with no ability to nourish variety or to survive a blight afflicting their singular purpose.

Natural agglomerations do not survive getting spiffed up, moved around, or added to with big projects. Projects replace. They don't add. Once a garden is uprooted, it is hard to replant after the replacement falls short. Project Planning undermines the organic process, instead of nourishing it. Natural districts are misinterpreted today and translated into "themes" and "clusters" that never add up to more than "themes" and "clusters." Contrivances can't endure. Districts cannot be created or imposed. They can only evolve. The legendary 42nd Street evolved. Nobody planned it. No consultant picked its uses and screened its entrepreneurs. It grew in small and large pieces and, for a long time, adapted easily to constantly changing times.

THE SMALL PROJECT AS CATALYST

In the mid-1970s, major strides were initiated on 42nd Street between 9th and 10th Avenues, where seedy and sleazy uses rivaled neighbors on the more famous blocks just to the east. A modest nonprofit effort called Theater Row renovated a series of brownstones and commercial buildings, creating small theaters for off-Broadway productions, rehearsal studios, classrooms, commercial spaces, and restaurants. Edwin Wilson looked back on this in *The Wall Street Journal*: "...a cozy, inviting group of off-Broadway and off-off-Broadway theaters began to thrive."[8] Apartments were rented upstairs. A few offbeat restaurants opened. And strategies were devised to fill in some empty spaces and add to existing buildings on the block.

This was a small effort by New York's exaggerated development standards, but it illustrated the creative possibilities when conventional approaches called for only demolition and building new. This was a significant accomplishment at the time, and it gained a lot of attention. The success of Theater Row was doomed not to be repeated, not to be allowed to gain momentum and spread. Midtown New York became out-of-bounds for modest-scale change. Other agendas took precedence. Theater Row's vision was too small. Its innovations could not be translated into a "development" formula. It was not compatible with the real estate community that would come to dominate New York, as in so many American cities. Ironically, it served a purpose for the big plans. It seeded a portion, a fringe, of the garden and legitimized the Project Plans and formula investment that followed. How many downtowns have seen this modest beginning interrupted before full flowering had its chance? From the Gaslight District of San Diego, to Riverwalk in San Antonio, to Granby Street in Norfolk, such tales abound.

Big Ideas, Big Visions, Big Plans—and the big public subsidies they require—had taken root in the collective mind of New York and downtown America's political, planning, design, and development establishment and in the downtowns across America. Forty-Second Street became the new focus and the unfortunate beneficiary of French architect Le Corbusier and his Super-Bloc/Tower-in-the-Park, "first kill the street" theories that gave birth to the raze-and-rebuild beginning of Project Planning. "The idea, adopted from Le Corbusier, was to create cities that suited the needs of corporation managers—cities that were, however, unlivable for everyone else," says Dr. Vincent Scully. Le Corbusier changed the view of cities. Buildings became machines. Cities were dehumanized.

Forty-Second Street had evolved in small pieces, reflecting changing entertainment tastes, architectural fashions, and builder/impressario egos, and it gracefully absorbed big and little changes in the entertainment industry. Somehow, this world-famous gathering place had successfully weathered transitions from the 1920s right up to the 1960s: from vaudeville, to music halls, to legitimate theater, to first-run movie houses, where movie stars came for glamorous openings and crowds gathered to watch. Through all these decades, the illicit and illegal co-existed with the acceptable, periodically provoking expressions of moral outrage. But, after 100 years, only the big solution appealed to government, guaranteeing years of expensive planning, debating, legislating, negotiating, and taxpayer incentives...and *the killing of place in the name of saving it. This was the new way to rebuild cities.*

No one in any city arguing for an alternative approach wanted to preserve pornography or the negative uses that went with it. Architecture critic Robert Campbell, in a 1995 *Boston Globe* column wrote about that city's deteriorated theatrical heart, Washington Street, and the impending demolition of two historic theaters, "yet another gap in a street that is already becoming very gappy." What he also said about Washington Street can, of course, be said of 42nd Street and dozens of other plowed-under urban hearts:

> The argument I've had with the city folks who want to get rid of these buildings on Washington Street—they say, "Oh my God, it is pornography! We have to clean it out." But it seems to me that tearing down these buildings to get rid of pornography would be very much like solving the bedbug problem in your house by demolishing it. It doesn't make a great deal of sense. And we think of very, very badly deteriorated neighborhoods in other cities...the Marais in Paris, the Covent Garden Points area in London, an appalling slum at the turn of the century...Columbus Avenue in New York[9] and many, many others. *From among the very worst neighborhoods in cities some of the very best neighborhoods, without demolition, have been created.*

Campbell noted about Washington Street: "Like similar hearts of other cities, it's long been weakening. But there are encouraging signs." Things were already happening in this old retail and entertainment core, Campbell also wrote. College students were moving into downtown locations. "UMass, Northeastern and Emerson College—the latter with a major theater-arts program—are all nearby in the wings. Another neighbor, Suffolk University, announced plans to convert an old office building on Tremont Street into a dormitory."

Forty-Second Street could be flourishing today, if, in the 20 years since the Theater Row initiative began, it had been respected as the ultimate entertainment district, "cleaned up" through code and police enforcement to temper the most blatant of the sex uses, well patrolled to keep the sidewalks safe, and if the city had invested directly a fraction of the money given to real estate interests. Real estate values don't inflate as much if government promises don't raise expectations. Many smaller and innovative things could have happened. It is impossible to envision in what form 42nd Street would have evolved. Chances are that Disney would be moving onto the street in some form because the time is right for Disney to be entering downtowns, and where better to start than on this legendary street? "New York is still the place you open a show in, the 'A' place," says architect Robert A. M. Stern.

More than $350 million was spent just acquiring and vacating the buildings. Another fortune was spent relocating hundreds of existing businesses and residents, including a persevering group of artists who hung on until the end. The street was upzoned to a monstrous scale. Feature stories revealed the uniqueness of some of the old buildings as they were being demolished. News reports about the viable businesses and tenants forced out did not appear *until* the end. Stories about the project "moving forward" ran steadily for years. Some would call those stories a lie. Others, more kind, would call them factually challenged. By the time the public opposition and legal resistance (48 lawsuits) were overcome, the real estate market had collapsed (a frequent story with big projects everywhere). No way would the developer proceed as committed. A clause in the complicated deal between the city and the developer said the city could pull the plug on the developer, if the project did not proceed according to the promised time schedule. City officials refused to exercise the option, but agreed, instead, to postpone the tower development, if smaller buildings were built to house stores and restaurants *for the interim*. The developer had to turn over $241 million to the city to retain development rights.

Out of desperation, the city was thinking smaller. Architect Robert A. M. Stern had been called in a few years earlier to assess the restoration potential of the historic theaters. Stern was asked to come up with an "interim plan" of more modest and lively uses to move things forward and encourage long-term investment. Stern, a Disney Company board member, discussed with Disney head Michael Eisner the idea of a Disney theater on 42nd Street. The word got out long before the deal was sealed that Disney was coming. The gold rush was on, but *in small pieces*.

Ferrara's, the famous Greenwich Village/Little Italy coffee house, opened in a low-rise, landmark-quality building slated for demolition. A brewery restaurant opened. Two more historic theaters, the Apollo and the Lyric, have been combined into an 1,850-seat Broadway musical theater, the Ford Center for the Per-

Ferrara's Café opened in this landmark-quality Art Deco building scheduled for demolition, as part of the "interim" plan for 42nd Street. Note the man on the corner handing out flyers to a nearby adult club. Although chased from the area, these spots still exert an influence.

forming Arts. A 25-screen movie complex is going in behind the historic Empire Theater, a one-time burlesque house that is actually being moved 70 feet at a cost of at least $1 million to serve as the entrance and lobby. *The "interim plan" is what the whole plan could have been in the first place.*

Ironic isn't it? The most celebrated change is not a Disney creation, but a splendid historic restoration by Disney—but a restoration nonetheless. With or without Disney, the restoration of the historic theaters is the key, the centerpiece, the most talked about attraction. Theater restorations have anchored many downtown reclamations across America. Disney recognized this, to both its own and the city's benefit.

Disney gave investors confidence. There was no confidence in anyone or anything else. By destroying 42nd Street in order to "save it" (a commonly repeated pattern), no choice remained but a big project, and big projects need big anchors. *Disney is not the villain. The Project Planning mentality is the villain.* Disney, never a factor in the beginning but who could naturally have come to 42nd Street (where else in New York would it have come?), is saving the Project Planners from more years of failure. How many times have we seen good buildings and blocks demolished, Project Plans approved and the market fallen apart? That was supposed to have been one of the most important lessons of Urban Renewal.

Many people assume what has unfolded on 42nd Street—first the 1993 Interim Plan, and then the office buildings that followed—was all part of the plan. People are impressed that Times Square is finally changing, that so much money is being spent, that glitz and glamour are coming in a big way. At first and easy glance, the Project Plan appears to have worked. Not true at all. "...the project hung on despite itself, propped up by billions in tax breaks and real estate write-downs—and blessed with plain good luck," Todd W. Bressi wrote in *Planning Magazine* in September 1996. Fifteen years of a well-funded state development agency and a lot of legal support helped too.

The millions of public tax dollars spent over the years on plans, visions, property condemnation, and big incentives could have been better invested in the reclamation and reprogramming of the street's seven historic but deteriorated theaters (the original excuse, in the first place, for the massive Project Plan). Strengthening the existing viable uses, especially the theatrical support services that were part of the production of culture instead of the development of real estate, could have begun the process. Commercial uses would have clamored to follow, as they are doing elsewhere around the country where this strategy is followed. A zillion dollars of additional subsidies and decades of subsidies could have been avoided.

Instead, 42nd Street is rezoned for towers of unspeakably absurd scale, with tax incentives to go with them. The first office tower was built by a developer who said incentives were unnecessary. Development rights for this choice site were purchased from the first developer, who negotiated the public giveaways. A renewed booming citywide market and two willing tenants made the first building happen. Other developments are in the works, taking advantage of the enormous upzoning accomplished earlier. Public subsidies on top of public subsidies are already committed. As each new building is negotiated, developers are seeking still *more* incentives and additional tax breaks. Millions upon millions have been spent to stimulate development. Nothing made the new development happen until the market was ready and Disney led the way. In the meantime, productive local businesses have been chased away needlessly. Serious theater has shifted further off Broadway, scattered in small theaters around town whose increased or renewed activity is adding new social and economic life to those neighborhoods.

In the end, instead of strengthening what was good, discouraging what was bad, and fostering conditions to let the street flourish in new ways, the 42nd Street that had weathered natural change was destroyed by some good intentions, considerable ignorance, a lot of misguided visions, and greed to be rebuilt in a false way, never to add up to more than a poor imitation of its true self. The original 42nd Street was made up of components if not unique to New York, then a unique version of other things. The new 42nd Street is a combination of chain uses that would be at home in any mall and New York theaters. Only the theaters are authentic. Again, the parallel to so many American downtowns applies. Pizzazz and style can be manufactured, but the richness and yeastiness that is the fundamental appeal of a lively entertainment district, or any lively downtown, whether 42nd Street or elsewhere, cannot be created on a designer's drawing table, even in the multitalented Disney Studio, or sold in national chain stores. Disney will appeal to many, but Disney on 42nd Street eliminates a certain possibility, a certain evolution. Evolution is what enriches a city and keeps it healthy, like a garden. Both the good and bad have been removed. The baby with the bath water.

Even Disney's useful lessons go unlearned. One of the unfortunate ironies of Disneyland is epitomized in the picture-perfect, three-quarters-scale Main Street that American visitors have always loved. The appeal of Disney's Main Street resonates for most American visitors, but few seem to make the connection that the genuine edition—the one Disney copied—could be found in the backyards of most American visitors. But while they could relish the Disney version, they allowed their own local Main Street to fall to the Trojan horse of the larger and larger shopping mall, each more energy-draining and economically murderous than the last. They may have valued it, but surely lacked the tools to preserve it. After all, as noted earlier, most zoning, building, and fire codes prohibited that protection. In a similar way, New York and other downtowns are at risk of worshipping the Disney version of itself, forgetting that Disney has come to New York because, regardless of the city's woes,

New York is unique in the world. Even with Disney, 42nd Street will add up to nothing if it lacks local character, locally-generated life, and local economic activity. Some locally-generated life will come from office towers that could have been built as the market dictated.

Anything interesting and worthy of the urban label that emerges in the final reconfiguration of any downtown district will be there only because citizen activists fought Project Planners in vain, but achieved occasional restraint of scale and somewhat varied uses. Citizen activists fought for—and won—individual landmark designation for most of the districts' irreplaceable theaters after two of the best of them, the Morosco and Helen Hayes, went down needlessly for Atlanta architect John Portman's universally disparaged Marriott Marquis Hotel. Citizen activists fought to retain a semblance of the sparkle. And, by forcing builders to include illuminated signs, at least the illusion exists of the Times Square they destroyed. These were modest, sometimes empty, victories. But these are the qualities that will give the district genuine appeal. The so-called rebirth, widely acclaimed and now under way, may yet be one more act of smoke and mirrors, one veteran theater expert cautions. Spectacle, not theater. Ada Louise Huxtable, in the essay, "Reinventing Times Square," says it all. Her words specify Times Square but recall the policies and conjure up the image of so many American downtowns:

> ...It is hard to believe that no one understood that the combination of city and state initiatives meant wipeout, rather than salvation, for Times Square, that the sheer size and bulk of the new office buildings would turn it into just another big business district. It is easier to believe that this is exactly what everyone involved really wanted. It is certainly, eventually, what Times Square will get.[10]

This is Project Planning in its most exaggerated guise.

URBAN LIFE IS FOUND IN THE SMALL THINGS

Contrary to all the big visions, big plans, and bigger promises, and before Disney was on the scene, 42nd Street actually is being reborn step by step, landmark by landmark—Bryant Park, the New York Public Library, Grand Central Terminal, the Art Deco McGraw-Hill Building, the skinny, white terra-cotta Chandler Building, dating to 1914, next door to the New Amsterdam—and theater by theater. The New Victory, a sophisticated theater for young people, and the New Amsterdam, the showcase for Disney productions, were first.[11] Even the Gap, the kind of chain officials love, opened at the corner of Broadway and 42nd Street in 1992, *before* Disney's entry was a planner's dream. The Gap recognized the site's inherent potential—a large nearby office population, many tourists, great transportation linkages, and the area's rebirth potential. The store was an instant success. So before any of the big new stuff materialized, that Gap became one of the chain's high-grossing stores.

The center of interesting and unplanned urban life has shifted two blocks east to the genuinely *renewed* Bryant Park. Forty-Second Street and Times Square are being rebuilt, but Bryant Park was reborn. And, *when 42nd Street is all jazzed up and a great public attraction once again, it will still be the visitors and serendipitous activity that will give the place whatever life it exhibits.*

Civic activist Margot Wellington has noted, "Everything good we love in this city was fought for by ordinary people, paid for mostly with private money, and accomplished against the city's will. In a crazy way, that is why so many of us love this city. We are each responsible for saving at least a little corner of it."

Cannot the same be said for so many downtowns across the country?

Yes, in fact, the renewal of the larger 42nd Street is shaped by historic preservation, by Urban Husbandry, not by Project Planning. That is why it is finally showing signs of success. The life on the street will be as memorable as the entertainment inside.

THE LESSONS

The success of 42nd Street may, in the end, do the country and its downtowns the best favor. If the right lessons are learned, it may demonstrate the folly of developing "centers," the products of decades of planning and development thinking that turned its back on streets and brought life inside and killed it outside. Instead of centers of activity, the direction must go back to streets of life that evolve into districts and connect with the larger place.

Cleveland's theater district, Playhouse Square, for example, won't be a "district" until the entertainment of its historic theaters spills out onto the streets around it with restaurants, retail, and street-activity-generating businesses. The master plan calls for this, but gives no indication how it will happen. The test will be what small accretions are allowed and encouraged to evolve from this along Euclid Avenue.

Cleveland has turned its back on more than just the streets around the three historic theaters. Those theaters connect inside and can be reached from parking garages without touching Euclid Avenue, once the city's grandest of streets and front door to the theaters. Nothing indicates that Cleveland appropriately values Euclid Avenue, the central pedestrian spine of its downtown, which still has all the components of a grand urban boulevard. Life has been pulled away from Euclid to its periphery, to Jacobs Field on one side and the Rock and Roll Hall of Fame and Museum on the other. The historic train station, which was once at the heart of downtown life, had its historic guts torn out and has been turned into a huge vertical suburban mall, drawing away from Euclid Ave-nue the kind of life it once created. Regen-eration of the Flats, Cleveland's regional en-ter-tainment district, and the Warehouse Dis-trict start-ed spontaneously with artists and spread, like New York's SoHo. The same kind of life could be generated along Euclid Avenue. Yet, *official city energy appears directed everywhere but at the gen-uine potential life of its tra-ditional center.*

Above: "Warehouse District" in Cleveland. What type of develop-ment will take place between this exciting new residential area and the business district just a few blocks away?

Below: Woodward Avenue, Detroit. Nine lanes dividing a city. Photo: Alexander E. Zachary.

Detroit is trying desperately to attach the label of "district" to the five square blocks with nine diversified theaters (five in use), including several fabulous historic theaters, on either side of Woodward Avenue, once that city's spine of urbane and elegant activity with a trol-ley line in the middle. The first problem is the lack of assorted uses and varied buildings *between* the theaters that would weave every-thing together into what could then legitimate-ly be called an urban district. Demolition has erased the buildings that would make this pos-sible and left holes everywhere. The second problem is Woodward Avenue itself. Since before five freeways sliced through the city (three feeding downtown) and after the removal of the trolley in the 1950s, Woodward has been a nine-lane highway (including two parking lanes, plus one for turning), not a sur-prising circumstance for the country's premier auto city.

A few years ago, a broad coalition of for-ward-thinking citizens, including community

leaders, preservationists, downtown business owners, residents, university people, architects, and planners, promoted the idea of widening Woodward's sidewalks, narrowing the street, eliminating two lanes of traffic, and lowering the speed limit. Detroit rejected that opportunity, although it could still be embraced today. Traffic engineers fiercely resisted, as so many do everywhere, any idea that makes a thoroughfare less hospitable to speeding traffic and more user friendly for pedestrians. City officials worried the plan would jeopardize the state funding designated for repavement. Perhaps they were correct. But to secure that funding, the city is paying a high price. Until city officials initiate such a move and transform Woodward back into an avenue pedestrians can feel comfortable walking along and across without fearing death, life for the theater district will elude Detroit, as it will most of its downtown.

A varied assortment of landmark-quality and plain, but sound, buildings exists in the downtown core. Some of America's greatest architects are represented. Whole blocks of buildings remain in the compact, urban arrangement in which they evolved, an arrangement wise leaders in other cities now strive to reinforce. "Yet immense aspiration remains embodied in these monumental old edifices," Camilo Jose Vergara wrote in his extraordinary book, *The New American Ghetto*.[12] "This, the third largest concentration of pre-Depression skyscrapers in the world after Manhattan and Chicago, could become a source of pride for Detroiters," Vergara noted.

The tragedy is that Detroit actually has more of a downtown left to renew than most cities. Detroit just does not know what to do with this traditional fabric. Instead, piece by piece it demolishes itself and looks to the big Project Plans—stadiums and gambling—to resuscitate its urban core.

Detroit is the most symbolically important of our urban tragedies. Few people recognize the underappreciated, but sizable, downtown left to regenerate. The absence of the fundamental understanding of the economic and social intricacies of a working city cripples that city. Of course, as well, Detroit is home to the automobile industry that is so much at the center of the undoing of our cities, as will be illustrated later in this book. But even more significantly, Detroit is home to Renaissance Center (RenCen), the greatest urban redevelopment tragedy of the country, as good an example of the ignorance of urbanism as can be found. The biggest Project Plan of the absolutely wrong kind, Renaissance Center, built in 1976 at a cost of $357 million (estimated at $750 million in today's dollars by *The Wall Street Journal*), this glittering five-tower sprawling complex vacuumed out the shaky but active life of the downtown business district and encapsulated it in this hostile concrete-and-glass bunker, killing any possibility of the organic regeneration happening in many other places. It was the biggest creation of the fortress mentality that has swept this nation in the last quarter of this century.

When in 1995, photographer/ author Vergara suggested that the empty buildings of downtown Detroit be left standing as a monument to this country's urban decay, Detroit leaders were incensed. Vergara wrote: "I propose that as a tonic for our imaginations, as a call for renewal, as a place within our national memory, a dozen city blocks of pre-Depression skyscrapers should be left standing in ruins: an American Acropolis." Actually, Vergara was onto something, but I suggest a different variation: Empty out Renaissance Center. Let all that activity move back out into the city itself. Let it spill out onto the streets, back into the spectacular office buildings of an earlier era, when design had character and scale had a human face, and back into the high-ceilinged, big-windowed loft buildings and earlier commercial skyscrapers more appreciated in the 1990s than in the 1970s when RenCen was built. How rapidly genuine, active, and diversified life would return to Detroit and set a standard others would line up

Top: Renaissance Center, Detroit, an enormous project plan failure.

Above: Parked cars get the best view of the river in Detroit.

to follow. *Let Renaissance Center stand empty as this country's greatest monument to the killing of American cities.* Let ivy and hanging plants cascade down from its concrete balconies and let birds nest on its concrete columns and byways that showed signs of deterioration in 20 years that took old, empty Detroit buildings 100 years. An urban botanical garden of a new kind but surely, symbolically, this country's biggest Project Planning mistake.

This is not meant to be, of course. General Motors has purchased RenCen for a mere $73 million and is relocating there out of its historic and appealing headquarters midtown. GM has trumpeted its move as a catalyst for downtown rebirth. Catalyst it will probably be—for more demolition of the genuine urban fabric to be replaced by big Project Plans, not as big as RenCen, but no less suburbanizing. No one should be surprised, however. One of our biggest car makers, Ford, was the primary force behind RenCen's construction and another of the biggest, GM, is bailing it out.

There is an extraordinary irony in the GM move. GM bought the RenCen buildings but Ford retained the acres of waterfront parking lots. This means that parking is expensive for GM's suburban commuting employees. So...GM is actually recreating a mass transit connection, the kind an earlier generation of GM executives killed. A bus service will shuttle workers from suburban parking locations, and a defunct commuter rail line is being revived. Talk about an appropriate reinvention of the wheel!

Pieces, remnants, a few treasured landmarks, local businesses, persevering residents, and special uses remain in every downtown, the varied plants of the traditional urban garden. If not further eroded or totally rebuilt, the surviving plants can be cultivated into a garden again. Some downtowns have more surviving plants than others. They are the fortunate ones, best positioned to be the star performers of the 21st century. In each downtown, these enduring precincts, sustained functions, resilient businesses, committed downtowners, determined place defenders, community activists, neighborhood developers, landmark preservationists, and human-scale advocates will be the building blocks of a brighter future, the special offerings that will lend degrees of character and credential to what follows.

Grand plans and inflated visions will continue in new configurations. The need for public resistance will not cease. But advocates for more modest and appropriate visions, people who understand and use cities, are increasing in number and influence. Only if they succeed will downtowns survive. These are the instinctivists, citizen users, Urban Husbanders—the enlightened opposition to excessive Project Plans, the people who are the best experts about cities and towns.

This book celebrates those people everywhere—in or out of government, planning and design professions, citizens' and business organizations—who follow an unconventional path, reject Project Planning, and take risks and challenge the norm. They are paving the way for the genuine rebirth of downtown America.

---

1. Macro data do not reflect micro differences. Plans based on macro data do not consider the micro impacts. All macro decisions have micro impacts. A national or state decision based on macro data affects localities where conditions may be antithetical. Similarly, a citywide decision translates into neighborhood impacts. This will be explored later.

2. *The Death and Life of Great American Cities*, p. 434.
3. Id., p. 434.
4. Chapter 6. Urban Husbandry: The Economy of Wisdom, was contrasted with Planned Shrinkage (an early form of Project Planning): The Economy of Waste.
5. "Smaller Is Better: Condé Nast in Times Square," *The New York Times*, May 18, 1996, p. 21.
6. See *The Living City*, p. 372.
7. Disney demanded and received low-interest loans for 75 percent of the cost.
8. Dec. 19, 1995.
9. The rebirth of Columbus Avenue erroneously is attributed to a 1960s urban renewal project and the creation of Lincoln Center. I illustrate the falseness of this in *The Living City*, Chapter 13, "Streets Have Value: Lincoln Center Urban Devitalizer."
10. Id., pp. 361–364.
11. The New Victory, built in 1900 by Oscar Hammerstein, was refurbished by a nonprofit organization designated to redevelop six of the theaters and reopened at the end of 1995 to great acclaim. The New Victory is dedicated to theater for young people, the only such theater in the city. Restored by Disney, the New Amsterdam, built by Ziegfeld, is probably the most resplendent and abused musical theater in the district.
12. New Brunswick, N.J.: Rutgers University Press, 1995, p. 216.

TRANSPORTATION AND PLACE

The Great Survivor, the St. Charles Trolley in New Orleans'
Garden District, remains the neighborhood's lifeblood.

CHAPTER FOUR

DEATH AND REBIRTH OF
THE PUBLIC REALM

Public life can only be reclaimed by understanding, then prac-
ticing, its connection to real, identifiable places. This is not a
particularly easy way for most of us to think about public
issues. Thinking of politics in historical terms is second
nature, but we tend to be more dubious about the proposition
that political culture may be shaped by its place, as well as by
its time.

    Daniel Kemmis, former Montana state legislator and
    mayor of Missoula, in *Community and the Politics of Place*

Following the truck bomb attack on the federal office building in Oklahoma
City in April 1995, President Bill Clinton closed the two blocks of
Pennsylvania Avenue in front of the White House to all but pedestrian traffic to deter potential car- or truck-bomb attacks. This major east-west thoroughfare had been a traffic artery for nearly two centuries, sometimes carrying up to 26,000 vehicles a day. Known as the country's Main Street,
Americans have long gathered here to march, protest, and celebrate. Such
rituals would surely continue. But, suddenly, a new destiny was in store for
it as a genuine public place. It had the potential to become an extension of
adjacent Lafayette Park, a great magnet for pedestrians, a hangout, a haven
for cyclists and skaters, a meeting place, a great gathering place—and a
monumental headache for traffic engineers. Finally, the front of the White
House might find its proper setting, not a front lawn facing a street, but a
downtown plaza where the public over whom the President presides
would have the opportunity to mix, mingle, and meet in genuine democratic fashion.

    President Clinton, however, did not see it that way. In announcing
the move, the President said:

Pennsylvania Avenue has been routinely open to traffic for the entire history of our Republic. Through four presidential assassinations and eight unsuccessful attempts on the lives of Presidents, it's been open; through a Civil War, two World Wars and the Gulf War, it was open. And now, it must be closed...a responsible security step necessary to preserve our freedom, not part of a long-term restriction of our freedom.

I will not in any way allow the fight against domestic and foreign terrorism build a wall between me and the American people.

The truth is: The wall was already there in the form of a continuous stream of moving vehicles. This is a national condition. Everywhere in this country, the automobile has been eroding the public realm for decades. We have become a walled-in and walled-out society, and the car dictates who is in and who is out. It took the Oklahoma City tragedy to topple the one wall in front of the White House.

Editorialists and public officials all across the country, however, took only a dim view of the street closing, labeling the action another sign of our increasingly unsafe society. A number of senators and representatives were particularly critical, forgetting that several streets around the Senate Office Building are closed to traffic. Yet, as New York planner Joan Tally wrote in a letter to the editor of *Progressive Architecture* (August, 1995):

> Closing the street is not a loss of public space, but a great opportunity for increased civic engagement in one of the most prominent public staging grounds available to Americans. This is really a reclaiming of the public realm from the domination of the automobile. It is unfortunate that it took terrorist attacks to spur the creation of what should always have been a civic staging ground but was really a traffic thoroughfare. In many urban settings, public rights of way should be used to reduce traffic, not accommodate it.

No sooner was the street closed then the public quickly found uses for it, but Pennsylvania Avenue was much too wide, still a street that looks like a street blocked off with concrete highway barriers, not yet a welcoming place.[1]

One year later, the National Parks Service announced a $40 million design plan for the new front yard, one that returns to the pre-auto age when public space truly meant something. Harking back to Washington's original designer, Pierre L'Enfant, the plan called for a narrow, gently curving pedestrian promenade with fountains, broader sidewalks, and a narrow roadway for the inaugural parade. The idea for a lower wrought-iron fence around the White House was first conceived by Thomas Jefferson.

THE FIRST MOTOR AGE

This plan is in keeping with the period that traffic engineer Walter Kulash has identified as the "first motor age," the first era of the automobile when "we did not try to rebuild our cities to accommodate cars. We thought we could incorporate cars by adapting existing street forms."

Kulash is a Florida-based traffic engineer who loves "the smell of freshly laid asphalt on a cool winter morning" and spent the first 20-plus years of his career working "in the very normal traffic engineering direction of providing ever more capacity," he wrote in an article titled, "The Third Motor Age."[2] Today, he is an important advocate for overthrowing modern urban planning and transportation dogma in favor of the durable city designs of the First Motor Age, when streets were wide enough for vehicles but not too intimidating to cross on foot, when sidewalks were generous in size and graced with canopies of trees.

Speeding traffic, the absence of curbside parking, the cutting down of flowering shade trees, and the elimination of sidewalk furniture and plantings—all traffic engineering prescriptions—have degraded downtown streets. Street-level retail stores and the whole assortment of downtown uses don't have a prayer competing with malls in this unappealing condition. Instead, Kulash and other maverick transportation engineers and downtown advocates argue, narrowing streets, widening sidewalks, and adding curbside parking and sidewalk amenities all make downtown streetscapes more attractive to shoppers, workers, diners, and visitors. With this makeover comes "traffic calming," the slowing of cars in neighborhoods and downtowns to a 15- to 20-mile-per-hour range.

In the early 1990s, Kulash became intrigued with just this theory being promoted by a group growing in recognition, known as the "New Urbanists." Traffic calming and advocacy of traditional urban design had been around for awhile. In fact, urban advocates had been fighting for these principles since car-age planners disavowed them. But these ideas had never gotten the national attention they deserved until advocated by this primarily architect-based group. Kulash scientifically compared the performance of the grids of narrow neighborhood streets in existing traditional neighborhoods to the high-speed suburban arterial systems that carry traffic between residential cul-de-sacs. What he discovered surprised him and contradicted the basic assumptions traffic engineers use. His 1990 study, "Traditional Neighborhood Development—Will the Traffic Work," done for the American Society of Civil Engineers, contradicted accepted assumptions.

The "dense network of small streets outperforms the pattern found in suburbia," he concluded. The traditional urban grid of perpendicular streets allowed for slower travel speeds but similar travel times, because distances were shorter. Traffic was dispersed throughout the entire grid network, resulting in fewer congestion-caused delays on the primary streets. There is "no efficiency of scale in a large road," Kulash illustrated. In fact, there is a deficiency of scale. Traditional grid neighborhoods generated 12 percent fewer vehicle miles traveled overall and a staggering 25 percent fewer on arterials. Kulash also concluded, from observations, what environmental planners have argued for years: The more attractive or interesting the landscapes, the slower people will drive and the more pleasant the trip they will experience.[3] Conversely, stripscapes of vast parking lots and banal buildings encourage high-speed driving. Public opposition to continued road expansion, Kulash writes, has been increasing since the 1960s, when only farsighted urbanists fought proposal after proposal to mow down functioning neighborhoods and pristine farmland for bigger and bigger highways, wider and wider streets, and bleak commercial roadscapes.

"Local elected officials, primarily mayors, tell us that the cost of providing ever more capacity has been too high, financially as well as in terms of quality of life," Kulash writes. The pendulum has swung away from conventional traffic thinking, he says, and toward "a new motor age, one in which the goal of maximizing traffic speed and volume is being balanced against other goals for creating livable urban settings." He identifies this new period as the Third Motor Age.

Defenders of the status quo argue that current and increasing automobile dependency is simply the result of the invention of the car and cannot be modified. This view fails to distinguish between the different periods of automobile development that Kulash identifies. When cars were only one of a choice of transportation modes, communities were still being built with pedestrians and public transit in mind. A balance was in place. As cars and trucks replaced rail transportation, the country's physical and communal landscape was altered accordingly. Kulash brilliantly segments the 20th century into three motor ages. In the first, lasting through the 1920s and 1930s, Kulash writes:

> ...we did not try to rebuild our cities to accommodate cars. We thought we could incorporate cars by adapting existing street forms. The designs have proven to be enormously durable: Almost every city, for example, still has the twenty-four to twenty-six-foot-wide street type with generous sidewalks and plantings.
>
> Through this period, cities grew in a familiar fashion. Their form started with a few major streets, quite often inherited from pre-urban paths, waterways or livestock routes. Then, as the city grew, more pieces of fabric were added. The pieces didn't always match, and they were quite often under different political jurisdictions, but the process was very organic and natural. From a traffic engineering point of view the interesting feature of

this system was that it was a dense, highly connected network.
There were many ways to get from one point to another.

In those years, livable urban settings were essentially left undisturbed. A drive in an automobile was more a leisure-time pleasure—the Sunday drive or vacation trip—than a commuting or errand-running necessity. People either lived close to work or commuted by one or more connected transit systems. "Parkways" were landscaped to be visually appealing and "parklike" with curves to give travelers a variety of views. Commercial development was prohibited. Downtown commercial districts and residential neighborhoods were densely developed on walkable street grids. Trolleys, trains, and feet provided basic transportation.

VISIONARIES SHAPE A NEW DESTINY—
THE SECOND MOTOR AGE

Then, Kulash notes, in the 1920s came the "visionaries who concluded that we had to reconfigure our cities and our lives for the automobile...(and that) cities could no longer adapt to, or live with, the automobile." This was the era of Le Corbusier's "Towers in the Park" and Frank Lloyd Wright's "Broadacre ('everywhere is nowhere') City." The dominant features of today's road system took root at this time, with separated land uses connected by big arterial roads fed by traffic-restricted cul-de-sacs, suburban-type towers surrounded by "keep off the grass" lawns, and a hierarchy of roads from driveway to highway replacing pedestrian amenities. "The expected extinction of walking eliminated the need to have origins and destinations within walking distance of each other," Kulash writes.

It is interesting to note that at the same time, the basic urban planning and zoning theories operative today came of age. Unsurprisingly, urban planning and transportation thinking evolved on parallel tracks. They've been almost interchangeable since. The separating and segregating of uses is the common link.

As Kulash points out, this was an era of "visionaries," whose "visions" were totally out of touch with reality:

> From these visions certain things are missing. You never see a storage place for all the vehicles: where would they park? Where did people buy and sell things? The two activities that dominate our landscape today—parking and the notion that once you bundle people together on a road somebody is going to want to sell them something there—did not occur to (them).

This vision emerged during the 1920s and 1930s, but gained its greatest exposure at the 1939 New York World's Fair in "Motorama." That popular General Motors exhibit, with its elevated, wide highways going between buildings carrying well-spaced cars, and with no congestion, excited many people, but gave no hint of inevitable traffic or parking problems. Upon these visions—however disruptive of existing places and people—the future was formed. Until then, road and traffic engineering was the purview of the municipal engineer, Kulash notes. *Transportation was still intimately connected to broader community concerns and took into account all the components of a livable and workable society. Interdisciplinary thinking had not yet been replaced by singular-focused professions.* This second motor age, however, marked the emergence of traffic engineering as a profession singularly focused on moving vehicles not people. Transportation planning became disconnected from all other considerations.

In a 1955 Skyline column in *The New Yorker*, Lewis Mumford quoted a "one-time city planning commissioner" to summarize this prevalent attitude: "The main purpose of traffic (surely) is to enable a maximum number of citizens to derive all possible benefits from the use of automobiles as a means of transportation, for business, convenience, and pleasure." From then on, engineers responded to traffic problems, as Kulash observes, with "more pavement—wider lanes, more lanes, wider turns."

The Second Motor Age came into full bloom after World War II, with the shift of the country's economy to domestic production and the shaping and domination of that production by the auto and roadbuilding industries that had been gaining strength for more than a decade. Passage of the 1956 Interstate Highway Act sealed the country's fate. But today, new thinking is spreading way beyond the citizen activists who have fought highways, road expansions, and mass transit cutbacks since the 1960s. As Kulash notes:

> Now a growing number of mayors, commissioners and citizens are rephrasing the question. Isn't moving people, not cars, what we really mean to do? Can we move fewer people fewer miles? What about changing our land use or stopping the need to constantly flee from cities? Who says that vehicles must move at an unimpeded flow regardless of what that is doing to our cities? We've changed many types of standards over the years; isn't it time to rethink our standards on traffic?

Then Kulash harks back to an image Mumford used 40 years ago:

> We now realize that trying to cure traffic congestion with more capacity is like trying to cure obesity by loosening your

belt. We've loosened the belt for fifty years, but the problem has only become worse.

Vehicular traffic, not people or places, has been the dominant planning and design factor in downtowns for 50 years. Downtowns were bulldozed half to death for traffic arteries or transformed into vehicle-friendly environments. Few could recover from such mortal wounds. This is probably the most significant and underacknowledged factor in the decline of cities. What remained of downtown either deteriorated for all the conventionally understood reasons or, more likely, deteriorated because too many blocks of productive buildings had been destroyed, undermining the fine-grained connections that comprise an urban economy. A downtown is not unlike a table that needs four legs to stand. It is precarious with three and impossible with two.

Years ago I was in Buffalo, New York, where downtown life was a rarity. What I could see of it appeared traditional enough, an interesting and varied mix of buildings with some spectacular landmarks worth the trip. I was walking around trying to see what was missing, what ingredients had been removed. Then, a few blocks off the main street, I saw blocks and blocks of leveled land and then, the interstate. A postcard I purchased later of an aerial view of Buffalo in a snowstorm confirmed my impression. Half the downtown seems to have been leveled at the same time the highway was built, probably in anticipation of large development schemes that never materialized. How can any city hold itself together when so much of it has been purposely destroyed? Four-legged tables cannot stand on two. Aerial views of downtowns can be revealing, a good guide to understand what is missing and how much empty space needs to be filled.

It is no mystery why people today stay away from downtown or merely pass through it. In small ways and large, people have been chased. Cars have been welcomed. Traffic has been pampered, pedestrians hindered. Elaborately landscaped but empty plazas, winners of multiple design awards, proliferate. But creating "place"—a space to which human activity gravitates naturally—is rarely a high priority and few know how to do it. A genuine public space should not *need* a consumer activity to draw people. Order, efficiency, and security are today's standard imperatives. *The irony is clear. The more well-ordered, efficient, and designed-for-security that places become, the less safe they feel and the more safety becomes the bottom line.*

THE PARKING LOT COMES OF AGE—OR, THE DEATH OF PLACE

The dimensions of the destruction that occurred during the Second Motor Age, however, have not yet been fully acknowledged. The centers of community after community have been obliterated. Where centers have survived—and they have—they are treasured, well-used places that often suffer from overuse by a public hungering for more of them. Tragically, the "no there there" that defines too many locations is today a parking lot, the dominant "building type" of most downtowns, whether an open lot or a vertical garage. It robs the street of commercial uses, especially retail, and allows cars to cross over the sidewalk to enter or exit. The walking experience is made boring and unsafe. Yet, 40 percent to 60 percent of downtowns is commonly devoted to parking.

Columnist Calvin Trillin said it all when he wrote "Hail to the Suburban Devils," about a victory celebration in a parking lot in New Jersey, "the betting favorite in the morbid national race to become the first all-suburban state." The event, Trillin noted, was "a symbol for the disconnected nature of modern American life."

The hockey team that recently won the 1995 Stanley Cup long after the ice had melted everywhere else, the New Jersey Devils, did not have a traditional victory parade down Main Street. The Devils staged a celebration in the parking lot of the stadium they use, the Byrne Meadowlands Arena...

But if the team were to be honored by a parade down Main Street, which Main Street would it be? Like a lot of people in New Jersey and Long Island and Westchester County, N.Y., the Devils aren't exactly from anywhere. They represent a market rather than a place—a certain number of people with a certain amount of disposable income living within a certain radius drawn on a map around the Meadowlands. If sports teams were named accurately, the new Stanley Cup champions would be called the Suburban Sprawl Devils.

Given the fact, holding a victory celebration in a parking lot might have been appropriate. Parking lots are, after all, where a lot of fans of the Devils spend a lot of their time—the parking lot at the mall, the parking lot at the train station, the parking lot at the 12-screen cineplex, the parking lot at McDonald's and Burger King and Pizza Hut.

Am I just lost in nostalgia, or did the championship of professional hockey used to be celebrated with a winter parade down the main drag of some proud metropolis—the goalie waving to the fans in the office buildings...? Wasn't there a large chunk of time back there somewhere when a city's team was more or less permanently that city's team? For that matter, didn't there used to be cities rather than metropolitan areas? Was there a time when nobody would have thought of naming a team the Mall Rats?[4]

New Haven, Connecticut A widened sidewalk and the addition of a café with public seating have transformed this major corner from "nowhere to somewhere." Photo: Copyright © by Project for Public Spaces, 1996.

Ironically, in the suburbs, even with vast parking lots, an empty space is often hard to find. "It was once a given that suburban office workers could find parking next to their buildings," Mitchell Pacelle wrote in *The Wall Street Journal*.[5] "No more. As companies like AT&T shoehorn more workers into office buildings, suburban parking lots are overflowing. As a result, car commuters often face the day's most maddening hassles before they even reach their desks."

While the suburbs wrestle with where to put all those cars, downtowns seek to diminish the dominance of the car. In community after community, today, the automobile is being recognized as a major root of downtown problems. Project for Public Spaces (PPS), the environmental design organization mentioned earlier, works with communities trying to bring life back into downtown centers. In New Haven, across from Yale University, they widened the sidewalks and narrowed the traffic lanes by a few feet.[6] Curbside parking was already in place, but on one corner, at College and Chapel Streets, they eliminated five parking spaces, widened the sidewalk even further, added a telephone, public seating, and room for a café. Car traffic slowed slightly, but the number of cars did not diminish. In place of a few parking spaces, a pleasant public environment was created. The street was transformed from a traffic thoroughfare to a place, from "nothing to something," notes PPS president Fred Kent. It is now a popular gathering place.

In St. Paul, Minnesota, the main street, Wabasha Street, had been transformed in the 1960s into a one-way traffic artery feeding the ring of highways around the city. In this case, as in most, downtown suffered for the sake of the arterial. At PPS's suggestion, one traffic lane was removed, on-street parking and a bike lane added. Tree planting is next, and, possibly, a return to two-way traffic.

Tallahassee, Florida, is another typical case of surrendering a downtown to the needs and wants of traffic engineers, whose only concern is the needs and wants of motorists. "Traffic engineers," observes Kent, "are appalled by congestion even though in a downtown congestion is healthy. It means something is going on." In the end, at PPS's suggestion, angled parking was installed on Monroe Street, the city's main street, which is also an arterial. Approval had to come from the governor himself. Everyone wanted it except the city and state transportation engineers. The head of the city's planning commission was in favor, along with a variety of downtown groups and institutions. Monroe Street retailers complained that cars went too fast for people to stop and shop, and that there was not enough parking.

Angled parking filled both needs. When evaluated, this project, which included modifying the timing of traffic lights, succeeded in slow-

Holland, Michigan. Angled parking slows downtown traffic while providing more parking spaces for customers.

ing traffic, despite the fact that the design was poorly implemented: The angle is too perpendicular and makes getting into a space most difficult. The spaces for each car are wider than necessary, creating fewer additional spaces than could have been had. Cars go more slowly, but not slowly enough. The overall number of accidents is down. Local police complain that they still have to be the bad guys giving speeding tickets when, in the first place, the transportation engineers designed the roads for too high a speed. This highlights an interesting contradiction: Roads designed for speeds that break the law.

In some big cities like St. Paul, New Haven, and Tallahassee, angled parking is being introduced on a small, experimental basis. But in smaller cities, angled parking is being introduced as a downtown enhancement, illustrated so vividly in Holland, Michigan, where it works as part of a total approach. Holland's downtown is a model of physical and economic measures—trees, benches, plants, vest-pocket parks, public sculpture, local businesses, cultural attractions, restored and well-maintained storefronts, *and* angled parking—that make it so totally appealing.

THE PUBLIC REALLY DOES KNOW BETTER

What was done in St. Paul, New Haven, Tallahassee, and other cities was not easy and was never merely a design problem. State transportation regulations usually set minimum widths for urban streets. Compliance is not mandatory, of course, but state transportation funding is often withheld if standards aren't followed. Traffic engineers warn of dire traffic delays and urban planners predict congestion and increased pollution if those standards are not met. In each case, the negative impacts are often minor. A few minutes are added to the commute of the non-city resident.

Overwhelmingly, the results of slowing traffic have been positive. Downtown social and economic life is strengthened. Gathering places are reborn or created. And vibrant street life is either revived or given an opportunity to begin in that direction. The PPS methodology, originally developed by sociologist William H. Whyte (mentioned in Chapter 2 about Bryant Park), is to study pedestrian activity closely, conduct user surveys, and convene groups of citizen users to generate the vision and "design" of their own center. PPS then helps develop solutions in response to specific conditions and local needs. In community after community, they found that car issues are at the core of the dissatisfaction with the local quality of life.

Often the complaints are not identified at first as car-related. "They complain about small things," notes PPS vice president Steve Davies. "Cars drive too fast. You can't get across the street safely. Traffic lights change before you reach the other side. Empty streets feel unsafe. No places left to walk comfortably, wait for a bus or train, meet friends, shop, work, and socialize. There is no grocery downtown. Given opportunities to discuss these problems, light bulbs go on in their heads and they connect all these concerns to the car."

Downtown can't expect to encourage retail and other pedestrian activity without making it easier to stop to shop. This is dramatically obvious on major downtown streets, like Brooklyn's Atlantic Avenue, a six-lane thoroughfare, where on-street parking is permitted only between rush hours. During the morning and evening rush hours, the streets are cleared of parked cars and become highways. Atlantic Avenue is one of many New York City streets that have been totally and organically revitalized during the past two decades of extraordinary rebirth of adjacent and nearby brownstone neighborhoods. "Cars whiz by during rush hour," commented an Atlantic Avenue merchant. In this neighborhood, like so many throughout New York City and around the country, neighborhood residents and business owners are fed up with municipal unwillingness to slow car speeds. "Traffic must keep moving," transportation officials say. Observed one Brooklynite: "If people choose to hurtle through our neighborhood at 50 plus m.p.h., it's condoned by the Department of Transportation (DOT). If, however, they are intrigued by our retail and decide to park and shop, they must be constantly vigilant because a mistake of just a few minutes can mean either a severe fine or having the car towed or both. The message is very clear!"

This is an overly familiar condition. On a small shopping street in New Haven is a cluster of quick-stop shops, including a pizza parlor and florist. During rush hour, curbside parking is prohibited, just when people want to stop, run in, make a quick purchase, and continue home. Such customers will not likely take the time to park at a nearby parking lot and walk over. A sign in the window of one retailer bears the warning: "Beware: The car-towing vultures will get you."

Speeding traffic and pedestrian street life are antithetical and incompatible. Grass-roots traffic calming demands are growing and, in many places, local groups are resorting to civil disobedience and establishment of neighborhood-created, unofficial, unapproved traffic calming mechanisms. Guerrilla warfare is the way someone described the local activists in a Connecticut town, who took action into their own hands after being constantly rebuffed by local officials. En masse, they started curbside parking on a series of streets and dared officials to put up no-parking signs. Independent action, a polite term for guerrilla warfare, is what it will probably take in many localities where public desire for slower traffic is blocked by official intransigence. Local activists argue that speeding traffic will drive out all other activities, to the point, as one protester said, "they'll be able to say about this place what can be said about so many cities, that not much happens there but boy, does the traffic move." They are more right than even they realize.

BEYOND DOWNTOWN

Alex Marshall, a perceptive urban issues reporter for the *Virginian-Pilot* in Chesapeake, Virginia, summed up the generic conditions found in suburban and suburbanized urban downtowns in a story called "Lunchtime Dash."[7] He described the attempt of two women walking to lunch in the Lynnhaven area of Virginia Beach:

> In some other time, in some other place, this would have been easy, not to mention safe. But this is 1991, where the Greek sandwich shop lies hidden inside a brick and glass monolith across hundreds of yards of parking; where the glossy Mexican restaurant is a remote oasis across eight lanes of busy traffic. "We run," (notes the luncher). "When we walk to the mall, we take our chances."...
>
> All along Lynnhaven Parkway, other steel, stone and glass towers repose behind green lawns and pine trees, like a commercial version of plantation row in the old South...Like Greenbrier in Chesapeake, Pembroke in Virginia Beach, and Kroger Executive Center area in Norfolk, this is one of the region's suburban downtowns.
>
> But it is difficult to eat lunch, drop off dry cleaning, or pick up aspirin without driving. So it's normal to see women in high heels and men in pricey suits leaping berms and dashing across chasmlike highways..."Driving is so much part of our lives that driving (to lunch) doesn't seem foreign," said another office worker in the same building. "I guess what seems foreign now is walking somewhere."

Here, like everywhere, first and foremost, the traffic must flow. Thus, traffic engineers are the primary planners and shapers of the environment, in town or out. Traffic wins. The value of place, where people come together face to face, and where street life translates into economic life, does not matter.

"The center is the place for news and gossip, for the creation of ideas...for hatching deals, for starting parades," wrote Whyte. "This is the stuff of the public life of the city. This human congress is the genius of the place, its reason for being, its great marginal edge. This is the engine, the city's true export. Whatever makes this congress easier, more spontaneous, more enjoyable, is not at all a frill. It is the heart of the center of the city."[8] Up against traffic and Project Planners, the center never had a chance.

Place died during the Second Motor Age. Downtown's heart gave out, and with it went the public realm. There is no public realm without streets and sidewalks open and accessible to all law-abiding citizens. Streets, and how they function, are the ultimate distinction between a city and a suburb. And sidewalks are the lifeblood of streets.

On streets, public rules, not private dictates, impose limits. There is no public realm without a reason for people to be on those streets and sidewalks. Cars circumvent that impulse. This is why privately-owned malls can never replace the public realm. *A public street is a place of activity owned by its users; a mall is a private real estate and retail investment owned by investors. No one can be in a privately owned mall, or engage in any activity that would be legal on a public street, without the tacit or written permission of a private land owner.*

Urban downtowns and town centers are by definition inclusive. Malls by definition are exclusive. It is no more complicated than that. And when downtown is converted into a mall or into a series of malls or into self-contained private, automobile destinations, the public realm has no chance. By gradually, step by step, removing pedestrian activity from public streets, bringing it inside, underground, or on skywalks and shifting people from public transit to the private cars, the street, the common ground, the public realm is either diminished or eliminated.

Downtown erosion took the form of "traffic improvements." "Nibblings," Jane Jacobs called them. Streets were widened, sidewalks narrowed, trees uprooted, street furniture removed. Pedestrian-friendly Main Streets, with continuous storefronts tight to the street, were disemboweled. Streetfront buildings were demolished for "drive-in" eateries, banks, dry cleaners, and the like. Historic and useful buildings were destroyed for parking lots to lure drivers to a diminishing number of businesses. Car-bound shoppers demanded to park in front of a Main Street destination or they headed to the mall, where walking long distances across enormous parking lots somehow became acceptable.

When all of these traffic improvements that undermined downtowns are added up, is it any wonder why downtown America could not compete with malls? Clearly, a reversal of this process is a good place to start the downtown rebuilding process. If it does not *start* the process, making downtown less traffic-friendly and more pedestrian-friendly is an imperative component *of* the process. Traffic must be calmed and traffic engineers tamed (see next chapter). "Pedestrian Facilitators" (a profession waiting to be invented) must prevail over traffic engineers.

THE DAWN OF THE THIRD MOTOR AGE
Sadly, more than damage control is needed now. Whole industries, professions, zoning and building codes, mindsets, and community layouts are inextricably bound up in maintaining the status quo that evolved during the Second Motor Age. This is a serious and urgent challenge. Nothing less than the Oklahoma City bombing could have forced such a

dramatic rethinking of the nation's front lawn at the White House. When looked at against the backdrop of Kulash's three motor ages, the announced plan, harking back to the days of pre-auto-age livable places, makes total sense. As does the pedestrian-focused planning emerging among diverse advocate groups all over this country. But logic, good sense, and rational planning ideas are rarely sufficient to derail bad planning and development projects.

The highway projects halted in mid-construction or before construction in communities across the country were stopped by citizen protests that usually included long delaying lawsuits. Where highway projects were derailed completely or in midstream, downtowns and neighborhoods have held on or regenerated...if enough was left to do so.

An earthquake, not common sense, took down San Francisco's never-completed Embarcadero Freeway on the waterfront and redirected federal transportation funding into investment in the city's subway system. But citizens, led by a straight-talking Mayor Joseph Alioto, had stopped the freeway's completion first.

Alioto was outraged, he told a 1974 Senate hearing on the cause of our transportation crisis, by the placement of an interstate highway link along the San Francisco waterfront just to give cars access to the Golden Gate Bridge. "I wouldn't let them complete it," Alioto recalled. "I said tell everyone to slow up and enjoy themselves in this beautiful town...There isn't a view like this in the world. You don't have to zip through it." Alioto had wrestled long and hard with strong-arming highway builders. "That crowd would put a freeway through the Vatican if they had a chance and could save space or money," he said.

THE "IMPOSSIBLE" *IS* POSSIBLE

In August 1996, San Francisco's Central Freeway was closed to repair damage from the 1989 earthquake. Instead of the traffic nightmare predicted by road engineers, there were *fewer cars on the road*. Predictions of 45 miles of bumper-to-bumper traffic did not materialize. Instead, 80,000 cars a day *disappeared*. Transit ridership increased only slightly. Speculation is that other commuters are carpooling, bicycling, arriving and leaving work later, or telecommuting.[9]

A similar experience occurred in New York when a section of the West Side Highway collapsed in 1973 and "deferred" maintenance caused the closure of the Williamsburg Bridge in 1988. Predictions of traffic chaos following both events never materialized. Yet, environmental lawsuits and exposures of fraud, not common sense, averted Westway, a 12-lane highway planned for Manhattan's West Side waterfront. Highway funds then traded in for transit funds gave the biggest boost to the rebuilding of the city's subway system since support for that system was diverted to highway building decades earlier. This was the primary goal of the Westway opposition in the first place. Common sense could not do the same for the northern portion either, where removing an elevated highway and bringing it down to grade would have created Manhattan's only true waterfront park. Years earlier, only citizen opposition led by Jane Jacobs, not common sense, defeated the Lower Manhattan Expressway (see Chapter 13). That highway defeat made possible the emergence of SoHo.

If not for neighborhood and preservationist resistance, an unnecessary Presidential Highway planned for access to the Carter Library in Atlanta would have destroyed an historic, stable black residential neighborhood. Tragically, 750 homes in this historic Atlanta neighborhood were demolished before lawsuits forced a scaling back and redesign. A South Pasadena Freeway extension has been delayed for years by citizen resistance, but is still an active plan. One thousand homes, five historic districts, and 6000 trees are threatened—the equivalent of the destruction of a California earthquake. Countless communities have similar tales. Where highways were stopped, coalitions of residents, businesses, environmentalists, and preservationists did the stopping. Where stopped, real public places either have been spared or are being recreated, efforts that are adding new strength to their downtown or neighborhood surroundings.

The symbolic step taken in front of the White House is the most recent, highly visible, and perhaps most significant for the nation as the dawning of the Third Motor Age advances. In some quarters, however, small steps to reclaim public places for people instead of cars are already in progress. Significantly, many of the small, local steps are not identified as public place enhancements. Instead, they are transit improvements, downtown landscaping, Main Street rebirth, bikeways, historic preservation projects, or community beautification efforts. Only when looked at differently are they recognizable as the beginning of an incremental taming of the car—indirectly modifying traffic—that will make a big difference down the road.

Communities are rethinking what they want from their downtown. Some are going through a "visioning" process to determine how they want it to function.[10] Others seek to protect downtown from further mall erosion. Increasingly, many embark on historic preservation efforts to stem the loss of local heritage, functional buildings, and local economic activity. They pass a local landmarks law or designate an historic district or establish design guidelines, and sometimes all three, to protect the remaining functional place. These strategies are necessary to prevent the big demolitions and small nibblings advanced by Project Planners and think-only-big developers. These efforts are often as much about preserving the qualities of place created during or before the First Motor Age, as they are about preserving the buildings built at that time. Most preservation efforts are locally based, heavily tied to local suppliers and other segments of the local economy—a significant bonus. Many efforts aim specifically to transform downtown into a place where people activity dominates and automobile traffic is minimized. *Whatever people are doing to a downtown to make it more pedestrian-friendly, active, and aesthetically appealing and to revive street-oriented activity, taming of cars is inevitably involved. More and more people demand it.*

Rails-to-trails systems have become increasingly popular, and the idea is spreading. In fact, a rail-to-trail bikeway across the country is 70 percent complete or under way, according to Rails-to-Trails head David Burwell. This is 10,000 miles of rail corridor converted to multiple-use trails. Policies and programs must be directed to pedestrians, bikes, and transit. Such transformation is not difficult. The will to make that transformation is what is difficult. If downtowns are really going to support renewed activity, they must be more than a collection of parking lots and disconnected buildings. The hundreds of acres tied up in parking lots could contain buildings, recreational spaces, apartments, offices, and light manufacturing sites, in close proximity and accessible on foot. *Downtown streets need to be more than vehicular links between highways and driveways.*

BUILDING ON THE LESSONS OF THE PAST: TROLLEY-CAR NEIGHBORHOODS

Elements still left from the First Motor Age provide excellent lessons on how to piece back together active places in the Third Motor Age. Ironically, these remaining places date from the time when short-distance trolleys and long-distance trains were everywhere, the Golden Age of Urbanism. They are the trolley-car neighborhoods and streetcar suburbs of the First Motor Age, when an endless array of trolley lines were created, often right by or near the railroad, to carry the passenger the rest of the way home, or at least within a 10-minute walk. The intricate connectedness of streetcar neighborhoods contrasts sharply with the enforced "apartness" created by post-World War II suburbs, when the car replaced rail as the necessary connector.

During World War II, trolleys reached their highest use. Hundreds a day rolled on multiple lines around cities. Even the smallest downtowns often had trolleys connecting them to surrounding neighborhoods, and interurbans connected to other downtowns of the region. With an awesome efficiency and human scale, railroads, interurbans, and electric streetcars wove together city and city; city and suburb; home, work, and leisure; and downtown and neighborhoods. The efficiency and connectedness of the network was astonishing by today's standards. But by war's end, all systems were overused and in disrepair. After the war, dismantling, instead of repair, began. (Europe reinvested in transit; we disinvested.) As mass transit disappeared from our downtowns, the reconfiguration of the landscape to accommodate the automobile gained full speed.

Former streetcar neighborhoods all over the country have a lot in common, since they evolved in similar organic patterns. They even have the same things in common with many neighborhoods in foreign cities that grew along surface transit routes at the same time. Tree-lined streets. Tightly developed houses and multiple-family housing. Small front yards. Driveways to the side of a house, sometimes with a garage at the end. These are often clues to surviving neighborhoods built at that time. Their neighborhood commercial character evolved in the era before zoning and the idea of separating uses, so there is often a comfortable mix of street retail, office, and residential uses on upper floors and occasional institutional buildings or theaters. Streets are sufficiently narrow to provide visual access from one side to another. Stores have generous front windows, once, and sometimes still, filled with creative displays. Signage is modest in scale and often quite artistic. Cars park along the street. Landscaping and other amenities exist in different degrees. Traffic moves slowly and cars stop for pedestrians even without a traffic light in many places. Within walking or transit distance is a downtown or a major thoroughfare with larger stores, modestly-scaled but sizable office buildings, civic, educational, and institutional buildings. This is a multipurpose center with major buildings and lots of traffic, pedestrian, transit, and vehicular, a "wonderful chaos." The structured chaos of a city.

Some of the most enduring and popular streets in American cities and towns date from this era of building. The places and streets so many people find appealing today are those compact centers and streetcar suburbs of a pre-automobile era. The most livable communities were shaped at this time, before the notion of segregation of land uses by zoning took hold during the visionary Second Motor Age. Too many were sacrificed to the misguided visions of urban renewal.

Architecturally notable structures, from elaborate Victorians to modest bungalows, often characterize those neighborhoods. The tightly-placed bungalow, a particularly American-style house, was the predominant house style. Close to nature (even if it had a small yard), efficient, and cozy, with most living space on one floor, the bungalow had compact functional advantages previously limited to the rich, including built-in furniture and cabinetry to conserve space. Built of varied, mostly natural materials, such as wood, stone, and brick, the bungalow embraced architectural styles from Queen Anne to Art Moderne.

Modest, neighborly, close to the street, the bungalow "stood for a more civilized existence," wrote Clay Lancaster in *American Bungalow*. "Its heyday corresponded with the apex of democratic domestic architecture." "The bungalow became the rage at a time when many Americans were moving from rented housing to their own homes," wrote Robert Winter in *American Bungalow Style*.[11] "Five rooms, neat porch," proclaimed Sears, Roebuck when it introduced a mail-order bungalow, "The Crescent," in 1921.

Interestingly, the typical development pattern often saw the moneyed class facing the main streets. The poor, the immigrants, and the ethnic minorities were more modestly housed on the lanes and alleys, if they had even been able to leave the tenement districts downtown. "I knew we had arrived," remembers a black resident of a onetime streetcar neighborhood of Pittsburgh, "when we moved from the alley into a big house facing the street." This reflected a social mix rarely seen today. Adults may have kept their social distance when it came to invitations to one another's homes, but neighbors of different color and ethnicity were familiar and often friendly with one another in the neutral territory, i.e., the public realm, of the neighborhood sidewalk or shopping street. The kids played together and became friends. That period of residential and social integration is mostly forgotten today.

Trolley-car neighborhoods developed street grids of small blocks, often with service lanes behind them, as just described, to minimize disruption of the street proper. Building lots were small, forcing developer and architectural innovation that still has great appeal. Modest scale and intimacy went hand in hand. What is often missed by today's observer is the extraordinarily high density these neighborhoods often contain. Residents were only a few blocks and a short walk from a commercial street or from a small collection of convenience stores. Yet the surrounding density could support such local businesses. Even more importantly, perhaps, that density could support mass transit in a way low-density suburbs can hardly do. This notion apparently totally escapes observation by current planners, who are encouraging low-density, suburban-style redevelopment of inner city neighborhoods. The urbanistic attributes of these low-income neighborhoods are ignored and consequently destroyed.

Former streetcar neighborhoods today are commonly identified as historic districts because of the quality of their architecture and richness of their history. The more significant shaper of character than the popular building style or aesthetic quality of the buildings, however, was their street-sidewalk-trolley grid nature. Even in the most automobile-dominated cities, such as Charlotte, St. Louis, Denver, Seattle, New Haven, Atlanta, and certainly in the scores of cities and towns that are a combination of old and new, the much-loved remaining streetcar neighborhoods are cited by citizen activists and farsighted planners as the models of choice for future development. This makes perfect sense when one realizes that "streetcar suburbs" and transit-centered down-towns evolved when pedestrians were still the priority. This is the standard many people are demanding again.

The streetcar seemed to be the perfect mass transit conveyance. Cheap, fast, safe, convenient, and well-adapted to a street network, it carried millions of passengers a day. Streetcar tracks—described as a "fishnet pattern"—marked towns and cities across America. Four-story commercial buildings with apartments over locally-owned stores stood along trolley lines and single, two-family, and apartment residences were nearby. So intricate was the trolley network that, with several dozen transfers, one could travel from Portland, Maine, to Chicago on a "pocketful of nickels."

The country's extensive network of trolley systems, once one of the world's finest, was destroyed to give automobiles more road room. Stephen B. Goddard, in his revealing and extraordinarily detailed book, *Getting There*,[12] puts it bluntly: In the 1920s, General Motors, under the leadership of Alfred P. Sloan, "and his fellow automakers decided to do nothing less than reorder society to alter the environment in which automobiles are sold by replacing light rail systems with cars and buses. So in the early 1930s, GM approached railroads and electric utility companies, which owned most urban trolleys, and offered to buy their electric streetcar lines, which GM would then replace with buses."

Resistance was strong. Buses were a hard sell. They jolted, smelled, and were not nearly as comfortable as trolleys. Trolleys were smooth, efficient, and frequent. But they were badly in need of repair after World War II. During the war, all the effort that might have gone into maintenance and upkeep of many things like public transit was directed, instead, to military needs. GM and its cohorts could not even pursue a plan of replacing trolleys with buses until after the war, when manufacturing could switch to a domestic focus. Sloan would not be daunted. If the streetcar systems would not willingly sell, they would be taken over from within and dismantled. With Greyhound and Yellow Coach bus companies, Standard Oil, Phillips Petroleum, Mack Truck, and Firestone Tire Company as partners, General Motors secretly formed the National City Lines, which bought up streetcar lines in 83 cities. NCL cut services, left repairs undone, raised fares, and took money out of each system, instead of rebuilding it.

A 1947 court case later confirmed that this secret partnership had "schemed to create a motor monopoly in nearly four dozen cities across the country, taking over more than 100 electric transit systems in the process." The pattern was set. The momentum was in high gear. The direction was unstoppable. In a stark case of 20th-century waste, the light rail systems either built or on the drawing boards in many communities today are recreating the routes of the earlier transit systems.

The rhetoric regarding the virtues of the suburbs emerged during the streetcar suburb era. The opportunity to own a home, to get close to nature, and to escape the density, dirt, and perceived evils of the city made urban outskirts appealing. Access to this good life was what both the streetcar and automobile suburbs were supposed to offer. But that is where the similarity—or illusion of similarity—between streetcar and automobile suburbs ends. *With streetcars, pedestrian needs were still paramount. With automobiles, building highways and moving vehicles became the priority. Furthermore, streetcar lines were built by private land developers and electric utilities. The interstate highway system, however, was and still is the largest public works project ever initiated in the country.*

"Tenement slums were the scandal of the age,"[13] writes Sam Bass Warner Jr. about the impetus to leave cities for the outskirts accessible by streetcar. Was the same notion not behind urban dispersal after World War II? But during the streetcar era, sidewalks, small tight house plots, small front yards, alleys, lanes, street trees, sideyard driveways, and "continued need of close proximity for daily work" dictated municipal rules of development. "Economic life still depended on physical proximity," Warner observes.

One need only visit the Garden District of New Orleans today to sense the hallmarks of the everyday neighborhoods of the streetcar era. The St. Charles line is the world's oldest continuously operated street railway with regular service provided by an aging but well-maintained fleet of cars much celebrated in photographs and song.[14] Tourists ride it for novelty. Residents ride it for convenience.

The refurbished 1920s cars, "durable as tanks," offer the incomparable comfort of operable windows and wooden slatted seats that are reversible, so that a group or family of four can face each other for the ride. Live oaks grace the sidewalks. Lushly landscaped antebellum single- and two-family homes tied graciously into the street are interspersed with institutions, short patches of local commercial services, restaurants, corner stores. New buildings are pedestrian-accessible, fashioned in the street form of the earlier era. Loyola and Tulane universities appear comfortably integrated. Small hotels and garden apartments coexist. The variety is rich but the overwhelming feel is of a residential, comfortably scaled quarter of a density that would probably alarm people today if just the numbers were looked at. Macro numbers never reveal the micro stories.

Cleveland, Ohio, fortunately, still has one of its early streetcar lines that connects to some of its longtime appealing, early suburbs like Shaker Heights. Cleveland resident Ryan Mackensie captured the essence of these very urban suburbs in a personal essay about living "car-free in

Cleveland" that appeared in the March 1996, Surface Transportation Project newsletter.

> The automobile is so much a part of the culture, the economy, and the landscape of Greater Cleveland, that everyone assumes that a successful graduate in his mid-20s should own one.
>
> I've learned the public transit system, overcome my ignorance of city neighborhoods, come to love the convenience of my corner store, and discovered what a joy car-free living, even in an auto-oriented city like Cleveland, can be.
>
> I live on a street of 1920s Victorian houses and stately, old trees. My apartment has a front porch, high ceilings, inlaid hardwood floors and beautiful woodwork, and is less than two miles from downtown. A five-minute walk takes me to the bus stop, where they come so frequently that I don't bother checking the schedule. Eight minutes later I am at the center of downtown, with work, shopping, restaurants, culture, the best library in the region, and convenient access to intercity buses, the airport, and locations throughout greater Cleveland. I grew up in a family of three cars. I was marooned until I had my driver's license. And then had to drive in order to do anything.

Mackensie acknowledges that the car-free lifestyle "means limiting choices and what some would consider *freedom*." He has given up shopping at the Wal-Mart off the freeway, like his father, and chooses instead to pay a little more nearer to home; a trade-off, he says, that evens out with money saved on car ownership. "And while some of my friends claim that their cars give them freedom," he notes, "I observe that they're spending so much on monthly payments, insurance, maintenance, gas, parking, and unexpected repairs, that they're worrying more (and working more) just to keep their heads above water." It takes him slightly longer to get places, but his "travel time is of much higher quality with no worry about traffic, accidents, or breakdowns," a luxury enjoyed by transit riders lucky enough to live near a well-maintained, comfortable, efficient, and frequent system. On the rare occasion when he needs a car, he rents, but looks forward to the day American entrepreneurs follow the European model and establish rent-by-hour companies. Mackensie is not out to take anyone's car away from them. He appeals to policy makers, however, to make possible the desires of people like him for "honest lifestyle choices, true affordability, and the local control of decisions that can make car-free freedom possible."

The popular new residential planning and design movement, the New Urbanists mentioned earlier (for whom Walter Kulash is the most important traffic engineer), draws on the design principles most common in early trolley-car suburbs. In New Urbanist communities, however, the mass transit is not necessarily developed first or at the same time, and the density created usually is not enough to sustain it. While transit and commercial centers are planned for, their development is not assured, could take decades, and, in some new developments, does not seem possible at all. Such plans are a limited variation of the old streetcar urbanism, a new-old art but without the defining features: Houses close to the street. Modest front yards or small lawns. Sidewalks and shade trees, the primary nemesis of traffic engineers. Curbside parking, as both a discouragement of vehicular speed and a protective separator between cars and pedestrians. Grand front entrances, frequently broad entry stairs, porches, verandahs, picture windows, all features that connect neighbors. Driveways on the sides of the house. Garages in the rear, if at all, sometimes with a second-floor space convertible to a workspace, "in-law" residence, or rental apartment. Neighborhood shopping districts within walking distance, oriented to the local, walk-in trade. These are the essential elements of community and place advocated by New Urbanists and long advocated by traditional urbanists. Absence of public transit, density, and the broad menu of housing alternatives prevent any existing or new community from matching the strengths of the streetcar suburb model. Without significant population density, low-rise multifamily apartment houses, three- and two-family homes, commercial streets with upstairs apartments, connections by transit or foot to other similarly structured but differently populated neighborhoods, the result is a better designed suburb still wholly dependent on the car.

We knew this once. All the right guidelines exist in surviving places, from which it is easy to learn. Relearning is not only possible, but is also happening at the grass-roots level in neighborhoods and downtowns all over the country. This is simply the old urbanism valued anew, built around frequent, low-cost public transit. *It is, in fact, more important to strengthen or renew the neighborhoods and downtowns already exhibiting these principles than to build new suburbs on the same principles. Repair and rejuvenation of existing places is the highest form of sprawl containment.* Centers already exist near operating transit. If the transit has long been removed, the model remains to rebuild the fabric to justify transit again. These already evolved organic places contain empty space left from demolition eras to be filled in with new buildings and needed uses in the appropriate scale. This filling in or infilling would provide the next layer of development in the organic process. Urban Husbandry at its best.

1. "In London's financial district, auto restrictions invoked as countermeasures against terrorism have cut traffic by one-fourth, road accidents by a third and bus travel times by more than half without displacing traffic to adjacent districts, winning plaudits from shopkeepers, residents and commuters and prompting similar moves elsewhere in London." Tri-State Transportation Campaign Newsletter, August 8, 1997.

2. *Places* Magazine, Vol. 10, No. 2, Winter 1996, p. 42.

3. This has been my own experience. Whenever possible, I avoid thruway driving. When my husband and I drive to our weekend house in upstate New York, we choose to take the Taconic Parkway, an early, noncommercial road from which one enjoys splendid country vistas, instead of the New York State Thruway that has every negative aspect we have come to expect of interstate highways. Thruways are being made ever uglier and more boring with the installation of concrete buffers and horrid 15-foot-high walls necessary to protect communities from traffic noise. It is like traveling in an endless tunnel. How much worse can it get?

4. "Hail to the Suburban Devils," King Features, July 7, 1995.

5. "In the Suburbs, Job Strife Starts in the Parking Lot," October 1996.

6. "It was the funniest negotiation I've ever been in with traffic engineers," recalls Fred Kent. "We argued over every inch."

7. Jan. 19, 1992.

8. *City: Rediscovering the Center* (New York: Doubleday, 1988).

9. Tri-State Transportation Campaign Newsletter, October 18, 1996.

10. "Visioning" is an increasingly popular tool for community planning that involves more genuine grass-roots input than earlier planning practices. Planners, architects, Main Street consultants, and others who use it give provocative slide shows at public meetings in which alternative streetscapes, open spaces, storefronts, parking facilities, and the like are shown. Viewers register preferences and priorities. The resultant Visual Preference Survey (VPS), originally developed by architect Anton Nelessen, reflects public preferences and is used to build consensus for future direction. The images most consistently rated negative, Nelessen reports, are those that were created after 1938.

11. New York: Simon & Schuster, 1996, p. 31.

12. *Getting There: The Epic Struggle Between Road and Rail in the American Century* (New York: Basic Books, 1994), p. 126.

13. *Streetcar Suburbs: The Process of Growth in Boston (1870–1900),* Second Ed. (Cambridge, MA: Harvard University Press), p. 33.
14. "The Crescent City: Looking Forward," *Passenger Train Journal,* August 1991, p. 16.

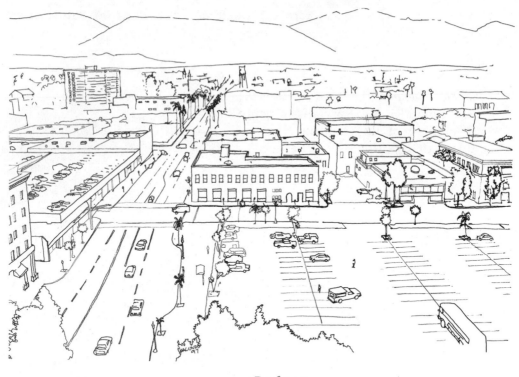

Before

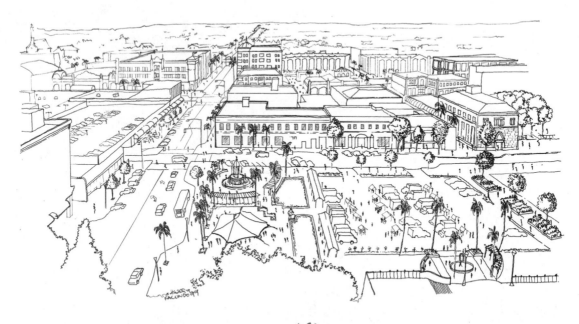

After

**Returning a center to San Bernadino:
from parking lot to place.**

CHAPTER FIVE

REBUILDING PLACE, VALUING TRANSIT

Places have an impact on our sense of self, our sense of safety, the kind of work we get done, the ways we interact with other people, even our ability to function as citizens in a democracy. In short, the places where we spend time affect the people we are and can become.

Tony Hiss, *The Experience of Place*[1]

It is difficult to design a place that will not attract people. What is remarkable is how often this has been accomplished.

William H. Whyte

REVERSING FORMULA THINKING

San Bernardino, California, did everything possible to kill its downtown. Its story parallels the undoing of most of the country's currently dismal downtowns. Over a period of decades, the old main street, Third Street, was completely demolished and replaced with a 1-million-square-foot enclosed shopping mall that totally turned its back on the street.[2] Streets were widened to facilitate speeding through traffic. A civic complex was built featuring elevated plazas and walkways, and leaving a parking lot (for future development) right at the main corner of downtown. Sidewalk cafés and street vendors, activities that bring people onto streets, were prohibited.

In recent years, however, San Bernardino has set about reversing these misguided alterations with modest, achievable projects that could be implemented quickly. All were accomplished on a "demonstration basis," since they broke local transportation and zoning regulations. Most innovative improvements in any downtown today usually have to be on a demonstration basis because of crippling codes. The parking lot was converted to a public square in less than one year's time and is evolving back into the "heart" of the community. Local residents and workers gravitate to it. Crowd-gathering activities, from concerts to markets and even weddings, now take place at this town square. What a positive reflection on the appeal of this square that people consider it a choice location for a wedding, something surely no one predicted or planned.

A bus stop was upgraded. Businesses around the square are attracting more customers because more people are walking. Diagonal parking was introduced on the wide streets. Traffic has been slowed. Opportunities for incubating local entrepreneurs were developed in the square. Now there is fun, street life, and a sense of place where only recently there was just asphalt. On the first street where diagonal parking was introduced, the number of parked cars increased by 25 percent and the number of people walking on the sidewalks doubled. Drivers report one minute added to their trip, but some note the trip is now more visually interesting. San Bernardino has begun to reclaim the public realm.

"Short-term projects get people interested and motivated," observes Kathy Madden, PPS vice president, who worked with San Bernardino to create this strategy.

Years of big plans, false hopes, and broken dreams have left most communities appropriately skeptical. When people see positive change quickly, no matter how small, they begin to believe in the future. Small steps invariably lead to bigger ones. Small, manageable steps are rarely included in conventional plans. Yet, early modest accomplishments build public confidence that big changes can be accomplished step by step.

Sometimes a community starts with the big picture and looks at how all the pieces fit together. Many communities are alarmed enough to be taking a fresh look at the direction of their communities' growth. Mary Newsom, editorial writer for *The Charlotte Observer* (March 2, 1995), reported on this happening in Davidson, North Carolina, a town with a traditional downtown increasingly under pressure from encroaching sprawl. Life has changed in Davidson, Newsom observed, and so it has in the countless places that used to function in a similar manner. Newsom writes:

> Now most commerce takes place along The Bypass, a generic strip of Burger Kings and Wal-Marts and Food Lions, possibly a shopping mall, and probably an abandoned strip shopping center belly-up in a sea of asphalt. What used to be the center of town might hold a historic courthouse, lawyers' offices, a few small shops and a lot of vacant storefronts.
>
> Out beyond The Bypass are subdivisions...all belching cars onto...multilane highways into or out of Charlotte. Davidson has seen its future, and it is frightened...(and) is the first municipality in Mecklenburg County trying to stare down suburban sprawl...

Its Main Street, the spine of its village-sized downtown, is also N.C. 115, which the state plans to four-lane. Double its traffic, speed it up, and you've pretty much gutted the ambiance downtown.

With the help of University of North Carolina at Charlotte consultants David Walters and Robert MacLean, Davidson began rethinking the town's zoning codes, subdivision ordinances, transportation services, and general land use regulations—all the rules that created the current conditions. The goal was to strengthen the existing downtown and to resist state transportation plans for road widening, tree removal, and increasing speed limits through town.

Davidson developed a new vision. A variety of housing types on less land closer to downtown. New construction on empty lots in existing neighborhoods. Street networks dispersing traffic, rather than funneling it onto one thoroughfare. Sidewalks, streets, and building scale meant to reinforce, not overwhelm, the village-like atmosphere. Density added to the center without overwhelming it. Varied housing and cost levels to provide opportunity for starter families and the elderly in need of smaller homes within walking distance of basic services. This kind of development creates the critical mass necessary for local businesses to evolve or remain stable.

More and more communities seek this scenario for their future. The efforts are widely scattered, often small, and just beginning. Many efforts have not yet had a visible impact. In a significant way, these efforts contribute to the undoing of sprawl (see next chapter), even if the first step is just slowing its momentum. With the undoing of sprawl comes the rebuilding of place. San Bernardino, Davidson, and other communities like them are rebuilding place.

It bodes well for future development nationwide. As these preferences percolate up, transportation officials and policies *might* change. In fact, they *must*.

As planner and architect Anton C. Nelessen notes:

One of the most important benefits of increased citizen participation has been the discovery that community is fundamentally pedestrian-based. More and more citizens are rejecting the notion that streets are the exclusive domain of the automobile. Instead, they are redefining their streets as important public spaces and reclaiming them for a multitude of community functions, such as artistic expression, commerce, recreation, communication, and social interaction. As a result, planners and citizens alike are beginning to understand that streets provide the unique visual, cultural, and spa-

Boston, Massachusetts. (Newbury Line) Coffee shops are opening in train stations, helping transform transportation sites into gathering places. Photo: William Pignato.

tial characteristics of a community, that they define each community's unique sense of place.

True community involvement does not suit most traffic and transportation engineers.

TRANSIT STATIONS CAN BE COMMUNITY CENTERS

Transit stops can be safe, clean, operationally efficient, and deadly as places. Transit stops can be physically upgraded, beautifully ornamented, architecturally appealing, and deadly as places. Or, transit stops can be all of these things—safe, clean, operationally efficient, physically upgraded, beautifully ornamented, architecturally appealing *and* be active public places. But to achieve this, stations must be thought of as extensions of a community. Station and town must connect.

Train stations along surviving and revived commuter lines, most noticeably in the Boston vicinity, are sprouting coffee bars, enlivening waiting rooms, making them friendly meeting places for both transit riders and downtown users. Local businesses are opening across from the stations. New and old ones benefit from the increased pedestrian traffic. Neighborhood health and day care centers and other social services are locating in or next to train stations around the country, reinforcing the stations as centers of community instead of being just a "stop." South Station in Boston, 30th Street Station in Philadelphia, the Union Stations of Washington, D.C., Chicago, and Los Angeles, and, of course, New York's Grand Central Terminal are not only being restored to the grandeur that defined them as gateways to great cities, but they are also being celebrated and revived in their respective cities as great public spaces. Renewed stations are serving the dual function of rebuilding public places *and* encouraging transit usage. They defy prevailing rules.

More typically, recent transit stations have been designed only for easy access of the bus or automobile, not for the comfort of the traveler. Security is the ubiquitous priority, but it is security as conceived by the prison architect—stark, bare, devoid of activity. Only drug pushers and the homeless are there by choice.

Transportation officials think only about getting people on and off a transit mode. The idea of a transit stop as a real place, a desirable destination on its own, a center of community activity as opposed to just a "stop," is alien. It shows. *When the rules address only the vehicle needs, the traveler pedestrian loses as much as the downtown street pedestrian.*

GETTING IT RIGHT BY DOING IT WRONG

A new bus transfer center with a long, open-sided shed attached to a small building in Corpus Christi, Texas, however, broke all long-established regulations and illustrated that it *is* possible to creatively go beyond the realm of what a transit agency normally does. The new depot was built on an empty site, what was the original center of Corpus Christi. But before a pencil touched paper on a designer's drawing board, surveys of area bus users and retailers were taken, as were time-lapse photos, to

Corpus Christi, Texas. A bus depot and a public place...a winning combination. Photo: Copyright © by Project for Public Spaces, 1996.

Top: Woodbridge, New Jersey. Before. Graffiti-covered, dimly-lit, weed-filled entrance did little to attract customers. Photo: Copyright © by Project for Public Spaces, 1996.

Above: Woodbridge, New Jersey. After. A canopied walkway, clear signage, new lampposts, small store combine to make a more inviting place for commuters. Photo: Copyright © by Project for Public Spaces, 1996.

record how the area was already used for transferring between buses. Design decisions grew out of understanding those user actions.

Prescribed space requirements for bus turning, parking, and loading were reduced. Less square footage of concrete saved money, slowed buses to a safer speed, increased the number of bus spaces, and created more public space. Seating, shading, water fountains, information displays, landscaping, and refreshment vendors were added. The new Spanish Colonial-style building, with tan stucco and arches, complements the architecture of the historic buildings on the block. A traditional-style clock tower is an architectural centerpiece and focal point. Public art was integrated into the design process. Architect John Wright and artist Ed Gates organized 1500 community residents—including children, seniors, and the mayor—to design the handpainted ceramic tiles for the depot's planters, light fixtures, and building. The result is a building with a familiar South Texas style.[3] The public was involved throughout. Community pride, awareness, and usage are high. Transit ridership has increased, as well. Again, all this was accomplished as a "demonstration" project. The Corpus Christi depot illustrated that getting it right often means doing it "wrong," by breaking official rules geared only to vehicular needs.

Evidence is appearing of enlightened new thinking. Amtrak recognizes the value of focusing on the untapped ridership potential of development around train stations that provides for more than parking lots. Amtrak has helped establish the American Station Foundation and has given it $2 million in seed money to advocate and support efforts to upgrade stations and to use them as anchors for rebuilding civic places around transportation centers.

Similarly, New Jersey Transit, overseer of the state's train and bus systems, set about to increase commuter train usage and reduce management costs by turning train stations into community centers and real places instead of mere parking lots and sterile refuges for the homeless.[4] At the Woodbridge station, a modest new canopied walkway replaced a graffiti-covered, dimly lit, and threatening tunnel entrance and space was created for two new businesses to create a presence, a sense of security, and an inviting entrance. Clear signage, historic lampposts and benches, bike racks, new pedestrian walkways to parking lots, and landscaping put a new face on the station and transformed it into an inviting place. The station again feels connected to the adjacent downtown and has become a place asset, as well as a transit stop.

TRANSIT, PLACE, AND EQUITY

In Los Angeles and Chicago, community-based efforts around transit sites have become starting points for larger, ongoing community issues, like housing, employment, and entrepreneurial development. In Chicago, a city-suburban coalition defeated a proposed demolition of the 100-year-old elevated train, renamed it the "Green Line," and crafted a planning and reinvestment strategy around rebuilt stations. Infill home ownership and job creation have followed. Community-based organizations along the whole route are, for the first time, wrestling over future regional strategies.

Poor and moderate-income neighborhoods around the country are acutely aware of how central accessible transit is to the more widely-discussed issues of their lives, such as welfare, jobs, and family stability. Yet current transit service continues to decline for the poor, like salt on the wound. Transit alternatives to the car are rapidly diminishing or disappearing altogether. No one suffers more under these conditions than the poor.

Approximately 10 U.S. cities have installed new light rail systems in the last decade, and several are expanding existing ones. Portland, Denver, San Jose, San Diego, and Baltimore have become models of light rail as a stimulus for better land use and urban design. But light rail systems are expensive at a time of transit cost-cutting, and few serve low-wage workers most dependent on transit. Worse, expensive new rail systems are sprouting up at the same time service is diminishing and fares are increasing on more and more public bus systems serving the car-less poor. Support for public transit should not mean a choice between light rail lines and ongoing bus service. Both are critical and they are competing for the crumbs, while roads get the cake.

Of broadest significance is the struggle in Los Angeles by the Labor/Community Strategy Center (LCSC), under the dynamic leadership of Eric Mann, to make bus service more available and less expensive for the 350,000 daily riders who earn less than $10,000 or the unemployed who seek jobs accessible by mass transit. Mass transit in this country is predominantly bus transit, as LCSC points out. Of 8.4 billion transit trips in 1994, 5.4 billion—64 percent—were on buses. And, as Mann says, "bus service can provide all the mobility of rail and does not have to tear up neighborhoods."

Mann charges that the much-celebrated recreation of rail transit in Los Angeles is "more about construction projects and developing real estate than about transportation," and that the city's "bus system has been gutted to move money to rail projects." While this undervalues the potential of the renewed Los Angeles rail system, the cost overruns of the rail construction are notorious and, as one MTA board member acknowledged, "special interests have taken over the MTA." In a lawsuit against the MTA brought by LCSC and other groups, for example, figures show a $38-per-rider subsidy for suburban Metro Link and a $1-per-rider bus subsidy. In an out-of-court settlement early in 1997, the MTA agreed to all sorts of improvements to the bus system, but soon after the agreement was enacted, further hurdles and delays were created. This is a potentially explosive issue, as the isolation of the poor is exacerbated. The charges articulated in the Los Angeles case parallel conditions in many communities. "An inferior, overcrowded, high-fare, poor-service bus system serves 94 percent of MTA's total riders, who are 81 percent people of color and 60 percent with incomes less than $15,000," says Mann. The rail system, however, serves predominantly suburban riders, with incomes averaging $60,000. Another observer noted: "The bus system takes people to places where they can spend money, not where they can make it." Diminishing bus service is nothing less than a national disgrace.

How tragically ironic! In Montgomery, Alabama, where Rosa Parks sat down on a bus in 1956 and catalyzed the civil rights movement, the bus service she fought for the right to use in dignity has been cut to an outrageous minimum, as it has in Birmingham. One has to wonder how coincidental this is. In many localities, such service has been discontinued altogether. In even more places, poor communities are served only during weekday business hours, leaving them stranded on evenings and weekends. How backward it is when the poor must depend on expensive taxis or private car services to get to work, shop for food, attend school, seek medical attention, or go to a movie. At the same time, billions of everyone's tax dollars build new highways and repave old ones, keeping it cheap and easy for the rich to do anything. Efforts like those of Mann in Los Angeles to organize bus riders and Gene Russianoff, head of the New York Public Interest Research Group (NYPIRG), in New York to sue transportation agencies over the imbalance of transportation policies are bound to spread. One has to marvel that the issue has not exploded in violence.

Increasingly, riders are paying a larger share of operating costs at the farebox. *New York Times* columnist Clyde Haberman noted in 1997 that in New York City, the $1.50 subway and bus fare covered a "whopping 88 percent" of the operating cost. The New York Public Interest Research Group (NYPIRG) and the New York Urban League sued over the lack of racial fairness of the 1995 transit fare increase. Subway riders were already paying a greater portion of their travel costs than commuter rail users. The 1995 fare increase was 20 percent for city transit and only 8 percent for suburban. Eventually the suit was settled, with the MTA agreeing to fund a study of equity in the distribution of transit subsidies. NYPIRG said the suit at least helped gain increased transit aid and some fare discounts, although the larger battle remains an uphill fight.

Public places are essential for low-income communities, but impossible without public transit service.

PITTSBURGH RESISTS WASHINGTON RULES

Stanley Lowe, executive director of the Pittsburgh Housing Administration, gained national attention as a community activist a few years ago with his extraordinary success in turning around some historic Pittsburgh neighborhoods with a low- and moderate-income population. Working through the Pittsburgh History and Landmarks Foundation, Lowe developed home ownership programs that were supported by a consortium of banks needing to meet their Community Reinvestment Act (CRA) obligation and which are now profiting nicely. Because of his community-based work, Lowe brought to his city housing position a special understanding of the dilemmas of urban neighborhoods. No matter how nice the home and community someone might live in, he knew, isolated living doesn't work without a car. A car, of course, requires money, which is better spent by low-income families on other necessities.

As housing director, Lowe turned down a $26 million federal grant to renovate a dismal, deteriorated, and isolated housing project. No store, community, or recreation facility was within walking distance. The isolation, in fact, had contributed to the social and economic deterioration of the housing. "I knew," Lowe says, "that a beautifully upgraded apartment complex would still leave the residents too far from jobs, medical attention, schools, and recreational facilities. Buses are few and far between, stop altogether after 11 p.m. weekdays, and don't run at all on weekends." Even the $10-a-ride car service did not operate at night.

Lowe rejected the grant for that purpose and asked for more money to upgrade functional, transit-accessible inhabited neighborhoods to which these tenants could be relocated. In the meantime, the Housing Authority is starting a resident-owned bus company to serve isolated public housing.

In Pittsburgh, residents are lucky to have Housing Authority bus service. In many places where the mall is the primary, if not only, work or shopping site, low-income shoppers can't get there by public transit. Malls make sure to keep it that way. In a suburb of Buffalo, New York, a young African-American mother was crushed under a 10-ton truck after stepping off a city bus to cross a seven-lane road on her way to her part-time job at the Walden Galleria. "While buses from suburban towns and charter buses from Canada stopped at Walden Galleria every day, city buses were not allowed on mall property," *New York Times* columnist Evelyn Nieves reported in December 1996, after Cynthia Wiggins' family filed a wrongful death suit, with Johnnie L. Cochran Jr. as their lawyer, against the Pyramid Mall Company and others. "The No. 6 bus, which went from downtown Buffalo through largely black neighborhoods...dropped passengers off on a chaotic road 300 yards from the mall." After Wiggins' death, the public bus company released internal documents to *The Buffalo News* showing that it tried for eight years to get permission for the bus to stop in the mall's parking lot. A boycott threat eventually succeeded in gaining the stop. More deaths will probably occur before the full realization of and appropriate remedies to the degree that public transit deficiencies worsen the economic, social, and political divisions of the country. Without improved public transit, a healthy society cannot exist and the rebuilding of place doesn't have a chance.

TRANSIT IN NEW CONFIGURATIONS
Transit is a critical thread of the intricate fabric of place but is not enough to reweave the whole, if transit service is not frequent, convenient, on time, clean, cheap, and safe. Yet, many places no longer have any transit service, and without some form of it, the capacity to strengthen a downtown is limited.

Transit services are reviving in ingenious and experimental ways, bringing new shoppers and pedestrians to their downtowns, and, in the process, rebuilding place. These small, localized efforts are shaping transit to user needs. Shuttle buses are linking residential areas with commuter transit stops. Downtown circulators enable shoppers to park a car once and ride transit or walk around the center. New entrepreneurs are initiating neighborhood services that could grow into a larger network of transit. Piece by small piece, mass transit is being reconstructed—*at great expense.*

The most telling example of this is, ironically, in Detroit, the "Motor City," and involves General Motors. In 1997, GM started transferring operations and employees to Renaissance Center, the mammoth downtown complex it purchased in 1996. GM established free bus shuttles from suburban locations for the first 250 employees. "Since GM won't have to pay their parking fees," reported Nicole M. Christian in *The Wall Street Journal* (June 9, 1997), "it estimates a savings of about $200 for every employee who agrees to leave his or her car behind and take the bus." Individualized solutions are appearing in many localities.

In Eufala, Oklahoma, a resource team from the National Main Street Center recommended the establishment of a modest transportation system that would bring visitors from Marine Cove, a popular marina on Lake Eufala (the largest in Oklahoma), to the downtown business district a half-mile away. Partially state-funded, a 50-cents-per-ride bus system (four 25-passenger and one 12-passenger handicapped-equipped buses) was launched in 1986. It became so popular that it now transports senior citizens, schoolchildren, and other local residents to downtown, along with the originally targeted tourists. Ridership has been growing steadily. In fact, a whole new tour and charter business has grown out of this, expanding both the tourist business and local tax base. Most significantly, the system now operates "on demand," which means that one can call for service as needed. This is as user-friendly as it gets.

Atypical Transportation runs nine trolley buses in Scottsdale, Arizona, maintaining a constant stream of pedestrians into the downtown. It began with a 3.2-mile loop around downtown as a downtown promotion, and expanded to pick up tourists and locals at outlying resorts and bring them downtown. The downtown loop, subsidized by the city, is free for those who board and depart downtown. Suburbanites often drive to the resorts, park, and take the trolley to downtown shopping and cultural events. Ridership sometimes reaches 2,000 a week.

TROLLEYS STILL FUNCTION

A wide assortment of vintage trolley systems are being revived. Conceived and promoted as tourist attractions, these quirky, limited rail or bus lines are bringing people back to centers, increasing pedestrian activity and street life, bringing people to a downtown to which they don't think they have reason to go, keeping people downtown longer by making it easy to go from place to place, and introducing a car-born and car-bound generation to mass transit in a novel way. Cities like Dallas and Memphis have discovered what San Francisco, Toronto, and New Orleans, with their uninterrupted historic cable car and trolley lines, have long experienced. Comfortable, old-style streetcars have never lost their appeal and, today, they bring tourists aplenty.

Daniel Machalaba, in *The Wall Street Journal*, wrote: "The new old-style transit lines allow cities to avoid building costly transportation systems for short-haul intracity trips...Savings come from using older or vintage rail cars, which are cheaper to purchase than new models, and staffing the lines with volunteers."[5]

In Tucson, Arizona, for example, volunteers not only restored the tracks, but also operate antique electric streetcars between a university campus and a trendy arts and restaurant district. With a sharpened appreciation of transit, Tucson is also upgrading transit stops with bike racks, benches, bus shelters, landscaping, improved lighting, crosswalk upgrades, and sidewalk improvements along a two-mile corridor southeast of town.

It took 12 years for a coalition of merchants and property owners in Dallas to revive three miles of the McKinney Avenue trolley. Now, the trolley, with restored vintage cars, is an integral part of the city light rail system, with extensions in the works, and the trolley is already a catalyst for new economic strength. More than 500 residential units and a downtown university complex have been added, mostly in converted office buildings and former department stores. In Maplewood, New Jersey, a free town-operated jitney service to the train station was initiated, instead of adding more spaces to the station parking lot. The town's senior citizen shuttle bus is used for rush hour service. All this has worked quite well, which should not be a surprise. Transit agencies, however, resist shuttles.

In Syracuse, New York, City Express, a 4.6-mile intracity streetcar, was revived and is successfully transporting an increasing number of students, sightseers, and shoppers for $1 a ride. The line runs between Syracuse University, downtown, and the Carousel Mall. More people are coming downtown for the first time since the mall opened. Ironically, it was the Carousel Mall that sealed the fate of downtown less than a decade ago. Three downtown department stores closed, and much else disappeared with them, when the mall came on the scene. The local economy all but disappeared. Now, expensive public efforts are needed to revive it.

A spontaneous private rejuvenation has been occurring in an old Syracuse warehouse district. Armory Square has restaurants, taverns, small shops, and loft apartments, and is attracting the "mall rat" generation. City Express is aiding this rebirth by making downtown more accessible, bringing people down after Carrier Dome events, and providing new customers for local businesses.

This kind of transit service, rail or bus, has enormous potential for cities and towns with colleges within their borders or on the fringes. Universities have overcatered to student desires for car ownership. Enormous quantities of campus blacktop are required to service this privilege. This is extremely expensive, wasteful of often scarce campus space needed for buildings, and destructive of the campus landscape. Schools could return to the not-so-long-ago limitation on car privileges to seniors only, and institute instead a campus transit system that connects to downtown. Municipalities should be willing partners, since the economic benefit of a real connection between the campus and the downtown is obvious. Young people are important for any downtown trying to regenerate its public realm.

The University of Connecticut, in Storrs, experiences a typical campus parking crunch. In 1995, for example, 8582 student cars were registered for 4472 spaces, and 3400 faculty cars for 3000 spaces. That is a lot of asphalt for a college "campus." In 1993, the university and nearby town of Mansfield in eastern Connecticut developed a transit alternative with a novel twist. The university and the town prepaid fares (the university $15,000, the town $5000) for their constituencies to provide a free 13.5-mile ride to the downtown of the Village of Willimantic, among other stops including a shopping mall. Ridership has gone up 58 percent since its 1993 beginning and continues to climb. Shoppers, commuters, students, and faculty benefit. In three years, 126,674 people have ridden the bus. The village benefits from diminished car usage and increased downtown activity. A similar program is in use in Amherst, where five colleges subsidize bus fares. If colleges limited car privileges, traffic would ease, fewer parking spaces would be necessary, and more students would take advantage of the transit.

TRANSIT DOES NOT AUTOMATICALLY REBUILD PLACE

The re-emergence of light rail systems in downtowns today does not automatically signal the strengthening of a downtown in the reconnecting, reintegrating, reweaving, and renewing sense. In Cleveland, for example, the new light rail connects primarily tourist sites, a great convenience for the suburban or long-distance visitor. This expensive new light rail line was supposed to serve downtown office workers, as well as tourists and suburban visitors. Not unpredictably, it does not work as promised. Office workers are unwilling to give up the convenience of their cars for transit that requires a long, windy walk to their offices.

This city's string of much-celebrated alleged "revitalizing" projects starts with Gateway Sports Complex, conveniently situated for drivers between the Inner Belt and the southern fringe of the business district. Here are Gund Arena, Jacobs Field, and two parking garages. An underground walkway connects Gateway to Tower City Center (a once grand railroad station and city gateway, now a three-story suburban shopping mall). The waterfront rail line starts here and whooshes people to the next tourist site, the Flats (a SoHo-style loft and entertainment district), along the riverfront to the lakefront and the Great Lakes Science Center at North Coast Harbor, and, of course, the much-ballyhooed Rock and Roll Hall of Fame and Museum. *The light rail line does not even connect to the city's street network but instead ends in a parking lot, not an easy walk away from the business district.*

The Rock and Roll Museum's waterfront site is clearly the wrong place to help strengthen the core of existing downtown. Originally, a smaller-scale version was slated to be built behind Tower City Center on the main thoroughfare of Huron Avenue and overlooking the Cuyahoga River.

This is the site that would have helped to tie the downtown together. As *Cleveland Plain Dealer* art and architecture critic Steve Litt observed, at this site, the rail line could have connected to the city and suburban lines originating at Tower City Center and formed "a real transit hub, a people magnet. It would have been building on what was there." Instead, due to apparent disagreements between the museum and Tower City Center, the I. M. Pei-designed pyramid structure was transferred to the waterfront site, an example of what Litt aptly describes as "plop architecture."

Cleveland's new transit is thus not the kind that is part of the fabric of the city—transit that is a necessity, not an amenity, that links all kinds of places and people within the city and connects businesses, suppliers, customers, and services. Sadly, there is no evidence of official interest in regenerating the kind of urban economy in Cleveland for which such a transit system would be helpful. An intricate and richly productive fine-grained urban economy is usually the first casualty of Project Plans.

The light rail does not approach Euclid Avenue, Cleveland's onetime equivalent of New York's Fifth or Chicago's Michigan avenues. A proposal for a new four-mile light rail line from downtown to University Circle along Euclid was killed a few years ago.[6] Euclid was once the central spine of the commercial, retail, and entertainment activity of downtown Cleveland. Its decline paralleled that of Fifth, Michigan, and all primary urban retail avenues during the exodus of retail to the suburbs. Fifth and Michigan avenues are again filled with retail. But the street-level retail that was once Euclid's hallmark is now primarily found in Tower City Center and the Galleria downtown. The Euclid Avenue retail that survived the long pull of the suburban mall now has been drained by the enclosed mall downtown. To add insult to injury, the mall is named "The Avenue."

Euclid remains a spectacular urban boulevard, despite its state of neglect and disfavor. Here is an avenue with three unique 19th-century arcades, one of which is a famous masterpiece. Arcades, covered pedestrian walkways lined with small storefronts, serve as destinations, walkways, and a birthplace for new local businesses. One has to wonder what the hidden agenda is for the still-exemplary shopping street when current arcade tenants report they are rebuffed by Euclid landlords when they try to move onto Euclid to enlarge their businesses. These arcades connect Euclid in two directions to new and long-standing civic attractions. Upstairs in all the varied buildings along Euclid, great potential for office and loft conversion exists. But what chance does Euclid have when new enclosed malls are the downtown retail form of choice?

DOWNTOWN NEEDS CARS

Recognition of the necessary "role reversal" or balanced transportation policy can go too far. Cars should not be banned from a downtown.

Handled properly, cars can be a positive thing. They provide action and movement. They belong downtown. Cars are essential for some pickups and deliveries and, certainly, for servicing downtown merchants. But regulation of hours for car use, slowing traffic to a pedestrian pace, locating parking lots behind stores and not in front, instituting angled and parallel street parking instead of prohibiting on-street parking, and placing great value on sidewalk amenities all can go a long way to keeping the car from undermining a downtown street.

Streets should almost never be totally closed to traffic. This might work on some short, narrow streets that would not attract much traffic anyway. Closing streets to all traffic for the sake of creating a pedestrian mall has proved unsuccessful in most places for this very reason. Many pedestrian malls have been reopened to vehicular traffic. Oak Park near Chicago; State Street in Chicago; Riverside, California; Milwaukee; Dubuque and Burlington, Iowa; and others have put the street back but added amenities and traffic calming.

Exceptions exist, like Santa Monica, California's Third Street Promenade, which is a "faux street" and generates the activity and sense of excitement of a town square. At one end, the enclosed mall, Santa Monica Place, built in the 1970s, makes Third Street a dead-end street. The enclosed mall was meant to revitalize this area of downtown but, predictably, killed it instead. The Promenade came to life organically and despite the mall, as small, ad hoc uses, such as a farmers' market and used book stores, emerged slowly. As variety and popularity increased, the Promenade brought new energy downtown. Some stores have shifted to the Promenade, leaving a question mark about whether the renewed activity is enough to spread beyond the Promenade. Santa Monica Place, the enclosed mall, remains a deterrent to this broader economic regeneration.

In Santa Monica, it wasn't until movie theaters opened on the Promenade and downtown housing was built that the Third Street Promenade became, almost overnight, a big success. Ironically, the enclosed mall benefits from the Promenade, probably more than the rest of downtown. It was supposed the be the other way around.

Pedestrian malls that provide for limited traffic can work. Burlington, Vermont, permits vehicular access during off hours. During the day and on weekends, the four-block closed stretch of Church Street serves as an interesting public space. Like Santa Monica's Promenade, Burlington's Church Street Mall functions more like a town square, a public gathering space where the action is more than about consumption. This is a public domain, not a private enclave. This Burlington success, especially given the cold Vermont winters, contradicts those who argue the need for enclosed malls in cold-weather climes. But downtown Burlington would still be wonderful without it. The closed street is not necessary for downtown Burlington's liveliness.

Car traffic must be slow. The slower the better. Car speed should coincide with a walking pace. Main Street's appeal is its human scale. The scale, character, and pace are perfectly suited to the pedestrian. Take that away and little is left. Cars, although important, must be secondary to the human scale; otherwise, the appeal to people erodes. When they move slowly, drivers and passengers look at store signs and windows and decide to stop or, perhaps, return. This is happening where communities decide not to let the car dominate their community life.

GRASS-ROOTS TRAFFIC RESISTANCE GROWS

In Takoma Park, Maryland, local residents and merchants lost patience with Washington commuters racing through their streets looking for ways to avoid the traffic. Speed bumps, those little mounds of pavement across a road that cause a dramatic bump if traversed too quickly, were added to a few of the most traveled streets. Predictably, the traffic shifted to the bumpless streets. Speed bumps were then added there, and the pattern continued until speed bumps were added all around town.

Speed *humps* rather than *bumps* are, increasingly, the preferred technique for this purpose. They are less exaggerated and less jarring on impact, but equally effective. Some places have had them for years. Fort Lauderdale, for example, has had them for more than 20 years. They've been so appreciated that other communities have followed the pattern. In response to the growing traffic calming demands of New York City neighborhoods, Transportation Commissioner Christopher Lynn took the bold step of ordering installation of speed humps at 12 locations around the city, a first for New York City, whose policies for years have been weighted in favor of car drivers. Speed has been reduced by 25 percent, from 42 mph to 31 (the official speed limit is 30 mph), still too fast for some. The city gets 2 letters a day from citizens, police, community groups, and politicians requesting speed humps. "Where traffic signals can take years to be installed and cost upwards of $50,000, humps can be installed in a matter of weeks at a cost of $3000," the Tri-State Transportation Campaign weekly bulletin reported in August 1996.

In one of two *New York Times* columns on the issue (December 10, 1996, and April 25, 1997), Clyde Haberman posed the question:

> Do you realize that a New York pedestrian is statistically more likely these days to be killed by a stranger driving a car than by the spector of the urban nightmare, a gun-toting stranger on the street?

More than 40,000 people die yearly in car-related accidents—20 to 25 percent of them are pedestrians, according to the Federal Highway Traffic Safety Administration. In 1994 in New York alone, Haberman points out, 249 people died as a result of 12,730 vehicle-pedestrian collisions, one every 41 minutes.

> If carnage on that scale were the result of terrorist actions, the entire city would be in an uproar, demanding that City Hall and the police do something. When did wholesale death by automobile become an unavoidable natural phenomenon? Yet for some reason the problem draws scant public attention...

The police, Haberman notes, seem more focused on parking tickets than speeding motorists. In recent years, he wrote, police average only 44 speeding summonses a day on local streets, but more than 6,500 parking tickets.

Charles Komanoff, an economist specializing in energy and transport policy, calls this "both a quality-of-life disaster and an unacknowledged crime wave." Government officials, Komanoff adds, often blame the victims and resist improved enforcement policies. Yet, Komanoff writes, "aggressive enforcement of traffic codes and licensing laws has cut pedestrian fatalities in London by 50 percent, and the fatality rate in Paris and Tokyo stands at half of ours."[7]

A coalition of approximately 60 New Jersey communities has been battling the state transportation department over a strong local desire to install "yield-to-pedestrian" signs in the middle of a road where there is a crosswalk. Local officials have had to battle county officials on county roads as well, and one locality went to court to secure local control. The state legislature passed a law giving this authority to localities, but only if an engineer certified conformity with national standards that don't even include mid-crosswalk signs. This could sabotage the idea while appearing to endorse it.

New Jersey, the country's most densely populated state, is more prone than other states to pedestrian accidents. Almost 24 percent of all traffic deaths statewide involve a pedestrian, compared to a nationwide average of 13 percent.[8] Equally startling is the statistic that half of traffic deaths suffered by New Jersey youth are of children walking. A 1988 report of the federal HWA found that crashes were twice as likely at places without sidewalks or pathways.[9] Cars kill more kids in the suburbs than guns kill kids in cities, Jane Holtz Kay points out in *Asphalt Nation.*

The pedestrianization of downtown is a growing phenomenon, and slowing cars is a centerpiece of the multiple efforts. Numerous people walking on the sidewalk and slow cars passing by can be signs of downtown health. Similarly, cars parked along the street provide a frame for the streetscape and a barrier between moving vehicles and people walking on the sidewalk. Wide streets offer the opportunity for angled parking, giving the street a narrower appearance, providing more spaces than parallel parking, and slowing passing traffic. Alternatively, and sometimes in addition, wide streets can be an opportunity for a creatively landscaped median strip with trees, benches, and gathering places.

Birmingham, Alabama, narrowed a few downtown streets under a program called "Birmingham Green." Four traffic lanes were maintained, but the 100-foot-wide street was narrowed to make room for widened sidewalks and a landscaped median. Traffic islands, median strips, and sides of roadways make for ideal areas to be adopted by special community and garden groups, as are the many different planting areas. Much can be made of a little.

THE PARKING PRIVILEGED

Downtown merchants and their employees park in front of their stores and complain they lose business because parking space is insufficient downtown. Downtown residents, whose neighborhoods border a commercial district, have difficulty finding parking spaces to leave their cars because commuting business-district employees use their community as a parking lot. In big cities like New York, construction workers, government employees, transit workers, and police—yes, police, who can ride transit free and whose presence on the subway could provide additional security—have whole blocks of curbside or open-space parking reserved for them. In transit-serviced cities (New York is a prime example), planners have been dramatically increasing off-street parking opportunities for years, making worse their own responsibility to manage growing congestion. Portland, Oregon, of course, is the star success of the reverse policy. Portland froze its number of parking spaces and built a light rail line. Within five years of its opening in 1986, $800 million in office, retail, and residential development occurred near train stations.

Traffic commissioners resist the curbside parking that adds so many spaces without losing economically productive buildings to construction of parking garages. Parking has become such a lucrative business that large new development projects are financed based on a preconstruction garage commitment. Government agencies subsidize new development projects by underwriting the construction of an enormous new garage as part of the project. The more downtown space devoted to parking, the less "place" exists.

Yes, we have a parking problem all over the country. But it is not the parking problem most people assume exists. Parking experts say plenty of parking exists, *Wall Street Journal* reporter Heidi Evans observed, "if you are willing to pay or walk—two activities that are anathema to American motorists." Marie Witmer, editor of *Parking*

Professional, told Evans: "People want to park within 17 feet of their destination, and are frequently unwilling to either pay for the privilege or use a free, vacant space several blocks away. It's not that there is a shortage of spaces, just a shortage of free spaces where people want them to be."

Millions of dollars, probably more like billions, are spent subsidizing free or discounted parking. A 1991 Metropolitan Washington Council of Governments study found that area employers provide employees with free or discounted parking worth $240 million a year, that eight of 10 commuters park free, that thousands of drivers view their space as a right, and that one-in-a-car commuters make no effort to carpool or take transit as long as parking is free.[10] Jane Holtz Kay notes in *Asphalt Nation* that 95 percent of Americans who drive to work and 99 percent of those taking all other trips park free. Is there any wonder traffic problems get worse instead of better? Commuters would rather drive than switch. Transit service is underfunded. Transit advocates are overpowered by the auto lobby. And use regulations encourage car-dependent development. None of this will change while parking is cheap or free.

Given this set of circumstances, rebuilding places remains a struggle.

TAME TRAFFIC ENGINEERS

Safety has been the excuse for almost every unfortunate traffic improvement that has eroded downtowns. But safety for whom? Safety for cars—speeding cars, in fact—is the answer. If that were not the case, the most effective safety program for cars and pedestrians alike would be the lowering of vehicular speed. Using the traffic engineers' rule of thumb for safety, no real place can survive. People-friendly places are antithetical to traffic speedways. People-friendly places, however, can be hospitable to moving traffic in a manner not threatening to the pedestrian, as experience in European communities shows.

More and more communities seek slower traffic. And as more places do, they discover that an extraordinary power over the shape and future of their locales is in the hands of transportation planners. It is staggering how many people both of us have encountered in recent years who report how their efforts to rebuild downtown streets and public spaces were thwarted by transportation planners unwilling to bend their standard rules.

St. Paul, Minnesota, for example, was classically transformed with one-way streets, a ring of highways around the city, and a series of second-floor, enclosed walkways guaranteed to kill street life. St. Paul Mayor Norm Coleman eliminated a lane of traffic and added parking and a bike lane as a first step to reviving downtown street life. Variances, however, were required from the state, releasing the city from state regulations that set minimum widths for urban streets. Any locale can ignore those regulations, but doing so clearly jeopardizes its share of gas tax revenue, a powerful enforcement club.

TRANSPORTATION PLANNERS ARE RELENTLESS

Transportation officials' inclination to widen roads continues unabated. This is probably the biggest threat to historic districts across the country. Whitewater, a southeastern Wisconsin city of 10,000, is a classic case. Whitewater has a heavily traveled two-lane Main Street that, like so many Main Streets, is part of a U.S. and state highway route. The state transportation department sought to widen it to four or five lanes. "That would have wiped out hundreds of majestic maples and oaks along the street, part of which is a National Historic District, and devoured generous terraces that set off this lovely stretch of 19th-century homes," editorialized *The Milwaukee Journal.*[11] "Talk about destroying the village in order to save it!" A spirited citizens group demonstrated that traffic congestion and gridlock were exaggerated, that a scaled-down version would serve traffic needs and avoid most of the damage, and that a planned future bypass would make the widening unnecessary. But logic and problem solving were not what this Project Planning proposal was all about. The "real motivator...appears to be money," the *Journal* editorial observed. State and federal road, sewer, and utility repair funds, $3.5 million worth, would be lost if the road widening project was abandoned and the community preserved. "A Faustian bargain," the *Journal* called it, noting that: "This is how the road-builders traditionally have put locals over a barrel: Do it our way or you won't get the money...History and leafy streetscapes are at least as important as smooth traffic flow."

The tenacious citizens at least diminished the traffic engineers' damage. "DOT operates with a straitjacket," reports opposition leader Robert Burroughs. DOT wanted five 12-foot lanes. The opposition showed three would be sufficient. The result: four 11-foot lanes, 150 trees saved out of 200 threatened, and the street and sidewalk realigned to go around some trees. "Common sense, not to mention federal law, compels a better balance between street improvements and preservation," noted the *Journal* in the 1992 editorial. That goal is far from reach. Damage control is the best to hope for when communities are held hostage by state transportation engineers. This happens everywhere.

CALMING TRAFFIC

Traffic calming is the art of setting the needs of walkers and transit users as the priority while still permitting car use. The term emerged in Europe to describe a full range of techniques to slow cars as they pass through commercial and residential areas. These techniques, such as lowering a speed limit, planting trees, or installing a tree-lined median or traffic circle, are low in cost, can be installed on an experimental basis, and are easy to change and modify. Traffic calming establishes a balance among users of the street—cars, trucks, public transit, bikes, and pedestrians. Studies of traffic-calmed streets show a decrease in injuries, deaths, and air pollution, little or no decrease in volume, and no significant time added to the drive. Safety takes on a new meaning. People, not cars, become the priority.

Only recently has "traffic calming" as a policy or program become an issue in some American communities. In fact, most Americans have never heard of the term. This has been changing rapidly. In fact, in August 1996, *The Wall Street Journal* ran a front page story by Mitchell Pacelle on traffic calming, spotlighting Walter Kulash as one of the chief advocates of the idea. Traffic calming has been a familiar and well-appreciated concept among downtown advocates, preservationists, environmentalists, and assorted like-minded groups, but the *Wall Street Journal* article surely placed it in the mainstream.

Evidence that traffic calming adds value to downtown real estate is a message that resonates for the *Journal*'s readership. The appeal of this turn-the-clock-back approach is growing among mayors, Pacelle notes, who have found nothing else that works as well to renew downtown life and economic energy. St. Paul; Milwaukee; Portland, Maine; Providence, Rhode Island; West Palm Beach, Florida; and Birmingham, Michigan, were some of the places Pacelle pointed out that had instituted or were planning traffic calming policies.

When informed of traffic calming, Americans often react with disbelief ("You can't get rid of the car") or fear ("You want to take away my freedom to drive"). The object is neither to get rid of the car nor to take away the freedom to drive. *Traffic is doing that instead.* The object of traffic calming is the creation of transportation and life style alternatives, of which this country does not offer many. Actually, transit alternatives should be a self-interest priority for car drivers. Some people can never imagine themselves traveling any other way but in their car. Fine. But wouldn't they like it if other drivers could switch from cars to transit and leave more road room for them?

EUROPEANS ARE WAY AHEAD

In total contrast, most European countries do offer those alternatives. And, while some European countries seem in a race to catch up with us in our economy's overdependence on the automobile and highway building industries, none have either sold off their train networks to private interests or dismembered their delicate mass transit systems to the degree we have since World War II. Denmark, Australia, the Netherlands, Germany, Switzerland, and others have many programs reflecting a whole spectrum of success that seeks to support compact growth plans, minimize congestion, and keep transit reliable, frequent and reasonably priced. Many German, Swiss, Dutch, and Scandinavian cities have special auto-reduction standards per year.

Everywhere in Europe, gas prices are higher than in the United States. In fact, gasoline is probably the *only* consumer good that is cheaper in real dollars in the United States than it was before the 1973 gas shortage. A 1995 Mobil Oil newspaper advertisement displayed a chart for inflation-adjusted gasoline prices, $2.21 per gallon in 1920 and $1.17 in 1994. Under it was a headline: "America's best bargain." In 1990, Christopher Flavin, energy expert at the Worldwatch Institute, noted: "It costs less now to drive 100 miles than almost ever in our history." Nothing, of course, is for nothing. The real costs have been shifted in a multitude of ways, for which society is now paying a very stiff price. Reversing this condition is imperative.

Pedestrianized communities often have the strongest local economy. In the Dutch town of Houten, where 50 percent of all shopping trips are on bicycle, two-thirds of household budgets are spent within the town, including a reported 100 percent of food purchases and 50 percent of other merchandise.[12] A Netherlands policy directs businesses to sites that aggravate traffic congestion the least. Businesses with high turnovers get sites with good transit and pedestrian access, while those depending on freight service are matched with highway, rail, or port access.

"The key is not to punish people, but instead to give them better choices," says Hank Dittmar, executive director of the Surface Transportation Policy Project (STPP), one of the nation's leading advocates of diminished auto-dependency and increased pedestrian and transit-related development.

Examples abound in Europe, but Denmark has one of the best track records in both small towns and large cities, and even in modifying long distance highways and arterials to calm traffic and reduce congestion. In Copenhagen, one of the world's most civilized and best loved cities, 2 percent of the city's parking has been removed each year for 30 years. Car traffic still flows smoothly through the city and has increased as more people come. Traffic has surely not increased as much as it would have if limiting measures had not been in place. Stability reigns. The economy thrives. No periods of overheated growth, no massive demolition, and no high-rise overkill has occurred. *People often don't notice change that has occurred gradually.*

In some Danish communities, when parking spaces become scarce, the price for parking is raised. (Toronto does the same thing, using the price of parking as a traffic control measure.) Transit has been systematically upgraded for 30 years. No parking lots at all are provided at schools. Students bike or walk. (The United States is probably the only country in the world with an expensive, single-use rubber tire transit system devoted exclusively to transporting children to school. It is a monumental burden for local public school budgets.) Every American public official, planner, or traffic engineer at all interested in promoting the stabilization or rebirth of American downtowns should visit Danish communities.

Koge, for example, a city with a population of 40,000, is one of the largest suburban towns outside Copenhagen. A 30-minute train ride from the city center, Koge is a living example of any American community's wish list of desired conditions. Charming, historic, and fully modern in function, Koge is a medieval town with the eras of its history remaining clearly evidenced in buildings and sites from an earlier time, but all functioning in up-to-date fashion side-by-side with recent editions. Every storefront is occupied with a successful business serving a primarily local population. A modest public square, one block square in the center, combines a park, car and bike parking, an occasional open-air market, food vendors, and a transit stop. Across from the square is City Hall. Half a block away is a well-used, even crowded, library. Hardware, groceries, clothes, and gifts are available within a short walk. Street trees and bike racks line sidewalks. People stroll in the street. Pedestrians and vehicles travel at the same pace.

On a visit a few years ago, I was walking down the middle of the street, marveling at a scene ahead of me. A small delivery van was slowly following directly behind three women, one of whom was pushing a stroller. All three were deep in conversation. The women were oblivious to the vehicle's presence. The driver did not honk, but just waited for them to reach a corner at which he was turning. I pointed out this scene to one of my walking companions. "Look behind you," he said to me, smiling. Sure enough, I was being followed in similar fashion by a "walking" vehicle whose driver was undisturbed and unagitated.

Amazingly, studies in Denmark and elsewhere in Europe where this scene is not uncommon show that calming traffic through towns reduces the speed, not the number, of vehicles and that only one to three minutes are added to most vehicular trips. Drivers accept the limitations. Bicyclists proliferate. All kinds of safety statistics improve. More significantly, traffic calming is much cheaper than building more bypasses that bring short-lived congestion relief, and it does not open new land for sprawling development.

We think of this as foreign, except when we are tourists. The idea that these conditions are not as applicable to where we live as to where we choose to visit is bizarre. *The choice must be better than between living an auto-bound daily life and separately enjoying a pedestrianized leisure life.* No legitimate reason exists to prevent the advantages existing in each part of our life. The principles are universally applicable. The car, in fact, has become an impediment to both mobility and community. The only choice is to undo excessive dependence on it. As *The Economist* concluded in its extraordinary issue devoted to the car:

> There are lots of little things that can be done (and are being done) to make the car easier to live with, but only one thing that would make a big difference: using it less. That can happen only if all the costs incurred are fully identified and charged to its users. Only then will public transport improve, because it will compete on equal terms. In the end, putting economics in the driving seat is the only magic solution, however unwelcome.[13]

1. Alfred A. Knopf New York: 1990, p. xi.
2. Enclosed malls in warm, sunny locales with year-round good weather baffle me. The power of formula thinking is extraordinary.
3. The project won a 1995 Federal Transportation Design Achievement Award.
4. In keeping with the transportation schizophrenia of many states, New Jersey's Department of Transportation is relentless in pursuit of new roadway projects that widen existing ones or add new ones, at the same time as state transit agencies are pursuing more enlightened policies.
5. "To Boost Economy, Cities Give Old-Style Railways a New Twist," February 24, 1995.
6. Cleveland, like Detroit, has two centers, a downtown business core and a second center, where educational and cultural uses, among others, are located. In recent decades, both cities have let decay or erased the varied urban network that once connected the two centers. Detroit, like Cleveland, defeated a rail line plan for its downtown spine, Woodward Avenue.
7. Komanoff, "A Fitting Memorial," *City Limits*, April, 1997, p. 26.
8. David W. Chen, "For Safety's Sake and Their Own, Towns Learn to Pamper Pedestrians," *The New York Times*, July 23, 1995.
9. Tri-State Campaign Newsletter, April 19, 1996.
10. Stephen C. Fehr and D'Vera Cohen, "Subsidized Parking Fueling Area Traffic," *The Washington Post* Metro section, April 18, 1991.
11. October 2, 1994.

12. "Buses, Bicycles, and Small Town Revivals: How smaller European cities are out-competing the automobile and boosting economic vitality, safety and quality of life," by Bruce W. Hammond, Policy Analyst, Natural Resources Council of Maine, for the German Marshall Fund of the United States.

13. "Taming the Beast," *The Economist*, June 22, 1996, "A Survey On Living With the Car" on the 100th Anniversary of the Auto Industry.

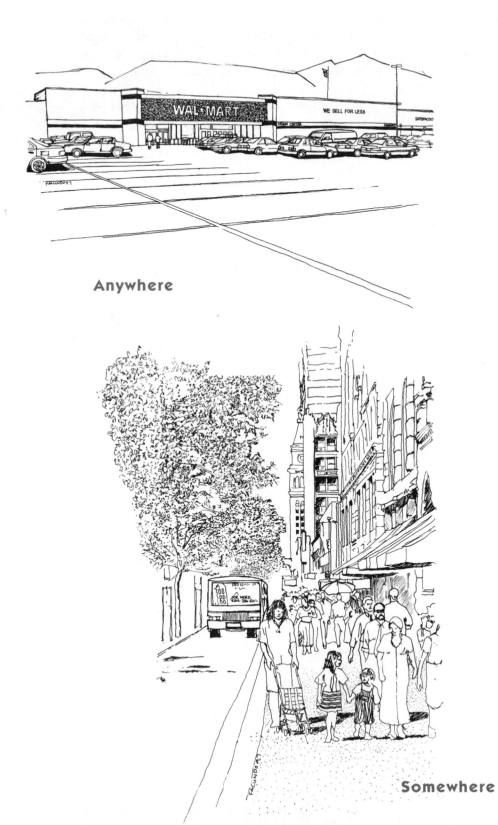

WAL★MART

WE SELL FOR LESS

Anywhere

Somewhere

CHAPTER SIX

UNDOING SPRAWL

> Though people talk about "urbanization" as the process that ushered in modern ills, many urban neighborhoods at mid-century were in fact fairly communal; it's hard to walk into a Brooklyn brownstone day after day without bumping into neighbors. It was suburbanization that brought the combination of transience and residential isolation that leaves many people feeling a bit alone in their own neighborhoods. (These days, thanks to electric garage-door openers, you can drive straight into your house, never risking contact with a neighbor.)
>
> *Time Magazine*, August 25, 1995.

When the above paragraph appeared in *Time Magazine* in a cover story by Robert Wright, "20th Century Blues," one knew the tide had turned. *Time* is hardly the voice of fuzzy urban radicals or tennis-shoed preservationists. This is mainstream. Maybe, the myth that the suburbs are the refuge and cities the generators of problems is coming apart. It is about time. Neither the myth of the uplifting and idyllic suburb nor the perception of the violent and alienating city fits today's reality, as if they ever did. But now, the nation has a suburban majority and many of those suburbanites are experiencing a nightmare of new frustrations.

The nightmare has a name: *sprawl*, the low-density, land-consumptive, automobile-oriented development that has been moving farther and farther out from the fringes of existing urban and town centers. Fueled by a combination of public policies and private development practices, sprawl is synonymous with postwar suburbanization. Our vast spaghetti network of postwar highways is the lifeline of an endless assortment of residential enclaves with "no identity other than the one developers gave them"[1] and usually named after the landscapes they replaced—Elm Court, Vineyard Fields, Orchard Lane, Old Farm Road, Meadow Estates, Blueberry Hills, Valley View, Heritage Hills, Meadowlark Cove.

Rationalized as the price of progress, the unavoidability of sprawl is a myth. Growth, progress, and suburbs do not have to come with sprawl. Sprawl is the reality that grew out of a tangle of myths that must be dispelled. Downtown America depends on it. The nation's social health depends on it. The national economy depends on it. Taming sprawl and rebuilding downtowns and local economies go hand in hand.

Sprawl is not about progress. Sprawl is not cheap. In fact, sprawl is extremely expensive. Sprawl is not unplanned. Malls are no substitute for real downtowns. Americans have not flocked to the suburbs out of pure choice. Conventional explanations of sprawl do not fit reality. And, *for a nation so obsessed with efficiency, sprawl is the most inefficient, least cost effective form of growth imaginable*. Awareness is growing and the momentum to undo sprawl accelerating. The myths, however, are solidly entrenched.

By now, sprawl has become a household word. Instinctively, many people recognize it as a problem with impacts on entire families. As Jane Seaberry noted in *The Washington Post*, "Suburban developments are so sprawling that in many places neighborhood games are all but obsolete. Children have to be driven miles to play with friends, requiring intricate planning and plenty of time."[2] Long, stressful commutes strain family life. School budgets are strained by the cost of serving a sprawled-out population. Unsupervised teenagers, parking garage crime, carjackings, and sexual assault plague shopping malls.

Calls for alternatives increase. "Studies by real-estate economists of Baltimore, Dallas, and Oakland, California, show that when you strip away all the other factors known to influence home prices, buyers are willing to pay a steep premium for a home in a well-preserved traditional neighborhood," noted *Consumer Reports* in an extraordinary article highlighting the economic and social values that come with the purchase of a home in compact, walkable communities.[3] Sprawl is a consumer issue. It puts a social and economic tax on us all.

A San Diego suburbanite visited her Brooklyn cousin in one of the many New York neighborhoods where young professionals and families with young children have been increasingly settling for more than two decades. The San Diegan was stunned to see the solid elegance of her cousin's 19th-century, four-story rowhouse, but was really left breathless when she compared the value of his Brooklyn home to hers. Both properties cost about the same to buy, but his property taxes were slightly less than hers. He rented out half of the building but could expand into it in the future. He was within walking distance of every convenient shopping need and a 20-minute transit ride from his work. He didn't own a car. More than the economic differences, she loved the "friendly, small town feeling of the neighborhood."

In a similar vein, an ironic but telling Endnote, titled "Small Town, U.S.A.," appeared a few years ago on the editorial page of *The New York*

Times. The message underscores what an upside-down and inside-out world we have created.

> Not long ago, a New Yorker looking for a simpler world journeyed to a small town. This town had once resembled those on Christmas cards and in children's books: here the grocery store, there the fishmonger, the shoe repair shop to the north and the newsstand to the south. All one needed to sustain life was concentrated in a few blocks—unless one was looking for madder music and stronger wine, in which case, forget it.
>
> Now the town looks more than ever like something on a Christmas card: Money's moved in and touched up the houses, resodded the lawns, gone wild with hydrangeas. But this is no longer a simpler world, with necessities at hand.
>
> Within a block of the house in which the New Yorker was staying were three antique shops and a store that sold "country collectibles,"...Buying a quilt would have taken a two-minute walk. Buying a can of beans, however, was a three-mile drive to the supermarket. The grocery stores were gone...Watch repair is 17 miles to the north, and fresh vegetables involve a trek to the back roads. True, the town's new deli sells paté, but where is the butcher of yesteryear?
>
> Once back home, the New Yorker took a new look at her neighborhood. It will never make a Christmas card, although it has more than once made a cops-and-robbers movie.
>
> But there they were: the grocery store, the fishmonger, the shoe repair shop to the north and the newsstand to the south. It was the simpler world she'd longed for, with all one needed to sustain life concentrated in a few blocks. To find the kind of small town she remembers, it seems, the place to look is in the city.

SIDEWALK URBANISM

Several years ago, I was speaking in a small northwestern city set in one of those celebrated landscapes that boasts mountains, inland and coastal waterfronts, forests, campsites, hiking trails, and great biking terrain—not unlike too many of the country's growing areas with great landscapes being gobbled up by car-dependent development.

I had been driven through several recently built developments earlier in the day. Curved roadways. Houses set back. Two or three garage doors comprising the bulk of the front façade. Front door entrance set back from garage, almost lost in scale in its narrowness. Utility meters and exposed pipes affixed to the front façade. The day was sunny and warm. Not a person was visible, on the road, on the lawns, at the front doors. Enclave after enclave looked the same, with occasional variations in house type: mock Tudor, mock Colonial, mock Victorian, mock ranch. Surely, on this glorious spring day, people were outside somewhere, perhaps in their backyards, away from the street and public interaction. The only neighborhood in which I saw any communal life was in a low-income community of garden apartments, modest density, and a simple playground that actually had parents and children participating in shared activity. All of these highly planned developments were fanning out from a charming, but struggling, traditional downtown that had old life to it and signs of new, innovative additions filling old buildings and creating modest new ones. But between downtown and the residential enclaves was Strip Sprawl U.S.A., drawing auto-bound people out of the center. This is not a description of a unique American location. It is everywhere.

The discussion following the lecture revealed the dilemmas of this landscape. People in the audience voiced their frustration. The distance for a quart of milk or to the mall. The commute. The distance to after-school or weekend programs. No nearby recreation. Not enough informal communal interaction. This community, like thousands of others, was going through a year-long Vision 2000 process, wrestling with how to cope with the growing problems, how to shape the future, and how to rein in sprawl. Earnestly, people were searching for solutions, the easier and quicker the better. No such thing exists, of course, but that does not mean a beginning step shouldn't be taken. Something always leads to something else.

One woman in the audience reported proudly that her enclave succeeded in getting sidewalks installed. The residents considered it a significant advance. I applauded the effort. Sidewalks have become the most comprehensible and visual feature of the compact, walkable community so many people want, almost a metaphor for the human interaction they hunger for. Sidewalks are, in fact, the lifeblood of a community. But, I asked the speaker, "After the sidewalks are installed, where will you walk to?"

She had no answer. No shared, communal place, no park or playground even existed. No commercial center, corner store, or entertainment facility was within walking distance. Surely there was no public space. The closest transit stop for the hourly downtown bus service was at least a mile away. Yet, one can expect, with sidewalks installed, the far-sighted residents who identified the sidewalk void might come up with another addition of consequence. Step by step, they will figure it out. It is not mysterious and, when given the opportunity to articulate their needs and preferences, they can lead the way to rebuilding *real* connected communities.

The starting point of the unsprawling process does not matter. Communities are like jigsaw puzzles. When all the pieces fit, the picture is complete. Everything connects. The missing pieces become apparent no matter where the process begins.

BREAKING HABITS

The unsprawling process has a certain logic but it is not easy. A *walkable* community does not guarantee a *walking* community. Sidewalks without interesting things to walk by and destinations to walk to will not easily draw pedestrians. Wide traffic arteries to cross, empty parking lots, blank walls, and empty store windows to pass and the absence of visible human activity on the street discourage pedestrians.

And habit must not be discounted.

Savannah, Georgia, for example, is one of the most beautiful, pedestrian-friendly places imaginable. A city that combines the ambiance of a small town and an historic urban neighborhood, everything is within a 15-minute walk. All pedestrian-friendly essentials are present: small landscaped squares filled with graceful trees draped with Spanish moss and inviting park furniture, each square different but a model of a small open space that provides visual delight and stimulates social interaction. Historic architecture of great variety on both residential and commercial streets. Storefront shopping streets with the variety of retail opportunities that so many traditional downtowns are struggling to rebuild. Yet, Savannahians drive even a few blocks.

"We do it by habit," a life-long Savannahian told me. "I was raised going everywhere by car and now I do it automatically."

The old trolley-car neighborhood of Roslindale in Boston has a wonderful 11-block downtown of small streets and appealing local stores. In 1987, the commuter train line to downtown Boston was revived. Within a stone's throw of the station are various conveniences, from a drugstore to a shoe repair shop, and more than 100 businesses. But of greatest appeal are an assortment of ethnic bakeries reflecting the rich variety of immigrant groups living in the vicinity. Commuter trains are clearly attracting riders. Yet, downtown observers and merchants report that not many commuters are taking advantage of the walkable amenities, driving to and from the station parking lot instead.

People raised in a car-dependent life style don't alter the habit easily. A transit-oriented community does not assure a transit-riding community. Advocates of more roads argue that mass transit is not cost-effective because not enough people ride it. *Mass transit will not attract mass ridership outside of dense cities as long as driving is cheap, parking is free (nothing can compete psychologically or economically with free parking), transit service is inconvenient and expensive, highway subsidies exceed transit support, and low-density development patterns continue. The more density, the more walking. It is as simple as that.* "Life attracts life," Jane Jacobs wrote. It took a whole generation, almost two generations, raised on cars to forget the appeal of alternatives. It took a half century to reshape the country for the car. Change never comes quickly.

SPRAWL DID NOT HAPPEN OVERNIGHT

Sprawl is the outcome of foolhardy public policies of the post-World War II economy, fueled by the building of suburbs and manufacturing of cars. Sprawl was intended and planned (just read any zoning code); the problems of sprawl were not.

The Interstate Highway Program, which began in the 1950s, shaped federal investment policies from housing to transportation.[4] Highways were intended to disperse population and empty cities for defense purposes. The 1950s, after all, were marked by fear of atomic bombs. The U.S. government moved research and defense industries out of cities. Veterans Administration loans were limited to *new*, single-family homes. No apartments and no rehabilitation were allowed. In other words, no existing housing in center cities. Home ownership and suburbia became synonymous. To Levittown without looking back. This can only be defined as a conscious government decision to fund suburban growth, and car-dependent development at that.

Car ownership became the goal of many in an increasingly prosperous nation. Car dependency was the unwished-for, unintended consequence. The myth of America's love for the car took on a life of its own. No choice was offered. Mass transit systems (both long-distance and local) were allowed to decay as public investment shifted to the open road. Alternatives were removed, slowly but surely. Railroad service was undermined by highways built on adjacent routes intentionally located to directly compete.[5] Trolley systems were ripped up to eliminate competition for rubber-tired transportation. Trolley-car suburbs and highway suburbs should not be confused, as we saw in Chapter 4. They are like night and day. Trolley-car suburbs connected well with and functioned as extensions of downtowns. Highway suburbs clearly did not.

The voices of challenge were drowned out by the euphoria of a postwar building boom. William H. Whyte, in a still-seminal 1958 book he edited, *The Exploding Metropolis*,[6] wrote: "Already huge patches of once green countryside have been turned into vast, smog-filled deserts that are neither city, suburb, nor country...This is bad for the farmers, it is bad for communities, it is bad for industry, it is bad for utilities, it is bad for the railroads, it is bad for the recreation groups, it is bad even for the developers." It is cheaper to build when infrastructure costs less.

Lewis Mumford's critiques of urban density and praise for countrifying cities, on the one hand, fueled advocates for new "greenbelt" suburbs and the whole suburban fever. But his *The Highway and the City*,[7] on the other hand, was and remains a cogent condemnation of auto-dependency. As the massive interstate highway exchanges (cloverleafs) spread across the countryside like weeds, Mumford disdainfully declared in 1961 that the Concrete Cloverleaf should be named the national flower. Jane Jacobs' pioneering 1961 critique, *Death and Life of Great American Cities,* challenged all the city planning principles that rationalized the "sacking of cities." This seminal work was welcomed by the public and ridiculed by many planners. Jacobs noted that the new development patterns were "reducing city and countryside alike to monotonous gruel."

Public investment in a new and sprawling landscape was what government was about in those days, when attention was concentrated on converting a vast war machine to domestic service. The automobile and construction industries were the primary beneficiaries and as long as they were fueled, the thinking went, prosperity would continue. That thinking was, in fact, formed by the auto industry. Since 1932, when General Motors established the National Highway Users Conference with Alfred P. Sloan as president, the staggering power, influence, and control of the highway/auto lobby on the American political system have held firm. The consequences of the damage to the environment and removal of investment from existing communities were secondary.[8]

THE MYTHOLOGY OF SPRAWL
Myths emerged to rationalize this national transformation. Market forces shape everything. People love automobiles. Automobiles define freedom. Everyone wants a new house in the suburbs with a lawn. Old houses are out of fashion. No one wants to live in cities. Developers follow the people. You can't stop progress. And so on. All kernels of truth encased in beds of myth. Simplistically explained, conveniently ignored, totally underestimated, or craftily interpreted are the whole web of government and corporate actions that drive these trends, what environmentalist Henry R. Richmond, chairman of the National Growth Management Leadership Project, calls the "tilt of existing public policy."

Today, persistent myths get in the way of small cures.

The myth of the open plains Americans love to drive on is the most potent, as depicted in all the car commercials that only show open roads. Environmentalist Jessica Mathews wrote:

Ninety percent of our auto trips are less than 10 miles long, and most are made between rows of concrete, not waving grasses. The myth is no more connected to people's everyday choices than are the bucolic country roads of the television auto commercials or the Marlboro man's horse and lariat. We drive and drive not because of a collective national memory of the Western frontier, but because we have piled subsidy on top of subsidy to encourage the use of automobiles over every other form of transportation.[9]

The myth that America has the best transportation system in the world undermines efforts to revise American thinking about our transportation policies. We surely have the *biggest* system. We do not have the best. Many experts say, in fact, that we have the worst in the industrialized world. Germany, Japan, France, Norway, and others have more efficient and balanced systems, where transportation choices are offered and development patterns are directed away from auto-dependency. Europe rebuilt its worn-thin transit systems after the war. We dismantled ours and set about building only roads.

In Europe, transit is subsidized as generously as highway travel, so that transit can compete with the car in cost, comfort, efficiency, and frequency, although even in some European countries, this is changing for the worse. In most European countries with better systems, transportation respects and reinforces existing patterns of community and commercial development. In the United States, auto-based highways plowed through cities, destroyed existing communities, and then forced all development to follow them. No country exhibits sprawl to the degree of this country, and no country subsidizes its oil-consuming car culture as generously as we do.

Popular myth identifies sprawl development as unplanned and undesigned. Not true. Local planning and zoning codes, design guidelines, building codes, and transportation systems shape all development. The plan for every new shopping or office center, every industrial park, every garage or carport, every road connection, or any car-accommodating project is a legally-mandated, sprawl-enhancing design. *Every project that continues automobile dependency and does not provide a transportation alternative is a planned and designed sprawl enhancer.* Transportation planning and Project Planning are synonymous. Together, they have brought us to where we are.

"Transportation is only about mobility" is probably the most misleading myth of all. As noted earlier, everything connects to transportation like spokes on a wheel. Community development. Downtown stability. Farmland preservation. Business locations. Local economies. Clean air and water. All environmental, planning, design, and preservation issues lead to transportation. Senior citizen housing. Job development and access to jobs. This last item is particularly relevant with the pressure to transfer people from welfare to workfare. The poor are the most dependent on diminishing transit schedules and increased fares. As refreshingly enlightened Milwaukee Mayor John O. Norquist has written, "...Many people on welfare don't have reliable, affordable ways to reach jobs. Policy makers are slow to catch on...the average cost of car ownership (is) $6500 a year. That's far beyond the reach of households at the poverty level. And without cars, or affordable public transportation, many jobs will remain beyond their reach." Ironically, in fact, welfare to workfare is forcing government on all levels to come to grips, *at great expense*, with the demise of public transit that once served neighborhoods now lived in by the poor. The Clinton administration has asked Congress for $600 million to fund programs to get welfare recipients to jobs, and encouraged a multicity experiment to identify programs that work. New Jersey's Governor Christine Todd Whitman announced a free bus and train pass program for new workers, but had to add funds for counties to help these workers even get to the buses and trains. The Transportation Innovation Fund, the new county funding agency, was named. More localized efforts are under way in many places, such as East Baltimore, Minneapolis, and Chicago. These mushrooming costs don't show up on any conventional balance sheet. Most surviving and new mass transit serves suburban residents going to urban jobs. Before the welfare-to-workfare initiative, all governmental agencies could ignore the transit-deprived condition of most low-income communities.

Even educational opportunities are intricately entwined with transportation in unrecognized ways. Many educational facilities relocated out of downtowns to campus settings over several decades, and newer ones located out of town to start. In the city of Hudson, New York, for example, a large poor population lives downtown, typical of the kind of poor population that remains poor because urban areas have lost the improvement opportunities they once offered. The community college, however, is three miles outside of downtown. A downtown bus exists to take visitors and employees back and forth from the railroad station to the county hospital located in the downtown, but no such facility exists to take car-less downtown residents to the college. The one opportunity for job training in the vicinity is denied to the population needing it the most.

"After all, what good is a school if students can't get to it?" asks Joe Montoya, Sr., writing in *STPP Progress*.[10] Montoya and a group of other retirees in the South Valley of Albuquerque got together "to devote the rest of our lives to brightening the prospects of our young people by providing them with better educational opportunities." In an area of 60,000 people, "poverty-stricken barrios, 400-year-old Spanish settlements, a few middle-class neighborhoods, and an Indian reservation," Montoya and his colleagues created a community college branch of the Albuquerque Technical Vocational Institute (TVI) for vocational and other employment training classes. They renovated an abandoned school building, secured all credentials, supplies, and teachers, and opened the doors. Transportation is their biggest problem. The nearest bus stop is a mile away. They convinced the city to extend the bus three-quarters of a mile to the school, but it comes *every other hour and ends service at 7 p.m.*

My favorite sprawl myth is the homebuilders' mantra that they only build what the public wants. If builders were correct, how can one explain

Georgetown, Beacon Hill, Back Bay, the Upper East Side, Brooklyn's Park Slope and Brooklyn Heights, Philadelphia's Society Hill, Grosse Pointe, Coral Gables, San Antonio's King William District, Vieux Carré, Charleston, San Francisco's Nob Hill, Pacific Heights, and Victorian District, Seattle's Capital Hill, Atlanta's Virginia Highlands, Morningside, Garden Hills, and Inman Park, Charlotte's Dillworth, and the endless list of other cheek-by-jowl, super-expensive urban neighborhoods? And how to explain the "Back to the City" movement of the past two decades that has seen home buyers choose the value of historic urban neighborhoods over suburbs?

And how can one explain the favorite summer vacation destinations of historic, tightly built old towns, from Edgartown to Mendocino and from Fire Island to Carmel, where biking and walking are the preferred transportation modes? Or the newly built Seaside, Florida, or recently rediscovered South Miami Beach? "Resorts Gain Civic Seriousness," *Architecture Magazine* proclaimed in an introduction to an issue devoted to "New Urbanism/Old Urbanism." Historic they all may be, but they are also the kind of coherent communities loved by residents and visitors alike. Most of them did not start out as resorts, but as fully functioning communities that evolved into resorts because of their inherent appeal. Friendly streets, diversified architecture, comfortable density, and easy, non-car-dependent accessibility to most needs are common denominators for all of them. Erroneously, these vacation spots and historic neighborhoods are dismissed as curious throwbacks, but they surely go to the top of the list of public preferences. Authentic places have become tourist attractions because of their rarity. Sadly, people believe these appealing qualities can only exist in tourist towns.

The most desirable residential neighborhoods and the most valuable real estate exist in long-established, mostly pre-car-dependent communities. Builders, however, are geared to build what they have been efficiently building for decades, namely, postwar single-family suburban housing. Zoning laws dictate street and sidewalk widths, minimum setbacks, mixture of uses, and variety of dwelling sizes. Those same zoning laws prohibit the community design more and more people seek. And institutional lenders are totally synchronized with builders' formulas and zoning prohibitions.

The New York brownstone is one of the most popular, efficient, and appropriately urban housing forms ever built. It can serve as either a single-family residence or multiple dwelling and, in many New York neighborhoods, that row house form and its many variations serve the various purposes well. Incredibly, the New York brownstone and its row house cousins could not be built today under the city's building code and the state's multiple dwelling code. New York architect Peter Samton pointed this out in a *New York Times* letter to the editor[11] following the announcement of a sweeping new city plan to encourage new residential construction. Samton wrote:

> By making changes that would permit one staircase instead of two for a typical four-story apartment building with a maximum of eight apartments, we can recreate the 21st century version of the 19th century brownstone (now illegal), still one of the most efficient, attractive, and least expensive housing types in the city. Modern fire codes and materials already contribute to assuring more fire-resistive buildings, which makes this proposal reasonable. Furthermore, nearly all the major cities of Northern Europe contain substantial non-elevator housing of this type—where a single, centrally situated means of egress for a mid-size building is deemed adequate for fire safety and is viewed as desirable for security and for enhanced social contact.

Currently, suburban housing projects seem to be the city's preferred style of choice, guaranteeing a de-densification that will continue to undermine formerly urban neighborhoods.

REALITY IS COMING INTO FOCUS

Where we are now has been pointedly capsulized by none other than the Bank of America, the California giant whose 1995 report, *Beyond Sprawl: New Patterns of Growth to Fit the New California*, was nothing short of a stop-sprawl manifesto. In partnership with an unlikely coalition—the California Greenbelt Alliance, the California Resources Agency, and the Low Income Housing Fund—the Bank of America report noted:

> ...as we approach the 21st century, it is clear that sprawl has created enormous costs that California can no longer afford. Ironically, unchecked sprawl has shifted from an engine of California's growth to a force that now threatens to *inhibit* growth and degrade the quality of our life...
>
> This acceleration of sprawl has surfaced enormous social, environmental and economic costs, which until now have been hidden, ignored, or quietly borne by society. The burden of these costs is becoming very clear. Businesses suffer from higher costs, a loss in worker productivity, and underutilized investments in older communities.
>
> California's business climate becomes less attractive than surrounding states. Suburban residents pay a heavy price in taxation and automobile expenses, while residents of older

cities and suburbs lose access to jobs, social stability, and political power. Agriculture and ecosystems also suffer.

In the short run, the report noted, new residential and commercial development on the fringes and outskirts of our established centers, in fact, may be cheaper for builders, but "the ultimate cost—to those homeowners, to the government, and to society at large—is potentially crippling." No bank, it would seem, has done more in recent decades through its loan policies to finance the very condition it is now so boldly criticizing and, in fact, the bank did not declare an end to sprawl investments. This report, however, put the spotlight where it belongs and added momentum to the political will for change. Many financial institutions and builders associations were quite unsettled and, reportedly, let the Bank of America know it.

Other ominously worded studies have been just as revealing.

In 1992, New Jersey passed a statewide plan to contain sprawl and direct new investment into and close to traditional urban centers, much the same way states like Oregon had done with the creation of Urban Growth Boundaries and growth management plans. A study by Robert Burchell and the Center for Urban Policy Research of Rutgers University compared the costs over 20 years between today's sprawl development patterns and this alternative plan. The conclusions were staggering. The state could save $1.3 billion in capital costs alone—roads, sewers, utilities, schools—and $400 million in operating expenses. The New Jersey plan articulated sprawl containment goals, but the impact on state policies seems to have been minimal. Municipalities and state agencies are not required to comply. In 1994 and 1995, more than 60 percent of the state's share of federal highway money went for *new* roads and new highway lanes.[12] So much for fiscal responsibility! Road widenings, mall access roads, and new bypasses continue to proliferate. In at least one known case, a site designated as rural and environmentally sensitive by the plan was designated a "center" to make possible approval of a huge development. Declaring an empty site a "center" is a corruption of the English language.

The Regional Plan Association of New York issued a 1996 report, *Region at Risk*, calling "uncontrolled growth," or sprawl, the greatest threat to the three-state New York-New Jersey-Connecticut region, noting that land was devoured 12 times faster than the population grew. The RPA recommended rebuilding New York state around its transit in order to revitalize its economy.

In a 1989 monograph for the Urban Land Institute, James Frank, associate professor of urban and regional planning at Florida State University, estimated a $48,000-per-house sprawl "premium" for providing services to a three-unit-per-acre development located 10 miles from central facilities and employment centers. A 12-unit-per-acre development costs half as much.[13] The New York town of Pittsford, a bedroom suburb near Rochester, agreed, in the summer of 1996, to raise $10 million through municipal bonds to save seven farms and 1200 acres of land—about 60 percent of the tillable land remaining in the town—from development. The cost to the taxpayer of new sprawl development is what motivated voters to support the bond issue. The program will cost the average taxpayer $67 a year over 20 years to pay off the bonds. But the calculated savings that represents is staggering. "If these same properties were to develop, it would cost the same household $200 annually, forever, because of the increased costs in schools and services," town supervisor Bill Carpenter told Anne Raver of *The New York Times*.[14]

A 1995 report of the American Farmland Trust focused on the cost of sprawl to California's Central Valley, one of the nation's most productive agricultural regions. The region will lose 1 million acres of productive farmland by 2040, if current patterns (three homes per acre) continue, but would lose only 474,000 acres if a compact alternative (six homes per acre) is followed. The alternative would add nearly $70 billion to the agricultural economy and save taxpayers $29 billion, which would be spent extending sewers and other services to newly developed areas. "The cost of providing the current level of public services to low-density sprawl would exceed the revenues of the Central Valley cities by about $1 billion annually, necessitating a reduction in services or an increase in taxes. Compact, efficient growth would produce an annual budget surplus of $200 million, enabling services to be maintained or slightly improved."[15]

Newspapers across the country have written in-depth series on the impacts of sprawl on their region: the *Sunday News Journal* in Wilmington, Delaware (Gannett),[16] the *Kansas City Star* series by Jeffrey Spivak and Chris Lester, "Divided We Sprawl,"[17] The *Chicago Tribune* series, "A Nation of Strangers."[18] A *Denver Post* poll in 1995 revealed that uncontrolled growth was the number-one concern among the majority of respondents. A popular Colorado bumper sticker reads: "Don't California Colorado." A similar sticker is appearing in Utah. In Oregon, "Don't Californicate Oregon."

Ironically, California, the perceived inventor of sprawl, with car dependency its primary feature, seems to be leading the nation in understanding sprawl's negative consequences and in coming to terms with it. In 1996, I attended the annual conference of the Local Government Commission, an organization of primarily California officials. Over the weekend, I listened to diverse appointed and elected officials from towns and cities of all sizes wrestle with sprawl issues and share both successful and unsuccessful experiences. Stopping or undoing sprawl was their primary concern. I was impressed with how much on the cutting edge most of these government representatives were, especially those willing to confront the issues when their communities had not yet reached the same point of understanding.

The year before, Jim Sayer, executive director of the California Greenbelt Alliance, cited in a speech several local studies revealing sprawl's added costs to local homebuyers and taxpayers. Two nearby towns compared their costs, acreage, and population, for example. The one with one-third less population spread over 15 percent more acreage had 50 percent higher annual service costs. The city of Fresno, in 15 years, doubled its population in a sprawled-out manner. The cost of services increased by twice the amount of the income derived from new development.

The facts are painfully clear, yet officials duck the issue and, as noted, sprawl issues fail to enter the national debate in a meaningful way.

THANK YOU WAL-MART, THANK YOU DISNEY

The good news is that public awareness and public opinion seem to be ahead of most local, state, and national officials. Ironically, the biggest help in turning the tide came from two of the nation's biggest and most visible giants—Wal-Mart, the largest retailer, and Disney, the largest entertainer. With Wal-Mart's announced national 1997 strategy to continue to open new discount stores and supercenters on the already "overstored" countryside, and Disney's proposed 3000-acre real estate development in 1994 that included a 400-acre theme park near the Manassas Battlefield in Prince William County, Virginia, the realization of the enormity of sprawl's impact spread like wildfire.

Wal-Mart and Disney actually did the country a favor, much more important than offering cheap underwear and Mickey Mouse. They provided the wake-up call all Americans could understand.

Popular bumper sticker created by Sprawl-Busters.

The extraordinarily well-focused and determined opposition to Disney in Virginia and to Wal-Mart in countless places gave voice to the enormous dissatisfaction with the changing character of American cities, towns, and villages. The citizen army against sprawl finally got its national act together, spurred on by Disney and Wal-Mart to new levels of activism and sophistication. The first meeting of the national "Sprawl-busting" network occurred during the annual convention of the National Trust for Historic Preservation that took place in Boston in October 1994,[19] when participants shared war stories, gave hints to newcomers, and learned from each other. "Sprawlmarting" is becoming a household word and was used against Disney side by side with the debate over treatment of Civil War history.

"Our opposition is not focused on the theme park itself," Richard Moe, president of the National Trust for Historic Preservation, told a U.S. Senate committee.[20] "What we oppose is the scale of the overall project and the intensive additional development—the sprawl—that is sure to follow in Disney's wake, and that is sure to destroy the beautiful and historic countryside of the Northern Virginia Piedmont." Under Moe's leadership, the Trust assumed a central role in the battle against sprawl, armed communities with the tools to fight, and, importantly, showed that alternatives exist that don't trade community values and a real place for the price of a deceptively cheap suit.

Moe, a Civil War scholar and author, organized the committee of historians whose vocal opposition to the "Disneyfication" of American history drew the most national attention under the articulate leadership of historian and author David McCullough. But at the congressional committee hearing, Moe noted: "Disney's arrival will…send the region into a chaotic spiral of speculation, construction, and congestion." This is an apt description of sprawl itself. Anywhere. It differs in each place by degrees.

Comic strip artist Garry Trudeau, who knows a national issue when he sees one, connected Disney and Wal-Mart in a "Doonesbury" series, depicting Wal-Mart as the more benign option. "The most irresponsible idea ever hatched in the Magic Kingdom," *The New York Times* editorialized.[21]

Until Disney, the debate remained local. But suddenly, the giant of giants, the most American of corporations, became the object of national resistance and, by extension, the case was made for the specialness of every place, with or without a Civil War battlefield. Sprawlbusters everywhere were empowered by Disney's withdrawal. Many saw the parallels to hometown proposals in Disney's 3000-acre scheme—a 400-acre theme park and parking lots, surrounded by 2300 units of suburban housing, 1.9 million square feet of mall development, two golf courses, a waterpark, campsite, and more, all made possible by at least $163 million in tax dollar road improvements as the first installment of public subsidies that were sure to follow. The battle was joined and it was equally significant, if not infinitely more significant, than whether Disney would do justice to the heroes of battle.

Let's be clear. The national outcry in Virginia was not against Mickey Mouse, but against Mickey's entourage—the deadening traffic, the sprawling new suburbs, the endless mall culture, the destruction of local economies, the loss of historic buildings and working farms. This was an outcry against the car-dependent, pave-over development that has been mangling America.

If the opposition had been just rich, hunt-country NIMBYs (Not-In-My-Back-Yard-ers), as some editorialists claimed, the effort would have failed. Everywhere, handfuls of rich people oppose development in their own "backyard." But they don't win without broad support. In fact, this issue attracted as broad a spectrum of America as any issue can generate. The National Trust published an open letter to Disney as an ad in *The Washington Post*. A coupon was included soliciting opinions from the public. More than 4000 responses were received from that one ad in opposition to the proposal.

Sprawlbusting is a genuine and growing grass-roots movement. Disney gave it a needed boost. "Disney was a national turning point," notes Constance E. Beaumont, director of state and local policy at the National Trust for Historic Preservation and leading strategist of the organization's vigorous sprawlbusting efforts. "This was a victory that said you can take on the big guy and win," Beaumont adds. "The biggest hurdle in these fights is the feeling that you can't win, so why try."[22]

In the Disney editorial, *The New York Times* identified the opposition to the Virginia scheme as "the passionate nationwide outcry that carried a clear message." That may have been the first time it was heard nationally, but it is heard frequently locally in battles against the newest sprawl proposal. People recognize the problem everywhere. They don't always define it broadly.

CHANGING THE RULES FROM THE BOTTOM UP

Defeating local sprawl development proposals is urgent. Communities are waging these battles daily, and with increasing success. In town after town and neighborhood after neighborhood, planned development proposals, and the official rules that encourage them, clash with community preferences exhibited in the visions emerging from community planning efforts that genuinely involve people in a public planning process. Change is increasingly called for. Many long-entrenched rules need to be broken and grass-roots efforts mobilized.

The nation took note when little Westford, Massachusetts (population 17,500), 20 miles northwest of Boston, defeated a Wal-Mart in 1993. Almost one-third of the population, 5200 people, signed a petition against approving a Wal-Mart application to locate there. This was the first visible, cohesive, and victorious fight. Wal-Mart agreed to pull out, for the first time living up to the now famous Sam Walton quote, "If some community, for whatever reason, doesn't want us in there, we aren't interested in going in and creating a fuss." Peter Jennings, on the ABC evening news, and the *Wall Street Journal* on its front page, turned the spotlight on Westford.[23] Wal-Mart was embarrassed. A month later, the corporate Goliath conceded defeat to another David, Greenfield, Massachusetts (population 19,000), a Connecticut River town 90 miles west of Boston. Greenfield succeeded in having a referendum on whether Wal-Mart should be allowed to open a 121,267-square-foot store (larger than the size of the entire downtown retail district) on the outskirts of town.

"Westford sent the message to a lot of people that they could fight and win," notes Beaumont. "Westford had a catalytic effect. More than 100 communities were fighting Wal-Mart at the time. The Westford victory spurred them on."

The onslaught of sprawl comes in many guises and with many corporate giants, but Wal-Mart is the most symbolic manifestation. "The quintessential modern icon of sprawl," planner Anton C. Nelessen calls Wal-Mart in his 1995 book, *Visions for a New American Dream*. "No one is as difficult, arrogant, secretive, and vindictive," says Al Norman, who helped many communities, including his home town of Greenfield, Massachusetts, resist Wal-Mart. He founded a newsletter, "Sprawlbuster's Alert," has a web site on the Internet, and works with hundreds of communities fighting superstores. In fact, seekers can use the search engine Yahoo to type in "Wal-Mart" and find Sprawlbusters as a next door neighbor to Wal-Mart in cyberspace.

Wal-Mart is, of course, the most ubiquitous symbol of sprawl, and the one with the biggest impact. Wal-Mart is the nation's largest retailer, with 1996 sales of $94 billion (sales were $1.2 billion in 1980) and, as of September 30, 1996, 2700 stores around the country (most of them 200,000 square feet), surrounded by 18 to 20 acres of parking. Within 10 years of Wal-Mart's move into Iowa, for example, almost half of the men's and boys' clothing stores in the state disappeared and a third of all Iowa's hardware stores and grocery stores closed, according to a study by Dr. Kenneth Stone, an Iowa State University economist, who has been studying and reporting impacts of mass merchants, especially Wal-Mart, since the mid-1970s.

CBS' "60 Minutes" focused on the 10-year impact on Donaldsonville, Louisiana, a typical Wal-Mart impact story. Glenn Falgoust, a former retailer who could not survive after Wal-Mart's opening, noted on the program that until Wal-Mart's 1983 opening, Donaldsonville averaged four business failures a year. In 1983 alone, 18 businesses closed. In the following three years, another 50 closed. "As middle-class owners of these stores closed, they left town," Falgoust said. Stores closed. Tax bases eroded. Services declined. The middle class left. And as competition to Wal-Mart ceased, the discount giant's prices went up, "33 per cent higher than at other Wal-Marts," Falgoust says. In many towns, with the diminishing middle class, Boy Scout troop leaders disappeared, church choirs shrank, financial support for local charities evaporated.

"There is no way to deny that some of the superstores do a better job than some local businesses," Kenneth Munsell, director of the Small Towns Institute in Ellensburg, Washington, told writer Richard Stapleton for an article, "The Superstore Syndrome," in *Land and People*.[24] "Penney's and Sears did not destroy the towns they entered in an earlier era. Their scale was not so huge that they precluded the sale by others of virtually all other merchandise." This does not compare to today's superstores. Communities that once welcomed Wal-Mart now publicly express regret and report the unanticipated consequences. And the sprawlbuster speaker network is filling up with representatives from towns that Wal-Mart killed twice, once when it opened and then when it closed and left town, leaving an empty store of its own and a legacy of closed stores around it.[25] Wal-Mart, as Sam Walton prescribed and wrote in his autobiography, often targets a large area for several stores, thoroughly saturating a market. Predictably, much of the existing competition in that market will either close or so change its character that the competition with Wal-Mart is virtually nonexistent. Wal-Mart then can close one or more of its stores, forcing dependent customers to drive farther to shop at the remaining stores. Resistance to Wal-Mart—or "sprawlmarts" as they are popularly known—is often a fight for the survival of free competition in a region and the kind of development that fosters it. (See Chapter 7.) Wal-Mart has become the lightning rod for the sprawl issue.

"Colorful, emotional, and very local and very national at the same time, the struggle has recast sprawl from an abstraction into something specific and visual, inciting citizens and catching the media's eye," wrote Arnold Berke in "Striking Back at Sprawl."[26] "The assault on superstores serves as a beacon to illuminate the broader crusade."

SPRAWL CONTINUATION IS NOT ABOUT LOGIC

It is truly difficult to understand why sprawl development persists at a ferocious pace. Local communities everywhere are fighting it. A few are winning. Individual battles are over specific projects, but the war is against sprawl. Nowhere is there much being written or said to justify sprawl, except by those with a financial stake in sprawl or those professionally invested in road and highway building. Zoning attorney Grady Gammage Jr. wrote an op-ed piece for the *Phoenix* (Arizona) *Gazette,* proclaiming his preference for the sprawl life style and annoyance with those "conducting a near-holy war against sprawl." Of course, the issue is not about forcing people like him to give up their suburban cul-de-sac or three cars. The issue is about giving others an alternative so this self-destructive national madness can be contained. Suburbs are not for everyone.

Equally important is the cost of sprawl, and even a sprawl partisan like Gammage posed all the right questions: "Sprawl does have serious consequences, many of which are negative to the point of threatening the very benefits of a low-density life style. But the challenge to Phoenix isn't to radically transform the 'sprawling' character of our growth patterns. It's to figure out how to deal with the specific negatives of sprawl. How do we pay for infrastructure? How can we make neighborhoods more livable? How can we reasonably provide more transportation alternatives? Can we make our skies spectacularly blue and clear again?" Positive answers to those difficult questions are impossible within a business-as-usual development pattern.

Most of what is written and said, in fact, argues against sprawl's continuation. Mainstream mass audience magazines, like *Time* and *Newsweek*, spotlight its drawbacks. *The Economist,* "60 Minutes" and NPR programs like "Marketplace" and "All Things Considered" have covered aspects of it. Architecture and planning magazines, real estate journals, transportation and conservation organization newsletters, and *Consumer Reports* have given it significant attention.

The costs of sprawl can't be minimized. The financial burden of servicing spread-out suburbs, with wide roads, big parking lots, expensive police and fire protection, and dispersed school districts, is straining local government budgets. Local budgets are, in fact, spiraling out of control. The debt service on local infrastructure bonds, for example, is loaded onto the cost of housing through property taxes, making home ownership more and more prohibitive. Local economies, once the foundation of stable communities, have been undermined, often wiped out. Too many long-standing local businesses have been lost without an equitable net gain. Too many local dollars have been lost to distant headquarters. Too much new taxable development requires an even larger public investment in new infrastructure, while an existing infrastructure deteriorates. One Vermont cost-benefit analysis of a proposed Wal-Mart determined that $3 in public cost would come with each dollar of public benefit. The bill for all this highway-oriented development has come due.

The Natural Resources Development Council reports that "passenger ground transportation consumes nearly $1.6 trillion annually—approximately one-fourth of the country's annual gross domestic product and much more than our total expenditures for health or education."[27] That expense primarily involves cars.

Sprawl continuation makes sense only with recognition that to tame it, stop it, unravel it, and dramatically alter a 50-year, entrenched national development pattern, an entire interrelated network of rules must be fundamentally changed. Inertia is the enemy of change.

"We're still building the past today," observes Robert Liberty, the executive director of 1000 Friends of Oregon, a Portland-based planning advocacy group that has been in the forefront of state-level growth management. "It takes a long time to start building something new," Liberty notes. The kind of places people are asking for is illegal by the laws of their own communities. Unraveling sprawl today means breaking, bending, or amending the existing rules under which building has occurred since World War II. From federal roadbuilding standards to most local zoning codes, the cards are stacked in favor of sprawl. "Understanding the policy roots of sprawl—as well as what isn't causing sprawl—is important," Henry R. Richmond, chairman of the National Growth Management Leadership Project, wrote in *Land and People,*[28] the magazine of the Trust for Public Land. "It means that sprawl and disinvestment are not the inevitable, unavoidable, and 'natural' consequences of market forces. On the contrary, when policy is understood as a major cause of sprawl, land use reform becomes an appropriate subject for corrective legislative action."

NATIONAL MOMENTUM BUILDS ON LOCAL EFFORTS

Sprawlmart resisters are the true advocates of change—appropriate, beneficial, and enduring. They advocate real progress, a move away from the patterns of development and transportation that have created communities and roads hostile to pedestrians and a countryside broken up into parcels "too big to mow and too small to plow." Transportation is the fundamental issue. Since the inception of the massive, heavily-subsidized interstate highway program in the 1950s, we have been destroying our culture from the interstate. Now the mauling by "malling" of America has reached every American's backyard.

More and more people recognize what has been lost. Some try to save what remains and build new to reinforce rather than replace it, Urban Husbandry in its purest form. Compact communities—where work, home, school, government offices, and entertainment are within walking distance or accessible by mass transit—are a rare treasure. Downtowns where the "there" still exists are hard to find, but much sought after by new businesses and residents. Suburbanites, like the woman identified in the beginning of this chapter, lobby for sidewalks and the development of a real town center, where life is not only about commerce and formula entertainment from 9 to 5. Many are even building town centers, or at least planning them. A genuine center takes time to evolve and develop, and must contain pedestrian-scale streets and transit to function differently than a mall.

Schaumburg, Illinois, a Chicago suburb west of O'Hare Airport "full of malls and highways and nowhere to walk," is "trying to find its heart...a sense of place, a sort of civic soul," Dirk Johnson reported in

The New York Times, August 7, 1996, by building a town square. The car will remain the lifeblood of such monolithic, white-collar suburbs, but that should not preclude any step in an unsprawling direction. The project "promised" for 1998, Johnson noted, was just some brick-and-cement posts that say "Town Square," and a 55-foot clock tower.

SOLUTIONS COME IN ALL SHAPES AND SIZES

Even if there were no Disney and no Wal-Mart, there would still be sprawl. And while resisting these kinds of plans prevents acceleration and worsening, it does not eliminate, or even modify, what already exists.

Efforts that undo sprawl come in many different guises. Undoing sprawl is rarely their stated purpose. Commonsense development is. Good planning is. Urban Husbandry is. Of course, the most effective strategy starts with rebuilding centers—the centers of cities and towns of any size where a core residential and commercial population, already-built resources, and an established community exist. Either architecturally significant or just well-constructed buildings exist everywhere an infrastructure exists. Plenty of empty space and parking lots also exist on which the new can be built as needed, again reusing the existing infrastructure. Rebuilding centers is quite possible, as we have seen. But less obvious techniques are either already at work and apparently spreading, or on the horizon.

If a community zones out superstores by limiting the size of new retail stores to under 30,000 square feet, directs new retail and commercial devel-

Denver Dry Goods has become a national model. Photo: Hooman Aryan.

opment to existing centers, and targets permit approvals accordingly, sprawl is contained. When a national retailer locates in existing downtowns, instead of on farmland, two important things happen. Shoppers are inclined to do more shopping on foot downtown, avoiding car trips, and the usual sprawling strip development that follows malls and superstores does not devour more countryside. Again, sprawl is contained.

"In larger towns and cities, the large floor plates of older buildings make perfect shells for superstores, and the floors above work as apartments and offices," says national developer and planner Jonathan F. P. Rose. Rose renovated the vacant 1897 Denver Dry Goods Store in downtown. The elegant red brick former department store was designed by noted architect Frank Edbrooke, designer of several Denver landmarks, including Brown's Hotel. Rose combined retail space for three national chains with commercial and residential uses in the refurbished six-story, 350,000-square-foot grande dame of department stores. Both low-income and market-rate apartments for 800 residents are included. Mixed-use buildings like Rose's provide a "defense during economic swings that affect one part of the economy," Rose observes. "We are always surprised that lending institutions prefer projects with one large tenant rather than many small ones. Time and time again we see large, single-use buildings in bankruptcy because Wal-Mart or IBM moved out and no one moved in. Projects that are flexible enough to serve a wide variety of users have much higher lifetime occupancy rates."

Big retailers returning to downtowns are not automatically a good thing. If they bring the suburban form with them, either in an enclosed mall or free-standing box surrounded by parking, they do not reinforce or strengthen the downtown. In fact, essential urbanism is further eroded. The car-dependent sprawl pattern is simply imposed on an existing downtown.

Suburban-style stores surrounded by parking should be zoned out of downtowns. Most local zoning codes, in fact, have codified all the car design and planning concepts that have evolved over the past half century. Every downtown code should be drastically overhauled to encourage pedestrian-friendly, instead of car-friendly, design.

Accelerating pressure on banks and other institutional lenders under the Community Reinvestment Act is helping to stabilize and strengthen city neighborhoods, a critical ingredient for undoing sprawl and easing pressure for outward migration. The banks are not being asked to make bad loans. Strict standards apply. CRA requires banks to make loans to qualified borrowers of all income levels in the neighborhoods from which deposits originate. If they fail to comply satisfactorily, they can be blocked from mergers or from opening or closing branches. New bank investment is an important beginning to redress some measure of the damage of earlier redlining policies that denied home mortgages and business loans to minority urban neighborhoods and used investment dollars earned in cities to build suburbia and the conditions described in the Bank of America's own report. Without CRA, first won by neighborhood activists in the 1970s,[29] bank executives admit they would never have discovered a profitable new market, underserved low-to-moderate-income homebuyers.

Hugh McColl, CEO of NationsBank in Charlotte, North Carolina, says he first viewed CRA as "interfering with our business." But with CRA pressure applied, NationsBank eventually "made a business out of community investment," quite profitably. "Banks had overlooked the market that was there all along," McColl added.[30]

In Massachusetts, a coalition of community groups helped pass precedent-setting legislation requiring extensive insurance data reporting and providing financial incentives for companies offering policies in underserved neighborhoods. The legislation requires insurance companies to report where they write policies, their losses and profits. Starting in 1997, for the top 25 insurance companies, the commonwealth commissioner of insurance reports the number of policies in each zip code and the number of policies canceled. Like CRA, this can be critical to inner city reinvestment. No insurance, no mortgages, fewer homeowners, more abandoned neighborhoods, further outward migration.

A new tool in the lending box, the Location-Efficient Mortgage (LEM), is on the horizon and eventually could have a dramatic impact on sprawl. Although still in the development and experimental stage, a LEM allows lenders to consider the transportation savings inherent in an urban setting with public transit and pedestrian access. The savings would increase a buyer's ability to afford a home closer to employment. Currently, the cheapest homes are farthest from the center, require the longest commute, and incur the highest automotive expenses. Less driving means more money in the consumer's pocket.[31] The national average cost of car dependency is $6500 annually. A Federal Transit Administration report noted that households located near transit stations save an average of $250 per month in car-related costs.[32] Buyers are limited in purchase opportunities because banks will grant mortgages based only on the borrower's salary. But if the transportation saving is factored in, the affordability rises beyond normal income limitations.

One of the most significant steps in the undoing of sprawl was the 1991 Intermodal Surface Transportation and Efficiency Act (ISTEA), a significant first step in loosening the stranglehold that the entrenched and powerful highway lobby has on the nation's economy. The name alone was a symbolic shift away from the annual National Highway Act to a broader transportation approach. This landmark legislation gave states and local governments unprecedented flexibility to use some highway monies for a wide range of alternative transportation projects, including bike paths and trolleys. The built-in incentive to go the highway route—the federal share for new highways was larger than for public transit—was eliminated. Local communities were brought into transportation planning in new ways and, significantly, funding was provided for projects to make localities and transit stations more hospitable to people than to cars.

The legislation was an extraordinary victory for a ragtag coalition of sprawl-busting transportation alternatives advocates that included the elderly and young who can't drive; preservationists who watched so much of the historic landscape of this country wiped out by highways; transportation workers who know how much more labor-intensive mass transit is than highway construction; downtown business leaders who watch their economies erode as business migrates to the cloverleaf; environmentalists who recognize vehicular traffic as the single worst source of pollution of all kinds; advocacy planners and architects acutely aware of the damage wrought by the traffic-moving-first priority; citizen groups fighting to preserve their communities; rails-to-trails advocates who value the endless miles of abandoned railroad tracks as a national treasure in need of protection; open-space and farmland preservationists who know no greater threat to the countryside exists than automania; and so on. The list could not have been more diverse. They formed a coalition called the Surface Transportation Policy Project (STPP) and, with Senator Daniel Patrick Moynihan as their legislative leader, stunned the highway/automobile lobby with their effectiveness. A coalition of losers, some called them, but they can't be called losers anymore. The time had clearly arrived, STPP executive director Hank Dittmar noted, with the Interstate Highway System completed, "to turn our attention to resolving the threats posed to competitiveness by urban and suburban congestion."

While it was clearly an important achievement, the national mindset and road-focused bureaucracy would not be dislodged easily. As Jane Holtz Kay wrote in *The Nation*, "Despite the knowledge that the old ways won't work, and the fact that the Clean Air Act is compelling us to change them, road barons and traffic engineers still move us in macadamesque ways, taking the time-dishonored route that has destroyed the landscape, gutted urban America, spread blight by mall and multilane mayhem, and polluted the planet."[33] While the highways-only, auto-firsters continue in full force to turn back some of the gains achieved under the first few years of ISTEA, the genie is out of the bottle and cannot be fully contained again. ISTEA could be one of the best sprawl antidotes.

Sprawl is clearly a national issue that has not yet specifically materialized into a national issue. Sprawl is the national issue most politicians seem afraid to confront directly by name. It has, however, been penetrating state houses for decades. The well-known leaders have been Oregon, which passed growth management legislation in the 1970s, and Vermont, which passed similar legislation, Act 250, also in the 1970s. Both states have been seeing salutary economic and environmental impacts for years. In 1995, the Oregon state legislature approved tax advantages for mixed-use, high-density development and tax abatement incentives for developers to construct compact, multifamily units. Oregon's urban growth boundaries don't stop development, but direct it to where it strengthens centers while protecting farms, forests, and rural country-side. Other states have toyed with the idea. Some have even passed more limited versions. More recently, governors of Maryland, Colorado, and other states acknowledged the devastating impact of sprawl. "Sprawl development is costing Maryland dearly," former Maryland Governor William Schaefer noted simply.[34] In fact, in 1977, under the leadership of Governor Parris Glendening, Maryland instituted a breakthrough "Smart Growth" policy that limits state funding for new public projects to locali-ties inside the beltway and with existing water and sewer systems. This does not interfere with any local ordinances; it just wipes out the assump-tion that, if approved locally, the state will financially support develop-ment with infrastructure additions. Time has not yet tested this innova-tive strategy but, again, it is a significant step.

Lewis Mumford predicted in 1958 that Americans would discover that the "highway program will, eventually, wipe out the very area of freedom that the private motorcar promised to retain for them." This warning has come to pass. Today, the car embodies the freedom to wait in traffic. Transportation choices hardly exist. Viable transit systems exist in only a few big cities, service is usually infrequent, inconvenient, and expensive, and is being drastically undermined by fare increases and service cutbacks. Gasoline is one of the few things that are cheaper today in real dollars than 20 years ago. Mass transit travel is many times more expensive. Development patterns make transit travel difficult, even for those who prefer it, and unavailable to most.

If the goal is to protect the vast public investment already made in water, transportation, and energy infrastructure, if the goal is to contain wasteful taxpayer programs, if the goal is to make affordable housing and workplaces accessible to people who need them, if the goal is to reduce air and water pollution, if the goal is to preserve existing and sta-ble communities, if the goal is to seriously tackle traffic congestion, if the goal is to preserve historic and cultural resources, then the place to start is with the car and the development patterns it stimulates. Sprawl fighters have long understood this. Disney and Wal-Mart helped more people catch on.

1. Philip Langdon, *A Better Place to Live*, U. of Mass Press, 1994.
2. "For Suburban Youths, Recreation Is No Longer Just Child's Play," *The Washington Post*, May 31, 1993.
3. "Neighborhoods Reborn," May 1996, p. 24.
4. A full treatment of how all this evolved is contained in the chapter titled "Urban Dispersal," in *The Living City*.
5. Stephen B. Goddard, *Getting There: The Epic Struggle Between Road and Rail in the American Century* (New York: Basic Books, 1994).
6. Edited by the Editors of Fortune, 1958.
7. New York: Harcourt Brace Jovanovich, Inc., 1953.
8. Goddard, op. cit., documents this well, as does the PBS series, "Point Of View," documentary, "Taken For A Ride," by Jim Klein and Martha Olson; produced by The American Documentary Inc.
9. "The Myth of the American Car Cult," *The Washington Post*, March 31, 1991.
10. Surface Transportation Policy Project, Washington, D.C., March 1996.
11. December 27, 1997.
12. "NJ DOT Favors New Highways," *Mobilizing the Region*, weekly bulletin of the Tri-State Transportation Campaign, October 11, 1996.
13. Cited by Kevin Kasowski, "The Costs of Sprawl, Revisited," September 1992 newsletter, *Developments*, of The National Growth Management Leadership Project Newsletter. This is one of the best overall reports on the costs of sprawl.
14. "Saving the Family Farm Means Giving Up Something, Too," October 10, 1996.
15. "Alternatives for Future Urban Growth in California's Central Valley: The Bottom Line for Agriculture and Taxpayers," American Farmland Trust, Washington, D.C., October 1995.
16. November 26, 1995.
17. December 17, 1995.
18. December 29, 1996.
19. This meeting was organized by Trust staffer Constance Beaumont. It grew under the sharp leadership of Al Norman and is run out of the Conservation Law Foundation in Boston.
20. Subcommittee on Public Lands, National Parks and Forests Committee on Energy and Natural Resources, June 21, 1994.
21. Sept. 30, 1994.
22. Beaumont's 1995 guidebook, *How Superstore Sprawl Can Harm Communities, And What Citizens Can Do About It,* published by the National Trust, has become a popular tool for local communities confronting superstore issues.

23. *Wall Street Journal*, September 16; Peter Jennings, *ABC World News Tonight,* Oct. 1993.

24. Fall 1995. *Land and People* is a publication of the Trust for Public Land.

25. Many communities complain that Wal-Mart won't sell a closed store to a competitor, forcing shoppers to travel a longer distance to the nearest Wal-Mart instead.

26. *Historic Preservation Magazine*, September 1995.

27. "Stop the Transportation Insanity," *The Amicus Journal*, Spring 1995, p. 5.

28. Spring, 1997.

29. Gail Cincotta first led protests against redlining in her Chicago neighborhood, then formed the National People's Action, a national coalition of redlined neighborhoods. Under her leadership, an anti-redlining campaign and lobbying efforts led to the Community Reinvestment Act of 1977, forcing many banks to revamp their neighborhood disinvestment policies.

30. Interview with Hugh McColl by Mary Newsome and Dan Chapman, *Charlotte Observer,* May 12, 1996.

31. The National Resources Defense Council's *Amicus Journal*, Winter 1995, issue, reported: "An NRDC study of California neighborhoods showed that, if neighborhood A is twice as densely populated as neighborhood B, its residents will drive 20 to 25 percent less."

32. *Mobilizing the Region*, newsletter, Tri-State Transportation Campaign, June 8, 1996, p. 3.

33. August 3/10, 1992.

34. Quoted in *Livable Places Update*, "Emerging Trends in Community Planning and Design," November/December 1995, published by the Local Government Commission of California, Sacramento.

BIG, LITTLE, AND PREDATOR

**A superstore fitting in, respecting the place,
pedestrian friendly and not car dependant.**

CHAPTER SEVEN

FREE COMPETITION OR
NO COMPETITION?

America does not believe in fair competition. We talk about
competition as the cornerstone of American culture but we
strive for monopolies in order to raise prices. The goal of
American business is to create a monopoly and then sell it or
take it over. We want to be unfettered at creating monopolies.
This is a paradox.

   Larry Lund, Chicago retail consultant

There are still those who cling to the notion that the issue of malls versus downtown, corporate giants versus small independents, national
chains versus local economies, big monopolies versus small entrepreneurs is all about the good old American tradition of fair competition.
That notion is quaint and simplistic. It is also dead wrong. To dismiss
widespread discomfort with superstore[1] proliferation or to argue that
"fair competition" is what it is all about avoids confronting the complicated issues and profound national implications of the superstore
dilemma. Dramatic shifts in the national economy, in retailing, and in
real estate shape the superstore debate. Glaring examples of "killer competition" make a mockery of "fair competition" and diminish or eradi-
cate consumer choice options. The old notion of fair competition is out
of date.

   "Superstore growth is more about Wall Street than retailing," notes
retail consultant Benjamin Fox. "Many of the specialty stores that have
sprung up in recent years—boutiques, discount, big box chains—are
products of IPOs [Initial Public Offerings]. Going public raises money to
finance expansion. Now, these are big corporations listed on the stock
exchange. Stockholders need to see growth and sales volume. The sales
of particular stores are not increasing in many cases. But growth is
defined as the opening of more stores."

   The continuous opening of new stores thus takes on enormous
importance. Even the rebuilding and expanding of older ones counts.
Each of these moves has local impacts. Retail analysts observe another

nationally damaging piece to this spiral. Easy expansion with Wall Street money meant overexpansion for many chains. Stores proliferated. Inventory swelled. Debt accumulated. No problem. Chapter 11 provided a handy way out. "Reorganizing," it is euphemistically called. Weed out the underperforming stores. Close the stores many localities resisted in the first place. Cut the jobs for which communities traded local values. Keep the better stores. Make customers travel farther, by car, to reach you. Bankruptcy laws made lease obligations meaningless. Each store is its own corporation, so when one store files for bankruptcy, the national corporation walks away with no responsibility.

The nature of real estate development and finance, notes national developer Jonathan F. P. Rose, also has transformed the venue of retailing. By the 1980s, community lenders who knew the builder, the retailer, and the market had been supplanted by volume-driven lenders who understood none of that. Volume-driven lenders, says Rose, "followed the Wall Street model and made loans based on the credit of project tenants rather than the record of the developer." Physical and financial formulas have replaced lenders' flexibility. Lenders resist, for example, the mixed-use loans that would finance the apartment-over-the-store developments that downtowns were built on and for which a new market now exists. Rose's own project mentioned earlier, the Denver Dry Goods, was totally stymied by this roadblock. Only his creativity at putting a variety of financing mechanisms together in a new way, together with the cooperation of the city of Denver and his experience as a developer, could overcome this. The Denver Dry Goods has since become a national model, but has not changed lender policies.

Changes in retailing are equally dramatic. Money manager James J. Cramer, writing in *New York Magazine*,[2] observed that the era when "women dressed differently from each other" by age, profession, geography, or financial status has gone the way of "the great tasteful democratization of the women's look" inaugurated by the Gap. There is no "raison d'etre," he argues, for the large number of "now-generic women's-apparel stores that line the innards of a mall." Noting that Sunglass Hut stock was a big retail winner in 1995, he wrote: "These days, sunglasses are about the only way women of the great middle class can tell themselves apart." With widespread merging, retail observers and finance professionals agree with Cramer, who added: "...big chain retailers now face only one another as competitors. The result is a carnage uglier than anyone could have anticipated." The "coming consolidation nightmare" Cramer anticipates will parallel the merger and consolidation of traditional department stores a decade ago that left multi-anchor regional malls with shuttered anchors. In some of them, the concrete was barely dry.

MYTHS COLOR DEBATE

Within this rapidly changing picture of overcapacity, high Chapter 11 usage, and ever-changing tastes, localities of all kinds are asked to make excruciating, community-altering decisions. Even worse, because of destructive existing zoning codes, decisions are made without communities being asked or despite community preferences. And as the levels of complexity are examined, the notion of "fair competition" recedes in relevance to the point of myth. The superstore debate, wherever it is currently raging, appears laden with myths, "fair competition" being only one.

The myths of convenience and of consumer advantage are popular. Malls and superstores, according to the argument, are convenient because people can drive to them, park, and drive home. Downtown, in contrast, has no place to park, prices are high, and choices limited. In reality, this is backwards. Distance, private cost of travel, public impact costs, and a whole host of other expenses (many of which were outlined earlier) are conveniently left out of the calculations.

As also noted, mall shoppers are willing to walk a considerable distance from a parking lot to their destination. Downtown, they demand parking in front of the store. Car ownership is mandatory for mall shopping. Where is this cost included? The poor, the elderly, the young—in other words, the car-less consumers—must rely on expensive taxis. Where is that cost included? Comparison shopping is either expensive, distance- and time-consuming, or impossible. Where is that cost included? Add all these uncalculated costs, and product price savings shrink. The costs are, in fact, hidden in infrastructure maintenance and other sprawl costs, and the public does not *feel* them directly. The public, in effect, carries the cost for temporarily cheap goods. The temporary nature of this is often overlooked. Does anyone really believe prices don't rise in a monopoly? Does anyone really believe the stores for which these dramatic accommodations are being made will last longer than an historic blip? Has the proliferation of Chapter 11 protection escaped notice?

"Yet as the retailing cycles flash by, communities must ask: Do we need these guys?" Neal Peirce wrote.[3] "The concern is that big boxes, like dinosaurs," Peirce continued, "may rule the earth for a time, but then, like all fads, be gone. And that their rotting hulks will be left for the rest of us (i.e., the taxpayers) to clean up and remove."

The myth of job creation is similarly popular and misleading.

"Category Killer X will create much-needed jobs" is seductive. *These are not new jobs, but shifting jobs.* New stores open, old ones close, but only the new jobs are counted. Does anyone really believe, in fact, that all those "new" jobs will even last? The net gain, if at all, is minimal.

WAR GAMES

For good reason, some big discount superstores are called category killers. They don't mean to *compete* with existing businesses. They mean to kill them off and *monopolize* the market. They are succeeding. These retailers don't mean to fit into the community they are entering. They mean to stand apart from it. They have a formula to impose. Period. Community values, community landscape, community economy, community scale be damned.

Burying the competition is the superstore's priority. New store location strategy is carefully planned to undermine existing businesses, eventually putting them out of business, to control the market territory. With domination come product mix changes, price increases, and staff cutbacks. Economist Thomas Mueller points out that this killer strategy is observable. Category killers and other superstores know pretty well, Mueller says, what level of sales per square foot they can anticipate. If one then looks at the sales figures for the market area of the existing business near which they are locating, one can see they aim to be the only one serving that market. The market normally may be large enough for more than one specialty store, but not at the scale the category killers build. This approach parallels that of the mall developers of the last generation, many of whom are still going strong.

I first observed this pattern at close hand in 1990 with the Pyramid Mall Company, then the largest mall developer in the Northeast, when I wrote an article for *The New York Times Sunday Magazine*, "Malling the Northeast." The Syracuse-based company's daily 6:30 a.m. meetings were legendary in the northeast region. In a boardroom equipped with the best of telecommunications, the whole Pyramid partner network was electronically connected at the same time each day. Overcoming fierce local resistance was the daily challenge, not unlike that of today's superstore. After sitting in on one of these meetings, I wrote: "So, like generals conferring on how to motivate troops and manipulate treacherous field conditions, Pyramid executives work out the daily strategies before the local opposition has had a chance to open its war-weary eyes. To these executives, field conditions at the different sites appear the same, all variations on an unholy alliance of local merchants, mall competitors, overanxious environmentalists, and citizens afraid of change, resisting what *Forbes* magazine called the Pyramid 'mall-building' juggernaut."

Is this scene repeating itself in superstore boardrooms today? By 1990, larger and larger malls were altering the American countryside and restructuring the national retail economy as significantly as mergers and acquisitions were altering the national corporate landscape.

Some companies use the language of war for their internal planning. Careful advance work identifies the successful businesses to be "knocked off." Store locations are selected with this goal in mind.

"Attack" teams are put together for the first few months of operation of a new store. If a new store is meant to operate with 100 employees, the "attack" team will contain 150 and will include friendly, helpful salespeople for the first several months. The first-time shopper at the store has a positive experience and saves money...at first. Customers are won early. Local stores close. Some try to reposition themselves to fit a new market. "Adjust," they are admonished. They try, without access to Wall Street funding or helpful politicians. Some succeed. They change their product mix, emphasize service and specialty goods. Many fail. Some hang on only to see the business they've built up over the years drastically diminish. Maybe they remain in business, but barely.

Then, as the category killer's smaller competition disappears, so do many of those helpful employees, the ones whose jobs were counted in the number boasted about in the press releases when the store opened. Some of these employees, in fact, were hired away from their old, long-standing jobs, accounting for their product knowledge. Call it layoffs, downsizing, settling down, anything. Whatever one calls it, the result is the same: diminished service and increased prices. As for the employees lured from existing businesses and then "downsized"...well, they bet on the wrong horse. In the meantime, alternative shopping options have disappeared. The competition has been killed. The consumer is captive.

Jack Hitt wrote in *The New York Times Magazine*:

> When predatory capitalists talk shop among themselves, they call superstores "category killers," for their destructive efficiency. Nowadays such talk is candied with P.R. sugar about how "we can all compete together." But not long ago a superstore tactician told a newspaper reporter that when hunting for a good corridor of wastage in which to roost, he searches in a strip that is "overstored" or "over-malled" because "the more stores we have in the area, the better. We call it cannibalizing." No reporter will ever get that quotation again.[4]

Category killers are masters at "variable pricing" and will undersell a one-time, single-purchase item. Such items were once called "loss leaders." A customer is impressed by the price saving and deluded into thinking all savings are comparable. On the bigger, multiple-purchase items, the price is often higher, but since comparison shopping has gotten more and more difficult, many shoppers are unaware that they are paying more. A clever approach works with items that require a series of accessory items to make it work. Copper piping, for example, may be priced well below typical market price, but the fittings that go with it are only a few percentage points different or more expensive and may not be of the same

quality. The price saving may disappear. With products like shoes, manufacturers often make a cheaper version of a style for the superstores and
a better-made, standard-price version for the independent shoe store.

The car-bound consumer already functions in a world where comparison shopping is difficult. On traditional urban shopping streets (in
some cities, these don't exist downtown anymore), and in many small
towns as well, comparison shopping is a genuine and convenient option.
Competing stores are often within a short walking distance from one
another. A friend of mine, actor Jordan Charney, was a habitual comparison shopper, roaming among the wide assortment of choices in our
upper Manhattan neighborhood. When he moved to Los Angeles, this
habit was constrained by the car. The distance between options and traffic discouraged this ritual. "There is a joy to shopping and comparing
prices," Charney explains. "But I would spend as much in gas as I was
saving on purchases. And it took so much more time. It defeated the purpose. There was still the satisfaction that I was not being taken, or taken
as much, but it was not as much fun. You're much more in control walking
in the city." In some places, choices don't exist, except at long distances.
*In the car-dependent economy—rural, suburban, or urban car-dependent—
the retailer is in control, not the consumer.*

COMPETITION AIN'T WHAT IT USED TO BE

When a category killer locates near an existing specialty store serving
the same market, how do you know which will be the surviving entity?
economist Thomas Mueller asks. That is where a combination of superstore advantages comes in that includes flexible pricing, capitalization
potential, technology capability, product domination, and the superstores' ability to buy cheaper from manufacturers or to produce private-
label goods. The pricing policy of some category killers and big box
retailers varies from store to store, especially the many chains among
them that don't depend on local advertising. This permits individual
stores to drastically cut the price on some goods, just to undersell competitors. Targeted competitors can be established downtown stores or
other malls and superstores. This requires the up-front cash that high
capitalization brings. To finance underselling and to take this risk, a
company must be big enough to have the ability to go public and raise
money through stock offerings and better credit. A superstore with that
capacity can then undersell and wait out the demise of the competition.

Technologically, category killers can restock their shelves overnight.
"Computers allow them to keep very little inventory in stock," explains
Mueller. "Each sale is conveyed to the warehouse by computer. A supply truck can deliver that night to have the shelves restocked by morning. This permits efficiency of scale that makes it easier to monopolize
a market."

Scandalously large trucks and the chains' distribution system make this efficiency possible. Those trucks have an enormous and costly impact on the national infrastructure, especially interstate highways and local streets. Infrastructure costs of local budgets are primarily road maintenance paid for by local taxpayers. Truck and gas taxes don't begin to cover that enormous public cost.

Superstores gain a great price advantage from manufacturers, but it is not obvious like standard price-fixing methods. The bigger percentage of shelf space given to that manufacturer, the bigger the discount. The bigger the store, the more space given each manufacturer. Isn't that another form of superstore price advantage? Call it "size-fixing"? Is this a justification for big boxes to gobble up more of the landscape? More containers of soap or more shelves of radios in exchange for trees, open land, or existing downtown buildings?

The most common pricing edge given superstores is the minimum order. A 100-pair order is necessary to open an account with some shoe manufacturers. An independent shoe store in any downtown that wants to try a new line may only want to start with 12 pairs or 24 pairs, but is thus closed out of this market. Is this what can be defined as a level playing field to compete on? What irritates many independents is that they are the ones who fueled the growth of these manufacturers, from the small unknown to the national name.

This country has never experienced an era of competitive retailing like this. Sears and Penney's did not destroy either the local economies or the competition in the towns they entered. Local businesses existed side by side with national chains. A town that had Penney, Sears, Woolworth, Kress, Kresge, Walgreen's, or any of the chains of the time also had local stores competing with the nationals. Many downtowns had several department stores *and* a Sears and Penney's. Coexistence, not annihilation, defined competition.

Mueller adds a different dimension to this view. "Sears and Penney's did not think in the same terms that category killers think today," Mueller says. "The psychology has changed. The capacity to operate at current scales was not possible. The technology to do so was not there, nor was the ability to raise the necessary capital. The pressures were not there to dominate a market. This is not the normal idea of competition. Monopoly means to dominate a market. A store does not have to be the only one to sell something in order to dominate. Competition is fine, unless it leads to monopoly. That is why some constraints are necessary." The implications and layers of problems these issues raise are endless.

If a locality resists a superstore and refuses to approve whatever special permits are necessary, familiar bully tactics become evident. Dirty tricks, they call it in political campaigns requiring large sums of

money. Phony citizen groups are formed to advocate approval, well funded by the superstore home office. Supportive political candidates are
generously backed in the next election, with the goal of reversing the
decision. Just the threat of a lawsuit by a superstore is often enough to
gain acquiescence from a local regulatory body. Local officials fear the
personal exposure and the public expense of a lawsuit, even if they have
the best chance of prevailing. Exercising available and legitimate local
constraints is not as easy as it seems, even though it is a crucial necessity. If local political leaders back the change, new pressures arise. Civic
groups are often warned that they risk loss of government funding if they
oppose the policy.

Threats and intimidation are not always necessary. Local politicians don't want to appear to be against growth. Politics demands support for job creation, construction, prestige, and growth at any price,
even if the promises are deceptive or fraudulent. Subtle and not-so-sub-
tle implications are easy to ignore in the face of simplistic appearances.
Local politicians and citizens alike easily get caught up in the appeal of
the latest trend, the power of a name, and the excitement of the moment.
Reality remains buried.

A common attitude among local merchants when they hear of plans
for a superstore coming into their territory is problematic. "I just won't
carry what they do and I won't try to compete," is the comment Mueller
frequently hears. Or, "I'm known in the community, I provide service
they can't." Naïve is what Mueller calls such thinking. A rude awakening
awaits such merchants. If a category killer, or even a general retail superstore, wants to put a particular store out of business, it has the capacity
to do so, with merchants very poorly armed to survive the invasion.

GOVERNMENT FUELS THE FIRE

What makes this state of affairs truly insidious is that it is aided and
abetted by government. This is true at all levels of government.
"Infrastructure investment" is the favorite term for publicly supported
highway, road, crossroad, local street, traffic management, parking
garage or lot construction, sewer, fire department, or water service
"improvements" or "upgrades," all supporting the superstore trend.
*Rarely is there a regional mall or superstore development of any scale,
whether it is commercial, industrial, or residential, that does not require a
local zoning change or special permit. Without permits and infrastructure
investments, none of these superstores could happen.* These are the constraints to which Mueller referred. Superstores *follow* well-planned highway and road improvements. A soothsayer is not necessary to predict
what will happen on the open fields adjacent to any highway inter-
change. This action is fully anticipated, hoped for, and expedited by the
government agencies promoting the "infrastructure improvement."

Public investment, therefore, fuels superstore advantages. The cheap land is cheap only to the developer and the retailer, not to the local tax-paying consumer.

In many localities, tax incentives, utility cost write-downs, reduced-interest bonds, or other direct financial sweeteners are added as well. Any one of these financial additives makes the idea of fair competition a joke. Isn't this a form of corporate welfare? The level playing field is a thing of the past. Superstores, national chains, all descendants of regional malls created by the Interstate Highway System, have the weapons and financial support of government on their side. Private enterprise pitted against private enterprise with government taking sides.

FROM CORNFIELDS TO INNER CITY, THE BATTLEFIELD BROADENS

Nowhere is this better illustrated than in our own home town of New York City, where Project Planners have long been adopting policies that both erode the very urbanism that makes New York distinctive and give developers advantages with which to accomplish this erosion. While suburbs and already suburbanized cities like Los Angeles seek to undo the imbalance created by auto-dependency, New York appears to be accelerating the post-World War II planning path of over-accommodation of the car. (The same can be said of most other major cities, like Detroit, Indianapolis, Atlanta, Cleveland, and Charlotte, where, like New York, one of the easiest developments to finance these days is a parking facility.)

New York Project Planners, like their counterparts across the country, and their supporters accuse opponents of being stuck in the 1950s, nostalgic for a city that can't still be, against progress, or just selfishly protecting their own backyard. They fail to see the outdatedness of their own viewpoint. They fail to recognize the damage wrought by their policies. And they fail to see that if New Yorkers—and urbanism defenders in other cities—did not protect their own backyard and the city's urban attributes, the suburbanization of all our cities would be further advanced. Many planners who shape urban policy today are products of the suburbs. Their disdain for genuine urbanism is clear.

Notes Vincent Scully, former dean of architecture at Yale and one of the wisest critics of American development patterns, "For close to a century now, the auto has gnawed at the city. It has destroyed everything that has to do with the definition of place. There are places where the auto makes sense, where it doesn't, and where it doesn't is in the city. What we must do from now on is to design against the auto." Ironically, the names of long-time urban sages like Vincent Scully, Jane Jacobs, William H. Whyte, and, on transportation issues, Lewis Mumford are continuously invoked by Project Planners. The consistent and collective wisdom of these critics, however, is either misinterpreted or ignored by them. Citizens fighting Project Planners apply the wisdom well.

New York's wrestling with the superstore issue reflects the national dilemma of how to accommodate mega-scale retailers in small and large downtowns. But while the New York controversy mirrors the nationwide conflict, New York has an added ironic dimension. New York is one of the few U.S. cities left with a large number of dense neighborhoods where residents are not car-dependent and can walk, take public transit, or drive to a wide selection of shopping opportunities. Department store shopping bags are a daily sight on every subway and bus line. At the same time, New York is one of the last corners of the national landscape unsaturated with malls and superstores. Not yet, at least.

The administration of Mayor Rudolph Giuliani proposed allowing developers to build superstores of up to 200,000 square feet (five football fields) anywhere in the city presently zoned for manufacturing, without any permit or public review necessary. This proposal, while defeated by the City Council, contained several extraordinary elements, devastating to any city desirous of staying urban or of recapturing urbanism after years of erosion. A City Council version provided for 125,000 square feet and some community input. The average Wal-Mart in a cornfield is 180,000 square feet. Imagine the traffic that comes with either size in a manufacturing district dependent on truck deliveries or near a dense urban residential neighborhood.

At any size, placed in an industrial district, these stores jeopardize the manufacturing that brings the kind of jobs most necessary in an urban economy. No one calculated the inevitable loss of some of the current 800,000 industrial jobs in manufacturing neighborhoods where the jacked-up land values and enormous new traffic congestion would surely push out industry. City officials who manipulated a lot of data to rationalize this policy did so most outrageously, with the argument that New York has an excess of empty manufacturing space. A City Planning Department study of the condition of local industry referred to 22,000 acres of underutilized manufacturing land.[5] This number was heavily reported and cited in editorials supporting the proposal. Left unsaid, however, was that 70 percent of that land is in Staten Island, the most remote borough of the city, and that the number *included* JFK and LaGuardia airports, railroad rights of way, a landfill, wetlands, and underwater land, along with once-thriving manufacturing neighborhoods, such as SoHo, Greenpoint (Brooklyn), and Clinton (on Manhattan's West Side), that are now heavily residential. The Planning Department staff never would reveal how many of the 22,000 acres were in these categories.

The erroneous assumption was promoted that zoning, and its time-consuming process, is a barrier to superstore development. However, more than a dozen new superstores opened while officials argued that the process hampered openings. Some took advantage of zoning loopholes. Others opened in areas appropriately zoned for commercial uses and, for the most part, well served by mass transit, not in conflict with industry.

The assumption that people will not shop in the suburbs as much, if any city gains more superstores, is flawed. The stores that come might not be the ones consumers want. More likely, people who never drive to the suburbs to shop will now drive in the city to shop, adding to the already unmanageable level of congestion. In fact, the staggering vehicular consequences in an already traffic-congested city of this proposal were ignored.

The mayor and planners cited seemingly compelling evidence that the city was losing $3 billion in retail sales to the suburbs to which New Yorkers were allegedly driving to shop. This reported "fact" was repeated in print so many times that the public totally accepted it. Ignored was a critical fact: The study presenting this "fact" was commissioned by New York's largest superstore developer. The study's data, gleaned from interviews with 1000 city residents, was then used by the city for its own report and zoning proposal, "A Comprehensive Retail Strategy for New York City." That the lower sales tax outside of New York City (New Jersey tax is 6 percent, New York City, 8.25 percent) might be the great consumer draw was either ignored or played down.

The tax influence was made clear later, however, in a January 1997 experiment when New York City lifted the sales tax on clothes and shoes for one week. The result was a shopping frenzy exceeding all expectations. Ironically, columnist Evelyn Nieves of *The New York Times* went to the Newport Center Mall, an "Everymall...neither small nor enormous" in Jersey City that week to see if business had diminished there. The city residents she interviewed were all there because they were already in Jersey City for other reasons. The only one who was there exclusively on a shopping expedition was an elderly resident of Greenwich Village who came because of the easy mass transit access, "a safe and pleasant" 15 minute PATH (New York to New Jersey subway) ride, she told Nieves.

SUPERSTORES AND DOWNTOWN CAN BE COMPATIBLE

As in many communities across the country, the superstore proposal generated the most debate of any issue in years. Overshadowed was an essential truth: *New York and any downtown can have big box retailers, national chains, and all other large-scale consumer offerings that officials are over-convinced urbanites want. But a city does not have to accept the suburban store building form so disruptive to urban shopping districts.*

Big, efficient, appealing, and competitive supermarkets and big box retailers can be designed to benefit rather than destroy neighborhoods. A one-level megastore, surrounded by asphalt to provide long-distance shoppers with parking, is a blueprint for disaster. A one- or two-story-plus-base-

ment or second-floor store, on the other hand, a sort of neighborhood Macy's or supermarket with limited parking either behind or nearby, adds healthy competition and reinforces neighborhood shopping streets. Add to this provisions for supermarket home delivery (reducing the need for cars) and you have a healthy prescription for neighborhood growth and retail strength. A municipal subsidy for home delivery, a genuine job creator, would cost less than the inevitable indirect subsidies required for undermined shopping districts. Improved bus access or even licensed van services (another job creator, see Chapter 5) should be considered as well.

The issue should be how to bring affordable shopping to any traditional downtown. "A sound economic development strategy would induce retailers to go where the people are, not force people to go great distances to where retailers are," wrote Tom Angotti, an urban planning professor, and Ron Shiffman, then a member of the City Planning Commission, in a *New York Times* op-ed article. "New York has the nation's largest mass transit system, and, to boot, more people travel by foot in this city than any other American city. This means that the city government should encourage big retailers to situate near mass transit while eliminating parking."

Here again, Project Planners are not setting out to *solve* a problem, but to impose a project approach that *does not solve the problem* and is inappropriate to the existing place. An alien plant undermining the ecology of the urban garden. Project Planners manipulate macro statistics and care little of the micro impacts.

For example, New York officials, believe it or not, argue that New York is *understored*. If you take a national standard of measurement geared to the development of suburban malls, i.e., so much population should have so many square feet of retail, then you can say New York, or any city, is understored. *National standards distort local differences.* New York City stores, for example, sell more merchandise per square foot than suburban stores. This stands to reason. Like the city itself, urban stores are more compact and efficient than their suburban cousins. New York has great downtown shopping districts and long, robust, and accessible shopping streets. The very compactness of the city's retail centers and neighborhood districts penalizes the whole city when measured on a national suburban standard.

Championing this style of shopping reinforces the false and insidious notion that city shopping requires a car. The elderly, the poor, and the young, after all, are too often car-less. What shopping they now have within walking distance will be jeopardized. The fundamental challenge is to create an urban form of retailing for the 1990s and beyond that doesn't duplicate the problem-filled suburban model of the 1970s and 1980s—the dinosaur mall that is already lumbering toward extinction. In addition, to argue that superstore congestion will not impinge on functioning manufacturing districts reveals an ignorance of how industry functions.

UNDERVALUING INDUSTRY

Project Planners across the country devalue the critical economic role of industry. Worse, they don't recognize signs of rebirth or know how to nurture it. This unfortunate circumstance puzzles many industry analysts. In recent years, real estate development has become the overriding goal. Stimulating "development," i.e., building projects, is what planning is primarily about these days. Again, big plans, big projects. Only big manufacturing plants, for cars or other high multiple production, fall into this category and catch official attention. Yet, a multiplicity of small factories is where the heart of manufacturing lies.

"That is what New York always had," notes writer Pete Hamill, for a long time one of the most articulate voices to spotlight the economic and social value of industry and, until recently, editor-in-chief of the *Daily News*. "We never had the big stuff. It was our great assortment of small factories that brought us through the Depression." Most of the so-called gains of the heady development days of the 1980s, for which New York and so many downtowns gave such incentives, were wiped out when the real estate market fell apart at the end of the 1980s and early 1990s. But interesting and incremental gains have been building in the small manufacturing sector that defy old definitions and escape appropriate notice. (See Chapter 13.)

One interesting explanation, Hamill suggests, is the absence of media interest in labor. "Newspapers don't cover labor as a total thing anymore," Hamill says. "Sure, they're there for a union corruption story or a strike but that is it. The last great labor reporter was Abe Raskin (NYT)." At one time, Hamill adds, New York alone had Murray Kempton and Richard Montague (*New York Post*) and Victor Riesel (*New York Mirror*), plus Raskin. Hamill adds: "The country has had a celebrity focus since the 1970s. You never see a factory worker on the cover of a magazine. But if there is a movie about one, the star (Sally Field, 'Norma Rae,' or Danny DeVito, 'Tin Man') will get the spotlight."

Meadville, Pennsylvania, once a manufacturing mecca, rebuilt its local economy on such businesses and today is known as "The Tool and Die Capital of the World." The invention of the zipper occurred in Meadville, giving rise to a flourishing industry. In their heydays, Talon and Avtex (acetate yarn) employed more than 7000 people. Both giants left town, but in the early 1980s, the city of Meadville, in partnership with Crawford County, set about rebuilding that local economy by cultivating and transforming the skilled toolmakers and local craftsmen of the former industry into new entrepreneurs. Their knowledge of precision steel parts, heat treatment, metallurgy, chemistry, cutter sharpening, engineering, design, and quality control contributed to the formation of *150 spin-off companies*. Meadville now has the most tool and die firms per capita in the United States and provides the world's original equipment manufacturers (OEMs) with finely tooled and machined essential parts. Many components went into this economic rebirth. Brownfield cleanup. Refurbishing and developing abandoned industrial space into industrial parks. A business incubator providing low-cost start-up space, shared services, business development assistance. Maintaining a one-mile rail line with links to long-distance systems. Road improvements. A whole range of additional things are included in this success story, including day care for industrial park employees and a nature trail encircling the park.

Sidney Grossman built the largest lumber and home-supply retailing operation in the New England region primarily by providing do-it-yourself home building kits. He sold the business in 1969. When he died in December 1996, the *New York Times* obituary reported that Grossman's "grandest scheme" was the "recycling of entire towns abandoned by textile mills and other employers." Grossman rescued such towns by luring smaller industries to fill the vacated factories, sometimes helping arrange financing. One such town, the article by Robert McG. Thomas Jr. pointed out, was Sanford, Maine. In 1954, Burlington Industries bought and closed the Goodall Sanford Mills, moved the operation south, and threw 3500 of the town's 15,000 residents out of work. Sanford became known as "the town that refused to die." With a population today of 23,000, the town thrives with a diversified assortment of small industries, none employing more than a few hundred people.

New York City has witnessed a growth in new and small industry, either unacknowledged or undervalued by conventional experts and Project Planners who view manufacturing neighborhoods as sites for new nonmanufacturing development projects. This gained public attention, predictably, through a non-expert, citizen activist organization. Linda Cox, director of the Planning Center of the Municipal Arts Society (MAS), has been developing forward-thinking public forums and programming for several years and, starting in 1993, brought the issues of manufacturing in the city to a very interested public. MAS is New York's leading citizen group involved in urban design, historic preservation, and planning issues.

Cox, not surprisingly, started with a question. "The City Planning Commission was proposing a big new waterfront plan making it easier for superstores to locate in manufacturing districts," Cox explains. "With changes proposed for industrial areas, we asked ourselves, 'What is actually going on in these neighborhoods?' We had no idea of the answer. The assumption was that the residue of manufacturing would soon be gone, that it will go away naturally and that this was the tail end of a trend."

Through on-site inquiries, panel discussions featuring manufacturers, and good, old-fashioned probing, Cox discovered that, contrary to Planning Department representations, considerable industry remained, a lot of new companies were forming, and real growth was occurring. What they found totally "obscured from view," however, was how much industry still "made sense to be in New York but could be driven out" by misguided public policies. Public forums were organized around this issue and the Planning Center found itself overwhelmed by the size of the interested audience showing up. At one, Cox sat with a high-level economic development official of the city, who looked around, amazed that he knew few people in the audience. "Who are these people?" he asked incredulously. The subject matter and people present did not match the official image of the city as primarily a white-collar city. This economic development official knows the real estate community well, but the manufacturing community hardly at all.

In the course of the ongoing exploration, the Planning Center discovered both a long-standing and newly emerging furniture industry, with young furniture makers setting up shop all over the city, particularly in Brooklyn. "Manufacturing, to exist," Cox notes, "must be based on assets, and New York's greatest asset is it is the center of the world of design." But designers, Cox also discovered, were losing awareness of what manufacturing capabilities and fabrication processes were available to them in New York. "Old links were weakening," she says. "We decided to work to create new links to bring designers and manufacturers together."

Cox worked with a quasi-public agency, the Industrial Technology Assistance Corporation (ITAC), through public programs, exhibits, and tours of factories, to strengthen awareness of New York's design-oriented manufacturing capacity. ITAC provides technical assistance to small manufacturing businesses of all kinds and is their chief advocate in the city. Sarah Garetson, ITAC director, is forever extolling the rich manufacturing resources that she observes, including the design fabrication field.[6] A goal was to show the diversity and quality of items made in New York, from carpets for the White House to shop window mannequins. This, of course, is economic development and planning of the best kind—problem solving, not Project Planning. In many places and in some states, "Made In" stores have been opened to display and promote locally

This cut-out sign announces the "Made in Virginia" products that are finding favor among consumers.

made products. New York could fill a department store with such items, dispelling the myth that manufacturing is dead or dying. That, however, is not what New York officials define as economic development.

DOING THE RIGHT THING

Nationwide, superstores and national chains are locating in downtowns. For their own sake, they *must* go downtown. The suburbs are "overstored," and retail giants are knocking each other off left and right in the oversaturated markets. Tamsin Carlisle, writing in *The Wall Street Journal* (March 11, 1997) about the restructuring and loss of big tenants in the world's largest mall, described the previous five years as "a period of takeovers, closings, and disappointments in the retail real-estate business. Malls that once appeared to have bright futures lost tenants and closed, and some were even razed." These retailers *need the cities more than cities need them.* They need the existing downtowns across America. They do not need incentives to come.

When McDonald's and the franchise craze broke on the scene years ago, they all claimed they had to have their drive-in formula. Today, McDonald's and a whole assortment of eating franchises can be found in historic buildings from Freeport, Maine, to Juneau, Alaska, in colonial houses and downtown storefronts, in new buildings and old, where the only formula piece still visible on the outside are the Golden Arches painted on a windowpane. But this is happening only where the locality sets the rules to reinforce, not undermine, pedestrian shopping streets and holds firm against threats to go elsewhere.

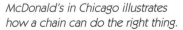

McDonald's in Chicago illustrates how a chain can do the right thing.

Most big box retailers don't know how to be urban, even when they locate in a city. They don't understand that the urban pedestrian shopper does not require the same things as a suburban car driver. They don't even realize that they may have more customers within a 10-minute walk than they are used to having within a 10-mile drive. In fact, for some superstores in New York City, foot traffic has accounted for greater sales than anticipated. Urban stores don't have to draw from as big a region when they locate in high-density downtowns.

Unfortunately, as well, most national retailers don't know how to stimulate impulse buying with eye-catching window displays, because they are locked into a formula store layout designed for huge, one-floor suburban sites. They are used to blank walls. The art of the window display seems to be dying, except for small stores in traditional downtowns. Kmart, for example, put cash registers, shopping carts, and wheelchairs in the window of its new 34th Street Manhattan store by which thousands walk daily, instead of dresses, toys, kitchenware, or linens that consumers might buy.

Above: Staples, a big box retailer, shows respect for the historic nature of a neighborhood, Broome Street, SoHo.

Below: Kmart, 34th Street, wastes the marketing potential of its large display windows in front of which thousands of people pass every day.

*Advertising playing cards and pill box given away
by the original Siegel-Cooper Department Store (1896).*

What a wasted opportunity! Urban design standards in traditional downtowns could actually teach suburban chains the art of window display, help them learn how to stimulate the impulse buying of the passing pedestrian, and, in the process, help them be more successful. Perhaps, superstores should hire an "urban consultant," an urban dweller to educate them about urban habits.

When pressed, national formula retailers can do the right thing in a downtown. This is happening all over the country. They knew how to do it on Manhattan's Sixth Avenue, where all the old department stores are now filled with vertical superstores. How ironic! Not only are these 19th-century buildings restored and reused for the same purpose for which they were built, but they would also not be standing today if determined historic preservationists (Urban Husbanders) hadn't successfully fended off the Project Planners of an earlier decade, who viewed the old store buildings as anachronistic and expendable for new development.

Superstores most often have to be taught, persuaded, and, sometimes, forced to be appropriately urban. They rarely regret it. The first successful superstore on Sixth Avenue almost evolved in a suburban mold. Owners of the classic 1896 Siegel-Cooper Department Store originally planned to hollow out the block-long building for a mall-like atrium, creating the typical inward-focused suburban mall instead of the street-directed urban store. They were persuaded, instead, to drop the mall idea and retain the traditional streetfront entries. Bed, Bath and Beyond, the first tenant, opened in only part of its current space, was an instant hit, expanded soon afterward, and has been followed in the building by T. J. Maxx and Filene's Basement. Before long, a number of others opened wherever space was available, all following the traditional pedestrian focus and all succeeding beyond retailers' expectations.

Similarly, superstores knew how to do it in Denver. As already noted, developer Rose showed them how to fit comfortably on a pedestrian shopping street and devised a new approach to financing that would permit it. The refusal of financial institutions to allow creative variations to suburban development formulas of all kinds is nothing short of a national scandal. Rose had to put together a unique and complex financial package to overcome institutional resistance and prove them shortsighted.

"Interestingly, it was local banks who made construction loans and were helpful from the beginning," Rose says. "The problem was finding permanent loans. That's where the national market went cold. In the end, a local bank made the permanent loans."

Even Wal-Mart learned how to locate in the downtowns of Bennington, in a former Woolworth's, and Rutland, in a rebuilt shopping center, that chain's first successes in Vermont after a decade of trying. The Gap does it with small stores scattered in one neighborhood, each almost a separate department—adults, kids. Safeway knew how to adjust its formula for a new store in a downtown plan for Boulder, Colorado, which the community then killed, fearing that a supermarket would bring too much new traffic to an already burdened downtown. Pathmark knew how to fit in on Harlem's 125th Street. In fact, some city neighborhoods, like my own on the Upper West Side, have supermarkets on two floors. And Zabar's, also on the Upper West Side, one of the most jam-packed, ever-popular, and internationally famous food emporia in the country, has two floors.

In New York, superstores are willing to forgo acres of parking only in Manhattan. At a Queens site close to Manhattan, Home Depot was one of the first, and one of the most controversial, because the pattern of killing the competition was obvious. Home Depot came in under a tricky provision that exempted hardware, toy, and stationery stores from the 10,000-square-foot limit in manufacturing districts. This was clearly a loophole in the zoning code. And it is a stretch to define Home Depot as a hardware store.

One substantial lumber and hardware business survivor of this onslaught reported meeting with Mayor Giuliani to argue against city assistance to Home Depot and other superstores. "There is room for competition, the mayor told me. I tried to explain that this is not a level playing field. This is an 800-pound gorilla, and the city is helping it along. I've been building this business for 35 years, breaking my neck, paying taxes, employing local people, paying a decent wage, and all of a sudden the city makes it possible for this gorilla to cripple, if not kill, me.

"If you survive, and for argument's sake, your business drops from $100,000 annually to $35,000, they say, 'Well, at least you are still in business.' Then they tell me I need to find a niche. Well, I had a niche. Home Depot took it away. It is one thing to say okay, come in, sit at the table, play the game with the same rules. But they sat at the table, changed the rules, and then ate my lunch and the city gave them the platter to eat my lunch on. They altered the zoning to make it all possible and gave them financial incentives in addition." (Many of the superstores received tax abatement and infrastructure adjustments.)

This particular survivor keeps running into former competitors of his who did not survive, New Yorkers who had built businesses that went under with Home Depot's entrance into sections of the city. After decades of owning and operating their own businesses, they now work for someone else. Several industrial businesses near Home Depot have closed.

Many negative economic side effects spin off this cycle of events, but one pointed out by my survivor friend is particularly unfortunate. "A secondary impact," he says, "is that it discourages people like me from either opening new businesses or expanding existing ones. I've passed up several opportunities to expand around the city for fear that Home Depot would follow me and wipe me out." The old American entrepreneurial spirit is dampened and, with it, a fundamental underpinning of our economic system.

Some argue that this pattern is contradicted, or even mitigated, by the many new businesses opening up around the country, many by a younger generation. These are separate issues. New, small start-ups do not undermine existing commercial areas. They add to them. The endurance of this trend is what is renewing many downtowns now. One of our celebrated national traditions is the building up of a business and passing it on to the next generation to continue building. Our survivor above, in fact, has a son now working in the business, but he is dubious about the future for his son. That tradition is undermined. Building a business to have something to sell for retirement is another undermined tradition.

A similar issue was highlighted by small supermarket owners, many of whom would have been happy to have the access to capital that would allow them to expand and serve their community better. "Through savings and high-interest loans," as *New York Times* columnist David Gonzalez reported, these independent merchants filled the void of the earlier food stores who abandoned the city for the suburbs. They had "moved into those empty stores, shunned by bankers but often financed by food wholesalers and others who made them pay high interest on short-term loans." They stuck it out through the neighborhood's hard times, but never had the opportunity of a level playing field. Instead, as they reported to Gonzalez, "their dealings with officialdom are often limited to maddening encounters with health inspectors and code enforcers who are quick to dash off a summons for the slightest infraction."

"We came in aggressively and financed it privately," Bronx grocer Luis Salcedo told Gonzalez. "Now the big supermarkets see us thriving in here and they want to come back. But they need special zoning and benefits we don't get. I don't think that's American...Why not offer the opportunities to the people who went in with their own dollars and risked everything? I don't want something for nothing. I just want the same opportunity." Why not? is right. That would surely be American, wouldn't it?

The implications for downtowns of this erosion of the American entrepreneurial ethic is profound. Survival is difficult at best. Yet, over the long haul, downtowns have a better chance of survival than super-stores. Retail analysts note that some markets are already oversaturated. Increasingly, the war is between the national giants in proximity to each other on the strip. As money manager Cramer says, "The super-stores are on a rampage."

The closing of the last generation of big stores can be seen across the country. The small ones anchored by the big ones are closing as well. The question is which and when—not whether—will be next. Their empty hulks will be the taxpayers' burden.

WHEN BIG IS GOOD

Big does not automatically mean bad. Small does not automatically mean good. Value is not in size measurement. Genuine communal value is the standard against which downtown change should be measured. How does a use, a project, a building, a business fit into the physical, social, and economic structure of a place? How is it individualized? How does it reflect the locality? These are the essential questions.

No greater evidence of the strong public desire for renewed public gathering places exists than in the lounge chairs, around the tables, and on the floors of both the mega-bookstores and individualized independent bookstores proliferating around the country. What a paradox. The car is supposed to have provided freedom. Cyberspace is supposed to make urban agglomerations unnecessary. The home entertainment center is supposed to help families enjoy leisure time at home together. Everything in this modern age is supposed to make our need for the unruly, overcrowded, uncontrollable center unnecessary. Yet the crowds gather at public markets. They gather in the gritty, SoHo-like warehouse districts of our downtowns wherever they still exist (see Chapter 13). And they are overflowing bookstores. More than ever, the technically advanced connections of the Internet era *increase* the human need for personal interaction.

Many independent bookstores have long been important gathering places and centers of intellectual and literary life. The erosion of public places, however, has created a new void. Barnes & Noble and

Borders are the leading bookstore chains that capitalize on this need by providing the simple amenities of seating room, coffee bars, extensive magazine browsing, and author readings. When they don't bring their suburban building type, surrounded by asphalt, into downtown sites, superstore book chains are often part of the vanguard return to public spaces. Public and university libraries are cutting budgets and hours. Bookstores help fill that void. Some bookstores are as much an individualized, public meeting space as a private enterprise can be. My office is four floors above one.

I work in a marvelous communal workspace, the Writers Room, probably this country's first urban writers' colony. For some writers, working at home alone is not an option. Limited space, family distractions, and the same assorted daily intrusions avoided by people who work in offices all conspire to impede a writer's work. And, like most people, writers need the social interaction that comes with a workplace. In the Writers Room, 35 desks and four private offices serve 200 writers at different times, on different days, seven 24-hour days of the week. Located in Greenwich Village on Astor Place, equidistant between Cooper Union and New York University, the Writers Room occupies a sixth-floor office of a small commercial building where Barnes & Noble fills the first two floors and a basement.

On the second floor of Barnes & Noble is a Starbucks, with a limited, but sufficient, sandwich, cakes, and coffee menu. Its 30 tables are rarely empty, even late at night. Students with computers, notepads, and book bags dominate the crowd, a puzzlement to me when you think about the fine libraries that the two neighboring schools have. But people of all ages, some with infants in strollers, enjoy magazine browsing, book reading, quiet conversation, or solo writing work. It reminds me of many a "study hall" I worked in as a student. Even the voices are kept reasonably low. This is my frequent meeting place where I arrange to have coffee, lunch, or an interview, if I want to stay conveniently near my writing office. The store may be a chain, but the crowd and personality are local. This is a private space that invites individuals to invade and make theirs. *A private space made public? What a reversal!*

No chain store, however, can match the individuality of the independent bookstore run by the involved, knowledgeable owner. Carla Cohen, who had worked in Washington, D.C., as a "convenor" in government, bringing citizens and bureaucrats together, opened Politics and Prose in Chevy Chase, Maryland, with the idea of still being a convenor. "Book buying should be fun, an event," she says. "It is not like buying cereal." With this in mind, she has created a unique institution, a "Great Good Place," as sociologist Ray Oldenburg (see Chapter 1) would call it, that social gathering place that is neither work nor home, but a necessary addition to both. Politics and Prose offers a four-time-a-year newsletter with reviews and recommendations, readings and discussions, a café, and an unpredictable assortment of services that includes people seeking book advice or help finding information, the kind of questions that one might ask a reference librarian. In 12 years, Politics and Prose has become a destination, a community anchor, a regional institution, the kind of personalized bookstore that national chains can learn from but not duplicate. Chains cannot match the quality of the locally-owned bookstore that is both a fixture and shaper of a community.

Similarly, Joyce Meskis and her Tattered Cover bookstore have been involved participants in the rebirth of Denver's LoDo. The Tattered Cover is a Denver institution and important downtown anchor. Tattered Cover started as a small bookstore (950 square feet) in the 1970s in Cherry Creek, an early streetcar suburb with a long, vibrant commercial center. As it expanded, Meskis always had her eye on the old warehouse district of downtown, but timing was always problematic because of Denver's oil-based boom-or-bust economy. "I've always had a love affair with old buildings and my business district customers were always urging me to open there," she says. "The scale and warmth of the buildings were always more suitable to our presentation."

By 1989, Denver's real estate prices were as low as they could get and the bookstore's need for expanded warehouse and office space was great. Downtown was "percolating," as Meskis puts it. She joined a partnership to buy adjacent warehouse buildings with the idea of developing affordable housing and a restaurant, along with a second bookstore site and increased back-office and warehouse space. By the late 1990s, the full measure of the vision had come to fruition ("these things always take more time and money than you thought"). The Tattered Cover occupies 35,000 square feet on three floors, plus more back-office space. Ninety-four rental apartments were created, three-quarters of them low-income, and a restaurant is open on the alley between the buildings. This is more than a bookstore. Different in form but similar in substance to Poetry and Prose and scores of independent bookstores, the Tattered Cover is an integral part of Lower Downtown's rebirth, a community participant and anchor at the same time.

Interestingly, in the small city of Holland, Michigan, with a thriving downtown of all locally-owned businesses, two independent bookstores, Readers World and Booksellers on Main Street, do well, despite bookstore chains in nearby malls. But Holland is unique for its local economy, has extraordinary character, and draws both strong local and visitor customer bases. The interesting assortment of all kinds of independent retailers in Holland creates its own appeal.

The popularity of both the personal, independent bookstore and the increasingly ubiquitous chains is as much about meeting a need for public gathering places and being a community contributor, as about bookstores.

The sociable hangout of varying kinds—the corner coffee shop, the small café, the neighborhood bar—has been disappearing from downtowns for years as blocks of varied-size buildings are replaced with mega-office buildings. The corner coffee shop is a victim of proliferating corporation cafeterias and upscale restaurants. Even educational and cultural institutions have been depleting the public and pedestrian realm as they have created, *inside*, their own cafeterias, stores, and underground/overground connections. Such eating and meeting places were once a mainstay of downtowns. The "Paris Café" is as alien to most downtowns now as the hot dog stand. Where it is reemerging, in the older neighborhoods and commercial districts, local businesses are emerging, street life is coming back, and communities are growing anew. Suburban populations, as well, hunger for such places. For many, the only source is the big chain bookstore in the shopping center that gives them inside what the mall form does not permit to occur in a combined inside/outside urban form.

Big or small, bookstore or dress shop, independent or chain, the standard against which businesses should be measured is how individualized and localized they are, what they add to communal life, how pedestrian-friendly they are. Offering short-term cheap goods to the consumer is not enough. The long-term costs get added to the tax burden in added infrastructure costs and loss of local economy, as this book illustrates throughout. Contributing occasionally to the Girl Scouts or United Way fund drives is not enough. Being a community participant, involved in the PTA, civic affairs, the block, the neighborhood, the Little League, the Girl Scouts, or any local community building block is equally, if not more, valuable. Certainly, enhancing an existing downtown or neighborhood commercial center, creating a gathering place, and enlarging the public realm uniquely contributes to the social currency of society. This does not even enter into the equation we too easily refer to as fair competition. But it should.

1. The terms "superstore," "big box retailer," and "category killer" are used interchangeably. Commonly, they range in size from 90,000 to 200,000 square feet, located as often as possible near highway interchanges or exits, use the same windowless box store design with several acres of a single-floor layout, and require vast surface parking. Usually, they shun downtown locations unless they can bring this suburban design with them. Specifically, category killers are large-volume retailers and often have direct relationships with product manufacturers. "Power centers" (250,000 to 750,000 square feet) are congregations of superstores.

2. The Bottom Line, "Bargain Basement," October 9, 1995.
3. "When Big-Box Retailers Fail, Who Pays?" Washington Post Writers Group, December 4, 1995.
4. January 23, 1994.
5. *Citywide Industry Study: Industry Trends Technical Report*, NYC Dept. of City Planning, January 1993.
6. In the interest of disclosure, this is my husband's business, a metal fabrication business, and a long-time, well-known furniture and sculpture producer founded by his father. This has given me a birds'-eye view of small manufacturing for more than 30 years.

Watt & Shand—a classic downtown department
store in Lancaster, Pennsylvania, until bought
by a surburban chain

CHAPTER EIGHT

YOU DON'T HAVE TO BE
WAL-MART TO BE WAL-MART

Bon-Ton is a 64-store retail chain with locations in New York, New Jersey, Maryland, Pennsylvania, and West Virginia. Bon-Ton emerged as a regional "killer" of downtowns. So far, the Pennsylvania communities of York, Reading, Harrisburg, Allentown, and Lancaster and Buffalo, New York, have been "Bon-toned," a word not yet in the vocabulary but destined to get there. Definition: a downtown with its retail heart willfully ripped out by a predator retailer. The following tale unfolded in the southeastern Pennsylvania city of Lancaster, after a variation already had occurred in the other communities named above.

Lancaster, centrally located between Philadelphia, Baltimore, Washington, and New York, is a city of 58,000, with three newspapers; 600 downtown businesses, including a variety of shops and restaurants, in 10 square blocks; 10,000 employees; insurance companies, government offices, and cultural attractions; one of the most historic thriving farmers' markets in the country, Central Market; an historic and expanding 1880s Fulton Opera House, beautifully restored and offering first-class entertainment; and close-in and walkable, appealing neighborhoods.

With a sizable financial community, large hospital, the Pennsylvania School of Arts and Design, and the Academy of Music, Lancaster's downtown does not suffer the feeling of emptiness and diminishing life visible in so many downtowns. Four successful used book stores reflect a less obvious, but unusual, appeal. The 1940 WPA Guide for Pennsylvania described Lancaster as "the most beautiful city in America." Its strong appeal endures. This is a neat and well-tended city. Modest lawns are all trim. Houses are painted. Litter is scarce. Corner stores endure. Architectural treasures are everywhere. Considerable downtown property was purchased and upgraded in the early 1980s with historic preservation tax credits, and a genuine upturn momentum was generated.

The city should not be confused with Lancaster County (population 443,000), with its extraordinary concentration of Amish and

Mennonite farmers and in which the city sits. State and county tourism marketing programs give the city short shrift. Most attention is focused on the county, specifically on a dismal and chaotic strip of Route 30, a collection of tacky strip malls, outlet stores, fake historic theme attractions (Dutch Wonderland, Fulton Steamboat Inn, wax museum), and mobile homes. Route 30 is the antithesis of the county's authentic farms and downtown's genuine urbanism.

There are five Lancaster highway exits on Route 30, none of which indicates the best one for downtown and nothing that signals downtown's culture-rich historic district. (This condition will sound familiar to the thousands of downtown boosters elsewhere who struggle to raise awareness that a downtown business district exists.) The state's Department of Transportation claims that such a sign would be a safety problem. Why, then, are there so many highway signs across the country telling drivers where the mall is? The average tourists go just where they are led, and no further.

In 1992, in a $10 million package deal, Bon-Ton purchased the downtown and suburban mall stores of Watt and Shand, the mainstay department store at the very heart of the city of Lancaster's downtown. (This story was reported in great detail in the local newspapers.) Everyone was immediately nervous about the downtown retail landmark's future, but Bon-Ton was reassuring.

Watt and Shand, started by Scottish immigrants in 1878, quickly became known as "the New York Store," a characterization that, according to reporter Jack Brubaker of *The New Era*, lasted well into the middle of the 20th century. There were, as well, a "Boston Store" (Leinbach's) and a "Lancaster Store" (Hager's), and where one shopped was apparently directly related to social status. In 1898, Lancaster's best-known architect, C. Emlen Urban, designed a four-story Beaux Arts structure of light gray brick, terra cotta, and marble that was expanded several times to its present 226,000-square-foot L-shaped configuration.

Downtown Lancaster, like so many Pennsylvania towns, is characterized by a small central square, in which a significant monument is located. Penn Square has been the heart of the city from the early 18th-century settlement period up to the present day. The community's four key thoroughfares branch out from this central point like arrows on a compass, creating four central L-shaped corners. Since 1898, Watt and Shand anchored one of them. The Grand Old Lady of Penn Square, it was called. And it was considered one of the most significant structures in Lancaster County, both architecturally and culturally. The store name was delicately etched into the glass on the transom above the front door. Its interior restaurant, the Rendezvous, was a favorite meeting place. A huge, yellow neon Watt and Shand sign sat on the roof since the 1940s. A seating area was inside one of the entrances for transit travelers waiting for their buses. And a three-story Christmas tree on its façade, heavily decorated with colorful lights, was downtown's most important holiday symbol.

Until Bon-Ton's 1992 purchase, this full-service department store, the city's last, continued under family ownership and survived the proliferation of suburban malls. Three years after the purchase, Bon-Ton closed the downtown store, blaming insufficient parking, crime, and the downtown community for not supporting it. Bon-Ton's president later admitted that actual crime was rare, but that the perception was otherwise. The downtown store, a press release said, was a victim of the "migration of consumers and businesses to the suburbs." Bon-Ton executives *claimed* they did all they could to keep it open. Bon-Ton's *behavior* tells a different story, one that can only slip into a killer category of another kind. Interestingly, the details of this sorry tale were well reported in Lancaster's three newspapers, *Lancaster Intelligencer Journal, Lancaster Sunday News, The New Era*, making the real store more apparent than the similar demise of downtown stores in communities where such reporting is no longer available. Understanding the deception of the official Bon-Ton story, one has to question how many other downtown department store closings with the same explanations were similarly deceptive. Downtown's inferiority complex is not always deserved.

In the first year of ownership of the Lancaster store, Bon-Ton reported a loss of 46 percent in sales, which already indicates the new owner was doing something radically different, and not doing it well. Different it was. The high-quality, upscale merchandise Lancastrians were accustomed to buying was removed. Upscale had been the Watt and Shand trademark. Downscale, discount goods were substituted. Sales staff was dramatically reduced, frustrating customers. Popular promotions were offered at both downtown and mall stores. Buy $30 worth of cosmetics, get a free gift. But downtown, after the special promotion purchase, customers were told to pick up the gift *only* at the suburban store.

Newspaper ads confused customers about downtown offerings, but clearly promoted the suburban store. Bon-Ton even refused to spend $125 to participate in a downtown business district promotion. No holiday shopping hours were offered downtown. The once-easy parking ticket validation process was made burdensome for shoppers. And, as a final insult, Bon-Ton refused to put up the Christmas tree on the building's façade, an old downtown tradition. If downtown merchants paid for the installation, a Bon-Ton spokesman indicated, the decorations could be erected.

Michelle Mink, a vice president of Dauphin Deposit Bank, led a fund-raising effort that raised $2300 from seven businesses in a day and a half to cover the installation fee. "The outpouring from the business community was incredible," Mink told *New Era* staff writer Todd R. Weiss. "It was really neat to see the whole business community come together." Then, Bon-Ton refused to pay the liability insurance. Again, the rest of the business community stepped in, and the lights went up.

After the closing announcement, the mayor told the *Lancaster Sunday News*, "They have a lot of excuses why they haven't turned a profit, don't they? We've been doing our part. There are more police downtown now than ever before. We've addressed parking concerns...They have a garage connected to their building which isn't always full...the city has done everything but run the downtown store for them." An offer of city financial assistance for renovating the store was refused. In 1994, when Bon-Ton announced a $52 million upgrade for the suburban store, no similar plan for the downtown store was included.

When the end came and Bon-Ton announced a $3 million loss and 46 percent drop in sales, downtown merchants and other observers said this could only have happened intentionally. "How could you buy a store that the year before was doing $12 million worth of business, lay off 100 people, buy smarter and cheaper, and not make money?" boutique owner Moirajeanne Fitzgerald told *Philadelphia Inquirer* business reporter Virginia Wiegand. "I'm not a genius," she added, "but some of us have just had our best year ever. If I'm making a good living here, I don't understand why Bon-Ton couldn't." Only 10 of the 300 storefronts in Lancaster's shopping district were empty, Wiegand reported, and the city's tallest office building, the 15-story Griest office building, was full after years of high vacancies. And while crime had risen 30 percent in the prior decade, it had dropped 63 percent in the four previous years.

After the closing, Bon-Ton refused to sell the historic building to either a retailer or an office developer. Even the city was rebuffed in purchase overtures. This is a known tactic of various chains, the inclusion of restrictive covenants preventing the buyer from selling to another retailer. So much for even letting downtown retail *compete*. Once again, so much for fair competition.

According to newspaper accounts in Lancaster and other cities, the same pattern was followed in each downtown Bon-Ton entered. In York, Pennsylvania, the building remained empty for 12 years, a downtown eyesore, until the city was able to buy it for conversion to government office use, but not to retail. Under normal conditions, this might have been fine, but York is one of those downtowns seeming to go too far in the office-use direction, while letting its retail base continue to erode and ceding to suburban malls all retail dollars.

Downtown as office center doesn't foster the kind of diverse activity a downtown needs for a stable and balanced economy. First floor retail, a whole mix of uses, is critical to downtown life. Filling street-level space overwhelmingly with banks, offices, or social service destinations deadens downtown. Where retail does exist, it is often off the street, in a mall, or in the atrium-*cum*-mall of an office building. Official policy sanctions, or even encourages, this. No wonder so many downtowns have few pedestrians on the street and few destinations to draw them.

In Harrisburg, Pennsylvania, the Strawberry Square retail mall adjacent to Bon-Ton tried to purchase the vacant Bon-Ton building. Bon-Ton refused, and sold the historic building to a developer, who bulldozed the building to create a parking lot. In Reading, Pennsylvania, the closed store sat empty for seven years.

None of these downtowns have a review procedure for demolition permits and none have historic preservation ordinances, any of which could have assisted the political leadership in each place to pursue its articulated intention of trying to save the stores. At one point, with considerable negotiation and involvement of all levels of Pennsylvania government, a complex, publicly supported $12 million deal was announced in Lancaster. The plan called for Harrisburg Area Community College programs to occupy the closed department store, along with county offices and possibly some small stores. A 1950s-60s warehouse, at the building's rear would be demolished for parking. (An earlier Bon-Ton proposal would have demolished 90,000 square feet for parking, including part of the rear of the landmark building.) The college had been looking to relocate, and had rejected two suburban sites for this location. Even this reasonable plan fell through.

This policy of either chain retailers or suburban mall builders owning downtown buildings and refusing to allow new retail uses is more frequent than realized, because it is often subtle and not apparent. Few downtown advocates we encountered across the country could say for sure that this was a policy they definitely observed. But many could identify former stores held empty and resisting specific purchase proposals from potential retail users. In Burlington, Iowa, for example, a former Kresge building had been empty for years. The Main Street manager had been unable to get anyone in the home office to even pay attention to proposals. Eventually, a fast-food restaurant moved in.

Calmetta Y. Coleman wrote a story in *The Wall Street Journal* (February 6, 1997), "Shuttered Supermarkets Prompt Civic Protests," identifying a policy of some supermarket chains of keeping buildings they vacate empty to prevent a competitor from moving in. Coleman wrote, "Across the country, real-estate brokers and community leaders tell of similar situations. In the rapidly consolidating supermarket industry, location is often the biggest factor distinguishing one chain from another, and few choice sites remain in many densely developed markets. For the leaseholder, paying rent on a closed store can be less costly than losing market share to a competitor."

MALLING THE CENTER, KILLING DOWNTOWN TWICE
Yet another model of this regional killer of downtowns is also found in a Pennsylvania city, Scranton (population 82,000), once the fourth largest

city in the state. The central player in the Scranton tragedy is the regional retail chain, Boscov's, builder of the typical downtown enclosed suburban mall. But by no means did Boscov's do the damage alone. Boscov's had all the political help possible, led by 35-year Republican congressman, Joseph M. McDade, then the ranking minority leader of the House Appropriations Committee, and one of the most powerful congressmen. Lined up right behind him were then-Governor Robert P. Casey, a Democrat, a series of Scranton mayors, two Scranton newspapers (of which only one survives), and just about the whole political apparatus of Scranton, both Republicans and Democrats. These issues are nonpartisan.

The only ones to stand bravely in opposition and to fight with every tool at their command were a hearty band of historic preservationists, architects, planners, residents, and local businessmen who knew the value of the downtown their city had, knew the local economy was in better shape than officials maintained, and recognized the city's need for modest, incremental projects to accelerate the rebirth momentum already evident. They lost, and now Scranton is one of the most unnecessarily undermined downtowns that either of us has seen in years of traveling around the cities and towns of this country.

The resulting project is an enclosed shopping mall. An overpass above a raised railroad bed connects the mall to a new railroad history museum on unused railyards. This might have been just another sad tale of a once-viable downtown destroyed by an enclosed suburban mall plopped into the center of it, if not for the control of McDade, a legendary powerhouse of the old school of strong-arm politics. Under pressure from McDade and with close to, if not more than, $100 million in federal and state funds, the National Park Service was reluctant to create the railroad museum, Steamtown. Historians and museum curators around the nation call it a "second-rate collection on a third-rate site."[1] The train collection around which Steamtown was created had earlier been rejected for acquisition by the Park Service because it lacked sufficient historic importance. At the same time this new museum of little substance was being created, respected, long-standing museums across the country

Before: Scranton, Pennsylvania. Eighty individual 19th-century buildings, the heart of the Lackawanna Avenue Historic District, are imploded to make way for a typical enclosed mall. Photo: John G. Carling.

were experiencing severe federal cutbacks. Clearly, this was a model Project Plan thinly camouflaged by a cloak of history.

Eighty buildings of assorted size, age, and condition, occupied by dozens of mostly locally-owned businesses, were bought, vacated, and scheduled for demolition to make way for the mall. This was the heart of the Lackawanna Avenue Historic District, an assemblage of appealing and functional commercial

After: The mall.

buildings listed on the National Register of Historic Places. The irony that Scranton would rip up its authentic history to create ersatz history escaped notice.

I first visited Scranton in 1989. I was invited to speak by the Architectural Heritage Association of Northeastern Pennsylvania after publication of *The Living City*. This group of citizens of varied backgrounds and professions were realists. They knew the downtown had seen better days. They knew help was needed. But they knew instinctively that the demolition of so much and the addition of a mall were not a solution to a problem. They also knew this proposal would destroy a great city resource, local entrepreneurs occupying interesting, historic, and functional buildings. Scranton should be a lesson for any downtown looking to a suburban mall as a palliative for downtown needs. On my 1989 visit to Scranton, I was stunned. The proposed project, with its layers of government subsidies, destruction of the kind of locally-owned businesses and historic buildings so many downtowns yearn to have again or have and are working to strengthen, and inclusion of such a fraudulent park project was bad enough. But what was really criminal was that Scranton was still an essentially intact city that could have truly made itself a model of urban endurance and economic rebirth—the kind of success cities, like Lancaster, may still pull off.

A substantial and functioning county courthouse is a centerpiece in the city's central park. Law offices and accessory small businesses, at that time, occupied buildings around the park. Investment in businesses and buildings was evident throughout the 20-square-block business district. Long-time businesses were side by side with new ones and city investment in sidewalk, lighting, and sanitation improvements added to the feeling of positive change. A healthy collection of retail shops was nicely scattered along the traditional downtown streets, which included a surviving but struggling local department store, the Globe, much loved by the community. Restaurants, many run by second- and third-generation family members, were more abundant than fast-food franchises. Hundreds of local businesses were evident alongside chains, the kinds only found in viable downtowns. Benetton, for example, one of the hot retail chains of the day, was doing well on a prime spot.

A local developer, Brian Murray, had begun restoring and converting historic buildings. A 10-story, turn-of-the century Romanesque Revival brownstone corner office building now had ground-floor retail, two floors of offices with five floors of apartments above, including apartments renting at $800–1200 a month (in 1989), a Manhattan comparable. This building had a waiting list for its apartments. There were two surviving local newspapers, both located downtown. Architecture offered a strong visual advantage with grand public buildings scattered among fine examples of almost every period of commercial building. The wide variety of age, size, and interior configuration of the buildings offered endless opportunities to a variety of new business ventures and residential styles. With creative leadership, Scranton's could have been one of the great success stories of the 21st century.

"A downtown has to find its own economic strength, and build upon it on its own urban downtown terms, and in doing so, to be different from the suburbs," wrote Scranton-born Jane Jacobs in a letter to the city opposing plans to build a mall. "This is true of all successful downtowns with staying power," she added.

Scranton has a rich history rooted in iron ore and coal mining, iron rail production, transportation services stemming from its several railroad lines, and assorted entrepreneurial ventures that emerged from this combination. In 1906, an extravagant Indiana limestone train station was built with imposing classical columns, a glass skylight, a barrel-vaulted ceiling of leaded glass, terrazzo tile floor, and interior faience panels of countryside scenes. The impressive edifice reflected the robust economy of the region and proud cultural heritage and served as a focal point of the city. The last train passed through in 1970 and the building, empty until 1982, was impressively restored by private investors and reopened as a Hilton hotel. Today, it stands as a strong symbol of the enduring city that might have been.

Instead, the mall continues to cost Scranton dearly. An expensive second-floor walkway was built to connect the local department store, the Globe, with the mall, to guarantee the department store's future. A realist would have known the opposite would happen. The Globe closed three months after the mall opened. More than 100 downtown businesses have folded. Some local businessmen and property owners formerly on the mall site were harassed and threatened until they sold. A 1993 FBI investigation of the mall's financing, questionable blight study, and fraud charges (local headline: "Mallgate!") came and went. Scores of government promises were made and broken. The private investor, Brian Murray, whose upgraded buildings with apartments and offices had waiting lists now has vacancies. The city, to meet mall needs, spent new money redoing streets and streetscapes it had just done a decade before. Downtown traffic was reconfigured; new traffic lights installed.

Expensive, publicly-funded parking built for the mall was made free by Boscov's to avoid paying the city the $10-per-car fee that all other garages pay. A score of plans to restore the former Casey Hotel for residential use were announced but went nowhere. The Casey, its windows left open to accelerate deterioration, was one of the downtown's best sites for recreating a downtown residential population. In 1996, the talk was of using it for welfare recipients or blowing it up, another symbol of the many rejuvenation opportunities Scranton ignored. As this book goes to press, the proposal is to tear down the Casey for a mixed-use project—including a hotel sure to undermine the existing Hilton. All kinds of government offices filled vacant, renovated space within walking distance of the mall. Could it be that McDade's power on the House Appropriations Committee helped persuade these agencies to open here? Predictably, big, expensive, government-funded projects like this lead *only* to the need for more big, expensive, government-funded projects.

Something else, however, is happening, many blocks away from the mall. Young, creative entrepreneurs and architects have found some of the vacant, underutilized buildings too good to resist. They've purchased them and imaginatively renovated them. They have attracted or started small businesses. Residents have moved into upper floors. Closer to the mall, a sports bar in a former red brick warehouse draws bigger crowds than anything in the mall. But closed businesses and empty buildings are everywhere. The best hope for Scranton now is that before more bulldozers move in, more young people and downtown partisans see the opportunities the vacant buildings offer and continue to purchase, restore, and reuse them. Surely, there is enough left of a genuine city to work with. This same new generation is reclaiming downtown after downtown, resettling what is left of traditional centers, and putting down the roots for the lively downtowns of the 21st century. If, over time, the shift occurs in Scranton as it is happening in so many places (see Chapter 13), Boscov's mall will become dated and wither, the traditional streets will experience new, up-to-date change, and Scranton may once again come alive.

JUST SAY NO

Communities across the country are learning how to say no to wrongheaded Project Plans.

Denver set design guidelines for its Lower Downtown Warehouse District that limited new building heights and prohibited enclosed malls. One of the country's biggest enclosed mall developers refused to comply and threatened not to build. Denver refused to buckle under, stood firm in its prohibition, and the mall developer did leave town. But another developer came and developed according to the guidelines, with streets open to the sky.

Multiplex movie theater companies wanted to locate in Santa Monica, but not near the three-block Third Street Promenade, where the rebirth of the downtown was evolving. The 80-foot, overly wide street was a dead pedestrian mall until sidewalks were widened, autos were brought back on a limited basis, and sections of the street bed were turned over to pushcarts, street performers, sidewalk artists, and other people activities. The city council banned movie theaters from being built anywhere in the city of 80,000 other than on the Promenade. The theater companies resisted. The mayor invited theater executives to discuss it over lunch at a restaurant on the Promenade. The executives were amazed at the street's rebirth, vibrant activity, and the numbers of people already there. They located on the Promenade happily. More crowds followed.

Similarly, in Sacramento, movie theater executives sought approval for a location out of town. A 28-screen movie complex[2] downtown on that city's K Street Mall was already in the works. The K Street Mall is another once-moribund pedestrian mall reopened to limited traffic and a new light rail line. The city council gave the downtown proposal an edge by banning other movie complexes for three years. A wonderful historic 1930s movie theater, the Crest, was already restored and active.

San Jose did something similar with new hotels proposed to be built near the airport. In recent years, San Jose has been making great strides at strengthening its center, including the development of a light rail line that draws people into downtown. Hotel developers were eyeing the out-of-town airport as the site of choice for new development, something that is happening around many airports, to the detriment of existing centers. San Jose said no airport sites, only downtown ones. This, of course, does not guarantee street-friendly designs that enhance public spaces but it is a start.

Even a really small town can find the wherewithall to resist the most formidable of trends. *The Los Angeles Times* described Sierra Madre as a "10,767-strong community with a single police detective and volunteer firefighter is without a modern supermarket, a multiplex theater or a drive-through burger joint."[3] In the fall of 1996, Sierra Madre joined that very small group of communities to ban drive-through restaurants. With a basically intact two-block, pedestrian-oriented downtown, Sierra Madre already had a small drive-through bank branch. People were determined, however, not to allow the "McDonaldization" of their much-loved downtown. The drive-through debate reportedly became more of a hot-button issue than anything else, even in the middle of a presidential election, and resulted in a 3–2 city council vote. West Hollywood, noted *The Los Angeles Times*, banned new drive-throughs at its incorporation 12 years earlier, and Burbank and South Pasadena had experimented with moratoria. Undoubtedly, this will become a hot-button issue in downtowns everywhere seeking to either protect a pedestrian-friendly character or to create it.

Most occasions for "just saying no" reflect conflicts with traffic and transportation planning rules. Saying no to new and widened highways is obvious to many people, despite the continued proliferation of new beltway proposals. Less obvious are the traffic-related "nibblings," the kind that erode pedestrian life because engineer road and street standards require traffic and speed-enhancing designs. The 12-foot street width requirement, which encourages high speeds downtown, should be resisted in favor of the 10-foot width that slows moving vehicles and makes pedestrian crossing less intimidating. Rules requiring tree and planter removal were written to remove vehicular safety hazards ("killer trees"), but studies show that a more attractive landscape encourages slower, more enjoyable driving and better safety for vehicles and pedestrians. The standardized federal and state signage and traffic light regulations and the banal cobra-head street lights, designed for parking lots, produce a tangle of confusion and ugliness on downtown streets and road crossings. Well-designed street signs and signals more appropriate for walking streets—and less of them—would add appeal to any locale. Local, individualized touches could be an added bonus.

Guilford, Connecticut, rejected nearly $1 million in federal and state highway money to improve a local road because the much-loved scenic road would have to be widened and straightened, disrupting the landscape. Federal road standards required a roadbed of at least 30 feet, twice the present width, with an additional 15 feet cleared on each side. The damage, they concluded, was not worth the supposed free money. The road, like many in towns everywhere, is narrow and winding, shaded by 100-year-old trees and bounded in places by stone walls. "People perceive a town through its roads," noted a local opponent who argued it would undermine the character and value of the community.

The heart of the problem are the design guidelines established by the American Association of State Highway and Transportation Officials (ASHTO). ASHTO is a formidable force in all of these cases, despite its nongovernmental nature. ASHTO's "one size fits all" approach to road design is accepted as gospel by government officials. "No engineer would dare design a project that didn't meet ASHTO guidelines," one transportation engineer reported, "lest insurance companies or government officials reject it."

Another Connecticut town, Redding, turned down $347,000 in federal and state funds to rebuild a picturesque 1895 stone bridge on a designated scenic road lined with 18th-century homes, many with lily-filled ponds. The existing bridge is about 15 feet wide and would have had to be widened to 24 feet. The height would have to be raised and approaching roads similarly widened. The town rejected the grants and, with local funds, repaired it. In a letter to the local paper, the town selectman commented on the inflexible standards: "It's a sad commentary when historic preservation, neighborhood aesthetics, and common sense are replaced by cookie-cutter requirements, standardization without regard to local custom and usage, and the 'bigger is better' philosophy." This particular story is repeated all over the country.

Needless to say, both Guilford's road and Redding's bridge required considerable less funding than the federal standards would have required. And they certainly did not meet ASHTO standards.

For eight years, the Fort Worth, Texas, community group, I-CARE (Citizen Advocates for Responsible Expansion), battled federal and state highway authorities over a proposed freeway that would not only increase traffic gridlock but also endanger much-loved landmarks and the Philip Johnson Water Gardens. They succeeded in gaining a tree-lined boulevard instead that, when completed, will fill vehicular needs without destroying the environment.

A similar battle ensued in Westminster, Maryland, 25 miles west of Baltimore, with an interesting twist. A citizen protest, initiated by one determined resident, Rebecca Orenstein, was organized when a road-widening project threatened the town's historic Main Street, with its more than 40 mature trees. The campaign involved schoolchildren who hung valentines on trees marked for demolition. The town, of course, was reluctant to resist the state plan lest it lose this and other needed state and federal road funding.

Orenstein was undaunted, appealed directly to state transportation secretary James Lighthizer, and pleaded with him to visit Westminster personally to understand the harm that would ensue. He did, immediately halted the project, and organized a task force that included Orenstein to develop an alternative. The result spared the trees, and the state planted 118 new ones as well. Noted one MDOT official: "We only needed to reconstruct the road. The irony is that by applying a certain standard, we would have widened the road but without achieving any additional capacity...It would have been a disaster." The episode brought much-needed new thinking to the state's transportation agency.

Whether it is the formula of a mall developer or the one-size-fits-all standards of the highway engineer, such homogenizing practices destroy places. The national corporations and retailers that demand to impose formula development wherever they choose are the equivalent of national planning agencies that take all voice and choice out of the hands of local communities. The same is true of transportation engineers applying the "anywhere" formula everywhere. Just saying no is imperative, if the distinctions of places are to have a chance.

When the community will is there, anything is possible.

1. "As 'Steamtown' Grows, So Does Parks Debate," *New York Times*, November 23, 1991. This is an excellent, detailed account of this enormously expensive, publicly subsidized project.
2. The size of movie theater complexes is getting way out of hand. Their megamall scale brings too many people to one place, mostly by car, and precludes the possibility of the smaller-scale entertainment anchor in other districts.
3. Richard Winton and Nicholas Riccardi, "Order Canceled," September 26, 1996.

Farmers' market, Syracuse, New York—
life returns to place

CHAPTER NINE

TO MARKET, TO MARKET

For the past few years I've spent most Saturday mornings in my
local farmer's market. It has become a kind of ritual, a changing
drama that focuses the eyes unmistakably on nature and its seasons in a time when the rest of life seems increasingly enclosed
and controlled—climate controlled, color coded, cocooned by
the plastic surfaces of modern secularity.

In the market is life, vitality, health, abundance, grit, prime
produce, color. In markets lie the thick of things, sociability,
the throb of human community. They provide links with the
past, and all indications suggest that farmers'-market networks will create far-reaching and revolutionary changes in
the ways we shop and eat—alterations that will affect agriculture's future.

So begins food writer Judith Olney's book, *The Farm Market Cookbook*, a
wonderful combination of market vendor recipes, guides to markets
around the country, interviews with farmers, and wisdom reflecting the
essence and importance of markets. Enough cannot be said about the
multiple levels of significance of farmers' markets, which are usually seasonal and in the open air, or public markets, which are usually year-
round, inside, and offer more than food.

Most important:

❖ They encourage and support a local economy, giving birth
to new local businesses and keeping consumer dollars circulating locally. Public markets offer opportunities to more than
just farmers, but all markets showcase small, local enterprises that can grow.

❖ They bring together, in the most democratic of atmos-
pheres, the groups of people that development patterns have
been separating in recent decades: young and old, white and

black, native and immigrant, millionaire and food stamp recipient, resident and visitor.

❖ They support and save traditional family farms that would have been lost to large, corporate agriculture and rapacious suburban bulldozers. Small farms cannot survive selling to national wholesalers. Seventy percent of Greenmarket farmers in 23 New York City locations, for example, say the market is essential to their survival.

❖ Markets are changing the way America eats, increasingly providing a fresh, unpackaged alternative to the plastic-wrapped fruit and vegetables grown for size, color, and long-distance "truckability." In response to consumer demand registered through the one-on-one relationship between farmer and consumer unique to markets, farmers are increasingly going organic, broadening their produce mix, and expanding their operations.

❖ Thus, markets reflect local character the way no collection of chain stores can. Markets foster the personality of place and they nurture the kind of new growth needed to repair the devastation left by sprawl.

Farmers' markets are probably the most successful tool for the strengthening or regenerating of downtowns of any size, from the smallest Main Street to the most rubble-strewn inner-city commercial center. Aaron Zaretsky, a public market consultant based in Asheville, North Carolina, points out that surveys indicate that many people who go to a mall to shop don't buy anything, and many people who go to markets for other reasons wind up buying. "The pulse of life draws people to markets," notes Zaretsky. "That is what makes them so successful. People are bored with malls. The growth in mall sales has barely kept pace with inflation. Market sales have been growing at 10 to 14 percent a year."

Today, across America, so many markets are taking root, with great success and multiple benefits, that one does not need to go far to find an example from which to learn. Twenty years ago, for example, fewer than 200 farmers' markets existed. From 1994 to 1996, their number increased from 1775 to 2400, a 38 percent increase. Farmers' markets mostly occupy open-air sites on plazas, streets, or parking lots, requiring very little site improvement and financial investment. According to the 1996 USDA Farmers' Market Survey Report, fruit and vegetables alone account for more than $1.1 billion in sales. Markets serve more than a million consumers a week, and 21,000 growers rely on markets.

Markets activate every place they occur. They provide a generic road map to the regeneration of downtowns and reactivation of public places. Markets are the antithesis of Project Plans.

Multiple definitions of markets can be found. The emphasis here is on public markets that primarily, but not exclusively, feature farm-fresh food plus nonfood items. Local variations are endless. Markets defy generic categorizing. Individuality and local personality distinguish each from the other. Like authentic places, no two are alike. Market consultant David O'Neil, who guided Philadelphia's famous Reading Terminal Market to a renewed life in the early 1980s, makes the following distinctions.

Farmers' markets are the most basic and pure, sell farm products directly from the farm, and are mostly in the open air. Simple market sheds provide a roof over a farmers' market, but may be used for other events.

Public markets have an intentional, broader public purpose beyond the commercial function. Stimulating social interaction, fostering new local businesses, preserving historic buildings, stabilizing downtown districts or small commercial neighborhoods, any number of public goals may combine in support of a public market. Public market halls, in which many markets still take place, are old buildings that often evolved at the place where producers came to sell to consumers. Bringing producers and consumers together again is a current public market goal. Public markets function year-round and have a mixture of long-term and day stalls available to producers. Many public markets in market halls include adjacent farmers' markets. The market buildings often house fresh-food vendors, who may buy wholesale. Some markets have existed for long periods, with varying ups and downs. Others are recent creations or a revival of a disappeared market.

Street markets can be a combination or variation of all three. Half sheds coming off the façades of buildings along a whole street cover the sidewalk, creating a shed feeling, as with the classic 9th Street Italian Market in Philadelphia, which runs along six blocks and spills over to neighboring streets. Flea markets, which sell everything from antiques to crafts, or street fairs have proliferated in urban neighborhoods across the country in recent years. Farmers sometimes park their trucks along a street or in a parking lot and sell from the rear.

Each kind of market has its own rules for who can sell what, and these vary according to who runs them. They all can function as economic anchors and activity generators for otherwise desultory public spaces and commercial centers, drawing people downtown who might otherwise not come. Each one is different and cannot be reduced to formula. The scale is human and comfortable. Markets offer an appealing alternative to the increasingly standardized retail landscape and create a tourist attraction, while first and foremost, serving a local clientele and encouraging local entrepreneurs.

Union Square Greenmarket, New York City. Christina Bulich Walsh (left) with her daughter and cousin, are the third generation to run the family farm.

At markets, shopping is an event, not a chore. The scent of the season's freshest fare teases the senses. A melon seller instructs a shopper on how to determine a ripe one. A farmer offers a listener a favorite recipe. Elderly patrons share stories of times past with farmers and offer words of wisdom to young cooks. Business people meet and munch while they walk and talk. People watchers watch. Shoppers sample new produce as they ponder an unresolved menu. Friends meet and mingle, while strangers encounter each other on neutral territory. The multiple levels of activity are endless. A more egalitarian activity center is hard to find.

UNION SQUARE GREENMARKET

New York's Union Square Greenmarket exhibits the most important characteristics of farmers' markets. Even on a rainy July day, Greenmarket customers are there in full force. Corn enthusiasts are peeling back husks to peek at the first local crop of the season. Two elderly women advise a New Jersey farmer about cooking spinach correctly. Several stands are filled with similar assortments of vegetables and fruit, making it difficult to decide where to make a purchase. The cherries are so enticing that a pound to munch on while shopping is irresistible. Fresh-baked breads, cookies, and pies and homemade pretzels test the willpower of a weight watcher. Vendors are eager to engage in conversation. One farmer stands amid an impressive array of garden plants, waiting for inquiries as to which need sun and which prefer shade.

The varieties challenge the shopper who comes with a menu in mind or a thought-out shopping list. Christina Bulich Walsh happily explains the distinctions among the five varieties of mushrooms grown by her family's Catskill farm, noting that Portobellos were added to their crop variety only six years ago due to customer requests. She and 10 of her 11 siblings are the third generation to run the farm. One sister works for a printer in Rhode Island but does the farm's advertising and printing work. The farm was founded by their grandfather as a dairy farm and was taken over and eventually transformed into a year-round mushroom farm by their father and two of his 12 siblings.

Walking through Union Square Park to get to Greenmarket at its northern edge, one can't help but marvel at the mix of people. People who would cross streets to avoid one another share park benches. Some read, others chat, many eat, and all watch each other. Lines of red-shirted children from a day school group file past bench sitters, bringing smiles to many a face.

Union Square once served as New York's answer to London's Hyde Park, the favorite site for political orators and protestors. When 14th Street was still a major retail hub, Union Square's traditional park functions continued. Surrounding retail diminished in direct proportion to the growth of suburban shopping, and Union Square increasingly was taken over by drug dealers, prostitutes, and the homeless. This accounts in part for the considerable skepticism directed at founder Barry Benepe's vision for a farmers' market. His persistence paid off and, in 1976, Greenmarket opened on the northern edge with 15 farmers. Marketers gradually displaced some of the unsavory users, providing the enduring lesson that *the best way to make public spaces safe and appealing is to provide an attractive activity.* Newly convinced, city officials responded with a full redesign and renovation of the park, which today, with a flourishing Greenmarket as its prize attraction, is the valued centerpiece of an entirely renewed neighborhood.

Greenmarket is actually the trademark for what is now a network of 23 farmers' markets scattered around New York City. They attract 200 farmers, and register annual sales of $20 million. Half of that sales total is registered at the Union Square Greenmarket, the only one to function four days a week, attracting 5,000 daily shoppers and 20,000 on a busy Saturday.

Benepe grew up on a farm in Maryland, where he worked part-time alongside his parents. Armed with an M.I.T. architecture degree, Benepe went to work as a town planner in upstate New York and witnessed firsthand the displacement of economically faltering family farms by suburban development. Grasping for a means to keep small farms viable, Benepe, together with Robert Lewis, now chief marketing representative of the New York State Department of Agriculture and Markets, conceived of the farmers' market he called Greenmarket. He overcame an endless array of naysaying "experts" and general skeptics. Community leaders, residents, and merchants worried about traffic, garbage, rats, noise, crime, and competition, but, year by year, most worries have evaporated with the positive impacts and increased retail sales of adjacent businesses. The loudest complaints seem to come from food stores, afraid they will be put out of business. This does not seem to happen. If anything, the existing stores benefit from new consumers.

Fees from farmers support the administration of the Greenmarkets, run by the Council on the Environment of New York City, a privately financed nonprofit organization that operates out of the mayor's office. With a budget of $500,000 a year, or 5 percent of the farmers' gross, Benepe and 18 staff members find the farmers, rent the stalls, check on participating farms to verify that all produce sold is grown by the seller, enforce market regulations, and, when necessary, battle city agencies or City Hall.

The color, activity, sociability, and local economic stimulus Greenmarkets provide to their neighborhoods have come to be expected today. The sustenance given New York and New Jersey farmers is less recognized, but offers a glimpse of the economic impact that extends way beyond the border of any farmers' market. Eighty percent of the Greenmarket farmers depend on it to exist.

For example, in the upstate historic town of Kinderhook, not far from the state capital of Albany and a short drive from the Hudson River, the Samascott farm would have sold its 1000 acres for development if the Greenmarket outlet had not changed the farm's balance sheet. "The impact on the village of what could have been 1000 units of housing would have been devastating," observes Benepe. "It would have changed the nature of the village entirely." Preserving the character of farm "places" is yet another market benefit. Farming is the defining landscape of many regions. These working landscapes appeal to residents, businesses, and visitors, are factored into property values, and are sometimes the only protection against the encroaching look of Anywhere, U.S.A. Their survival is an insurance policy against sprawl.

In Benepe's office is a giant topographical map with blue-tipped pins locating the points of origin for Greenmarket produce. The impact of the market on the farm counties of New York, New Jersey, and Connecticut is clear. Sixteen thousand acres of farmland are represented, grossing more than $4000 an acre of the tilled acreage. Two-thirds of the acreage is in vegetables, and the remainder in orchard fruit. Forest, pasture, and water resources producing syrup, dairy products, meat, and fish are not included, nor are greenhouses. This was Benepe's original dream. Now, experts all over the country acknowledge the significant impact of farm markets on farmland preservation.

"The best part," Benepe adds with a satisfied smile, "is that the children of these farmers are now helping to run the farms or taking over the operation," instead of leaving altogether.

Before Greenmarket served as the catalyst for the rebirth of this neighborhood, no safety-conscious person would walk through Union Square Park. It took a while, but slowly, restaurants started opening around it. Proprietors and chefs found the easy access to farm-fresh products irresistible. The undervalued, underoccupied variety of old commercial and industrial buildings started filling up with new tenants. Young people nested. New and modest-sized businesses found office space. Night life got livelier, the neighborhood more chic. Now, the area is often referred to as the restaurant district because of the proliferation of stylish, popular restaurants in the vicinity. High-fashion and chain store retail have replaced discounters and outlets. Rents and property values have doubled and tripled. Home furnishings, upscale house-wares, books, toys, and sporting goods are now all represented in the neighborhood, an old-fashioned downtown retail mix. But a food identi-ty supersedes the rest, thanks to the market and the stylish restaurants.

Many regeneration stories parallel Greenmarket's. They differ in kind and scale, but illustrate the same regenerative power of markets. "This particular form of commerce has restored the kind of intimate, personal exchange that the city has lost over the years," says William H. Whyte, author of *City: Rediscovering the Center*.

PASCO, WASHINGTON

Pasco, Washington, represents the opposite end of the scale from Union Square. Pasco (population 18,000; regional population 140,000) is simply a

small-town version of the com-mon tale of Main Street's demise across America. Suburban malls opened. Downtown businesses closed. Vacancies multiplied. The number of shoppers dimin-ished. The psychology of fear that follows the loss of pedestri-an activity outpaced actual crime statistics and kept people away. Downtown investment declined. Deterioration contin-ued. All this changed with the opening of a farmers' market, an idea hatched, like so many suc-cess stories, serendipitously.

The Greenmarket in Pasco, Washington, is credited with turning the downtown around.

In 1985, the Pasco Downtown Development Association, started by local businessmen concerned about downtown's future, sponsored the first Cinco de Mayo Festival, inviting area farmers to participate. The fes-tival was so successful that the city agreed to a PDDA proposal for a per-manent market site, designated a city-owned parking lot connected to the main shopping street through a plaza, contributed $45,000 to the construction of a simple but permanent steel shed, and retained the parking function for non-market days. Market days draw 4500 to 6000 people downtown. The simplicity of the steel shed is key.

High design often interferes with simple public functions. Enhancing the activity, not the look, is most important. Markets are relatively easy to set up and low in cost. The most successful are those that start small in the open air. Those that start in fancy sheds are more prone to greater financial difficulties and sometimes fail. Markets are not a built activity. Focusing on a building first or too early often leads to failure.

From the outset, the Pasco market has grown, and with it has come the rebirth of downtown. A second shed was built to accommodate more vendors. The PDDA created a business incubator in a vacant building nearby with room for six businesses. A micro-brewery supplier has succeeded well enough to move out to its own space. A jewelry business has doubled in size and is planning to move out. Two antique shops, a gift business, and a wine and beer store remain and additional entrepreneurs seek entry. The PDDA is now opening a café nearby. Clothing stores exist for the first time in decades. Growth has taken hold. New businesses are emerging out of the market, a renewal of an age-old but timeless economic process, sometimes called "pushcart urbanism."[1] Pasco's traditional Fall Festival has been renamed the Fiery Food Festival in recognition of Pasco's distinction as the largest area grower of chili peppers. Attendance has jumped from 10,000 to 40,000.

An important social goal is being achieved in Pasco as well, which parallels patterns observed in other market successes. The Pasco region is home to strong Black, Latino, and Anglo-American groups. Historically, nothing has overcome the divisions among them. Until the market. This has become the one regular place where they mix and mingle harmoniously.

Across the country, rejuvenation follows markets.

The North Market in the gritty Short North warehouse neighborhood of Columbus, Ohio (where Katherine Glover found the bread man, Dennis Howard and his Pane—An Italian Bakery, for Mansfield) is a market of long standing that has been a central cause for an extraordinary rebirth of its historic district. The original 1876 building burned in the 1940s. The city refused to rebuild, but market merchants financed a new large Quonset hut themselves. The market flourished in spite of the building's notorious flaws. With the market as its anchor and biggest draw, the nearby warehouse neighborhood has been gaining in SoHo-like popularity for years.

In the early 1980s, a citizen preservation group, Friends of North Market, formed to protect the area from city convention center building and area development plans. They formed a nonprofit development authority to take over the market and to plan for its future. The popularity and value of the market had gained citywide recognition, enough

*Although very small in size, the Firehouse Market in
the Cedar Park neighborhood of West Philadelphia
has become a major neighborhood anchor.*

so that the city helped to secure a two-level, turn-of-the-century warehouse for market expansion. National chains generally are not allowed,
and even regional franchises are discouraged. Vendors offer a full array
of specialty foods and, outside, 36 farmers comprise central Ohio's
largest farmers' market.

In the Cedar Park neighborhood of West Philadelphia (population
21,000, average household income $29,000), the Firehouse Market is
housed in an abandoned 1903 red brick firehouse at a central site where
several streets intersect. This modest market has become the anchor for
a mixed-income, racially integrated (86 percent black, 11 percent white)
neighborhood struggling to strengthen itself after decades of financial
and institutional disinvestment. Markets like this need what David O'Neil
calls "the invisible hand of support" to survive. The city-owned abandoned firehouse was provided free, and additional grants and loans were
secured. This was a wise public investment, since the spinoff will be
increased economic and social life for the neighborhood that will
increasingly shift to paying its own way.

The Firehouse is a "basic" model of a farmers' market—one baker,
a tiny restaurant that is more like a small lunch counter, one butcher,
one fishmonger, one produce vendor—all under one small roof. It is
amazing just how much can fit into a small space. The aisles are crowded, the space is dark, no real "design" is apparent, but who cares? It
works. There has been a high turnover here, which O'Neil says is to be
expected in this kind of market. But, he notes, management has been
smart in immediately taking over any failing business as soon as it

closed so as not to give the perception of failure and to keep it alive for a new entrepreneur.

MARKETS SPUR GENUINE GROWTH

Markets provide new local jobs, don't take jobs away from somewhere else, and bring customers to nearby businesses. The multiplier effect is an important economic attribute. Locally-owned businesses generally use area suppliers and spend much of their income in the local economy. Farmer vendors often expand their scope of business—start a catering enterprise, add homemade bottled goods, or diversify their product mix. Restaurants, cooking supply stores, or any number of unpredictable and non-food-related businesses start opening nearby, dependent on the steady and diversified flow of pedestrians from the market.

Arthur Burns, program manager for the USDA Wholesale and Alternative Markets Program, is way ahead of his Washington colleagues in recognizing the multiple values of farmers' markets and advocating, within the government, the nurturing of the market movement as an integral part of national farm policy. At a 1996 public market conference held in Philadelphia, Burns noted that farmers' markets give "business experience to those who have been without it" and help "overcome impediments to entry into a new business." Also important, Burns notes, is that markets provide semiskilled jobs at a time when the national economy is losing those opportunities at an alarming rate.

At the same conference, Philadelphia Mayor Ed Rendell welcomed the 350 visitors from all over the country and abroad and noted that the Reading Terminal Market, the largest indoor market in the country with its 3 million visitors a year, and the Italian Market, a classic street market with hundreds of stalls on sidewalks in front of stores and barely an inch to walk in, are great tourist attractions in Philadelphia. Rendell noted that the Philadelphia Housing Authority was encouraging farmers' markets in its projects to provide access to fresh, healthy food to underserved low-income communities at fair prices. Rendell also observed that Pennsylvania had the third largest number of farmers in the country. Somewhat apologetically, he noted the absence of the "big" farms, but one has to wonder if Pennsylvania's enduring tradition of many farmers' markets is not the reason it still has such a large number of small and medium-sized farms. Small farms, as Aaron Zaretsky also points out, have other advantages. Market farmers can make a living, he says, on 5 acres. Farmers who sell wholesale need big-scale acreage. The difference, Zaretsky adds, is between "product-based" and "community-based" farming.

Farmers' markets have long served a community-building and business-spawning function. A market in the upstate New York city of Ithaca 10 years ago attracted a farm woman, Peggy Kennedy, who worked as a seamstress. Every Saturday, she would bring about 75 articles of clothing to sell, all made from natural sources, such as wool and cotton. Each week, she would sell out. She turned it into a regular business, Angel Heart Design, and started selling in a downtown Ithaca store. Her clothes are now featured in 1700 stores around the country and are made in Ithaca and elsewhere. Also in Ithaca, in the mid-1970s, Penelope Gerhart and her cousin, Frank Kohler, started a business, Brown Cow Farms, selling yogurt she made on the kitchen stove. Gerhart and her husband owned a milk farm and she used only very rich Jersey milk, never homogenized, and used the cream that rose to the top for the yogurt. They took the product to health food stores, but were blocked by the health department for not having a license, so they turned instead to the farmers' market and found a great reception. They went to national food trade shows, found a national food distributor, and within four years, built a $5 million business and sold it some time later. Brown Cow Farms is now a major yogurt producer.

The logic of the market tradition and its economic potential is no less relevant today. It repeats a legitimate and timeless historic process. Countless communities trace their beginnings as marketplace sites. Thus, many Market Streets became main streets.

Public markets were often the centerpiece of urban neighborhoods as well, and many cities had several scattered around. Most neighborhood markets disappeared in the supermarket age of pre-packaged, long-distance goods. When supermarkets abandoned city neighborhoods for the suburbs, no new markets filled the gap. Some survive, however, as economic anchors, to which consumers come from afar. Others are catalysts for renewed growth. As Olney points out, the renaissance of Madison, Wisconsin, is attributed to the revival of the Dane County Market in 1973, which started with five vendors the first year. Some 200 vendors now line the sidewalks surrounding the state capitol at the heart of town, making it the largest open-air market in the Midwest.

Zaretsky cites the City Market in Roanoke, Virginia, as another example of a market that sparked the rebirth of a downtown. Roanoke's abandoned downtown, Zaretsky notes, had been taken over by crime, drugs, homelessness, and other typical downtown ills. Roanoke invested $5 million in infrastructure improvements in and around the market more than a decade ago, and now draws one million visitors a year and anchors a reborn downtown. Farmers line the curb of Market Street under an awning that spans the sidewalk. The historic Roanoke Hotel was restored and reopened. The First Union Bank built a new office tower and credits the regeneration of the market with drawing it back downtown. New local businesses have been opening within the vicinity for years, and there is no reason to expect that process to cease.

East Orange, New Jersey. You're never too old or too young for a farmer's market, probably the most successful tool for strengthening or regenerating downtown.

MARKETS FIT ANY SITE

Markets do not have to occur in a prized setting. They can often fill the neglected nooks and crannies of a place, require minimal site improvements, and, in fact, the battered corners of downtown spaces are often the best, as long as the foot traffic potential is real. In East Orange, New Jersey, for example, the unused, debris-filled space under the railroad trestle in front of City Hall gave birth to a growing multi-ethnic market. That market has now been moved to the front of City Hall on a rebuilt plaza, and has stimulated slow but steady new business growth and business start-ups in the nearby commercial street of this predominantly low-income minority community. Jazz concerts every other week from July through October are giving downtown more of a nighttime draw.

In Santa Fe, the challenge is to preserve what remains of an economy and a place that serves and satisfies a local population, not the tourists or seasonal visitors who have overrun this distinctive Southwestern town. In a parking lot at the railyards a stone's throw from the upscale shopping district, a farmers' market with more than 100 farmers is held three days a week. More than 20 farmers are regularly turned away. They asked for more space to expand. "All they need is a space to park their truck," says architect Steve Robinson, who has been advocating the market's expansion. "They just open the back and sell directly from it," he explains. In such a tourist-dominated place, the market serves both as a community center and a site for local entrepreneurs.

MARKETS SAVE SMALL REGIONAL FARMS

Long-time observers of the growth of farmers' markets date the new momentum to the 1970s, in response to the organic food movement and the increasing demand for field-ripened produce as alternatives to standard supermarket offerings. Remarkably, this movement—and it can be called a movement—is saving family farms in some regions, keeping hundreds of thousands of acres in production that otherwise would not happen, and, in the process, is redirecting, in small and large ways, the country's food supply. To sell wholesale, a farmer needs big acreage. To sell direct, a farmer can make a living on a small farm of five acres.

No big, expensive, disruptive, and lengthy urban renewal project can have as positive an impact, as appropriate in scale, as popular, and be as multidimensional as a successful market. Small change gives people reason to believe bigger, needed change can occur. Farmers' markets start modestly. Small-scale things happen in a short time. They do not interrupt existing economic activity. Invariably, they add to it. Some local merchants fear the competition and complain that market farmers don't pay local taxes. Significantly, merchants adjacent to or near markets report an increase in business on market days.

In some downtowns, and on particular sites in some downtowns, starting a farmers' market is not enough to regenerate local economic activity. In Charlotte, North Carolina, for example, a farmers' market was established in an unused park surrounded mostly by parking lots. The park was mostly unused for two basic reasons. Charlotte is not what one can remotely define as a pedestrian-friendly city. This particular park is not adjacent to anything from or to which someone would walk. To generate new nearby economic activity, a market must be primarily pedestrian-oriented.

Skeptics note, of course, the seasonal nature of most markets. Some function only one day a week. But even if it is a short season or only a few days, markets often get *something* started. And, like the Greenmarkets in New York, they can add days and locations as success builds. One-shot festivals and entertainment events are popular downtown events. They are often promoted as a way of getting people back downtown. They surely do that. No one, however, complains that they last only one day. And unlike one-shot festivals and events, markets animate a place on a regular basis, even if for a short season. The potential for a year-long activity generator is always there.

The seasonal nature of farmers' markets stimulates innovation, reflected in the evolution of year-round markets that offer a variety of goods, services, and entertainment throughout the year. In Roanoke, for example, the market is closed on Sunday, when art exhibits are scheduled instead. Local artists pay a minimal setup fee and gain exposure, recognition, and sales. The art must be original, created from raw materials (no kits), and sold by the creator. Roanoke's City Market is 80 years old and has 50 farmers doing business year-round. Several nearby restaurants started as small food booths and take-out businesses.

Genuine markets should not be confused with festival market-places. This term became widely used, almost generic, following the opening of Faneuil Hall Marketplace. Although Faneuil Hall Marketplace originally had a lot in common with markets described here, it no longer does. Chains dominate. Local businesses, once its backbone, now have a diminished presence. Pushcarts no longer incubate new businesses. The Boston Museum branch has long been replaced by commercial uses. The local feeling of the food court is about all that remains of its original feeling. And because of its convenient proximity to both official and residential neighborhoods, it still attracts local people as well as tourists, because it remains a great public gathering place. The now generic festival marketplaces that proliferated around the country trying to imitate Faneuil Hall Marketplace are malls, not markets. They are controlled by single owners, are rigidly planned down to the last design detail, are structured, predictable, artificial, devoid of surprise, the antithesis of enduring markets. The thoroughly pedestrian nature of Faneuil Hall Marketplace gives it an edge over most festival marketplaces that tried to imitate it, and will probably outsurvive them all because of it. The best thing that can happen— inevitably, in time, it will—is for Faneuil Hall Marketplace again to fill up with locally-owned businesses.

Any place, market or otherwise, that becomes an overly successful tourist attraction will eventually lose its local personality and local appeal. The tourist appeal diminishes eventually too, since local personality is what attracts tourists in the first place. The Westside Market in Cleveland, housed in a huge brick 19th-century Market Hall, is in danger of going this route, but so are a number of the best things happening in downtown Cleveland. The market already is a tourist attraction, with 85 percent of its Saturday customers coming from the suburbs. And although city representatives speak of "seeking a balance" between local and visitor, official city policy seems to be quite content to focus more on tourism and suburban customers than reviving Cleveland for Clevelanders. The adjacent and nearby neighborhoods have become increasingly popular and may help ensure a balance of locals and visitors.

PIKE PLACE PUBLIC MARKET

Markets being transformed by tourism should carefully study Seattle's Pike Place Public Market. *Pike Place Market is the number-one tourist attraction in the state of Washington. The goal of maintaining its local personality and local appeal persists undiminished and is pursued in innovative ways.* It purposely avoids catering to tourists. Yet, they come.

Pike Place Market is probably the most exemplary surviving historic market in the country that was, at one time, slated for destruction. It is in its own class, and while there are lessons to be learned from it, it can not be emulated by every locale. Scenically located high above the Puget Sound embankment, Judith Olney describes it as "probably the most stimulating and sensuously appealing market in America." Thriving in the midst of a hodgepodge of industrial, transportation, residential, business, cultural, and tourist uses, it puts the lie to repeated attempts by city planners to declare certain uses incompatible.

Many markets exhibit the same phenomenon, but none on such a large scale so successfully. If kept urban, if not oriented to cars, and if kept in balance, diversified uses can coexist. "It is a constant struggle to keep that balance," says market director Shelly Yapp. "Farmers shift from vegetables to flowers to dry flowers or from fresh berries to selling jam. The effect of tourism is difficult to control."

Authenticity maintains the market's tourist appeal. No advertising is directed at tourists and $250,000 is spent advertising to local shoppers, emphasizing local themes. No tours are conducted, just market classes giving instruction on selecting and cooking food. A school program for second to fourth graders, "How Does a Market Grow," aims to build local awareness and connections through children. Parking is purposely limited. On-street market district parking has half-hour meters. A half hour of free parking is directed at commuters who need to come in and out quickly on the way home. A "One Mile Market Plan" focuses on the great increase in downtown residents. New residents (names are collected from brokers) get a welcome greeting card from merchants. House parties are held in condominiums and apartment houses featuring market merchants. "We should be their supermarket," says Yapp. "We ask why we aren't and get opinions to learn from."

In fact, the Pike Place Market is a primary reason for the resurgence in downtown residential living over the past 20 years. Other than the gradual rediscovery of the nearby Pioneer Square area in the 1970s, downtown living was more a hallmark of Seattle's past than its present. The extraordinary appeal of the market and the strength of the public fight against its threatened loss was an important catalyst for a revival of downtown living. That is a critical lesson for the many downtowns that typically wiped out so many residential neighborhoods of an earlier era.

URBAN RENEWAL'S DEFEAT, URBAN REBIRTH'S VICTORY

In the 1960s, farmers' markets were in decline everywhere. Suburban growth, supermarket proliferation, refrigeration, the growth of corporate agriculture, and improved long-distance transportation changed how and where Americans shopped for food. Seattle officials saw little future for the market. An urban renewal plan determined that it had outlived its usefulness. This was an urban renewal misjudgment typical of its decade. High-rise apartment houses, a hotel, and a 3000-car garage were scheduled to replace Pike Place.

A group of citizens, led by Victor Steinbrueck, a professor of architecture at the University of Washington, organized the Friends of the Market and led a grass-roots opposition in 1964. By 1971, they forced a Save the Market initiative on the ballot, through which the public chose to retain the prized, but deteriorating, market and to create a seven-acre historic district around it. One can only ponder what other treasured sites, buildings, and uses might have been rescued from the bulldozer had citizen preference been sought. In the course of their five-year struggle, the view of the market as more than a collection of historic buildings and valued uses took hold. The expanded vision celebrated the "social ecology" of the market and valued social interaction over design.

"The farmers are the leading attraction in the market; if they ever leave, the market will truly be dead," Steinbrueck wrote in the introduction to his delightful *Market Sketchbook*, published in 1978 to help bring attention to the market.

Following the grass-roots victory, a complicated organizational structure was established in 1973 to oversee the preservation and restoration of the market and district buildings, to operate them over the long term, and to maintain the expressed public preference for retention of the social and economic mix. Protection of the "social ecology" was paramount. *Where preservation is as much about people as buildings, it succeeds meaningfully. But the approach to preservation that included progressive social values and appreciation of less-than-high-fashion design elements were bold innovations when first incorporated into Pike Place principles.*

The ongoing nature of a Market-supported health clinic, child care center, food bank, and senior citizens' center attests to the compatibility of progressive social policy and consumer capitalism. A day-old-bread outlet occupies prime space, a service appreciated by both low-income and upper-income consumers. Street people are not chased from the vicinity. And a nonprofit development corporation lends new farmers money for equipment, seed, and travel expenses. Old neon signs survive. The 1930s market-green-and-white paint scheme prevails. Some businesses date from the market's 1907 experiment. The original "experiment" was conceived by a city council outraged by high food prices set by controlling middlemen. Upon opening, five farmers drove up the "pike" with their produce, sold out immediately, and the Pike Place Market was on its way to becoming a city institution. The same need exists today.

Fundamentally, not much has changed. Although it keeps up to date and different aspects within the market change, it never strays from its initial principles. "Meet the Producer" and "The Farmer First" remain mottos. Activities dating from the market's inception continue, and many function in the same buildings. Social interaction and local entrepreneurs are given highest consideration. The "utilitarian esthetic" avoids the overdesigned look of the mall. Decorative column capitals, arched windows, brick pavement, flower boxes, and other design details have been retained without added embellishment. But the wealth of visual detail stems from the color, design, and richness of the market's commerce and human interactions, the juxtaposition of different elements, the casual layout and relaxed physical organization that cultivate serendipity, and the marked individualism of the farmers and merchants. Chains are forbidden. One fast-food operation opened on the edge of the historic district and eventually closed. People drawn to markets don't come for the standardized fare they get everywhere else. One Seattle restaurant from elsewhere in the city wanted to open in the market, but had to offer a different menu in order to get approval.

Twenty thousand to 40,000 people a day pass through the market. Nothing, beyond the limited parking, is done for the convenience of the automobile. Consequently, little interferes with the stimulation and excitement of the place. Most visitors enter on foot.

Pike Place is a public market in the broadest sense, with its wide spectrum of diversified social and economic activity. Yet, the food experience is the most distinctive one.

FOOD-BASED PROGRAMS AS BUSINESS INCUBATORS

Food-based businesses have an incalculable appeal and economic potential. They don't need a market connection to be a potent regenerator in a local economy and in a downtown. Poughkeepsie, New York, for example, is a Hudson River city that experienced typical urban decline. Big projects with big budgets poured into Poughkeepsie over decades, each one doing more damage than the last and none fulfilling the promise of "renewal." Judy Schneyer, a young, energetic, highly motivated employee of the Cornell Co-operative Extension Dutchess County, saw an opportunity for innovation that fit no prior model. The result, the Hudson Valley Foodworks, both reflects and nourishes the agricultural region surrounding it. The center provides local farmers with space to produce "value added" products and thereby diversify and add to their farm businesses. Value adding means taking food to the next step, turning apples—a big county crop—into apple sauce, cider, potpourri, and even pies and baked goods for restaurants or bakeries. Canning, in fact, turned out to be a tradition in Poughkeepsie that had disappeared but could be revived. And a major county institution is the Culinary Institute of America, a logical partner.

A downtown business group, Poughkeepsie Partnership, was eager to help and secure government support. With federal community development funds, a vacant Woolworth's was purchased at the neediest end of Main Street with two floors each of 20,000 square feet. Several federally approved kitchens were installed, a bottling and packaging room created, and storage space provided in the basement. Work spaces are rented by the hour or day. Tenants include restaurants that want to merchandise their most popular recipes, caterers, farmers who want to expand their businesses, homemakers, and some larger companies who need packaging help. A street-level retail store is planned to showcase products produced within. This effort is similar to Foodworks in Arcata, California, mentioned in Chapter 2. At Arcata's Foodworks, 15 food processors rent space in a shared facility where refrigeration, shipping space, and a state-of-the-art kitchen are available. A mail-order catalogue and a marketing effort directed at regional food markets assist users in creating outlets for their products. Another Arcata facility, Moonstone, provides a similar stimulus for local resource-based producers, such as furniture makers, potters, and jewelry creators.

FOOD FROM THE 'HOOD

In April, 1992, Crenshaw Boulevard, the commercial spine of South Central Los Angeles, went up in flames, part of what nationally was identified as the L.A. riots. In the Crenshaw district, however, these riots were also identified as "civil unrest" because the target was specifically the commercial corridor and its lack of local ownership and jobs. A few blocks from Crenshaw Boulevard and in an appealing, tranquil-looking neighborhood of modest homes and well-kept lawns, a quarter-acre student-cultivated garden grows on the grounds of Crenshaw High School (3000 students). Flowers, herbs, collard greens, cabbage, lettuce, and more gave birth to a community and entrepreneurial renewal project of unique dimensions. The small garden's vegetable crop and the selling of it at a nearby farmers' market inspired a small group of high school students to initiate an enterprise, Food From the 'Hood, that has changed their lives, the lives of a continuous stream of students, and, in the process, the life of the community. Until then, Crenshaw kids thought a business was something owned by someone else.

The story is best and quite simply told by the marketing brochure, "Great Things Are Growing in South Central L.A.," produced by this student-owned, student-run corporation, in the project's second year.

JUST A LI'L SOMETHING 'BOUT OUR BIZ...

We're Food From the 'Hood, a natural food products company located at Crenshaw High School in South Central Los Angeles.

We got started after the Los Angeles riots, when we turned a weed-infested plot of land at school into the greatest garden in the world. We wanted to do something to help rebuild our community, so at Christmas, we hooked up the needy with some organic veggies 'n stuff.

BUT IT WASN'T JUST THE HOMELESS AND HUNGRY WHO NEEDED OUR FOOD...

Our garden quickly became a popular get-together spot for people looking for quality produce. (There aren't many health food stores in our community.) Today, we sell our produce "straight out 'the garden" and at farmers' markets. And we still donate 25% of what we grow to people who really need it.

BUT WE WANTED OUR COMPANY TO DO EVEN MORE...

We realize that the best thing we can do for our community is get an education. That's why we use company profits to fund college scholarships for our student-owners. Although we make some money from our garden (we made $600 last year), we need to make a lot more if we're going to help send our 39 student-owners to college.

THAT'S WHERE THE SALAD DRESSING COMES IN...

It was a natural fit, really. After all, we grow lettuce, right? So we got together with some friends who know the game of salad dressings and mixed up our favorite herbs (lots of parsley and basil) to create our Straight Out 'the Garden Creamy Italian Dressing...It's all natural. The taste is kickin'. And the packaging is bumpin'.

Although the ingredients for the salad dressing do not come directly from the student garden, the inspiration came from the lettuce and herbs grown there. The recipe, basically created by a professional volunteer, was developed with the students.

A drive down Crenshaw Boulevard, with its chain stores and absentee owners, leaves no question why neighborhood youth would never dream of an entrepreneurial opportunity within their grasp. Paradoxically, the residential neighborhood surrounding the high school is a gem of a community—a neat, clean, and well-tended assortment of classic, 1940s Los Angeles houses. Enormous palm trees line the sidewalked streets. Driveways sit to the side of the modest houses set back from the street just far enough to create modest lawns. Each one looks as well cared for as the next, and few houses look neglected. The image contrasts sharply with news photos of the riots. The high school looks no different from most early suburban multilevel high schools surrounded by plenty of green, particularly the large sports fields. The national impression of

South Central leaves no room for such positive images and, surely, all of South Central does not look like this. But seeing it underscores the idea that the riots were as much about business ownership and entrepreneurial opportunity as about food, shelter, and jobs.

Crenshaw science teacher Tammy Bird gave the first adult leadership to Food From The 'Hood, but the student-run corporation evolved step by step from the ideas of the first class of 40 students. (The student-owner number is kept close to 40, with a quarter of the company graduating every year and being replaced by new student owners.) Former marketing consultant Melinda McMullen signed on as volunteer, and a series of professionals subsequently volunteered the necessary expertise. Modest start-up grants came from the city, Rebuild LA, and other foundations.

Ben Osborne, then a 16-year-old Crenshaw student who went on to Howard University, designed the label for the salad dressing, depicting a blossoming garden in the inner city. The kids work in teams, rotating through various responsibilities, from office work to weeding, gaining from the full experience. Profits are divided according to the number of hours worked, academic performance, and time spent on college-preparatory work and tutoring one another. The company meets weekly and decisions are reached by a vote.

From the beginning, the students did their own market research, learned what went into marketing a product, and, although professionally advised, went to meetings in person to pitch their product. Before long, 2000 natural product stores carried the salad dressing, nearly every supermarket in southern Los Angeles, and by 1996, the dressing was sold in 23 states. By 1997, the dressing was marketed to supermarkets nationwide. The $600 profit of the first year grew to $42,000 in 1995 and $32,000 in 1996. (The $10,000 drop was the amount the students invested in developing a new no-fat honey mustard product.) More than 40 students are on scholarships because of this operation. Students from the next class replace graduates, assuring a continuous benefit for new students.

The gains from this project are immeasurable. McMullen recalls the group's first visit to the farmers' market, where the students were looked at warily by white shoppers. "The kids thought they were jerks. The shoppers thought the kids were thugs. Finally, a kid said, 'Somebody has to have an attitude change.' When the ice melted, we became the hottest thing at the market."

None of these kids fit the perception, born out of distance, separation, and ignorance, of "inner city" youth. McMullen often reminds people that "it's not that the kids are special. It's that they've had the opportunity to do something special and they now know that if they work hard, they can achieve a goal." Food from the 'Hood defines the kind of self-help program that, over time, will produce new entrepreneurs, new enterprises, and new jobs. Markets are perfectly suited to nurture such activity.

ALL MARKETS CAN BE ECONOMIC GENERATORS

Markets other than food-based ones also can be significant economic generators.

In New York City, for example, an open-air Saturday flea market/ antiques fair has been ongoing for years in a parking lot at Sixth Avenue and 25th Street, a once-thriving manufacturing neighborhood that has seen manufacturing spaces converted to residence and offices in recent years and empty landmark-quality 19th-century department store buildings reoccupied by large retailers, as noted in the last chapter. Well-run, regular flea markets draw many people.

The presence of the 25th Street Antiques Market has given birth to a new antiques district, with nearby buildings now occupied by dozens of antique dealers where they never were before. With the changing real estate market, that parking lot will undoubtedly be occupied by a new building someday soon, but in the meantime, it has given birth to a new business district that had not been there before. Specialty markets can function in this way in many places.

Another New York market illustrates the unpredictability of urban growth. In midsummer, 1994 Mayor Rudolph Giuliani consented to demands of Harlem's 125th Street merchants and community leaders to remove hundreds of unlicensed street vendors, who, they claimed, were creating a "pedestrian hazard." This was an embattled issue. Pushcarts are, after all, an American tradition from which some of our biggest corporations grew. Many were quite popular on 125th Street. Some sold unique, hand-crafted items. But there were just too many. And the voices of protest were powerful.

A "temporary" relocation site was found, nine blocks south on an isolated, vacant city-owned lot at 116th Street and Lenox Avenue. Coincidentally, the lot is across the street from the Masjid Malcolm Shabazz, the mosque of the late Malcolm X and the anchor for this corner of Harlem for more than half a century. Under a contract with the city, the head of the mosque, the imam, agreed that the mosque would manage the open-air market. The city underwrote a repaving of the lot, new signage, and the bringing in of utilities. The vendors, mostly of crafts, clothing, and jewelry, pay $8 a day for a table.

The market opened in October 1994, and took a while to take hold. Many expected failure and, in fact, numerous vendors went elsewhere or nowhere. In two years, however, the seven-day market has evolved into a real attraction for both local people and tourists (25 tour buses weekly) with some of the 200 vendors heading for the next stage of business, a storefront. Plans are to improve the site further as a permanent market.

An unusual relationship has evolved, initiated by state officials, between the Harlem group and an Orthodox Jewish business group from Brooklyn. The Brooklyn group, with its history of small merchants evolving into larger businesses, is giving technical assistance and entrepreneurial training to the Harlem vendors, assisting the process of advancing market vendors to storefront merchants. Within two years, 20 vendors have moved from the market to nearby storefronts.

Another group of the dislocated 125th Street vendors was invited to set up shop in the Jamaica Market, a new Victorian-style market building in the heart of the Jamaica section of the borough of Queens. A food court with multi-ethnic offerings is already drawing customers. Market managers had been trying to foster more small entrepreneurs with specialized merchandise. The African import nature of many of the vendors is filling that bill and increasing the customer base steadily. The market is a community resource that has been growing in popularity slowly but surely as customers come from further areas around the city.

SMALL FAILURES, SMALL IMPACTS

Perhaps the most appealing and useful feature of public markets is the manageable dimensions of their failures. Every market is witness to a steady stream of entrepreneurial failures. Often, they are barely noticeable to the consumer and have little negative psychological or economic impact on surrounding vendors, unless their failure marks the beginning of a trend. What a novelty! When a corporate headquarters or an entire large business moves out of most downtowns, the occurrence reverberates negatively throughout the community, regardless of the size of place. Enormous publicly-funded projects fail to spark any sustainable economic growth, unless you consider further enormously publicly-funded large projects an acceptable spinoff. Worse than not delivering on their articulated goal of "downtown revitalization," many convention centers, stadiums, festival marketplaces, and entertainment complexes need a large, continuous flow of public funds to support their operation.

Public markets, on the other hand, offer the greatest return on the public dollar spent and lead to more genuine capitalistic, free-market activity than any big publicly-sponsored project. Further, markets don't promise more than they can deliver. A true public market emphasizing local food products, small local businesses, and public goals doesn't make big money. Its role as entrepreneurial catalyst and activity generator is a greater compensation than money. Nothing can be more important than regenerating the local economy.

The scale of public markets keeps the impact of any failures to a minimum. Small vendor space limits vendor growth or failure. A business born in the market must leave to continue to grow. Once it leaves, it is on its own. If a whole market fails, or even if it just stagnates, it takes nothing away from its surrounding neighborhood. Many districts have been undermined, but not killed, with the loss of their market. More, of course, have thrived with a market's growth and vitality.

The external scale of a public market, perhaps best of all, fosters the pedestrian use, civic intercourse, entrepreneurial nourishment, and serendipitous activity that must exist in a thriving downtown. Markets are as much about people as about produce, about reconnecting the larger social and economic fabric of the country pulled apart thread by thread during the past 50 years of highway building and social atomization.

Good things are possible without markets. Better things are assured with them.

[1.] See "Pushcart Urbanism," *The Living City*, p. 324.

DOWNTOWN ESSENTIALS

Warren County Courthouse, Warren, Ohio—
a downtown essential kept downtown.

CHAPTER TEN

PUBLIC BUILDINGS, PUBLIC POLICIES

When I was growing up, Ocala—located in North Central Florida—had a population of about 20,000. Most town activities took place in or around the courthouse square. The courthouse square was just what its name implied. A square in the midst of which stood the county courthouse. It was typically monumental looking, with a clock at its top. Surrounding the courthouse was a lawn planted with beautiful live oak and magnolia trees, palms, and azalea bushes. There were benches for passing the time of day with fellow townspeople. On the streets bordering the square were all the town's shops. Ocala was a town with a center, and that center was the court-house square.

More and more people came to discover Ocala and its gentle, friendly ways, and the town began to grow. Pretty soon, the courthouse was deemed inadequate and parking around it was simply not enough. Besides, its streets were too narrow and traffic was awful. The solution? The courthouse was razed—a new one built out on the highway. The square became a parking lot and the streets bordering it were widened.

Before long, "new is better" became the town's de facto motto. The post office—which looked a lot like the old courthouse—was the next to fall. Then, the pretty red brick public library, then the old hotel with its wide veranda across from the square. The shops soon followed—relocating in the many new shopping centers springing up in all directions.

Today, Ocala is much larger—being the hub of the third fastest growing area of the nation—but it is no longer a town with a center. It is a mass of gas stations, fast-food restaurants, and shopping strips. Old-timers speak of the old courthouse with fondness, and, lately, there has been some effort to save some of the Victorian homes in the neighborhoods.

Barbara S. Wright, then staff director for contributions at New York Telephone Company, told this story some years ago to a statewide conference of the Preservation League of New York State. She was hoping that conference participants from around the state would take heed of "the lesson learned too late" for her home town but not too late for those willing to work hard to prevent the same from happening in their communities.

But many of the attending preservationists did not then, and still don't, understand the profound significance of the phenomenon Wright reported. And, surely, the scores of people who regard historic preservation as a cultural luxury understand even less why Wright's story spotlights a serious American problem. *We fail to recognize the essentials that make up a downtown, that generate critical activity, the separate and distinct parts that together make a whole. We further fail to recognize that when you start removing them, one by one, small nibble by big bite, maintaining the downtown, sustaining a local economy, and retaining the center becomes difficult, if not impossible.* As important as essentials are, however, a few without context won't do. Landmarks or essential uses must have a variety of buildings and uses in between to fill out a functioning place.

This is not about historic preservation, although many of these buildings are often architecturally and culturally significant and worthy of survival as singular buildings. *This is about the public and private uses, the economic energy, the social and physical connections that form a downtown.* This is about the threads that tie a community together into a fabric of strong connections. The losses Wright was describing were of the crucial anchors to any downtown, what we call *downtown essentials*, the basics of a functional place. The placement of these essentials within close proximity of each other—a courthouse, post office, library, educational institution, hotel, theater, and stores—was not a plan designed by a trained professional of any kind. The placement evolved because of the pure logic of function and place.

Nowadays, all sorts of rationalizations are concocted by multi-degreed professionals, usually Project Planners of one kind or another, together with public officials and private investors with a new development agenda, as to why this arrangement is no longer necessary or appropriate, why the public desire for it is wistful nostalgia, why life is just different from what it used to be. They are, quite simply, wrong. Time and life have changed a lot of things. But they have not altered the basic logic of communal life and the connections needed by active, productive places.

This is not a choice between growth and quality of life, growth and historic preservation or growth and aesthetics. This is a choice between death and life. Economic vitality, growth as some would call it, and quality of life, historic preservation, and aesthetics all go hand in hand. This is the most important lesson exhibited in the downtown rebirth stories told in this book.

The value of downtown essentials is not easily assessed because the activity they generate is not neatly defined or measured. Essentials don't have a clear price tag. They cannot be quantified and packaged for lenders. A library or post office serves local businesses, stimulates the exchange of ideas, provides the social glue that helps to make residents part of a community, and adds to the activity of the public realm. This value eludes measurement. Yet, it is critical.

Essentials anchor the civic society of a downtown in the same way department stores anchor a retail district. But unlike civic centers, entertainment centers, cultural centers, and shopping centers, these individual anchors work as integral pieces of a whole place, not separate from it. They don't draw away from their surroundings, but weave into it. They are part of the ordinary workaday life and fabric of a place. Most importantly, they generate activity and diversity.

The importance to downtown of the essentials described here is underscored by the attempt to lure them to the enclosed arena of the shopping mall. "Battling outlet centers, Main Street revivals, catalogs, and all the Internet hype, regional malls are attempting to reposition themselves as America's town center," wrote Sharon Edelson in *Women's Wear Daily* (May 8, 1996). The country, experts agree, is over-malled. They can't survive "as mere shrines to consumerism," Edelson adds.

The movable essentials are the battleground of the next several decades. Downtown survival and rebirth depend on the continued or renewed traditional location of essentials at the center of a community. It is hard to believe what is already heading to the mall. The East Towne Mall in Knoxville, Tennessee, Edelson reports, has a chapel, a county clerk, and photography studio *with a 7,500-square-foot City Hall on the way.*

Sadly, one of the most destructive forces undermining downtowns has been both the movement of government buildings out of town for automobile convenience, and the demolition of downtown buildings adjacent to or near government buildings for creation of parking lots. The downtowns where this has either not happened or has recently been reversed are the downtowns in the best position to witness renewed strength in the coming years. If downtown is still home to what Donovan Rypkema calls "the institutional leadership of the community—local government, financial institutions, leading law firms, the newspapers, and others," it has a present on which to build a future.

THE POST OFFICE

A post office that residents, business people, downtown workers, and shoppers can walk to is an incalculable economic and social asset for downtown. A downtown business location increases in appeal with the variety of services available in close proximity. The post office, for some, is one of the most important services, along with banks, eateries, government offices, and office supply stores. The farther away from downtown such activities move, the more sprawl is encouraged and downtown undermined.

Downtown post offices are one of the most reliable community gathering spots, where business people and residents, young and old, visitor and native meet serendipitously. In small towns, it is a meeting place, like the barbershop, local diner, or general store. Friends meet. Commerce takes place. In 1994, *The Portland Press Herald* in Maine inaugurated a new feature called "City Life," meant to "provide an occasional glimpse into the unique aspects of urban Maine." One of its first columns spotlighted a Portland postal substation run by a husband-and-wife team with "a mixture of Maine cordiality and Yankee efficiency." As important as selling stamps and other postal services was the "dispensing of advice, gossip, and community news." The meeting place and sociability functions make the post office critical for community centers. It is often the most important anchor of a business district.

Essential to any downtown as a post office is, it is the government use most frequently wrenched out of downtowns. The impact is gaining national attention, from regional press stories to "CBS This Morning" and National Public Radio. Often, the announcement of a post office move comes quickly, by surprise, and without much opportunity for the locality to offer alternatives. A *Time* article ("It Breaks a Village," February 24, 1997) focused on the small town of Livingston, Montana, where the proposed removal of the post office could be a downtown death blow. "Those people [post office officials] gave us more say on whether the Elvis stamp would show the new Elvis or the old Elvis than they did on the future of our town," one resident told reporter Walter Kirn.

Unquestionably, the business of delivering the mail has changed radically since downtown post offices were built. Not surprisingly, the major shift paralleled transportation changes. Until the mid-1960s, most mail was shipped by railroad and sorted in mail cars en route. Upon arrival, mail was almost ready for delivery. Now, most mail is transported by air and by enormous trucks that have difficulty navigating any road narrower than an arterial, and certainly cannot easily maneuver downtown streets. Sorting does not begin until arrival at the post office, requiring sizable spaces for requisite equipment and work room. In 1995 alone, the U.S. Postal Service closed 239 facilities in 28 states. In the 1980s, the yearly closing average was between 150 to 180.

Writing about the "impersonal facility...laid out more for truck access and mail-sorting efficiency than for pedestrian comfort and for neighborly meeting and greeting," Philip Langdon noted:

The Postal Service has abandoned its historic role as architectural benefactor. No longer can you count on the Postal Service to provide buildings that elevate public life. Unlike distinctive, well crafted older Post Offices that added to the attractiveness of traditional Main Streets, new postal facilities tend to be uninspiring standard design.[1]

Handicapped access, increased space needs, parking requirements, and truck access are additional reasons offered for needing to vacate existing postal facilities and build new ones. Often, however, the most important factors include the inclination and personal preference of the regional postmaster, the involvement of a local developer, and the local political pressures favoring a move. Opposition to such short-sighted moves needs to be well-organized, broad-based, and early as possible. The location of a post office is more than a business and real estate decision.

Pine Plains, New York, a small rural village in the Hudson Valley barely holding its modest retail base, missed an opportunity to strengthen its downtown with a post office expansion. For decades, a two-story clapboard commercial building with big glass display windows on the front housed the post office, ideally located in the very center of town. Increased space was needed. Less than a half block away from the existing post office was ample room for an annex. The post office would have gained needed space and a void in the center of town would have been filled, adding strength to the core. Shoppers would have been able to walk from one store to another, eliminating the need for extra car trips and unneeded traffic. A real estate developer presented the post office with the opportunity to be part of a new commercial complex. Village officials could not resist. Although the post office is near the center, it is now just far enough away to be out of walking distance.

The threat to close the 1924 Five Points post office in Franklin, Tennessee, brought national attention to the downtown post office issue. The modest one-story brick building sits on a uniquely shaped trapezoidal corner in the heart of downtown. Franklin is an intact, tree-lined small town a short distance south of Nashville, with a classic variety of restored and well-occupied downtown commercial buildings and an effective historic preservation community. When a plan was announced in 1990 to move the post office out of town, a citizen effort, including petitions with 9000 signatures, took the post office by surprise. Among the most vociferous were the elderly, who depended on the post office being within walking convenience. The elderly testified that many don't drive, and those who do fear venturing out onto the interstate.

With the help of the National Trust for Historic Preservation[2] in Washington and a local Main Street program, the post office was persuaded to develop a new solution. The Postal Service contracted with a private provider to retain downtown service with mailboxes, window services, and stamp selling. This is believed to be the first time the Postal Service was persuaded to keep this activity downtown *and* do it in an historic building. Retaining some, if not all, postal activity downtown is now a spreading arrangement.

The threat of the disappearing downtown post office is one of the most frequent dilemmas for which localities seek help from the National Main Street Center. If some measure of postal activity cannot be retained in the historic building, the next best thing is a new use that generates activity comparable to the lost post office. Charlottesville, Virginia, turned its abandoned post office into a new central library. In a different twist, Culpeper, Virginia, converted a former department store into a post office. In Meadville, Pennsylvania, a vacated post office was turned into a dental office. Similarly, in White River Junction, Vermont, the former post office is a medical office building with doctors, dentists, and related professionals. Across the street is a storefront postal service, similar to the small one described in the Maine article cited earlier.

"In cities and towns from Maine to Wyoming, the story is the same: remote, often arrogant Postal Service officials swoop down to summarily relocate what to many heartland residents is the secular equivalent of steepled white chapels," Walter Kirn wrote.

LIBRARIES

New York City's main library at 42nd Street, the 1911 gem designed by Carrére and Hastings, is legendary as an anchor for downtown activity. One of the city's most treasured resources, the main library is a model gathering place, with exemplary programs of exhibitions and lectures. The appeal of what's inside is obvious, but the attraction of what's outside is a lesson on how to design a spontaneously lively public space.

All kinds of street theater, casual and formal meetings among people seated on the front steps, lunch eaters, and people watchers are observable on the

The steps of New York City's main library at Fifth Avenue and 42nd Street, a natural gathering place.

majestic stairway of the Fifth Avenue entrance. The Library is probably the most enduring activity anchor on 42nd Street. Even when the street was at its lowest, the Library assuaged the decline and never lost its position as a bright spot, though diminished for a while. The Library began a rebound ahead of all else and, in fact, helped bring the rest of the fabled street along. Andrew Heiskel, the Library's then-chairman of the board, added Bryant Park (located immediately behind the Library) to the Library's focus in an effort to strengthen the Library. One of the most successful reclaimed parks is the result, as noted earlier.

But the Library's usefulness at stimulating activity on the street has expanded in recent years, as it opened the Mid-Manhattan Branch across Fifth Avenue at 40th Street, in the former Arnold Constable clothing store, that includes a Library Shop, attracting pedestrian customers. Equally significant is the renovation and conversion of the former B. Altman's department store, the 19th-century landmark at Fifth Avenue and 34th Street. A newly created Science, Industry, and Business Library is now housed at the 34th Street site, along with Oxford Press and assorted offices.

In recent years, the Library has focused on upgrading its branch libraries, which are important neighborhood anchors. An "Adopt-A-Branch" program matches private donors with public funds to restore local libraries and has succeeded in doing so in a number of neighborhoods around the city so far.

Libraries can be significant catalysts for rebirth in the most seemingly hopeless communities. Such communities watch in horror the demolition of deteriorated but useful buildings that, in other neighborhoods, would be restored and reused gems. Chicago seems to be on a fast track to demolish neighborhood homes that could be productively reused, displacing long-term residents. Occasionally, grass-roots groups succeed in blocking such negative moves. Bronzeville, birthplace of Chicago-style blues, jazz, and gospel, is the heart of Chicago's South Side. Thriving black-owned businesses and banks once dominated. What a wasted resource! Here, a modest three-story 1930s commercial building, once the home of the famous black-owned newspaper, *The Chicago Bee*, stood empty for years. A few small commercial buildings stand on either side, but mostly it is surrounded by rubble.

Directly across the street is Stateway Gardens, one high-rise apartment house in the middle of the 40 blocks of lookalike public housing projects, that runs north to south on Chicago's South Side. Each has its own name, the Robert Taylor Houses being the best known. For years, residents of Stateway Gardens watched their once-thriving black neighborhood, Bronzeville (also known as Black Metropolis), fall victim to the forces of urban renewal, highway building, redlining, and assorted project building.

Bronzeville, once a place of economic opportunity, had a large, economically vital commercial center, filled with the same kind of black-owned businesses and residential neighborhoods once found in most black urban districts. After World War II, these districts began to weaken as people moved up and out, in a fashion that paralleled the rest of urban America. More of these neighborhoods, however, were systematically bulldozed than anywhere else. Redlining and the withdrawal of credit by financial institutions followed the transfer of businesses and property from white to black ownership. The exodus of businesses and capital cannot be separated from issues of racism. Government quickly followed the exodus. Decay accelerated. No tools or capital existed to reverse it. Piece by piece, the Stateway Gardens residents saw the businesses and residential buildings lining adjacent blocks demolished. Now, blocks and blocks of empty land await the next generation of overscaled, inappropriate visions, while small efforts struggle to retain and rebuild on the scattered pieces that remain.

Stateway Gardens residents had cleaned out the Bee Building, protected it from demolition, and initiated a campaign to save it. It was a diamond in the rough, to be sure. A few years ago, the city moved to demolish this damaged but intact gem. So much of this neighborhood had already been gratuitously demolished. The Stateway Gardens tenant association, led by its president of 15 years, Charles E. Reynolds, sprang into action.

They protested at City Hall, mobilized their political leaders, reiterated their need and expectation for a library and after-school educational center. The Bee Building, with its green-glazed terra cotta façade, large street-level storefront windows, and appealing Art Deco ornamentation, was perfect for the purpose. The ground floor of the apartment building had a tenant-run computer room and education center. More space was needed. Residents desperately wanted a real branch library, as well. They gained the outside support of such prestigious institutions as the National Trust for Historic Preservation and the Local Initiative Support Corporation. The city relented and eventually became an enthusiastic partner.

The Bee Branch Library and learning center now exist in the restored historic building and no better example illustrates the importance of a library as a gathering place, a community center. The facility is used by both children and adults for storytelling and learning programs of all kinds. The façade of the building sparkles.

Equally significantly, the Bee Branch Library is one of a half-dozen or so remaining Bronzeville landmarks used as starting points for the rebuilding of this sizable, historically significant, and potentially vibrant community. The grass-roots efforts are focusing on a few projects to contain basic downtown activity. The 1915 8th Regiment was home to the black-commanded Illinois National Guard Regiment, the site of great entertainers like Benny Goodman, and the social and political hub of the community. It is being restored as the city's first high school ROTC academy and the country's first black military museum. A three-story former bank building located on a central corner will house offices for local businesses and streetlevel retail.

Such projects generate the kind of activity on which downtowns can be rebuilt, step by step. And they are designated to occur in historic landmarks that will celebrate the history that has been undervalued. Highlighting that history reminds us of values lost and generates hope and confidence in future possibilities. The Bee Branch Library was the community's first hard-won success. Surely, it is just a beginning.

Big, new, or renovated center city libraries in downtown business districts attract more people and create new activity.

Virginian-Pilot reporter Alex Marshall, writing about the Norfolk, Virginia, debate on whether to move the central library to an auto-convenient site out of town, noted that some officials viewed the possible move as being "akin to relocating City Hall...It would acknowledge that the center of the city no longer resides downtown. It also would eliminate the opportunity to have an improved library contribute to downtown revitalization." Financially strained Norfolk, Marshall noted, had given more support to such project plans as the

Top: The Bee Branch Library is a faithfully restored, well-used community facility in the heart of Chicago's Bronzeville.

Above: No better example illustrates the importance of a library as a gathering place. The reflection in the window is that of the apartment houses directly across the street. (L to R) Harold Lucas, Henry Jackson, Charles Reynolds, and neighborhood kids.

downtown enclosed mall, MacArthur Center; to the performance center, Chrysler Hall; and to Nauticus, a cross between a theme park and a museum of the sea on a Norfolk pier.

"Nauticus, which cost $52 million to build," Marshall wrote, "and is a key component of the city's efforts to revitalize downtown Norfolk, draws 3000 to 4000 people to the waterfront on a good weekend. Virginia Beach's central library, which cost that city $7 million, on a good weekend draws twice that number to a strip shopping center district."

Libraries are important anchors both to a downtown and to a neighborhood center. Historically, libraries and early museums used to be part of City Hall. Now, they are cultural institutions in their own right, but should function as an integral component of a civic heart, not separate or removed from it.[3] Mayor Joseph Reilly of Charleston, South Carolina, proudly points out that the city gave land to house a new library and school board. The downtown location, Reilly notes, is important not just for the apparent downtown essential reasons, but to guarantee that such a picture-postcard city like Charleston remains a real place, as important for the Charleston resident as it is attractive to the tourist. In Burlington, Iowa, an 1880s Victorian sandstone library was sensitively added onto in 1989 in order to keep it downtown. Seven years later, further expansion was needed. With no room left on the site, a new building was judged to be needed, but the site would still be downtown.

COURTHOUSES

Downtown library fights seem easier to win than struggles to retain post offices, probably because the controlling government body is closer to home. Local agencies are perfectly capable of enlightened policies sensitive to the issues basic to downtown strength and community building. Often, it takes a local fight to accomplish the task. Sometimes, local officials need little prompting.

Many of the country's banal modern courthouses resulted from demands for interior advantages by judges with no interest in the exterior quality and public face or in the impact on the surrounding place. Warren, Ohio, is the antithesis, a win-win situation for everyone. (See illustration at beginning of chapter.) Warren, a northeast Ohio town of 52,000 between Cleveland and Youngstown, has the kind of downtown Ocala, Florida, once had. At the center is a town square, a mixture of green grass, trees, benches, a fountain, and a gazebo where a band plays on Friday afternoons in warm weather. On two sides of the square is a typically broad assortment of small, locally-owned stores, meeting resident needs, and a small hotel. Above some stores are recently created apartments, which are increasingly in demand. The third side of the square faces a small park that slopes down to the Mahoning River. And on the fourth side are government buildings, a county administration building, a jail, and the Trumbull County Law Library.

In the middle of the square sits the 1897 Trumbull County Courthouse, a massive Romanesque sandstone building with turrets, finials, a central dome, gables, arched windows, and a copper roof. This castle-like structure exudes a message of civic pride and government presence. The three-story courthouse contains five courtrooms, related offices, and support agencies. A few years ago, the state fire marshal declared the building in violation of every current code. But to the mayor and three county commissioners, this courthouse defined their community. Furthermore, to replace it in kind, they learned, would cost $50 million to $75 million.

Although everyone needed more space, a universal truth when it comes to government buildings, the judges and court staff all felt that keeping the courthouse as a courthouse and keeping it downtown was more important than the extra space. Faced with this challenge, the architects, van Dijk, Pace, Westlake & Partners from Cleveland, found new ways to be creative within the existing space. (Some of the most creative architecture comes out of these kinds of restraints.) The complete restoration and upgrading cost $8 million, included replacing 38 window air conditioners with a central system, and kept this important civic activity in the center of town. The support of the community was overwhelming, and the three county commissioners voted to impose a three-quarters percent sales tax on all products sold in the county in order to pay for the restoration and retention of the courthouse.

The law library was created with the same tax funding. The law library building is in the former Warren County Public Library, a Carnegie Library building, built in 1904. Unfortunately, when the public library needed more space, it was moved a half mile out of town into a new building. The library building was then cut up into a maze of offices and courts, primarily a juvenile detention center. To create the law library, the dry walls were removed, the plywood taken down from the stained glass skylight, and original ornamentation restored. And while the public library is no longer downtown, a combination of activity-generating uses (including a specialized library) fulfills the critical need for a civic anchor.

The jail, completed in 1997, was designed by the V Group of Cleveland to be compatible with the courthouse. Now, the 1960s pre-cast concrete county administration building located next to the jail is being redesigned to have a brick façade and reproportioned windows. "We're now fitting all the pieces of the puzzle together," says County Commissioner Michael J. O'Brien.[4]

INFRASTRUCTURE AND PUBLIC POLICY

Previous chapters have highlighted many shortsighted public policies that eroded the infrastructure of downtowns over the past several decades. The basic infrastructure in most downtowns, however, still exists. Repair of damage caused by vehicular-focused development is essential. As made clear earlier, cars are important to downtown, *but* people must come before cars. This sounds easy, but in most downtowns, the most power rests with the transportation department and its engineers. Road projects should no longer be sacred. Here, again, our earlier suggestion for the new profession of pedestrian facilitator is applicable. Every downtown should have one, someone who will both advocate pedestrian issues and critique car-facilitating proposals that diminish the walking experience. Facilitating activity in town is more important than facilitating traffic flow through town.

With this in mind, here are a few "people first" infrastructure essentials. A strong, repaired if needed, grid reflecting the downtown's traditional layout. Downtown grids vary, but their logic and form should be the starting point for the shape and character of the community. And, as transportation engineer Walter Kulash has shown, even traffic can be managed better with a traditional grid.

Undo one-way traffic, as much as possible. Two-way traffic makes getting around *in* town easier. Traffic is only sometimes slowed. Slower, two-way traffic at least doubles the number of people passing by local businesses. On-street parking, landscaped medians, traffic lights, generous sidewalks, sidewalk amenities—all these have been highlighted earlier. Infrastructure improvements should focus on reducing automobile travel needs.

Banish suburban, especially mall, parking standards from downtown. (The mall standard requires 5–6 spaces per 1,000 square feet of leasable area.) Mall parking facilities are built to accommodate the needs of the once-a-year Christmas season, and stand substantially empty the rest of the year. Downtowns cannot afford that and don't require it anyway. Everyone has to drive to a mall. Not true for downtown shoppers. Many are already downtown, working, living, and taking care of non-shopping business. Many walk to their destinations. Others arrive by car for another purpose and are already parked. Still others, if lucky, reach downtown by public transit. Main Street Center studies indicate that 30 percent to 40 percent of a downtown's retail customers already live or work there.

The Randolph-Wabash Self Park, in Chicago, contains retail stores at the ground level, providing income for the garage and allowing a shopping street to remain uninterrupted. Photo: Lucien Lagrange & Associates, Ltd., Chicago, Illinois.

Suspend the absurd, space-consuming, and destructive parking requirements for new or expanded development or businesses. The little bakery on the historic Main Street in Fairfax City, Virginia, seeking to put one table and two chairs out front should not have to create two new parking spaces because the move is defined under the zoning as an expansion of use. Too many downtowns have holes in their streetwall like missing teeth because perfectly functional buildings have been demolished for parking. Providence, Rhode Island, wisely exempts restored properties from parking requirements.[5] Chicago requires ground-floor retail for new parking garages, a critical requirement to ensure continuity of street activity.

However, such a policy, a tough battle in Chicago and elsewhere, should not unleash a proliferation of parking garages that both takes up otherwise productive downtown space and encourages excessive traffic. Less available parking encourages transit use. More available parking encourages automobile use. Ground-floor garage retail, in some areas now so unattractive to retail, may require below-market rents as part of the permit. Support for public transit infrastructure should replace parking requirements. This is getting back to basics in the most fundamental way. In traditional downtowns, walking once was assumed to be a form of mobility. It should be again.

A McDonald's, suburban style, on Main Street, downtown Houston, Texas. Photo: Kevin Milstead.

Reform parking policies, as well, for downtown residential neighborhoods, especially those close to commercial centers. Neighborhood streets should not be parking lots for commuters. If parking is easy, demand for transit doesn't have much chance. Local residents and business owners should have permit-only on-street parking privileges denied to visitors. Cities, such as Cambridge, Massachusetts, and New Haven, Connecticut, issue neighborhood parking permits, precluding the visitor influx that comes with university locations.

Other basics of a traditional downtown should be valued again:

❖ Short, rather than long, blocks.
❖ A consistent street wall, without buildings set back behind underused plazas.
❖ No curb cuts for businesses with parking in the front. A drive-in McDonald's on Houston's Main Street is one of the more ludicrous downtown uses we've seen. Curb cuts are unsafe for pedestrians, eat up sidewalks, and add to traffic.
❖ Open grill gates on storefronts instead of solid rolldown ones. An active downtown draws nighttime window shoppers when storefronts are visible and lit.
❖ Narrow alleys or lanes that help circulation, provide niches to fill with surprise uses, and remove loading and unloading activity from the street.
❖ Street-front store entrances that stay unlocked and in use during open hours. Too many new developments create ground-floor uses accessible both from an interior atrium and the street, but the primary street entrance is kept locked.

❖ Upper-level or underground walkways and blank walls should be prohibited for reasons that should now be clear.

❖ Downtown dwellers were once a natural part of downtown social and economic life and must be that again. They are essential for the critical mass that makes a local economy viable and a sociable place possible. Upper floors of downtown buildings are the most readily available and underused *existing* resource for increased residential opportunities. It should be easy but isn't. Most institutional lenders will not finance a "mixed-use" project (retail on ground floor, residences above), let alone one that is in a downtown. Federal mortgage guarantee programs present similar impediments. Reversal is key to rejuvenation. Similarly, many downtown zoning codes and master plans explicitly rule out the creation of upstairs residential uses, even though this was one of the pillars of downtown strength when downtowns were still strong. Revival is key today to downtown rejuvenation.

❖ Building and fire codes should be similarly reexamined, with stairs, windows, elevators, sprinklers, and exposed beams targets for updated thinking. Just the fire and/or building code requirement of two sets of stairs is enough to make upstairs apartments impossible in most places or prohibitively expensive to create.

Many of these changes are already finding their way back into downtown governance, change by change. This is not easy, however. This is still heresy to many conventional planners, traffic managers, and economic development specialists who worry most about accommodating parking or impose safety standards worthy of a prison. Yet they reflect common sense and help build business and community. It is getting back to basics.

DOWNTOWN TRENDS FEEDING DOWNTOWN ESSENTIALS

Some of the most interesting downtown trends observed directly in our research are not yet officially acknowledged by traditional planners, economists, or urban professionals, or even noticed in any way that we have found. If anything, these trends are dismissed as anecdotal and inconsequential. Yet these trends, as new and nascent as they may be, are feeding the rebirth of the downtowns that still exist. They are inconsequential only if one is unable to recognize the historic pattern of urban changes that more often than not start small. Nurturing these trends is essential to strengthening downtowns on a comeback.

Since World War II, we have been an increasingly mobile society. Families widely dispersed. Job opportunities taking people long distances. Yet, in renewing downtowns, young people are returning, moving back to be close to family, deciding the old connections had a previously unrecognized value. The more mobile we Americans have become as a society, the more rooted we want to be. Young people are moving downtown, where interesting and affordable residential opportunities exist, where entrepreneurial opportunities exist, and when the downtown is more interesting than the malled suburb or sterilized city they may have grown up in. Entrepreneurs look for local business opportunities downtown. Some have been cast off by corporate America and are applying their skills to a new business. Some watched their parents devastated by a decade of corporate firings. Others realize that the "security" of working for the "company" is a thing of the past. Still others are relocating an existing business. Whatever the motivation, more people want to be in business for themselves, want to work with their hands *and* their minds, and want direct responsibility for their economic futures. The willingness to start small is a common. Downtowns are incubators. Malls are expensive.

Downtown residential neighborhoods are also growing in appeal, mostly in the old commercial neighborhoods of downtowns or close-in historic, former streetcar neighborhoods adjacent to business districts (see Chapter 13). Planners and prophets of a few years ago who declared downtowns no longer appropriate for residential living were wrong. Some of the once-worst rundown neighborhoods are today the best residential areas, transformed without demolition. Any downtown that recognizes the increasing appeal of traditional commercial and residential districts, and that combines this with a strong policy of retaining and putting back downtown essentials, has a strong chance of enduring rebirth.

1. "When Post Offices Forget the Community," *Connecticut Town & City*, reprinted in *Nation's Cities Weekly*, June 2, 1997.
2. The Franklin post office was placed on the 1991 Most Endangered Historic Sites list. We want to thank Trust staffer Laura Skaggs for her research on this issue.
3. For museums, isolation has been particularly disastrous for drawing the car-less audience in need of access to them. In some communities, schools have to hold bake sales to raise funds just to cover transportation costs of class trips to the museum.
4. The other two commissioners are Joseph J. Angelo and Arthur U. Magee, who, along with Mayor Henry Angelo, led this civic preservation effort. We are grateful to Arthur Ziegler for bringing this story to our attention.
5. Unfortunately, downtown building conversions today require some parking be available nearby simply because the life of so many potential tenants is car dependant, even if it is not by choice.

Savannah College of Art and Design (SCAD) restored
a closed movie house downtown and revived an
element of downtown life that had been lost.

CHAPTER ELEVEN

BACK TO BASICS

COMMUNITY REINVESTMENT

Many communities, big and small, wait for a private owner or public agency to create the new attraction. Farsighted residents don't. They recognize a need, seize an opportunity, and get something started without waiting for public officials to move. Community-based investment, in fact, has the greatest chance for success, simply because local people treasure and nurture their own ownership role.

The Arcadia in Wellsboro, Pennsylvania, is a classic 1940s small, plain-Jane Main Street movie theater. Patterned brick and a traditional movie marquee form a modestly interesting façade, and the inside is plain. The Arcadia was on the verge of closing. Led by a major downtown businessman, Frank Dunham, the town bought it itself by creating 100 shares of stock. Stock is now handed down from family to family. An annual stockholders' brunch is the only direct dividend. But all investors know they saved an important essential of their downtown. This is an exemplary model of community reinvestment. As people increasingly appreciate their downtown assets, this kind of community investment probably will become commonplace.

Netty's Café, a small coffee shop on a street corner of the tiny, midwest town of Atwood, in central Illinois, is another example. This social hangout for the community was about to close. The loss to the social

Arcadia, Wellsboro, Pennsylvania. Rather than see it close, the community took it over, sold stock to town residents, and saved the theater and its function.

Top: Netty's Café in Atwood, Illinois, was too important for the community to lose, so it formed a not-for-profit corporation to run the business.

Above: Netty's Café—interior view.

well-being of the downtown community would have been dramatic. With no new owners in sight, Atwood's downtown leaders formed a not-for-profit corporation and purchased the business. The café continues as a social mainstay of downtown.

In tiny Bonaparte, Iowa (population 500), 50 residents invested $2000 each as seed money for the redevelopment of a sizable vacant retail property. The for-profit development entity, Township Stores, leased street-level space to a grocery, hardware store, and medical clinic, and created two residential condominiums above. It subsequently rehabilitated the town's historic Opera House for upstairs residential use and downstairs office and community space.

Sheboygan Falls, Wisconsin, is one hour north of Milwaukee and one hour south of Green Bay. Some of its long-standing manufacturers remain in business, but the most centrally located 19th-century red brick complex of three buildings (once a woolen mill) downtown were empty, an economically and psychologically damaging sight adjacent to a popular downtown waterfall. A local task force, including an accountant, a banker, and long-standing community leaders, concluded that the community could redevelop the property itself. Six local investors put in $25,000 toward the purchase of the property. Volunteers demolished what they could in the interior and stripped the façade, saving more than $5000 in renovation costs. Investors then renovated and selectively recruited tenants to achieve an interesting mix. A well-known local delicatessen being wooed by malls located there instead. A county manufacturer of picnic tables and gazebos wanted a showroom. Assorted small office users filled the second floor. In 1992, downtown had 50 businesses. By 1994, there were 84.

Increasingly, localities are willing to tax themselves for a nontraditional, worthwhile local investment. Local taxes for a new stadium or convention center are common, although the direct local benefits, if any, are obscure. Resistance to such expensive investments grows, but so does a willingness to tax for smaller, more comprehensible local values. Trumbull County, Ohio, broke its no-tax history to create a three-quarters of 1 percent tax to restore the courthouse described earlier. West Windsor, New Jersey, added two cents on a dollar to its property tax to buy and save open space. A land preservation fund is gaining more than $400,000 a year this way.

ENTERTAINMENT

Entertainment attractions are among the few things now easily understood as essential to downtown. Keeping existing ones, reviving old ones, and creating new ones are all another matter. Great historic theaters, and some plain but functional ones, exist in many downtowns, unused and in a state of continued decay. Without the determination of local citizens or the vision of elected leaders, their potential will be left unrealized.

Although some communities still miss out on the opportunity to rescue, restore, and reopen both the incomparable landmarks and plain useful ones, successful reopening examples are everywhere. The State Theater in Easton, Pennsylvania. The Ohio State in Columbus. The Renaissance in Mansfield. The Paramount theaters in Middletown, New York, and Oakland, California. The Fox theaters in Detroit and Atlanta.

Small towns everywhere occasionally still have them or have brought them back. Rangeley and Ellsworth, Maine. Fort Madison, Iowa. Callicoon, New York. Great Barrington, Massachusetts. Chatham and Millerton, New York. Sometimes, small theaters specialize in art films of foreign imports to establish a specialized appeal. The County Theater in Doylestown, Pennsylvania, does this and Time and Space, a theater created in a former bakery factory in Hudson, New York, similarly shows specialized films and often-forgotten old ones. Too many old theaters, however, still sit empty, a lost opportunity for recreating a downtown attraction. And too many downtowns lack any evening attraction, other than seedy or illicit uses. A downtown cannot be reborn without evening appeal.

EDUCATIONAL FACILITIES

A local educational institution often represents an untapped resource for downtown enhancement. Many schools and downtowns have long forgotten the historic beginnings of universities in city centers and the symbiotic relationships they used to have. Many universities abandoned downtowns during the same decades that people flocked to suburbs. Others stayed, but built physical and/or psychological barriers around them, a condition in some ways worse than honest departure.

Easton, Pennsylvania, for example, is home to Lafayette University, a fine liberal arts school, but one would never know it downtown. This represents a missed opportunity both for the school to secure extra space inexpensively and for downtown to have additional activity to support rejuvenation.

Vancouver, British Columbia, in contrast, has new life in its rather stiff corporate district with the inception in 1992 of the City Program of Simon Frazier University. Simon Frazier left the city center for a sprawling campus at the distant edge decades earlier, but recognized the market it was missing in the downtown resident and office working population. A downtown office building was converted for university use. The City Program provides a multidisciplinary treatment of urban issues and functions as a public forum for city issues, something many downtowns are lacking.

Worcester, Massachusetts, boasts of 10 institutions of higher learning[1] within the city but, until recently, not a shred of evidence of any of them was visible downtown. Two schools have recently rented empty downtown space, and they have all joined to form a consortium to explore ways they can use downtown for their advantage and downtown can benefit. One consortium proposal in the works is the Coalition for Venture Support, in which the colleges seek to encourage new graduates to set up businesses in downtown. Even before this idea was hatched, two W.P.I. computer science graduates opened a repair and consulting business downtown. Probably most significant, however, is the personal action of the president of one of those institutions, Richard Traina of Clark University, who took seriously the long-standing and common criticism of urban colleges for being isolated in ivory towers and removed from community concerns.

Traina recognized that downtown's problems were the school's problems, as enrollment declined and out-of-town parents were increasingly reluctant to send their children to a school in a city of closed businesses, abandoned row houses, and rising crime rates. Worcester, New England's second largest city, had followed the typical mistaken path of the enclosed shopping mall in the center of town that kept the lid on spontaneous rebirth for several decades. But Traina recognized the role Clark could play as a catalyst for that rebirth. He and his wife moved from their suburban home to a restored townhouse in an in-town neighborhood in Clark's shadow, where dedicated citizen activists alone could not overcome the usual blight-causing problems, including abandoned houses and increasing crime rates. A community-wide redevelopment effort was established, the University Park Partnership, including Clark, a local community development corporation, businesses, and residents. More than 100 housing units and 19 commercial storefronts were renovated with a combination of private money and government grants. New businesses were established and children's programs developed, including after-school tutoring and music classes and a mentoring program that puts local youngsters together with Clark teachers and students. As icing on the cake, Clark is offering free tuition to any student accepted who has lived in the community for at least five years. Crime decreased 13 percent in the target area, compared with a citywide increase of 1.3 percent. Local real estate values went up.

Just the presence of an institution in a neighborhood or downtown area can be an activity-generating anchor, if it is not in some way gated, "bermed," or encircled by other isolation-forming barriers. The Murray Hill neighborhood of Manhattan has been enriched by the youthful infusion from the masterful conversion of an 1894 power plant to the Newman Library and Technology Center, a library and classroom facility of Baruch College of the city's vast university system. A light-filled atrium has been artfully created in the seven-story building by the architects, Davis Brody Bond, and the building contains administrative offices and a conference center besides the classrooms, library, and computer center. In fact, all over New York City, institutions of higher education are useful anchors in some neighborhoods. Fordham and Lehman, in different areas of the Bronx. LaGuardia Community College in Long Island City, across the 59th Street Bridge in the industrial district in Queens. Brooklyn College in Flatbush and Pratt Institute, LIU, and St. Joseph's College in Fort Greene.

In Chicago, across the street from the new main library, DePaul University was looking to expand its presence and impact. The Catholic university purchased the long vacant Goldblatt's Department Store with one million square feet, converted the top floor of the 11-story building for student support facilities and an open deck, used the next six floors for business school classrooms and library, and leased the three lower floors to the city. The ground floor has been innovatively developed into retail space for small, music-related retail businesses only. DePaul has a strong music program, and viewed this as a way to add to its appeal and create a new downtown resource. Fifteen different stores exist, offering everything from sheet music to instruments.

Some educational institutions, such as Wayne State University in Detroit, can be overbearing and isolationist, even if they are located in the middle of a downtown area. Some do the useful thing of filling existing spaces vacated by others, but then turn a positive into a negative by filling in or painting over the ground-floor windows, creating a blank wall effect. I walk by many old loft buildings like this near my office that New York University converted in Greenwich Village. What could possibly be going on inside a classroom or library that a pedestrian should not see? Interesting windows don't have to come only from retail displays. When universities become so big, they often become a community unto themselves and see no need to relate to the community around them beyond what that community forces them to do.

Business school professor Lee Walker and his assistant, Jennifer Vickers, sought to overcome just this condition at the University of Texas in Austin. Walker observed that students in his entrepreneurial management class had a total mall mindset, didn't care about local businesses, had no sense of downtown's importance, thought downtown businesses were a thing of the past, and had no concept of what a lively urban place can be. "Their only understanding of what makes a good place came from their experience as tourists in cities like Madrid, New York, or Portland, Oregon," says Vickers. "In their heads, only tourist sites were alive, not ordinary urban neighborhoods or commercial streets. When we asked them to close their eyes and imagine the best street they had ever been to, they all cited European places." (This, unfortunately, is true of more than students. Too many people accept the assumption that where they live or work cannot have any of these qualities of vitality. Sadly, many students raised in suburbia don't experience a vibrant urban downtown until they visit Europe.)

The large university campus is fairly self-contained, and neither students nor professors relate much to the surrounding area. Right across from the campus, however, was a dying commercial street "with businesses screaming for help," says Walker, "and at the university were tons of talent and potential consumers. The university provides all kinds of help to city institutions a great distance away, but not in their front yard."

Austin has some wonderful, traditional downtown areas left, but shows no sense of truly appreciating and nurturing them. Walker and Vickers seized the opportunity to connect the university, its students, and the citywide networks, first through turning student attention to the commercial street facing the campus. It is the first step out of a cloistered mindset that could lead to connections of great significance for the larger city.

Savannah, Georgia, is probably the best example of the benefits to downtown a school can bring.[2] Savannah had witnessed one of the country's most notable citizen-led rescues that transformed this historical gem into an economically stable modern city with its incomparable historic fabric substantially intact. By the 1980s, Savannah was on the verge of being overwhelmed by tourists. Tourists still flock to this antebellum masterpiece, but their presence and impact is partially balanced by the Savannah College of Art and Design (SCAD). Founded in the late 1970s by Richard and Paula Rowan, SCAD started with a few dozen students in one modest-sized 19th-century commercial building. It now has close to 3000 students and 35 renovated buildings of all shapes, sizes, and ages. Extraordinary architectural treasures stood empty before SCAD took advantage of this incomparable resource at fire-sale prices, and other buildings had become vacant as SCAD grew. Because the SCAD buildings

*Wallin Hall in Savannah, Georgia: An elementary school
discard is a SCAD treasure. Photo: Wayne C. Moore,
Wallin Hall, Savannah College of Art and Design.*

are scattered around the approximately one square mile of the downtown core, they function like numerous dispersed anchors without overwhelming one particular district. They seed the whole city.

SCAD has shown how adaptable so many historic buildings can be. A furniture design studio occupies an 1880s warehouse whose floor was built on a slight slope so laborers could, with less effort, push bales of cotton the 30 feet from the side of the building, where the freight train dropped the bales off, to the end, where wagons transported them to waiting ships. Students love the space, despite the fact that they need to use a shelf that juts out from one wall as a true level. A classic roadside diner was moved to a parking lot across from one classroom building, serving again as a diner in a primarily residential area that had no local eatery. An 1890 power station serves as the video department. A rusticated stone jail is a computer center. A radio station vacated by the local CBS station because its parking lot was too small now serves as headquarters for the SCAD media department.

Ironically, SCAD occupies four former public schools that once efficiently anchored four corners of the downtown residential area. Like many other states, Georgia set standards for public schools that only a sprawling, out-of-town campus could meet. Savannah was forced to vacate these four 19th-century buildings as anachronisms. Of varying styles, they serve the purpose for which they were originally built quite effectively and stand in stark contrast to what SCAD preservation professor Marlborough Packard calls "the neo-penal-colony architecture of gates and grates" that marks most newer campus colleges.

SCAD programs and students have added cultural and intellectual nourishment to downtown's main shopping thoroughfare, Broughton Street. This retail street never experienced the resurgence the rest of Savannah did. Regional malls reigned supreme. Yet, Broughton exhibited all the advantages of an intact main street waiting for a step-by-small-step resurgence. SCAD took over an empty 1930s movie house, turning it into an increasingly popular performance space. Empty upper stories were converted to student housing. In fact, even a dismal gray brick 1960s Ramada Inn was converted to a dorm. Student bicycles and other paraphernalia fill the ugly balconies, giving this banal structure a character it never had. Galleries have opened and even SCAD graduates, charmed by the city's unending appeal, are beginning to stay beyond graduation to open new downtown businesses.

Broughton Street is not overwhelmed, however, by SCAD. With long-delayed wisdom, the city took over a small office building for city offices. An enterprising young restaurateur converted a small 1930s department store into a restaurant that has private dining rooms upstairs. A citywide citizen-led effort to restore the Lucas Theater, a nicely embellished 1920s movie theater, has succeeded and created a significant downtown entertainment center that Savannah hasn't had in decades, despite the construction in the 1970s of a typically banal convention center. In other words, Savannah is alive in many ways that can be directly traced to the presence of SCAD.

Schools provide a broader, more diversified benefit to a downtown than any new, unneeded convention center or sports stadium. And educational institutions provide some needed stability for a downtown during economic downturns. Students are a constant, even during recessions.

HOTELS

Downtowns have rediscovered the value of hotels to excess. Now, the unfortunate trend is to mindlessly cater to tourism at the expense of resident needs and a locality's genuine character and sense of place. The short-term gains will eventually be lost as, over the long term, residents depart. *Local residents and the life and economy they create is what gives a place the appeal to draw tourists in the first place.*

We are long past the day when skeptics predicted failure for the refurbished and reopened Hotel Benson in Portland, Oregon, or the U. S. Grant in San Diego, or the York in York, Pennsylvania, all catalysts for downtown rebirth. No one doubts their renewal value anymore. In Hudson, New York, the St. Charles, a 1920s hotel, facing the town square, closed in 1993, removing the only such facility from Hudson and from the larger Columbia County that lacks visitor accommodations. With critical financial help from the Columbia-Hudson Partnership, a local economic development organization, a new owner was found and the 38-room facility with ground floor restaurant, bar, and banquet facilities was fully renovated, recreating an important downtown activity generator.

A truly novel project was the conversion of the Association Home (Association for the Relief of Respectable Aged Indigent Females), an elegant red brick block-long building designed by Richard Morris Hunt in 1881. This solid-looking structure with its elegant dormers and gabled roof on Amsterdam Avenue on Manhattan's Upper West Side sat empty for years after it closed in 1975. Located in a primarily low-income neighborhood, the Association Home attracted no investors. Restored and converted to an American Youth Hostel facility, this incomparable landmark now houses an underserved visitor population for whom expensive hotels are not an option. It remains an important visual asset and activity anchor for a modest neighborhood.

In Buffalo, a hostel with 40 beds was created right on Main Street, out of a long-vacant six-story former women's clothing store. This was a beneficial addition to Buffalo's downtown, long suffering from the kind of mega-project planning that drained downtown vitality and demolished so many of its streets and variety of buildings. Unlimited potential exists for varied downtown uses—of more interesting consequence than the most common large-scale, one-activity, drive-in and -out uses. They give places character and local personality.

RETHINKING RETAIL

Downtown needs retail. Civic, entertainment, office, and industrial uses are not enough. Given the story of Bon-Ton in a series of Pennsylvania downtowns and Scranton's force-fed Steamtown mall, one must question some of the assumptions accepted today about downtown retail, if only for the sake of understanding that retail can succeed downtown today. Retail is a downtown essential.

The conventional wisdom indicates that traditional department stores died because of mall competition and that downtown retail lost its rationale because that economic activity shifted to the mall. That is substantially true, to be sure. But where is the consideration for the downtown department stores that were purposely killed by mall retailers wanting no downtown competition? What about the department stores closed because some retail chains decided the malls were the way to go and that while shoppers still existed in downtowns, those chains wanted their customers to follow them to the mall? What about the obvious evolution of national chains into one-formula-only concepts that could not handle the individual personality and local quirkiness of a traditional, individually-designed department store? What about the stores lost to unfriendly takeovers and subsequent bankruptcies? And what about the national chains convinced by mall developers that they needed to provide a parking space for every shopper, not something easily provided downtown?

When one sees the creativity today in converting old department stores into a new breed of large specialty stores and other uses, isn't it logical to ask, why was it not possible all along to have both? Retail financial analysts point out that many department stores closed during the heady Wall Street era of mergermania, leveraged buyouts, sale of assets, and so on. That was not about whether dresses would sell on Main Street. *That was about corporate spreadsheets, questionable assumptions, and shareholder expectations.*

Even the assumption that people avoided downtown shopping because of safety factors has to be questioned. Crime did not keep people away from downtown stores in the 1960s and 1970s. And, as noted earlier, Times Square always attracted visitors, regardless of its reputation. The *perception* of a crime problem grew faster than the reality and succeeded in scaring people away. It is a lot easier to be negative about anything. The perception was accelerated by the decrease in numbers of pedestrians on the streets as buildings were demolished for parking lots, as empty spaces outpaced filled ones, as businesses left downtown voluntarily or were pushed by relocation efforts, and as the onetime downtown residential housing stock was erased and the people living in these houses moved. Graffiti and litter spread, and so did the added perception that no one who cared was in control.

As corporations built interior-oriented headquarters with empty plazas and as they built their own lunchroom/cafeterias, fewer and fewer downtown workers had reason to be on the street. Most downtown changes were hostile to street-level retail. Pedestrianization diminished, like all else, in small nibbles. In large cities, where most people still move around on foot or on mass transit, interior malls frequently fail or perform considerably below expectations. In New York, the first major interior mall was created in the celebrated Citicorp Center at Lexington Avenue and 53rd Street. Being right on top of a major subway entrance did not help the mall, which enclosed a faddish atrium that was popular when it first opened in 1978, but not for long. Now, after years of underuse, Citicorp Center has undergone a major renovation of its retail spaces, and guess what was the first change being made? Street-front entrances to the stores.

In some communities, family-run department stores, like England Brothers in Pittsfield, Massachusetts, and Rockwell's in Corning, New York, went out of business because no younger generation stepped in to carry on the tradition or, if they did, didn't do it well enough. In contrast, in Wellsboro, Pennsylvania, Dunham's Department Store is still a thriving anchor in downtown, growing and prospering, because two sons learned the business well, took over from their father, and successfully continue the business today. More than just selling dry goods, in fact, James and John Dunham continue the family commitment to civic involvement. They completed the effort to save Main Street's movie theater, Arcadia, started by their father and initiated a similar effort to save the Penn Wells Hotel from extinction.

On Main Street in the upstate town of East Aurora, New York, not far from Buffalo, Vidler's has been a five-and-dime since the 1930s. East Aurora is the home of the Arts and Crafts Movement, with its greatest showcase, the Roycroft Museum, restored and reopened in 1995. Vidler's is run by Beverly Vidler, granddaughter of the original owner, who lives in a charming apartment above the store. Vidler's, greatly expanded, has remained the main anchor for the downtown that once had several similar "something for everyone" stores. It is a downtown landmark, run in a personalized way that Beverly Vidler says cannot be replicated. She is frequently asked to open another location. She resists, knowing that she needs to feel on top of everything all the time and feeling that any new version would be contrived. She's always rearranging, making things look fresh and new, and changing window displays.

The common assumption is that stores like Vidler's have died of natural causes, but that assumption cannot be universally accepted. Many things that undermined downtown retail are not commonly recognized. Zoning rules and transportation changes often added considerably to the survival difficulties of downtown retail. Elimination of curbside parking. Permitting curb cuts and the intrusion of drive-in eateries. Encouragement of pass-through driving. Initiation of one-way streets. All these nibbles diminished the walk-in business essential for street-level retail.

Questioning conventional wisdom regarding downtown retail is only useful today if it helps innovative thinking about new retail opportunities. Downtowns can still, or again, support retail. It is essential. Conversions of downtown department stores and other buildings should retain ground-floor retail for the sake of completeness and continuity of the street. This does not have to be a hard-and-fast rule and, for some buildings, this will not be appropriate. The standard, however, is not to let too big an interruption in street activity occur. Otherwise, like a parking lot, it will act like a stop sign to pedestrians passing by. Ground-floor spaces should not be hidden behind dark, tinted glass or closed Venetian blinds and, in new buildings, should not be set back from the traditional line of stores. Lifeless blocks of no interest to the pedestrian result. Lenders resist the mix of office and retail, just as they do mixing residential and retail. Conventional wisdom accepts too easily the myth that downtown retail doesn't have a chance anymore. Thus, anything filling in a vacated storefront seems acceptable. This is a mistake.

Yes, shoppers, in part, followed the stores to the suburbs but many downtown retailers could not get financing to stay downtown, even if they wanted to do so. Lending institutions redlined many down-town commercial districts in the same way they did downtown residential areas. Similarly, the renewed retail in many downtowns visible today started with small, individually-owned stores often without institutional financial help. Small efforts seed the market for the big ones to which lenders are willing to lend. But the small ones come first. The credit for rebirth, of course, goes to the big, visible stores who never would have opened if the small ones had not done so first and proved that a market existed.

Columbus Avenue on Manhattan's Upper West Side was one of the first major urban thoroughfares to be transformed by the current love affair of retail chains for downtowns. Long before the national chains even thought downtown retail was again feasible, Columbus Avenue had been transformed by locally-owned businesses over two to three decades of gradual rebirth. When the spotlight focused on its revival, chains started moving in, ready to pay higher rents than locals could manage. Big chains followed the small local stores.

The street "became captive to the corporate dollar, going up and down at the whim of Wall Street," notes Ben Fox, a leasing agent who specializes in retail stores. "Developers or building owners are impressed by names of chains," Fox added. "They see big dollars and seemingly successful formulas. Many chains give the illusion of success but wind up short-lived. Even though a chain will pay $120,000 a year in rent, it may be better in the long run to accept $85,000 a year in rent from a locally-owned business which is apt to be more stable. Better to have stability."

The downtown department store buildings of an earlier era are as useful today as they were then. They accommodate a very broad assortment of uses. The Portland, Oregon, Galleria was converted in the 1970s to an interior mall that functioned as much like a department store as a mall and felt like a department store on the street. The Galleria helped spark revival of the Old Town district. In Batesville, Arkansas, Shield's Department Store was converted to Home Furnishings. Thorn's in Northampton, Massachusetts, was divided into small, separately owned retail components. Such conversions succeed only when presented and merchandised with flair. Many developers buy and divide up stores but don't understand retail. Narrow corridors with shops, poor lighting, no pizzazz, any number of things done poorly can diminish chances for success. Retail still has its place downtown if it is done well. This was always the case.

CHARACTER AND HISTORY

In the end, the most essential need of a downtown is character. If nothing distinguishes downtown from the strip, the mall, the nearest megastore, or the formula-design chain store, why would someone bother to come downtown? Character is what old buildings contribute best. History disappears from view when they do.

Downtown after downtown repeats the recent mistake of upstate Endicott, New York, which permitted a shortsighted developer to demolish a recently restored and occupied two-story 1910 building to construct a formula chain drugstore. Drugstore chains seem to favor corner sites like this and are doing considerable damage in many downtowns. The Farmer's National Bank, a brick building with limestone trim, reflected a significant chapter of Endicott's history and was already a worthwhile contributor to the local tax base and job count. A 1939 theater and Victorian office building stood on either side, filling out an historical continuum that reflected an interesting slice of local history. With a little imagination and respect for the community from which the consumers would come, the modest building with its name carved in the keystone could have been converted to a drugstore with real character. A local landmarks law is in place but this building had not yet been designated. A vigorous citizen campaign to "Save the Bank" effectively educated the public to what was at stake. Expert guidance was provided by the New York State Preservation League's lawyer, Kathy Ridley. Nevertheless, the bank went down, a perfect all-too-often-repeated lost opportunity to enhance a downtown. Instead, a concrete box went up. Downtown is diminished. The developer could have made money either way. Local character has no price tag.

The most interesting downtown rebirth is, in fact, occurring in the cities and towns that have not malled or urban-renewed themselves into parking lot or corporate extinction. Long-ignored but now reviving downtown districts exhibit the character lost in the downtowns rebuilt with megaprojects. But this rebirth process is gradual, often slow at first, small step by small step, ad hoc. This is both the good news and the bad news, the good news because this is simply how it happens best, the bad news because the "experts" fail to recognize and value this style of rejuvenation until big developers or retail chains notice. When they do notice and move in with new, overwhelming projects, the hard-won character is in danger. Ad hoc is anathema to city planners.

Surviving districts with visible layers of history and growth have a different kind of downtown essential—a traditional downtown fabric with buildings of all ages, sizes, and styles, suitable for varied uses, convertible to innovative activity and a reasonable purchase or rental price. "The more variations there can be, the better," Jane Jacobs wrote. "As soon as the range and number of variations in buildings decline, the diversity and population and enterprises are too apt to stay static or decline, instead of increasing."[3] In addition, these streets have the opportunity to add new by filling in empty spaces, adding on to existing structures, or reconfiguring the interior spaces by combining or divid-

Union Square East. Blending the old and new retains character of place and works well economically. Toys R Us coexists comfortably with small stores on the block.

ing. The existing fabric and surviving uses are the most important assets. They are the foundation to build on.

Granby Street in Norfolk, Virginia, Carson Street on Pittsburgh's South Side, Colorado Avenue in Pasadena, Larimer Square in Denver, Newberry Street in Boston. Project Planners do not know how to recognize signs of early regeneration in these kinds of areas, nor how to nurture the new growth without stifling or overheating it. But, as we will see in the final chapter, these streets and districts hold the real future of downtown America.

ORGANIZATIONS

An organization of some kind is usually necessary to pull things together, stimulate new ideas, and encourage new business. An entity of some sort, whether a Business Improvement District (BID), a Main Street Program, a Chamber of Commerce, a Local Development Corporation, or Community Development Organization, must mold and guide any kind of program. Any organization can be too formulaic, too privately-controlled, too removed from public accountability, and can run the risk of pitting merchants against property owners. Not every type of organization is useful in every downtown. Fundamentally, any time an organization gets people to take control of a place and increase public interest and attention, good things are bound to happen. Downtowns often die from loss of citizen interest, caring, and attention. Whether one part-time employee or a whole organization, somebody has to be in charge, run the show, coordinate activities, and advocate on behalf of downtown. The process is only as good as the organization, the public involvement, and public accountability. The most important service any organization can perform is to bring together the expertise of separate disciplines in one process and to unravel the category thinking characteristic of planning practice of the past half century.

The element that so many organizations omit, however, is the marketing that is so essential to a downtown's success. A modest but growing program of the 34th Street Partnership BID has been partially responsible for the upgrading and regeneration of 34th Street, historically one of Manhattan's most famous retail thoroughfares. The stretch between Fifth and Seventh Avenues once connected some of New York's most famous department stores, B. Altman's, Macy's, Saks 34th, Gimbel's, Franklin Simon, and Ohrbach's. In between was a wonderful selection of smaller but significant stores that were sometimes as much a destination as the larger ones. With the suburban mall competition, mergers, and buyouts, the street lost its luster, significant destinations disappeared, and only because Macy's endured as the anchor did the street retain heavy traffic. Low-end merchants proliferated. Open storefronts became common, spilling merchandise onto the street. Oversized signs created unseemly clutter. Canopies covering the sidewalk from storefront to curb with more signs blatantly attached added to a cluttered sidewalk where the sun never shone. This overall condition is not uncommon on once-appealing downtown retail streets.

The 34th Street Partnership was formed in 1991, primarily to clean up, improve security on the street, and provide physical upgrades, not unlike many downtown organization efforts. Such efforts were directed at the physical and security elements because that is what governments and financial institutions know how to fund and what professionals know how to handle. Few recognized the need to work directly with merchants, however, or understood how to do so. Merchants are a varied and independent-minded group of individuals or retail chains. Gaining agreement among them is difficult. "Nobody tells me how to run my business" is the common attitude. This most difficult dilemma must be tackled with time, sensitive staff, and appropriate funding, if regeneration is to occur. This critical service is often omitted by downtown organizations.

In 1993, the Partnership added an innovative service to improve every aspect of retailing, working directly with individual merchants and landlords. Technical assistance covered everything from storefront design to merchandise quality and presentation, excessive signage and canopy removal, window display and signage improvements, marketing and promotion assistance, legal, retail recruitment, a newsletter, demographic data collecting, and public relations promoting positive changes on the street. Twenty-two canopies have been removed, signage has been upgraded, façades have been rehabilitated, vacancies have disappeared, and now big-name retailers are seeking a place on this rejuvenating street.

HISTORIC PRESERVATION

Some of the best downtown rebirth stories, as this book illustrates throughout, start as downtown preservation programs. As economic development and real estate consultant Donovan D. Rypkema says, "I have never visited a downtown with a successful record of economic revitalization where historic preservation wasn't a key element of the strategy. That doesn't mean such a place doesn't exist, but I haven't been there, I haven't heard of it, and I haven't read of it." We totally share this experience.

Every downtown should have some kind of preservation ordinance with teeth in it. In too many places, the undervaluing of existing buildings is permitting a nonstop erosion of downtown character, businesses, history, and sense of place. This shortsighted mindset is simply bad for business. Continued use of existing resources simply is prudent fiscal policy. This includes old buildings, many of which are architecturally and culturally valuable.

Historic preservation, however, should never take on an importance that makes it an overwhelming end in and of itself. It should be viewed as one tool in a large tool kit, and an essential one at that. A builder, after all, would not stop with acquisition of a hammer when he still needs a saw. Downtowners should no more think of doing without an historic preservation program than a builder would operate with a hammer only. But as has been shown throughout this book, preservation has to be about more than bricks and mortar. Otherwise, old buildings become only a façade, a costume, a cover-up for the erosion of citiness and historical continuity and a cover-up for the sameness engulfing the city and countryside alike. Preservation, as well, has to be about more than singular buildings. Every individual building loses immeasurable value when the context, setting, and social and economic fabric of a place disappear. Conversely, the social and economic fabric of a community loses immeasurably with the loss of its landmarks.

Historic preservation makes economic sense. The ribbon-cutting, big planning crowd fiercely resists this truth. Rypkema adds, "Any community that does not have a formal program of downtown revitalization with a strong historic preservation component cannot claim to be doing everything possible to save taxpayers' dollars." Building on assets already paid for, using existing infrastructure, strengthening one link that reinforces the whole, all these connected acts are financially prudent acts.

Critic Robert Campbell, speaking about Boston, observed that preservation makes economic sense for another, fundamental reason. "Why do people come to Boston?" he asked. "...Because it's a city that still feels like a city. The issue is what the advertising people used to call 'marginal differentiation.' You have to distinguish between Coke and Pepsi somehow." What differentiates Boston from Dallas or Phoenix, he added, is that Boston "possesses oldness, which they don't. It has a place in time, a sense of time having washed over it and layered up through it and given it that kind of richness and depth and patina. But it also has, more importantly, 'citiness.' Cities are made of streets and squares. Cities are dense and compact and multi-use."

BOOKS, BREAD, AND BARS

When Katherine Glover asked around Mansfield what stores people wanted to come to North Main Street, the three most frequent requests were a bookstore, a pub or coffee shop, and a bakery. This interesting combination could serve as a starting point for any downtown community looking to see what is missing. These businesses unavoidably reflect a community and give it character. They are basic connectors. It says something immediately about a place when a locally-owned bookstore exists downtown. Nowadays, bookstores serve as activity centers, offering substantive programs that are not mass market, and give residents an alternative to home entertainment, a home away from home.

In Blytheville, Arkansas, a Main Street bookstore called That Bookstore in Blytheville has become a community center in a novel way, beyond its variety of reading, lecture, and author visit programs. Owner Mary Gay Shipley decided to remove the aluminum siding from her building and restore the black Carrara glass dating from the 1940s, when it was a jewelry store. The glass was hard to obtain, so she opted for black tile and incorporated tiles designed by customers, friends, and area students. She staged a contest, challenged participants to draw an image of their favorite book, received 900 entries, selected 88, and had them specially fabricated. The project gained broad attention and was so popular, Shipley used additional designs for the interior walls and regularly has people coming in to show off their creations. At Christmas, Shipley mounts an Angel Tree on which hang angel ornaments with the name of a disadvantaged child and a book that matches that child's interests. Books are purchased at a discount and distributed by local organizations. More than 1,000 books have been distributed in the region through this program.

In Westchester County, New York, the much-loved and last of the county's old-time bookstores, Fox & Sutherland, closed after Christmas 1995. The community rejoiced when a new bookstore, the Mt. Kisco Book Co., was opened down the street by Westchester resident Irwin Hersch, a part owner of Coliseum Books, one of Manhattan's largest independent bookstores. But a fire destroyed the store just before Christmas 1996. The community was bereft, inundating Hersch with messages of sympathy and appreciation for what he had done.

Hersch, moved by the public outpouring and not one to be defeated easily, noticed that the former Fox & Sutherland space was still vacant and decided to reopen there, hopefully in time for Christmas. Suddenly, local volunteers offered help. A local furniture dealer installed carpeting immediately. A retired painter applied his talent. Employees from other stores pitched in after work. Hersch was overwhelmed. "The store's demise," wrote Trip Gabriel in *The New York Times*, "seemed to tap into the public's general affection for bookstores, for independent merchants in the age of megastores and for tough-luck Mt. Kisco itself, a working-class village surrounded by more affluent communities that has struggled to nurture a fledgling retail revival."

The bar, the pub, or the coffee shop is what Ray Oldenburg calls "the Great Good Place," the place where people connect, where community evolves, separate from home and work but a complement to both. A bakery serves local taste in a particular way. Roslindale, an early streetcar suburb of Boston, has nine bakeries, reflecting the diversity of that community's ethnic groups.

In Holland, Michigan, a town of 31,000 with a thriving, totally local-based economy downtown, Jack Groot owns and runs JP's Coffee and Espresso Bar, a 25-foot-wide by 100-foot-deep coffee shop that serves downtown in the best tradition of the gathering place. "I'm not really in the coffee business," Groot observes, "although I do serve coffee. My bar is a replacement of place, a social site." JP's is open from 7 a.m. until 11 p.m., already unique for a downtown eatery these days. All day long, the customer mix changes and includes what one observer called "from the 12-year-old getting a malted to the 75-year-old sweethearts holding hands and sharing a sundae." Early in the morning, the senior citizen walkers come first. Then the on-the-way-to-business crowd. Then, of course, the shoppers. Lunchtime draws from every group. After school and into evening is the nearby Hope College crowd, many of them lingering in conversation as if they were on the Left Bank. Many communities have similar gathering places (Netty's Café in Atwood, Illinois, is one) that embody its local personality and are essential to it.

WINDOWS AND TAXIS

Two very different things are sure signs a downtown encourages pedestrians, street life, and the full spectrum of activities that marks an interesting and lively downtown: individually designed window displays and a hail-a-taxi transportation system.

Taxis, in contrast to car services one has to call, are to be found only in large cities, such as Boston, New York, Toronto, Chicago, or San Francisco. Yet, few cities have such a luxury. Think of it this way. A walker can get around without help in a small downtown. In larger downtowns, a walker needs mass transit, usually a bus, to travel between somewhat distant destinations. In a large downtown, a well-performing transit network is essential.

In some large cities, an efficient combination of rail and bus transit still exists. But even with such a system, places inevitably exist in big cities that are not easy to get between by public transit. Several transit transfers may be required, which takes a longer time than many people are willing to abide. For those who can afford it, therefore, the option of hailing a taxi strengthens the no-car alternative. In many downtowns, people drive from one point to another to avoid an overly long walk or unreliable transit trip. Taxis offer a desirable alternative. Cruising taxis, therefore, complete a transit system.

Store windows are a different but equally pedestrian-directed element. Sadly, the art of the retail store window has diminished drastically in recent years. Sometimes, we walk around downtowns and wonder if it even exists at all. It is difficult to figure out, however, if it is the art or the financing that has disappeared. As individualized stores have been replaced by chains and malls, window displays have apparently been high on the cost-cutting list.

Store windows add interest downtown, where it matters most, on the street. Creative and individualized display adds character and reflects

*Thousands of visitors line up each year
to view Lord & Taylor's Christmas windows.*

local taste and sensibility. Without it, a store and, by extension, the street looks like any other.

There are no more famous window displays than the Lord & Taylor Christmas windows on New York's Fifth Avenue. Fairy tales or Christmas stories came to life in miniature-mechanized, exquisitely-crafted, humorously detailed, and imaginatively executed tableaux. They were magical. Out-of-town visitors made special trips to see them. Lines of patient, often freezing, viewers lasted well into the late evening. Annual visits with my parents marked my childhood. A walk down Fifth Avenue past Bergdorf Goodman, Bendel's, Tiffany, Bonwit Teller, Saks, Lord & Taylor, B. Altman, and, of course, Rockefeller Center with tree, skaters, and whatever graced the Channel Gardens, was our annual Christmas Eve ritual. My husband and I faithfully took our children for an annual visit to Lord & Taylor's windows, timing it for as late in the evening as the kids could stand. Whatever the hour, there were people. Intricacy, novelty, surprise, and artistry were worth the visit. The store could not have had better advertising for itself. Those windows were a unique draw. Only a few years ago, that Christmas window tradition was a victim of the buyout, merger, standardization and cost-cutting of merchandising. The specialness of the windows disappeared for a while. Happily, by Christmas 1997, a good measure of the uniqueness had returned. Again those windows are worth a special trip.

The loss of interesting window displays on all main streets has contributed to the overall loss of interest and appeal. Few recognize how important a part of street life it was. So nibbled away over time, merchants don't view it as important, and it is almost forgotten. When the reverse is true, when interesting window displays exist, one recognizes their value. In some towns, empty windows are turned over to historical societies or school art programs for exhibit creations. They become conversation pieces.

In Troy, New York, for example, Troy Architectural Program (TAP) created a program to fill empty windows with jury-approved art. Local artists create work specifically for the window in which the work is placed. This is part of a larger, ongoing program to create new interest, increase pedestrian traffic downtown, and provide exhibit opportunities for artists. Our favorite example is on a Greenwich Village street corner. Broadway Windows, a program of the NYU School of Fine Arts, contains rotating exhibits of truly fine student work on the ground floor of a 1920s apartment house. Tom Beebe has been the creative director for Paul Stuart Clothing in New York for more than 12 years, producing some of the industry's finest and most noted window displays. He is known as one of the masters of the craft. Beebe considers window display "street theater," a kind of "walk-by art gallery with the chance to stop passersby in their tracks. Windows are the billboard of the store." Although store windows are part of the urban experience, they are very much "separate from the real world," Beebe adds. "In the world of downtown, with its noise, move-ment, and intensity, a store window provides a rest, an intimacy, a time of quiet for the passerby." Good window display depends on windows first being as close to the pedestrian as possible, not set-back or off the side-walk, one more reason to protect the consistent building line of a down-town street.

We close with windows because they are probably the least appre-ciated, smallest, and least thought-about element of the many downtown essentials that must come within the focus of any rejuvenation effort. They also are the perfect vehicle to reflect local character and history, an essential so basic that it should be high on every effort's list.

Like so many downtown essentials, windows offer a small-scale com-ponent of the larger revitalization process. Essentials, after all, are pieces, not large projects. Windows, like all essentials, are unique in themselves and to the respective downtown of which they are a part. They require innovation. They are people-oriented and serve people in a more intimate, meaningful way. They combine the talents and resources of many people. They reflect the personality of a place, a community, and distinguish it from a consumer machine, a private mall. They are of a spirit, creative and fun. All essentials are easier to accomplish, in a sense, because they are more natural to their surroundings and, often, already a long-standing part of those surroundings.

Essentials are as essential as ever. Public money is drying up for big projects—the good news. Big projects are increasingly viewed as too expensive anyway and always fall short of expectations. Smaller projects are gaining in popularity. Their track record is being recognized. Small innovations are building blocks for real results (see next chapter). They are anchors. Anchors don't have to be big. These small pieces of a larg-er puzzle join together one by one to create a meaningful, distinctive whole. Essentials cannot be taken for granted.

[1.] Clark University, Holy Cross College, Worcester Polytechnic Institute, Worcester State College, Anna Maria College, Quinsagamond Community College, Assumption College, Becker College, Tufts University School of Veterinary Medicine, University of Massachusetts Medical Center.

[2.] See *The Living City: Thinking Small in a Big Way*, Chapters 1 and 2.

[3.] *Death and Life of Great American Cities*, Modern Library Edition, 1993, p. 279.

Timothy Dunleavy started his children's dress
company in an inexpensive upstairs space
in Hudson, New York—a renewed industry
for a renewing downtown.

CHAPTER TWELVE

INVESTING IN PEOPLE

Helen Rainforth ships tins of popcorn all over the country, grossing $1 million annually. She does this in downtown Lincoln, Illinois (population 16,000), her home town, the only town named for Abraham Lincoln with his consent. Her business is called Abe's Carmelcorn Shoppe. A tall, dark-haired woman with high cheekbones and a generous smile, Rainforth worked for various retailers, always with an eye for buying or starting her own business. "I wanted to control my destiny," she says.

In 1983, a friend put up for sale her downtown corner candy store, selling popcorn, candy, and drinks. Rainforth jumped at it, just to buy a store. One week after she took over, she understood why her friend had sold. There was no business. After a few months, she wrote 100 postcards to people that she knew in the area, offering a holiday shopping service. Ninety-two people said yes to her offer. She included her candy as, at least, part of every gift. She offered her candy and gift services to large corporations, spent a week in Chicago, and came home with a dozen new clients, including a hotel, manufacturers, insurance companies, and several corporations.

Business and need for space grew. She bought a two-story stone commercial building with a full basement, dating from the 1890s, located a half-block from her corner store. Each floor is 6000 square feet. The building was home to a newspaper first, then a funeral home. Carved ornamentation and stained glass windows had been covered over. From a business school point of view, Rainforth's building pur-

Abe's Carmelcorn Shoppe, Lincoln, Illinois, occupies a grand old commercial building.

chase probably was just another basic mistake. She failed to research the building in the same way she neglected to fully comprehend the bottom line of the business before she bought it. Intuition, creativity, and determination, however, more than compensated for bottom-line naiveté. Renovation cost $225,000, an amount clearly larger than she expected. She leased the ground floor to cover her mortgage.

She moved the production of her popcorn (caramel, cheese, and plain flavors) to the top floor. High ceilings accommodate tall storage shelves. Shipping is convenient. Trucks pull right up to the loading dock of the back alley with no interference from street or parking traffic. When the tenant left three years later, Rainforth moved her store in. More than half her business was corporate accounts by then, but she felt the retail presence on the street was important. "It's vital to display what you sell," she says. "Retail provides credibility."

Orders come in by fax and the Internet. She ships to every state. Her husband and son have since joined the business. She relies heavily on local resources. All boxes are made nearby. Corn comes from nearby farms. Estimating the number of jobs directly and indirectly created is difficult, but the spinoff economic impact of a local production business is significant.

For a long time, Lincolnites believed the return of a department store was what downtown needed to "come back," a typical assumption in many downtowns. So much money is spent on marketing and demographic studies aimed at luring a department store anchor or clothing chain store, like the Gap. People become disillusioned when their dreams of a return to the days of glory do not materialize. In Lincoln, following the success of Abe's, a bookstore opened next door, a specialty food store opened half a block away, and a gift store and antique shop followed nearby. Lincolnites don't think the department store is key anymore. A rejuvenation process has taken hold. A local economy is reemerging bit by small bit, but in somewhat different form from before. Some pieces will stay small. Others will grow. Some may fail, but the vitality continues as long as the process continues. This particular corner candy store developed into a national retail business. This is an American tradition that continues in the era of cyberspace and global markets. Macy's, after all, started small. In fact, R. H. Macy failed in five retail attempts before opening the "fancy dry goods" store that became the largest department store in America. F. W. Woolworth's story is similar. Zabar's, New York's famous specialty food store, started as the deli counter in a larger food store. Apple Computer started in a garage. Adam Gimbel began his career as a pack peddler.

Rainforth happened to buy a business that was already downtown and remained downtown because of the convenience and availability of the appropriate real estate and an ample labor supply. Downtown is the perfect incubator for emerging businesses, and locally-owned business-es are essential to any downtown.

DOWNTOWNS NURTURE BUSINESSES
THAT MOVE ON AS THEY GROW

Timothy Dunleavy designs high-quality children's dresses in a three-room workspace on the second floor above an antique store in Hudson, New York, a small city on the Hudson River, a two-hour train ride from Manhattan.[1] Dunleavy, 42, started his career in New York City, designing children's' clothes and off-Broadway costumes. His dream was to have a house in the country and to work as a designer for himself. The garment industry slump in the late 1980s provided the impetus. Friends in other professions were moving out and finding new trades. Dunleavy followed in 1990, bought a house in a small town near Hudson, started over from home, and, in less than three years, outgrew his house. A designer friend told him about a small space for rent in Hudson.

Dunleavy started working by himself in that one room ($125 rent) and now has 1500 square feet in three rooms ($600 rent) with huge windows, and two full-time and three part-time employees. He designs, creates samples, lays out fabric, and does everything necessary to prepare his creations for sewing elsewhere in the county and in New York City. With sales representatives in Texas and Los Angeles and twice-yearly visits of his own to children's shows in Manhattan, Dunleavy sells out his full collection and is featured by Saks Fifth Avenue and Neiman-Marcus. In 1996, he shipped 7000 garments (double the total of two years earlier) with gross sales of $500,000, up from $263,000 the year before.

Dunleavy is representative of the kind of new entrepreneur taking advantage of the undervalued spaces across downtown America. "The largest-growing area in American business is small business," Dunleavy notes, articulating an underappreciated fact. "I think more and more people are saying, 'I can't afford to work for anyone else. It is just too stressful.'"

Hudson is a typical small city that once had a healthy mix of man-ufacturing, retail, and residential uses, densely packed into a low-rise cityscape where no building exceeds the height of a church steeple. Although it is the only city in agriculture-based Columbia County, few signs of its farm-based economy are evident in downtown Hudson. Instead, what is evident is a slowly renewing downtown still losing old businesses but gaining a different mix.

Hudson's colorful history started when Nantucket and New Bedford Quakers moved their whale processing businesses to this river town in the late 1700s, safe from the British fleet. Warren Street, Hudson's linear commercial spine of eight blocks and its primary retail street, evolved from that period up through the 1950s. Block after block of textbook archi-tectural styles, starting with Federal brick houses of the early 1800s, line

Warren Street, Hudson, New York, block after block of textbook architectural styles.

a slow, gentle incline from the river. The largest concentration of buildings are Victorian commercial buildings dating from the period when manufacturing (dress contracting, long underwear, humidifiers, pocketbooks, matches) and industrial uses (cement, brick, coal) fueled the economy until the 1960s. Several manufacturers remain in Hudson and around the county, but their presence is not evident on Warren Street.

The buildings that line Warren Street are typical for downtowns built at the turn of the century, a period of rich individualized architecture. Few streets, however, display the completeness of Warren Street, the continuity of building styles, the great variety in details and color, and the diversity within a consistency of scale and design. A pleasant town green is surrounded by stores. Historic-style lampposts were installed as part of one of those 1970s federally funded streetscape programs. Side streets are mostly a tight fabric of single- and two-family residences with scattered corner stores. Pockets of emptiness exist due to fire or occasional demolition. And only a few drive-in uses mar the perfect streetscape. Warren Street's rare intactness represents what many main streets once had and lost. Also, typically, Warren Street is threatened by an outdated zoning code that makes positive change difficult.

Like so many downtowns, Hudson declined after World War II as manufacturing diminished. Businesses relocated to the strip. Retail shifted to bigger and bigger malls. Residential settlements sprawled out around the county and Hudson youth grew up and moved on. County residents gave up on Warren Street. Urban renewal cleared blocks of old buildings in one section of downtown to be filled with subsidized housing projects. Hudson property owners found a good thing renting downtown apartments to government-guaranteed subsidized low-income tenants, giving Warren Street a down-and-out personality. Investment all but disappeared. Buildings deteriorated. Decay continued.

Over the years, however, Columbia County, in which Hudson sits, gained appeal to New York City residents looking for an alternative life style or a second home in the country. Newcomers found Warren Street appealing, and some found the cheap space a great opportunity to open a new business. *Their view of downtown was not influenced by the memory of what used to be.* By the early 1990s, antique stores were filling empty low-priced Warren Street storefronts. More than 50 opened. Many bought and fixed up their buildings. Local residents scoffed at the trend catering to "outsiders," but then, they had given up on Warren Street a long time before. A new sense of community emerged out of an effort to restore as a community center and performance space the 1855 Hudson Opera House, a substantial building of modest architectural appeal that once housed City Hall and could anchor Warren Street with diverse programs. Before the Opera House effort, few cared about what happened on Warren Street and no community had rallied to downtown's cause. Since then, a community-based planning effort has been initiated, a local development agency is taking downtown seriously, and the political establishment is realizing something is happening they can't ignore.

A windshield view of Warren Street leads to the mistaken impression that only antique stores have moved to Hudson. But there is always more than meets the eye in any downtown, and in Hudson, plenty is not readily apparent. "Innovation," the late critic Brendan Gill pointed out, "is at first invisible when it is incubating." Furniture restorers, upholsterers, and designers have followed antique dealers. Art dealers and galleries have opened. Craftspeople of all kinds are gravitating and, slowly but surely, the professional base is broadening. A new men's clothing store has opened. A few of the long-standing businesses (photo supply, hardware, sporting goods, electrical supply) saw business increase. A fabric store opened, offering popular classes such as quilting, and found customers among shoppers who had not been to downtown Hudson in years. A young couple with a baby bought a building for her furniture restoration business, for expanding his landscape/nursery business (an empty lot is next door), and for an upstairs residence. Similar resident/entrepreneurs are following. Restaurants, an art film theater on a street parallel to Warren, Time and Space Limited, and a restored St. Charles Hotel (see Chapter 11) round out the elements appealing to new downtown enthusiasts, like Dunleavy. The Department of Motor Vehicles, an important downtown activity generator, almost left downtown in search of more space, but relocated instead to a vacated classic bank building. This gradually improving scenario parallels many in downtowns across the country.

Dunleavy finds a "real sense of community expressed on the street. I see a hundred or more small business people all the time, at the bank, at the post office, or just on the street."

MODEST INVESTMENTS/SIGNIFICANT RETURNS

Entrepreneurs like Dunleavy are, and will in the future, make downtowns come alive again, bringing in a new sense of optimism. Most significantly, they look at the upside of downtown, not the downside of what has disappeared. Too many long-time residents focus on decline, not on rebirth. Thus, new or younger entrepreneurs from within or outside the area are an essential to the rebirth of a downtown. *The challenge is to get new entrepreneurs to want to come, to identify them, to recognize their potential, and to figure out what it takes to nurture their growth.*

Some new business people, like Dunleavy, do not need much financial help. Dunleavy's start-up costs were small. A few sewing machines, cutting tables, material, and cheap rent. He was able to get a line of credit at the local Fleet Bank branch. He took advantage, however, of a Columbia County MicroBusiness program of the Columbia–Hudson Partnership that offered a seminar series on the basics of running a business and one-on-one consulting assistance. "I did not know how to make cash flow projections," says Dunleavy, "or how to plan ahead. The training was invaluable." He met others in the program to discuss problems with, to network, and to "share a sense of camaraderie." The program also offered start-up loans of up to $25,000, but the bank line of credit was more convenient and less cumbersome. Dunleavy had a business track record banks are willing to take a risk in. This is frequently not the case. Small alternative loan programs are crucial.

In Corning, New York, for example, Corning Enterprises, a division of Corning Incorporated, established the Corning Crafts Project, a low-interest loan program for craftspeople. Project staff assist craftspeople in locating downtown space in which they may work and sell wholesale. A condition, however, is that at least one-third of the space must be allocated to retail. For this, low-interest loans of up to $40,000 are available. In this case, a prerequisite is that the entrepreneur must have some business experience or knowledge of running a business.

Joan Reuning weaves on her loom in the window. Strollers frequently stop to watch, then enter her shop on Market Street, Corning, New York.

Joan Reuning, a woman now in her 50s, is a resident and business owner in Ithaca, 50 miles northeast of

Corning and home of Cornell University. Her store, Fibers and Fantasy, had been successfully operating in Ithaca for several years, carrying handcrafted goods from all over the country.

Reuning was looking to expand. Previously, she had opened a second store in Rochester, New York, that failed, but that, she knew, had more to do with what was missing from downtown Rochester (a city of 150,000) than her store's potential. She heard about the Corning program and was familiar with that city and its vibrantly revitalized downtown, as mentioned earlier. "The incentive was irresistible," she says. With the project's help, she opened in 1991, has been doing quite well, and has become a downtown destination for shoppers. "You know you can always find something unique in that shop," observes a long-time resident. She carries a full stock of knitted, woven, and batik clothes, jewelry, pottery, and a whole assortment of accessories. She, herself, is a weaver and placed a loom in the window on which she would work. Passersby frequently stop to watch.

OUT OF SMALL BEGINNINGS, LARGE INDUSTRIES HAVE GROWN

It is too easy to dismiss specialized gift businesses like Rainforth's, small dress businesses like Dunleavy's, or craft businesses like Reuning's as insignificant. This denies a little-recognized segment of the economy and an important element found in most downtown regeneration. Dismissing this trend ignores history. Most of today's big companies started small.

Simon Pearce, for example, is already a nationally recognized manufacturer of fine glassware and pottery, sold on Madison Avenue in New York City; Princeton, New Jersey; Bethesda, Maryland; Newberry Street in Boston; and other upscale shopping areas. The glassware is handblown and the pottery is handmade in two factories in Vermont that also have retail operations. Forty potters work in one factory and three glass blowers in the other. In Quechee, Pearce restored an historic woolen mill at an Ottauquechee River waterfall with a restored original hydropower system to electrify the building. In Windsor, a new 32,000-square-foot facility just for glass blowing was designed to resemble a classic Vermont barn and harnesses heat from the glass furnaces to distribute through the building. At both facilities, the public is able to view the potters and glass blowers working, and families regularly bring children to watch the process. Pearce, a glass designer and blower raised in County Cork, Ireland, trained at the Royal College of Art in London and worked all over Europe before establishing his operation in 1981 at the Quechee Mill.

Vitrix Hot Glass of Corning is another example on a smaller scale than Simon Pearce. Vitrix started in 1977 in the same 2000-square-foot storefront it still occupies on Market Street. A brightly lit, gallery-like retail space is in the front. Two or three glass blowers work in the rear. Shipping is done there as well. Ironically, Vitrix occupies part of the former Hawkes Crystal Glass building, one of the major glass companies, along with Corning Glass, of the 50 or more that once occupied Corning's downtown. Vitrix was the first new glass business in downtown since the early part of the 20th century. Since then, two other glassblowing businesses opened. Simon Pearce and Vitrix are both manufacturers *and* retailers. Old distinctions don't readily apply.

National Main Street Center director Kennedy Smith points out that the Internet, particularly the World Wide Web, is actually making it possible for many mom-and-pop downtown businesses to increase their sales by reaching new customers who don't live in the community's geographically-defined trade area. In Chippewa Falls, Wisconsin, Smith reports, J's Gourmet Coffee Shop advertises its Thursday evening concerts and poetry readings to customers via e-mail. Similarly, Norm Sobel, owner of a men's clothing store in downtown Kingsport, Tennessee, has customers from all over the world now via his Web site.

Forty percent of the Main Street Center's affiliated communities report an increase in the numbers of businesses using the Internet to advertise and to contact vendors. "This is an incredible new opportunity for downtown businesses to expand their trade areas dramatically," says Smith. "Even increasing sales by as little as 5 to 10 percent can make the difference between survival and extinction for many small downtown businesses."

Sometimes the impact is just as great, but closer to home. The Main Street Center, working with the Southwest Detroit Business Association, encouraged restaurant owner Omar Hernandez to pursue his dream of opening a bakery across the street from his restaurant in an underutilized three-story commercial building dating from the 1890s, once the Odd Fellows Hall. With design and financial analysis assistance, a façade loan from the city, and $24,000 in loan guarantees, Hernandez opened the Mexicantown Bakery. This modest business employs 9 people in addition to the 3 family members who work there, draws customers from all over metropolitan Detroit, is a popular gathering spot, and has been the catalyst for other private investments. It is becoming increasingly well known that nearly all of the net new jobs created in this country are in businesses employing fewer than 20 people—a wise investment for any downtown.

The economic significance of many small and different things is often unrecognized. Growth potential is ignored, as well. "The Invisible Factory" is what a study calls the crafts economy of western North Carolina.[2] The study revealed a $122 million contribution to the regional economy, more than half the market value of all agricultural products from the 20-county survey region and *four times greater than the revenue derived from raw tobacco production*. Retail sales make up 58 percent of the $122 million total, most of which occur either in downtown stores or at regional fairs. Those numbers cannot be minimized. But the significance reaches way beyond the numbers. The components of this economic sector seek no special treatment from government, no tax breaks, no site improvements, and no special infrastructure like improved roads, sewage, or drainage. A kind of low-maintenance economic development. And because they are spread around a whole region, their economic impact has a broad reach. The multiple levels of impact here don't register along traditional measurement standards and are mistakenly dismissed as too small to matter. *Nothing* is too small to matter!

How this study even came about is significant. Two women intuitively recognized the overlooked economic strength of the region. Experts challenged their assumptions, saying, "Show us numbers we can understand." Becky Anderson was then director of economic development for the Asheville Chamber of Commerce. She and her research assistant, Sassi McClellan, had been observing the economically viable craft component of the region for years. They applied to the Pew Charitable Trust's Partnership for Civic Change for support.

All over the country today, regional producers are making a broader and broader assortment of products that can be loosely identified as handcrafts, with variations of Reuning's Fiber and Fantasy selling the goods in revived downtown streets. We have found this to be true from Carmel, California, to Denver, to Santa Fe, New Mexico, to Hanover, New Hampshire, to Ybor City, Florida, to Brooklyn, New York. In fact, the "Made In..." trend is catching on. Stores selling products made in one locality, region or state are multiplying. Furniture of every kind. Dinner dishes. Linens. Clothes. Toys. Paper goods. Rugs. Lamps. Leather goods. Real products. This must be looked at as a nascent but growing new manufacturing economy. In fact, an increasing number of producers are joining together in organizations to exchange information, network, gain business advice, and get help reaching new markets. Sometimes the term "craft" is avoided entirely, as with the Creative Industries Development Council, based in a former grain storage building in Shelburne Falls, Massachusetts.

The definition of crafts embraces a broad spectrum, of locally made goods marketed at hobbies and craft fairs, contests, shows, galleries, and retail stores. Everyone in the field seems to offer different definitions, reflecting individuality within a big field, and similar to what we saw in Chapter 9 on markets with different definitions offered everywhere. There are craft centers, guilds, collaboratives, cooperative galleries, and local, regional, and state organizations representing practitioners. Whether alone or in groups, many of these small producers work and sell out of the same space, and often in a downtown. If it is not already in a downtown, these are among the kinds of businesses that can be encouraged to locate downtown.

Fifteen or 20 years ago, crafts businesses were looked down upon as "the hippie thing," notes Carol Ross, director of the annual Wholesale

Crafts Fair held at the Javits Center in New York City. The handcrafted products business has expanded so much that the annual fair has mushroomed to twice a year in New York and once a year in Washington, Boston, Chicago, Baltimore, Philadelphia, and San Francisco. An extensive section is reserved just for American-made goods. The growth is unmeasured, says Ross. "No one recognized the potential, so no one kept track."

Manufacturing, in both new and familiar guises, is also showing signs of new growth, to the unrecognized benefit of many downtowns. The accepted notion that manufacturing is dying and has been for decades is so ingrained that any deviation from that conventional wisdom is dismissed as inconsequential. In fact, even the accepted standards of measurement camouflage significant truths and prevent revelation of new trends.

How does one define manufacturing today? As noted earlier with Vitrix, the glass company located on Market Street in Corning, a product is manufactured *and* sold in their storefront. Is that manufacturing or retail? Vitrix glass is sold locally and across the country. Is that serving a local or national market?

Kinko's is a national chain of "copy centers." Is that a service business? Is it manufacturing? After all, Kinko's is a printing industry. How different is it from the "lost" pieces of the printing industry that fall into the category of lost manufacturing when today's version of the same product is the result?

A Brooklyn manufacturer of lamp parts is defined by a City Planning Department study as serving a local market. The implication is that it is not as significant as manufacturing that serves a global market. But the parts are going to a lamp manufacturer exporting around the world. That surely is global. So doesn't the original parts maker have a global function?

Traditional manufacturing, in which a product is designed, made, marketed, and distributed under one roof or within one company, is rare. Now, so much is fragmented into different entities and separately classified. Some businesses that used to be separate and distinct are now overlapping. Supermarkets, for example, are beginning to bake a lot of their own goods. Does that change their classification? Are they manufacturers now? And, if that is not enough confusion, look at printed T-shirts. If produced in quantity in a factory, they are manufacturing. If customized in a store, they are retail. Both are printed T-shirts. *More and more, technology is bringing the process to the customer at the store. This is the real technology revolution. It is called "mass customization." And it is good news for cities and for small downtowns as well. Smaller and smaller lots are being produced at decentralized, smaller sites, nearer the market. Empty storefronts, lofts, or unobtrusive neighborhood commercial sites are ideal.*

Relying on standardized, conventional measurements to know what is happening in a field or a place is less and less reliable. On-site observations, anecdotal reports, and streetside surveys warrant greater consideration. National measurement statistics totally eclipse micro impacts. Definitions of economic value need rethinking. Downtown value increases in such reconsiderations.

Everywhere, there are tales of new businesses started by talented people laid off by merged or shrinking corporations, many of them downtown. Even small local and regional banks offering low prices and personal service are on the rise again, *The Wall Street Journal* noted, calling it "the new wave of bank creation." In a March 4, 1996, front-page story, "Displaced by Mergers, Some Bankers Launch Their Own Start-Ups," Nikhil Deogun wrote, "As giant banks gobble up giant banks, they are leaving behind crumbs...experienced displaced bankers...are scrambling to reassemble the pieces." And why not? As corporations get bigger, more uniform, less local, and less personal, smaller services and products are bound to fill the gaps left at the bottom. And, as indicated earlier, a young generation is opening all kinds of enterprises, determined to be masters of their own future. This age of mega-industries, mega-projects, and global markets is blinding. Nothing *started* big. The combinations of small things provide vitality and stability.

Sidney Grossman, as noted, rescued entire towns by luring smaller industries to fill vacated factories. Meadville reinvented itself into many small producers after the one large one left town. On the Brooklyn waterfront, Greg O'Connell has turned abandoned piers and warehouses into a growing center of small businesses and singlehandedly proved experts wrong. No government money or program made this happen. Banks that for years wouldn't give him the time of day call regularly, offering loans.

Brooklyn's once-thriving industrial waterfront was long ago declared obsolete as a site for industry and shipping, not unlike similar locales around the country. Its death was prematurely declared in the 1950s, when Project Planners developed a new agenda for the area and promoted the idea that significant industry in Brooklyn had no future. The Port Authority of New York and New Jersey had begun development and modernization of the New Jersey waterfront that would attract Brooklyn seaport activity even though the Port Authority's original mission was to build a tunnel for freight trains from Brooklyn to New Jersey. No comparable investment was directed to the Brooklyn waterfront. Highway mastermind Robert Moses built the Gowanus Expressway, which bisected South Brooklyn and cut off the job-rich waterfront from the upland neighborhoods and the rest of the borough. Bustling streets and solid housing were cleared for the Red Hook Houses, a 28-building public housing complex with 8000 residents, half of whom are on public assistance. Acres of Red Hook land were cleared for big projects that never materialized. After the war, federal housing

Below: Greg O'Connell, standing by his truck, before one of his Brooklyn waterfront properties.

Bottom: Pier 41 revived on the Brooklyn, New York, waterfront.

mortgages, highways, and new suburbs drew heavily from the blue-collar population that included Italians, Irish, and Jews. The neighborhood gained a new name, Red Hook, because of its geographical shape. The 1990 census showed 11,000 people living where 22,000 lived in 1950; 75 percent of that current population lives in public housing.

Clearly, the nature of shipping and industry has changed considerably in 50 years, accounting for some diminishment of seaport business. Nothing, however, stood in the way of natural and positive change, if such dramatic Project Planning had not undermined what was there and reshaped the future. By the 1980s, city planners imagined mega-projects for the waterfront, luxury housing with spectacular New York Harbor views, and connections to Manhattan by ferries and hydroplanes. By the 1990s, superstores were added to the planning agenda. No bigger waste of a spectacular waterfront resource can be imagined. These were classic Project Plans, pre-ordained and devised by city planning department staff to meet a development and political agenda, not a solution emerging from a problem solving process.

While officials were busy planning to rezone the area, O'Connell, a former New York police detective, was quietly buying up neglected waterfront properties, renovating them, and leasing space to small businesses hungry for such space. O'Connell is a plain-talking man in his mid-50s with a boyish face and thick head of curly hair, who is normally seen dressed in work overalls and a T-shirt and driving around in a truck. O'Connell first made money buying small residential properties and improving and managing them. He did his bookkeeping in his truck, parked on the waterfront, of which he now owns 28 acres. The assemblage of Civil War-era granite warehouses and red brick piers captivated him.

In 1982, he bought his first waterfront warehouse, a three-story, 84,000-square-foot building, 12 percent occupied and housing five employees. Refurbished and rapidly leased, that building now has six new businesses—a furniture manufacturer, a leather goods manufacturer, a specialty door and wood molding producer, a furniture storage business, and two record retention centers. The purchase of three more substantial properties followed, similarly refurbished and fully occupied with manufacturers, distributors, custom goods fabricators, and importers.

Brooklyn is not unique. New manufacturing opportunities exist everywhere industry once flourished. The goal does not have to be one big company requiring expensive incentives that are a drain on the public budget. Modest, creative public investment is called for. *Nurturing smaller concerns, in fact, takes more skill and wisdom than public money.*

Scores of potential new businesses exist in most downtowns. Modest doses of public assistance often can make something happen that might not otherwise occur. Directly investing in the people whose businesses could add to the local economy is a downtown essential of great import.

Critical to the success of Mansfield's Carousel District and the slow but sure reinvigoration of the larger downtown area, for example, was a Chamber of Commerce-initiated start-up and working capital loan fund. Six banks annually contribute $250,000 each to a loan pool administered by Mansfield's Main Street Program, which also coordinates downtown promotions and aims to eventually stimulate development of more downtown housing. The bank contributions meet obligations under CRA (Community Reinvestment Act). CRA holds banks accountable for addressing the banking needs and concerns of citizens living in the banking district.

In the first six years of the program, 25 new businesses, with 200 employees, secured loans. The interest is pegged to the prime rate, like many bank loan programs. Loans range from $15,000 to $250,000 cover inventory, operating, or leasehold expenses, and include a 10-year payout period. The Mansfield program is comparable to many standard bank loans, but conventional bank financing appropriate to the nature of small start-up businesses is normally difficult to secure. Conventional financing terms are not geared to the particular nature of small businesses. A locally-administered loan pool can do what commercial banks won't.

FREE RENT AS ECONOMIC DEVELOPMENT

Many variations of local loan pools or government-sponsored loan programs meant to assist revitalization can be found. Some of them succeed. Many fail. And all of them make for interesting study by people who really understand the nature of downtown businesses and small entrepreneurial needs. Most common, however, are programs geared to only the physical and aesthetic aspects of downtown needs. Historic preservation and façade improvement loans. Urban design plans. New construction programs. Sidewalk improvements, tree plantings, street furniture, signage upgrades. But the additional critical piece, the marketing and tenant identification role illustrated by the work of Katherine

Glover in Mansfield, is rarely financed. The success of the physical improvement programs depends on this element, often missing from downtown strategies. *With all the private and public funds spent over and over again on economic studies, street trees, sidewalk cement, is there no way to invest in people? Cannot tying the local economy together again and creating a place of pride be accomplished at the same time?*

Banks are beginning to recognize, profitably, the new opportunity and growth potential. As banks become less and less the loan resource for big companies turning to Wall Street for financing, small opportunities are filling a void. Some nontraditional loan programs directed at downtown entrepreneurs are quite innovative. Their number is increasing.

ENCOURAGING NEW ENTREPRENEURS, NOT JUST CREATING JOBS

Al Dowe, a long-time jazz musician who plays the trombone and trumpet and has had his own band since 1974, had always dreamed of having a jazz club. Since the late 1980s, Dowe has also been teaching music in Pittsburgh public schools. Part of his jazz club dream was establishing a music school for kids, to create a student band, hire three or four teachers, hold open house for parents once a week, and offer summer outdoor concerts.

With the help of a new Pittsburgh loan program, Dowe received loan approval to purchase a modest, one-story vacant restaurant with a distinctive original Art Deco, black Carrara glass façade called the Club Café, just off Carson Street, the vibrant commercial thoroughfare (formerly a streetcar route) on Pittsburgh's South Side. The school was launched, starting with only a few students, but experiencing a demand already larger than he expected. A major new school of music could easily emerge out of this small effort. Clearly, Dowe's music school dream contributes something new to Pittsburgh and gives opportunity to both paying and nonpaying students.

The modest loan program was initiated by the Pittsburgh History and Landmarks Foundation (PHLF). For two decades, PHLF has pioneered, with enormous success, the rebuilding of deteriorated low-income neighborhoods through innovative historic preservation programs that foster home ownership and community development.[3] Local business development has always been included in its overall program, with its Preservation Loan Fund offering loans to scattered locally-owned businesses. In recent years, the fund has stepped up assistance to small neighborhood merchants with the goal of reinforcing existing local commercial corridors that provide walking distance shopping.

In 1995, a specific new program was initiated, WIN (Working in Neighborhoods), to direct small business loans to low-income neighborhoods. "Neighborhoods need local businesses to be complete neighborhoods," Loan Fund Director Howard B. Slaughter Jr. says simply.

This seems like such a simple truth. *Nowadays, however, so many housing programs focus only on housing production without helping to recreate the commercial centers that are critical to neighborhood strength and which distinguish urban neighborhoods from suburban developments.* Ironically, the WIN program is financed primarily by small suburban savings banks that wanted to meet their CRA obligations but did not know how. Slaughter had an extensive banking career before taking over the Loan Fund, and knew how to set up a program on terms the banks could accept. Eleven banks put in a total of $750,000 and the Preservation Loan Fund added $250,000. Loans are at market rate for up to 15 years, with a maximum of $75,000. The goal is to create entrepreneurs, not just jobs.

Every community now is filled with small entrepreneurs, each a potential downtown business, now operating out of a home, a garage, a single roadside building, or a strip mall. This **is** *the local economy, once represented in downtowns but now often floating, dispersed, uncentered, disconnected in an uprooted, unrooted, amorphous state.*

Lure to Main Street those disconnected pieces that make up the local economy. When stores fill up and customer traffic increases, new activity is generated. People return to Main Street for more than one errand. Each element feeds and reinforces the other. A critical mass of economic activity evolves, and the downtown whole becomes stronger than the sum of the parts. Every downtown needs it. Government, private financial institutions, or a combination of both could underwrite such an effort at far less cost than is now wasted on misconceived or overpriced programs of considerable less benefit. This should be viewed as an investment, not a subsidy.

For local communities, however, free or cheap rent would be the simplest, cleanest, and probably most effective "economic development" program for new storefront tenants and small manufacturers. This is a complicated concept to administer, but appropriate guidelines can be developed. Smaller sums of public dollars are involved than in most economic development programs that assist a few big projects. The qualifications can include needed services for the community, such as Al Dowe's music teaching classes. Many businesses, especially those related to the performing and visual arts and those that actually manufacture products, have educational potential—classes for young students and the elderly, downtown improvement services, or product contributions to community efforts.

Free or cheap rent may seem like a simplistic notion to be a stimulus for economic activity. Resistance in official circles to this idea, even on a small scale, is strong. Resistance to big giveaway programs that add nothing new to the economy is minimal. Economist Donovan Rypkema has examined trade publications, business statement studies, and Dun &

Bradstreet reports, seeking to understand what percentage of business revenue goes to what. In most small businesses, whether sales are $60,000 or $600,000, Rypkema notes, the percentage of gross sales that goes to rent (4 percent to 7 percent) equals the profit. A rent subsidy, in effect, provides the profit margin for a business where there might not be one, as solid an incentive as one can offer. The new business might not be so lucky to have a profit the first year, but the rent subsidy might make the difference between breaking even or going under. Few businesses take fewer than three years to take hold. The rent, Rypkema points out as an aside, is almost the only cost, other than advertising, over which a merchant has control.

Starting modestly underwriting Main Street rents entails a much smaller public investment than large, single-purpose projects. Some municipalities initiate loan guarantees or indirectly offer small business loans.[4] Even if a loan guarantee program worked well, 70 percent to 80 percent of the new businesses would still open without any kind of institutional loan. The application process and paperwork are often too intimidating for first-time merchants. Very few new businesses borrow from banks or other lending institutions in order to open. Many of them don't meet bank criteria for business loans. Instead, most new entrepreneurs use their savings, borrow from family or friends, or stock their businesses to the limit of their credit cards. Free or subsidized rent fits that mindset in a much more comfortable and encouraging manner.

For the local government, moreover, it is clean and simple to offer free rent for a year, with diminishing support for a few years after. This is a clear, targeted intervention that is finite, not a bottomless pit. If the business fails, the lost public investment is limited. Secondary benefits, at least, probably resulted, such as employment for local residents. Downtown businesses are interdependent, drawing customers for and from each other. Even if a rent-subsidized business fails, during its existence it has probably drawn some customers downtown from whom other merchants might have benefited and maybe captured. At worst, it is a failure with value.

SIMPLE ASSISTANCE CAN GET THINGS STARTED

In Meeker County, Minnesota, for example, Russ Bjorhus, a man in his sixties, left his job as state director of Farmers Home Administration to become director of economic development for the county, firmly believing in the importance of strong local economies for the health of the county and state. A Wal-Mart and Pamada had opened a few years earlier.[5] Scattered downtown stores closed. Bjorhus grew concerned about the ability of the seven county downtowns to survive, and was looking for a way for the county to nurture local economies. *Too many county development officials encourage development of new industrial parks with-*

in their *tax districts and under* their *control rather than nurture growth in an existing downtown that keeps its own taxes.*

In his own town of Litchfield, with a population of 6100 and approximately 50 stores, the megastore openings were endangering the future of the downtown's anchor department store, Boyd's for Boys and Girls, a traditional, family-run operation that had served community needs well. Like many such retail operations, the owner was nearing retirement age, hoping to sell when the time came. When a merchant like Boyd is put out of business, the idea prevails that "he was planning to retire anyway." *Forgotten is the fact that merchants invest years of their lives to build a business, counting on selling. The expectation is never to just close the door one day and call it quits.*

Boyd's two daughters decided to take over the store, rather than let it close. They made changes, strengthened personal relationships with customers, and added services. Boyd had never advertised and was "shocked" when his daughters did so in the newspaper of the neighboring town. And when the daughters put up a billboard, he was "horrified." They upgraded the quality of the merchandise to get out of direct competition with the megastores, experimenting with different lines.

While the Boyd sisters were showing modest signs of success, Bjorhus understood that something more was necessary for downtown Litchfield to both reinforce its strengths and protect against erosion. No organization is in place to promote the downtown, and many businesses are owned by "old-timers" nearing retirement, like Boyd. Four vacancies out of 50 stores is not panic time, but something new had to be seen as possible. Bjorhus surveyed the downtown offerings. A Ben Franklin variety store, jewelry store, gift shop, business supply and hardware store, along with Boyd's—a familiar assortment. But Bjorhus remembered the bakery that had closed two years before and had remained empty. Downtown was weak on food offerings and could support a bakery.

Bjorhus secured a $600,000 low-interest loan under a federal relending program for small businesses. The county pays 1 percent interest and reloans at 2fi percent below prime. Armed with this tool, Bjorhus set out to find potential merchants. His first project had to be successful to gain credibility and momentum. The bakery became the target. But he understood that having money to lend does not bring borrowers. Bjorhus talked to as many individuals as possible and addressed fraternal clubs, similar to what Katherine Glover did.

Following a Rotary Club presentation, four local businessmen—a restaurateur, an accountant, and two owners of a radio station—approached him. They borrowed $40,000, invested another $40,000, and hired two bakers and four salespeople. Bakery and Etc., offering fresh goods "made from scratch," found an appreciative audience and is flourishing. Not surprisingly, neighboring downtowns are looking to follow the example, and Bjorhus continues to talk up his program. He believes that many people have businesses in their homes that, with the right kind of encouragement and confidence-building, could be persuaded to expand into a downtown store. A carpet company also took advantage of the loan program and opened on Main Street. A local framer moved her business from her home to Main Street without a loan. She specializes in selling prints of local artists. The perception of downtown is slowly turning positive. And perception is half the battle. More people are coming.

Another variation works in Denver. The Denver Capital Corporation, funded by another consortium of banks to meet their CRA obigations, is a for-profit entity providing loans to promising small businesses. Many small businesses can pay regular interest rates, but need a longer than usual payout period. The quasi-public DCC can take risks that banks are either unwilling or unable to take alone. The DCC takes a business inventory as collateral. As of 1992, 40 new businesses had been created, most of them owned and operated by women and minorities. So far, the default rate is less than that of the business loans in the banks' conventional portfolios. Traditional financial institutions are not geared to lending this way, and few people recognize the potential value of such modest efforts.

None of the catalytic initiatives so far described would ever be enough to jump-start a downtown economy. *No one program can be enough.* But any single program can be a place to begin. Each must be tackled with innovative solutions. Everything is connected. Each piece helps another piece. The rebirth must be a process comprising of many components and many people. The many parts help build a whole but those parts must primarily be local for stability to take hold. This is Urban Husbandry.

No large-scale project is targeted. No outside business or developer is relied on. No big public financing is required. No big government subsidy is sought. Outside resources and people fit only as adjuncts to local efforts. Genuine local economic development is the goal and the gain.

If downtown is not strong, if a good proportion of local people are not in business locally, spending profits locally, hiring local people who spend their money locally, running for PTA president, or leading a church fundraising effort, then there is no foundation to build on, no support for the larger civic projects, a house of cards that falls unless artificially maintained at public expense. Big projects never cease their dependency on tax-dollar support. Small ones require little public investment. The regional impacts of small successes add up to a significant national impact.

1. The entire train ride is along the shore of the Hudson, offering spectacular views of this majestic landscape.

2. The study was conducted in 1994 by Dr. Dinesh Dave and Dr. Michael Evans of the John A. Walker College of Business at Appalachian State University with the support of the North Carolina Department of Commerce, the North Carolina Department of Cultural Resources, the Pew Charitable Trust, the North Carolina Rural Center, and the Z. Smith Reynolds Foundation.

3. See *The Living City*, pp. 74 and 286.

4. A municipality might write down the loan costs of a bank program but not make the loans directly.

5. Pamada is a large retailer concentrated in the Midwest. Both Wal-Mart and Pamada opened in St. Cloud, 42 miles from Litchfield.

IT'S HAPPENING

SoHo—the model for reborn loft and manufacturing districts across America.

CHAPTER THIRTEEN

THE SOHO SYNDROME

SoHo was one of the great forces of change
in this country.
  Dr. James Marston Fitch

The emergence of SoHo changed the way the country views and values
cities. The onetime New York industrial district was transformed with
little loss of its 19th-century buildings, without any suburbanizing
adjustments, without any diminution of its authentic urbanism, and
without large public funding. A more up-to-date, modern district cannot
be found in this country. SoHo epitomizes positive progress and enormous change.

A defeat of Project Planning and a victory of Urban Husbandry
made SoHo possible. SoHo's success led to scores of similar successes,
first in and around New York and then throughout the country. SoHo and
its offspring offer the best lessons for understanding, and even redefining, downtown's future potential. The downtowns where the SoHo syndrome has taken hold, or has just begun to take hold, are the downtowns
best positioned for successful rejuvenation in the 21st century.

Project Planners had designated the 45 acres of five- to six-story
factory buildings (no higher than a hook-and-ladder fire truck could
reach) in lower Manhattan, now known as SoHo, for extinction. Vast
highway networks and urban renewal plans were valued more than
organic, unplanned cities. A 10-lane expressway lined with huge apartment towers was planned to cut through the area to link the East River
bridges with the Holland Tunnel, facilitating travel between developing
Long Island and the rest of the country. The expressway had been
planned and talked about since the 1940s, but was formally unveiled in
1959. (The 1956 Federal Interstate Highway Act, with its 90 percent federal funding, gave highway planners the opportunity to implement scores
of road projects long on the drawing boards.) Four hundred sixteen
buildings, 2000 housing units, and at least 800 commercial and industrial

businesses would have been wiped out. Much of neighboring Little Italy and Chinatown would have been wiped out as well.

Citizen activists fought the Project Plans, defeated the highway, and rescued the district. It took a decade of fighting to kill the project.

A variety of industrial uses continued after the highway's defeat in 1969. Many manufacturers had already moved away due to the uncertainty and instability of the area. They assumed that their buildings would be demolished. Few expected the highway plan to be canceled. Defeating highway plans was unthinkable. New tenants were out of the question. What business would move into a doomed building? Functional buildings stood underoccupied or empty, but not because they were structurally unsound or unsuitable for productive use.

This is the *death threat syndrome*, also known as *planners' blight*. Any residential, commercial, or industrial area begins to die once a new destiny is planned for it. Property owners cease maintenance, anticipating condemnation and demolition. Banks won't lend money, even if property owners are inclined to invest. Businesses move out, not waiting for the battle to play itself out. Even if an announced Project Plan eventually fails to materialize, the announced plan can kill an area.

A highway plan is like a big billboard with a message to property owners: no future use for this area, disinvest in your property, cash in with a sale for a highway. City services diminish. Public resources are directed elsewhere. New investors disappear. Tenants and owner-occupants make plans to relocate. This happened to SoHo, with the death threat of the expressway plan hovering over it. This was totally unnatural decay. Many experts tried to identify it otherwise.

Manhattan manufacturing during the Depression decreased less than in the rest of the country. During World War II, it increased only moderately. The biggest cause of subsequent decline was the clearance for urban renewal at several sites, including the dozen square blocks south of Washington Square Park to Canal Street, where SoHo now starts, and east of City Hall in lower Manhattan for vehicular access to the Brooklyn Bridge. By the 1960s, decline had accelerated considerably, as highways made cheap suburban sites readily accessible.

Chester Rapkin, an economist and against-the-grain planner, led a study of the district in 1963 and discovered some 50 categories of industrial activity in the district, everything from furriers to the makers of dolls, rags, belts, pens, wheel hubs, and boxes. Most workers were minorities, almost half were women, and nearly all, he calculated, would be left unemployed if displaced.[1] Rapkin's report officially changed nothing. "Good planners are powerless," observes Jane Jacobs. The official word remained that the district was dead or dying, a collection of moribund, out-of-date, falling-down buildings. This is always the well-publicized, often-repeated official description of a district for which Project

Planners have written a new agenda. Probably every rejuvenated district in this country has been, at one time, declared moribund by the so-called experts, hired to justify the new political/development agenda. SoHo is probably the best known of them.

Hell's 100 Acres, the area was called by the fire department. Fires were common in the warehouses and small factories. Fire officials labeled the buildings firetraps. However, the activity in those buildings, not the buildings themselves, caused the fires. Code enforcement, not demolition, was called for. Factory floors were often piled with rags, garment scraps, bales of paper, open cans of chemicals, and other easily flammable objects. But fire officials' assessments fed right into the general public impression of the area as filled with derelict and discardable buildings. In the 1960s, the area became known as the Valley because its vast stock of low-rise industrial buildings lay between the skyscrapers of Wall Street and midtown. A distant look at the Manhattan skyline gives the impression of two separate cities, with a vast empty space between them.

Artists pioneered the organic rebirth of the district when they began filling the vacant lofts illegally, creating attractive, functional live/work space. The name SoHo emerged from its locational description, South of Houston Industrial Area. Houston (pronounced HOW-ston) Street is a major east-west crosstown street that, because of its six-lane width, serves as a clear separator on the northern edge, which is the southern border of Greenwich Village. Residential use in the industrial area was against the law. But landlords, unable to find industrial tenants for buildings scheduled for demolition, were happy to get any tenant. Elsewhere, artists' lofts and studios were being demolished, along with whole neighborhoods, by urban renewal, particularly in Greenwich Village (the artists' neighborhood in the 1920s and 1930s). The destruction there was halted with the designation of Greenwich Village as an historic district in 1969. Artist space was at a premium.

Coincidentally, contemporary art experienced a radical shift to large-scale work in the early 1960s. Lofts averaged 2500 square feet of open floor space. (Manufacturers remained longer in the bigger ones.) The large windows of cast-iron construction flooded each floor with natural light. Freight elevators provided useful access. Rents were affordable. A perfect prescription for artists. The transformation of SoHo had begun.

Not one dime of public investment or developer subsidy made SoHo happen. In fact, the defeat of a big, misplanned public investment made SoHo possible. The Lower Manhattan Expressway was conceived by the Regional Plan Association in its 1929 plan for New York that included an elaborate system of highways, bridges and tunnels, many of which were built in the decades that followed. Highway and urban renewal czar Robert Moses used this 1929 plan and added a whole network of New York State highways that gratuitously ripped through cities and set a pattern of highway building, centralized planning, and urban annihilation for the country. Only in the defeat of the highway did urbanism have a chance. Only in the defeat of Project Plans did SoHo have a chance. After the defeat, spontaneous regeneration took hold. Individual creativity rescued the beleaguered district that planners sought to raze. When not doomed by Project Plans, many urban and small-town districts could regenerate productively.

CITIZENS RESCUE SOHO

This pattern of planned urban destruction parading as renewal, set by Moses and his disciples, led to the sprawling, dysfunctional landscape with which the nation now wrestles. Urban defender Jane Jacobs, this century's most insightful urban critic and gutsy community activist, was Moses' most vigorous opponent. Jacobs led the fight against the Lower Manhattan Expressway, after being alerted both by Father Gerard LaMontagne of The Most Holy Crucifix Church on Broome Street and Greenwich Village resident Rachelle Wall. "Father LaMontagne told me about an expressway hearing," Jacobs recalls. "He was very articulate about how it would wipe out Little Italy and destroy a working industrial community. He was later punished by the church for his public role on this issue."

Rachelle Wall "realized early how this kind of traffic treatment would 'Los Angelize' the city. She understood how this highway would connect to others and how the ramps on and off would spread traffic

Friends of Cast Iron Architecture— the badge of honor worn by the SoHo pioneers.

around the city." Margot Gayle turned saving the Cast Iron District, now known as SoHo, into a significant historic preservation fight and, Jacobs notes, "alerted lots of people. She made people recognize the potentialities and value of the area. She was a great architectural educator." Artists began moving in early and were very important to the fight, Jacobs says, and Bob Dylan "wrote a song for us with a lot of street names in it that we sang at rallies. He was not yet famous." News coverage by the late *Village Voice* reporter Mary Perot Nichols was "critical," adds Jacobs, noting that Nichols, like so many people, first thought the expressway would remove traffic from the streets. Eventually, Nichols recognized what is now more widely understood, that highways breed traffic, not relieve it, and she covered the expressway and other battles as the urban wars they were. Nichols, who became a close friend of Jacobs', came to understand the national significance of these conflicts and wrote about them as the struggle for the future of urban America. Not many people understand the depth of that truth.

Jacobs is clear about sharing the credit for the fight against the Lower Manhattan Expressway, but she was its leader. It would not have been a movement without broad public support, instead of a one-woman crusade. But Jacobs gave that movement both the fire and substance. "Jane was our Joan of Arc," recalls Dr. James Marston Fitch, founder of the Columbia University historic preservation program (the first nationwide). In 1968, Jacobs instigated a major citizen protest at a City Planning Commission public hearing that is remembered by many veterans of Village conflicts.

"Moses and his gang," Fitch recalls with a satisfied grin, "limited official speakers to only those in favor of the highway. The audience was furious. Jane got to her feet..." At this point what Fitch remembers is clarified by Jacobs. "They weren't listening to us," she says. "So the idea was that some of us would just silently march across the stage and get them to pay attention. The stenotypist jumped up and grabbed the steno machine to her bosom—I guess she thought we were barbarians—and the tape fell out." Jacobs was summarily arrested.

Carol Greitzer, a long-time Village activist, a key leader in the expressway fight, and, for 15 years a member of City Council, identifies Jacobs as "the leading inspiration and major voice" in opposition to a series of raze-and-redevelop plans that would have erased much of what exists in Greenwich Village and SoHo today. "Many of us recollect that night scores of people waited outside the 5th Precinct while Jane was booked," says Greitzer.

Years ago, in an earlier interview with the author, Jacobs minimized the seriousness of this experience and laughed heartily at the memory. But Fitch recalls grave concern, even on the part of Jacobs' pro-bono lawyer. "She was getting in the way of powerful people," Fitch says. "That can be dangerous."

What most outraged Jacobs was that public hearings were always about "pieces" (commonly called "segments" today) of the highway plan, but never presenting the "whole" plan to the public for approval or disapproval. This is classic procedure for urban renewal and highway proposals. Today, officially, "segmenting" highway projects is not supposed to occur, but clever and more sophisticated maneuvers exist to accomplish the same thing.

Jacobs argued that the unplanned mix of uses is what constitutes a healthy urban district and sustains a viable urban economy. Such a sensible and observable reality was heresy when her first book, *The Death and Life of Great American Cities*, was published in 1961. She contradicted everything that the profession of planning was about and threatened power centers everywhere. This adds significance to the expressway defeat, a significance that reaches well beyond even the rescue and regeneration of SoHo. Urban districts should not be sacrificed for expensive, wasteful, destructive clearance projects, she argued.

Writing in "Metropolis" (December 1994), Greg Sargent noted:

> The confrontation turned SoHo into a battleground of urban ide-
> ologies whose outcome would transform the future of planning
> in New York and many other cities. Emboldened by Jane Jacobs'
> then-subversive attacks on large-scale utopian planning, a coali-
> tion of artists...and surrounding neighborhood groups emerged.
> In 1969, through marches and political pressure, they managed
> to block the expressway...The old tear-it-down, build-it-up idea
> of urban renewal, whose symbol had become the dreaded
> expressway, was defeated, and community-based planning,
> neighborhood preservation, and the "recycling" of buildings
> seemed to have triumphed. Riding the popularity of these ideas,
> preservationists in other East Coast cities managed to stall the
> bulldozers of urban renewal...

Here the lines were first drawn between the Project Planners and
Urban Husbanders, as described in Chapter 3. This was the biggest,
most widely publicized, and maybe even the first significant grass-roots
victory over top-down, autocratic planning. The reverberations had
national impacts. "This victory left a legacy of people energized to fight
harder if they were already embattled or to resist similar schemes where
the battle had not yet been joined," says Ron Shiffman, an advocacy
planner who, in his more than 30 years of work with communities in New
York and around the globe, probably has done more than anyone in New
York to put the ideas of Jane Jacobs into action. Recently, Shiffman
served on the New York City Planning Commission. Shiffman notes:

> Groups reached out to Jane and got her to speak in order to
> learn from the expressway fight. Community groups started
> coming up with alternative plans. There were other Jane Jacobs-
> type community leaders across the country but none gained the
> national attention that she did. New York, of course, is the media
> capital and there is always something happening in a communi-
> ty here that parallels communities elsewhere. Until then, only
> government officials and business leaders made decisions.
> They usually didn't live in the community and knew nothing of
> its vitality. If it was old, they just declared it a slum.

Shiffman heads the Pratt Institute Center for Community and
Environmental Development in Brooklyn, a technical assistance group
that, since the 1960s, has trained hundreds of community planners now
working across the world. Ironically, the center was established in 1963
in reaction *against* Jacobs, who had spoken out in Brooklyn against a

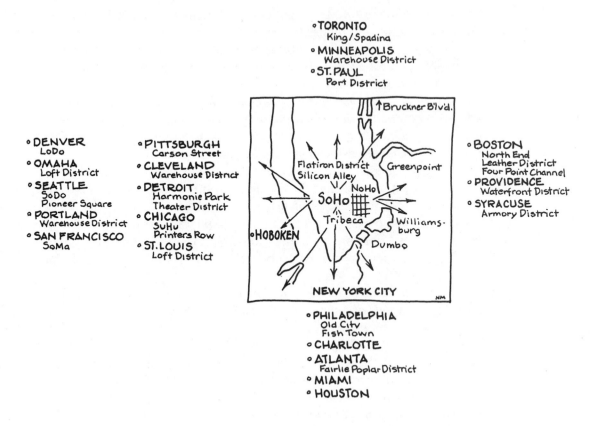

SoHo and its influence on other cities.

huge downtown Brooklyn urban renewal plan that would have wiped out what are today some of Brooklyn's prize neighborhoods within walking distance of its downtown. The Center's founders felt that an organization was needed to educate the public about the benefits of government plans. Shiffman was hired as the first director and *reversed the goal,* establishing the Pratt Center as the model facility for educating government about community needs and how development can *solve problems,* not just plan and promote projects.

Thus, the defeat of the Lower Manhattan Expressway had major impacts on redevelopment issues across the country. In addition, closer to home, it led to even more than the spontaneus regeneration of SoHo. That regeneration spread to other undervalued urban districts. Southwest to TriBeCa (Triangle Below Canal Street), northeast to NoHo (North of Houston) along the whole lower Broadway corridor, ESSO (East of SoHo), further northeast to the East Village.[2] Across the East River to DUMBO (Down Under the Manhattan Bridge) and Brooklyn's historically blue-collar neighborhoods of Greenpoint, Northside, and Williamsburg, where residential and industrial uses have long existed side by side. Up to the South Bronx along Bruckner Boulevard, a heavily-trafficked commercial thoroughfare. Even across the Hudson River into Hoboken, New Jersey. And across the country.

In effect, SoHo performed the classic function of a healthy urban neighborhood that provides an outlet for innovation, gives birth to new businesses, and adds new substance to the local economy and exports its people and innovations to the rest of the city and country.

As critic Jason Epstein has noted, "Artists driven southward by the redevelopment of Greenwich Village...accomplished, without having intended to, what decades of urban renewal had failed to do. They restored a neighborhood and became its taxpayers...SoHo's revival suggests that the spontaneous generation which once characterized New York's growth remains a possibility."[3] This observation should not be limited to New York.

Where the pattern of regeneration has been repeated, the downtowns and neighborhoods of American cities and towns have been reborn, SoHo-style, exhibiting spontaneous rebirth, increasing vitality, innovative growth, and productive change. New is added to old. Some pieces are replaced, but new does not overwhelm the whole. The layering process of history is continued, not interrupted. Most dramatically, the SoHo Syndrome has done more to retain the middle class in cities and stimulate new economic innovations than any planning or government-funded program.

Few people today understand the pivotal role of Jane Jacobs in the evolution of SoHo. SoHo might not exist if not for Jacobs. It is the clearest evidence of the underappreciated, but enormously positive, impact of Jane Jacobs on American cities. SoHo changed the way we view cities nationwide. But first, Jacobs changed the way we viewed SoHo. She subsequently provided in her writing what remains today the most clearheaded, commonsense, incisive understanding of how cities really work and how urban vitality evolves and survives. Ironically, her adopted city, Toronto (see Conclusion), fully appreciated her and embraced her teaching. Recently, that city discarded the long-standing planning and zoning regulations of its old garment district, with its rich assortment of loft and early office buildings. With Jacobs' total involvement in a public planning process, new guidelines, rather than rigid zoning policies, were put in place in complete agreement with Jacobs' prescriptions. This area, known as King/Spadina, of which the Entertainment District is a part, is Toronto's SoHo equivalent and is Toronto's hottest downtown district.

Zoning and density limits were eliminated. Building depth is limited, guaranteeing useful alley separations and preventing full block buildings. All non-noxious uses are permitted, as long as they are in an urban form. Design guidelines limit height, protect street wall, provide set-backs, and protect sunlight. Parking has minimums and maximums, with no open lots permitted. The market is the basic rule setter, but the city stands ready to step in with corrections as needed.

Radical? Contrary to convention? To be sure, by today's planning theory. But this has been the essence of Jacobs' prescriptions. For more than 35 years, she has criticized the planning profession and focused on the ills of zoning. Toronto heard the message, particularly its current far-sighted city planning director, Paul Bedford, who, with Mayor Barbara Hall, set out to fundamentally change things. Bedford viewed Jacobs' approach as perfectly logical, he says, when asked why. "She's simply right," he says, "that's the obvious thing. There are so many pressures put on a planning department that it is easy to be pulled in different directions to the point that the logic of things gets lost. I absolutely told myself I would not let that happen and that I would go the full measure to change things. The reality is that a planner is trained to do the opposite—to compromise. So we said, 'Let's experiment, let's trust the common sense of developers.' People are not going to do stupid things. Everything is always full of 'what ifs?' The system bogs down. The result is paralysis when you try to anticipate everything. That's what planners usually try to do. The public goal is positive change and we are getting those results incredibly fast. It is all perfectly logical. The proof is in the pudding." Such common sense is refreshing.

THE GENUINE SPREADS NATURALLY

The SoHo syndrome spread across the country slowly. First, the district recycled itself, step by small step, naturally, as an arts district. Gradually, artists' new settlement patterns and the creativity with which they converted manufacturing spaces gained media attention. Loft living became a trend in many cities. Every downtown wanted a SoHo. Today, almost every downtown that has any old manufacturing buildings and warehouses left either has a SoHo-style district or one in formation. And they take pride in citing the SoHo example. Some even mimic the name.

Denver's Lower Downtown is called LoDo. Seattle's South of the Dome is called SoDo, San Francisco's South of Market is SoMa. One of Chicago's loft districts, River North, north of the downtown Loop, has been dubbed SuHu because the popular conversions are concentrated around Superior and Huron Streets. Unfortunately for Chicago, in River North, now SuHu, developers tore down dozens of good loft buildings on speculation in the booming 1980s, just before the hot real estate market fell apart, leaving considerable vacant space. In many places, the Loft or Warehouse Districts are popular designations. Even Houston, the city of the car, mega-towers, an underground retail network, and sparse street life, has a growing loft district across the Bayou. Similarly, Omaha, which let so much of its SoHo potential be erased for construction of the sub-urban campus of ConAgra, has a reviving loft district.

Fairlie Poplar District in Atlanta. The Armory District in Syracuse. Lowertown, the port and railroad district in St. Paul. Carson Street and the South Side blue-collar neighborhoods of Pittsburgh. The Printers Row and Fulton River districts in Chicago.[4] The North End of Boston, once targeted for "renewal" by Project Planners. The Warehouse Districts of Minneapolis and Cleveland. The Waterfront and former Jewelry (now ProHo) Districts of Providence, Rhode Island. Pioneer Square in Seattle. The Theater District and Harmonie Park in Detroit. The Warehouse District in Portland, Oregon. The SoHo Syndrome appears to be almost everywhere. Even in Charlotte, North Carolina, a city that offi-cially exhibits no appreciation for traditional urbanism, random loft buildings are being recycled. Unfortunately for cities like Charlotte, with no gritty, tightly arranged urban fabric left, the SoHo Syndrome doesn't have much chance to bring new vitality to the center of downtown. But interestingly, slightly away from downtown along North Davidson Avenue, an arts district is emerging in low-rise factory buildings and storefronts. Eventually, this could become the most vibrant downtown district. The financial core has little room left for such vitality to take root. The few distinctive old buildings of various size and age remaining in Charlotte's core are doomed for demolition.

The newest frontier of regeneration going on is in the old financial and commercial districts, the former Wall Streets of cities such as Philadelphia, Boston, and Chicago, to name a few. In some places, tax incentives have accelerated the trend. In districts with buildings of the scale of 1920s skyscrapers, modest incentives may be justifiable, espe-cially since developers are now accustomed to incentives of some sort. The investment tax credits for historic buildings and low-income housing have served this purpose admirably for years all over the country. Local governments help when restrictions on residential and mixed use are lift-ed, live/work zoning prohibitions eliminated, new parking capacity is not required and public funds are spent on open space and infrastructure improvements. Early conversion districts, like SoHo, started without city help and despite government opposition.

In New York's Wall Street, for example, the recycling of the architec-turally incomparable commercial skyscrapers is developer-driven, and is aimed at creating a 24-hour financial district. Old office buildings, it should be noted, are built bigger than current zoning would allow replacements to be. This appeals to developers who seek to build the biggest building allowable. In fact, like most traditional neighborhoods, under current zon-ing this business district could not be built again. *Ironically, this is actual-ly a community-based process unfolding. In this case, the stakeholders of Wall Street and the real estate owners are the community, the people who know the assets of the area and the needs. They are very involved in the rebirth process. Participation couldn't be greater. Can the city learn from this model of Urban Husbandry and Participatory Planning?*

SOHO BROADENED THE HISTORIC PRESERVATION MOVEMENT

SoHo had a significant impact, as well, on the historic preservation movement. SoHo was the first gritty, working commercial district to be designated an official New York City Historic District, quite a contrast to the residential enclaves of Georgian, Federal, and other period houses championed by preservationists at the time. Georgetown, Greenwich Village, Rittenhouse Square, Beacon Hill, and similar treasured districts were the focus of the then-narrowly defined national preservation movement. "Few people even knew about Cast Iron buildings," remembers Margot Gayle, who founded Friends of Cast Iron Architecture ("a two-bit organization with a few volunteers," she describes it) and valiantly led the campaign to designate as an historic district the 26 blocks, now SoHo's core, by setting up tables in the area, circulating petitions, leading walking tours, and handing out magnets so the uninitiated could test if a façade was iron. (If it is iron, the magnet sticks.) Gayle, who was then working in the public relations office of the City Planning Department, remembers: "Preservationists were still focused on pre-Victorian periods. This was certainly true of the city's Landmarks Preservation Commission." SoHo has the largest collection of cast-iron-front buildings in the world.[5]

Remarkable buildings filled with vital businesses.

Thus, SoHo broadened the perspective of preservationists, helping them expand their focus to preservation of significant districts. The highway defeat gave heart to urbanists, community defenders, and all other opponents of misguided urban renewal projects. Thus, SoHo helped stem the automobile-focused development nationwide that has destroyed so many neighborhoods, architectural treasures, and cultural re-sources since World War II. Preservationists have always been in the vanguard of opposition to Project Plans.

SoHo survived the worst kind of planned impediments, and then flourished under strict government limitations imposed first by the Landmarks Preservation Commission and then the City Planning Commission. The landmarks regulations and zoning restrictions imposed on the area are the kind most people wrongly accuse of being "anti-progress," "anti-change." Under landmarks regulations, buildings cannot be torn down without a good, but hard to prove, cause. New buildings have to be in keeping with the height and context of the district. Ground-floor retail uses are limited to 10,000 square feet, preventing oversized stores from erasing the distinctions between spaces. Live/work spaces must be a minimum of 1200 square feet, offering some assurance that loft living will include work space. Lofts larger than 3600 square feet, a size still suitable for light manufacturing, require a special permit for conversion from manufacturing to live/work space. New eating and drinking establishments are limited to under 5000 square feet, averting the establishment of nightclubs. These are sensible restrictions that permit much to happen and prevent little that is beneficial. Such basic rules have simply protected the area from excessive and overwhelming change, not from change itself. These are not the harmful generic zoning regulations that ignore the diversity, integrity, and individuality of scores of distinct neighborhoods.

Property owners, developers, and tenants probably complain more about landmarks regulation than any other kind of city rules. Landmark designation is not the problem, however, although it is less understood and more easily opposed than building or fire codes. All bureaucracies create and impose unfair problems. The problems that exist are because they are bureaucracies, not because the mission is wrong. People always try to make an end run around bureaucracy because it is expensive and time-consuming. This does not mean the rules should be discarded. A ponderous permit process doesn't stop anyone when the long-term goal is worthwhile.

Discouragements to conventional development fundamentally helped SoHo's spontaneous metamorphosis. The restrictions were precisely what prevented wholesale alteration of the district and prevented a different development agenda from overwhelming it. Surely, no Project Plans were possible in the district.

Citizen activists stood ready to defend SoHo turf each step of the way. They lost few battles. When public opposition lost, as with the SoHo Grande Hotel, the project came out better under the pressure of the opposition. Citizen vigilance and participation legitimized a public process few city officials respected. No public funding, tax incentives, or zoning bonuses were necessary. The conventionalists, who once decried the messy mixture of urban uses in gritty districts, now celebrated the "mixed use" that SoHo epitomized. Now, they use the mixed-use character to justify an increase in maximum size for retail space to open SoHo to superstores. Superstores in SoHo would be a smaller version than the standard size, but still out of scale for the district.

INNOVATION AND ECONOMIC VITALITY ARE KEY

SoHo stands as a great example of spontaneous and positive urban change. It is a useful measure against which districts in other cities can be evaluated. But what may be the greatest significance of SoHo, besides its impact on the way the country views cities, is its birth and nurturing of innovation and new businesses, not just in the arts. SoHo has a long history as an incubator of the new and the productive. The 1963 Rapkin report listed approximately 50 categories of long-standing industrial activity. Innovative entrepreneurs are everywhere. A study today similar to Rapkin's of 35 years ago, if undertaken by people who understand manufacturing, would find a great variety of production-related businesses, both incubators and mature industries. Walking the district, probing beyond the surface trendiness, one discovers products, real objects, being made.

Today, no more vibrant, creative, economically productive, and action-filled district exists in New York, a model urban blend of art and industry. It is a gritty workplace, while, at the same time, an international marketplace for style and design. What is new anywhere can be found in SoHo and its environs.

"Anonymous ambition" is what the buildings of SoHo represented when built and still do, noted the late theater critic Brendan Gill, a sharp observer of the urban scene and an architectural historian. "The scale of the district is ennobling with its high ceilings, arched windows, and Roman columns. It ennobled and empowered all those who worked there. It was then and still is the heart of the city that really pumped," Gill added.

People on the street run the full gamut.

Every square inch of SoHo has something interesting to look at. Over-hanging cornices. Creative, well-designed signage. Artistic window displays. Varied store entrances. Classical architectural features of every variety, cast in iron and painted to look like stone. Finials, capitals, columns, brackets, arches, rusticated stone. You name it. You can find it.

Every visitor, resident, and user views SoHo differently. People on the street run the full gamut, from green-haired youngsters to blue-haired oldsters, from artist wannabes to suburban adventure seekers. Specialty stores, service businesses, and food emporia alternate between chain stores and art galleries. An air of mystery leaves the pedestrian wondering what happens in each building above the ground floor. Only scrutiny of the lobby tenant directory reveals the endless mix. In the early days, one knew an artist resided amid assorted factories when the "A.I.R." (Artist in Residence notice) was found above an entrance bell. Today, lobby directories list publishers, graphic artists, video and film companies, photographers, linguistic training schools, computer consultants, designers, jewelers. And, of course, artists and galleries. The list is endless.

SOHO'S EXPORTS HELP REJUVENATE OTHER PLACES

Change is a constant in SoHo. As it exported its innovations and innovators, new things have taken their place. The complaint today is that SoHo is losing its character as an arts district. As prices escalate, galleries and artists leave, chain stores move in, and tourists increase in numbers. City policies to allow larger retail stores would accelerate that change and more dramatically undermine SoHo's artistic character and economic value. Modest urban change, however, is both inevitable and healthy.

Nothing born or created in SoHo has been lost in the last decade of change. Whatever and whoever has left exists elsewhere. Chances are their art or business has expanded. The only losers, actually, are the residential or business renters, outpriced by the market. Many of the artists and entrepreneurs who left, left in better conditions than those in which they came. An artist friend of mine, for example, lives in a SoHo loft co-op. He was there 15 years ago when the building went co-op and bought cheap, as did other artists in the building. Several of his neighbors have sold their apartments, gaining financially, moving elsewhere to live more cheaply, using their financial gain productively, leaving town for greener pastures, or making other life changes of their choice.

Is this bad? It could be, if it weakens New York as a creative capital and if New York does not continue to regenerate and incubate new artists. But this incubation is still happening, very much so, in pockets all over New York. Some of the very people leaving SoHo and moving elsewhere are helping the process take hold in emerging SoHo-type districts in other cities. Some areas are a convenient train ride or a short drive from the New York City marketplace. Isn't this what healthy urbanism is all about? The nurturing and exporting of innovations and innovative people? *Both the incubating and the exporting must be happening at once for the process to be a healthy one.*

THE NATURE AND RATE OF CHANGE ARE KEY

The one urban constant is change. The fact that SoHo evolved from an almost erased manufacturing district into an extraordinary arts district could never have been the district's final chapter. Decades earlier, the West Village, as the section of Greenwich Village near the Hudson River is called, was an arts center whose arts orientation diminished, but didn't disappear. Trends change. Increased popularity alters the attractions of a place. The organic nature of cities, even if unimpeded or modestly intruded upon, includes shifts of different kinds.

The aim should be not to accelerate negative change and ignore or damage the existing assets of the area, but to let the process work but not let loose a stimulus whose scale is sure to dramatically alter it. Doubling the present allowance for retail would open the floodgates to homogenizing chains. This is shortsighted beyond belief. Chains are not what bring people to SoHo. If that is what it becomes, visitors will rapidly lose interest. SoHo will be like a million other places. The architecture will remain, but the character, the substance, the essence will be gone.

At the same time, some of the current SoHo shift must be recognized as logical on its own and is not simply due to the interest of big investors and national retailers in the area. For example, Paula Cooper, who opened the first SoHo art gallery in 1968, moved to West Chelsea in 1996. The far West Side district, wedged between the Hudson Riverfront and traditional Chelsea in the 20s, already had more than a dozen galleries—first-timers, foreigners needing a U.S. outlet, and SoHo refugees. During the art market slump of the early 1990s, approximately 30 percent of SoHo galleries closed. Some of those dealers reopened when the market turned up, but this time they opened in West Chelsea.

In the 1960s, Cooper was the first to represent the new artists who were creating monumental canvases and sculptures. The old manufacturing buildings were perfect in ways Madison Avenue spaces weren't. And, in fact, new artists had no interest in proximity to the old guard uptown. Recently, the nature of art has been changing again, away from large scale to video, installation, performance, and the like. Maybe a site change is also appropriate. And while the Cooper move—this time to an old garage—was cited as a sign of SoHo's demise as an arts district, perhaps it is more a sign that the never-stagnant art world is changing, is no longer highly concentrated, and the vanguard belongs elsewhere. The three museums, dozens of galleries, and art-related businesses will maintain SoHo's cultural character for years to come.

Art critic Amei Wallach, writing in the Sunday Art Section of *The New York Times* (May 12, 1996), observed, "Yet while SoHo as we know it may be on the endangered list, rumors of the section's imminent death as an art center are exaggerated. SoHo is going through changes that are generational, economic, geographical, and art historical, and the exodus is not likely to undermine it in the near future."

SoHo is far from over. Danger and damage lurk as city policies try to capitalize on the superstore trend, a short-term gain and long-term mistake, if not kept within urban constraints. If not undermined, SoHo will change, shift its form a bit, re-charge itself, and continue to evolve, an ability uniquely urban.

THE SITE SHIFTS, THE PROCESS CONTINUES

One block south of SoHo, the process continues in a different form, as it should when streets of usable buildings of all sizes, shapes, and ages exist. Just across the truck-filled east-west traffic corridor of Canal Street (connecting the Holland Tunnel from New Jersey to the Manhattan Bridge to Brooklyn and Long Island) is TriBeCa (Triangle Below Canal Street), bordered on the east by Broadway and on the west by Greenwich Street.

TriBeCa Park, although a mini-park, is as important to the neighborhood as a big grassy lawn is to others.

Nothing of SoHo's late-19th-century architectural consistency exists in TriBeCa. The many blocks of cast-iron buildings lining perpendicular streets that mark SoHo are unique to it. Instead, TriBeCa is a tangle of multi-angled streets, some short, some long, a wondrous mix of early 19th-century warehouses, tenements, factory buildings, occasional commercial architectural gems dating from the 1930s, and even the mini-oddity, history's gift to districts where change occurs incrementally.

A three-story narrow row house, elegantly painted deep green with white trim, for example, is out of character for the neighborhood and looks like a runaway from an uptown elegant neighborhood, like many of TriBeCa's current residents. Squeezed into the last few feet of a corner where four angled streets merge sits the long-established, and much-loved Greek-owned Square Diner, with a vintage 1950s interior. The roof of a two-story odd-shaped corner building sports a whimsical rendition of a terrace garden that includes a discarded phone booth.

Half a block south of Canal is a cobblestone remnant turned into a mini-park, as important to this area as a big, grassy lawn is to others. This quirky space, with nothing more than a generous arrangement of benches and trees, is actually an obvious leftover from when several streets were reconfigured to create the multilane Holland Tunnel entrance. Officially named TriBeCa Park, this cobblestone space acts like a public square and serves the useful purpose of blocking speeding through-traffic. A serendipitous traffic-calming device. At the same time, it is a pedestrian gateway into TriBeCa. Within the immediate vicinity is the mélange of distinct uses—restaurants, plumbing supply, wholesalers, a 1930s phone company skyscraper, new technology businesses, and film-related companies.

To walk the neighborhood with long-time resident, novelist, journalist, and professor Anthony Mancini is to observe one of the many singular New York neighborhoods reaping the benefits and burdens of the basic urban change spun off from SoHo. TriBeCa is decidedly different from SoHo, Greenpoint, Red Hook, or West Chelsea. Yet, in all these city precincts, the basics of urbanism prevail. SoHo's success exposed the folly of big replacement schemes. In the post-SoHo era, the basics of urbanism are increasingly valued and less vulnerable to big, destructive change.

Mancini, moved to TriBeCa in 1975. Newly separated, Mancini wanted enough space for his 4-year-old daughter, Romy, to have her own room when she visited. He wanted to be near both his office (we both worked at *The New York Post* then) and the civic center, where many stories he covered took place. The ability to create his own space at an affordable price had great appeal.

Artists and writers were already moving in, occupying many spaces illegally, but the area was still known as the Lower West Side by most and was a place where few people other than food wholesalers and small manufacturers had reason to go. After a few moves within the neighborhood, Mancini remarried and bought a top-floor co-op loft on Broadway, TriBeCa's eastern boundary, in what remains a wholesale fabric district. In fact, a fabric wholesaler still occupies the ground-floor space of the Mancinis' building. "Raw space" permitted the Mancinis to configure their loft to meet their needs.

"We thought of ourselves as real pioneers," Mancini says. "As new and younger people moved in, I figured they would just come and go. I never expected so many to stay like us."

Over time, as finances allowed, the Mancinis transformed their loft, adding a rooftop garden and sun room and another bedroom for a newborn son. Maria Cellario Mancini, an actress with an extraordinary talent for everything from carpentry to upholstery, did most of the work herself (with Mancini's help), served as vice president of the co-op board, and now serves on the board of the community's greatest asset, Washington Market Park.

Many bars that were offbeat artist hangouts have either disappeared or been discovered and transformed. The pool table at Walker's that drew Mancini for one of his favorite pastimes was removed to make way for more tables and chairs. Walker's, once a working-class bar and hangout for cops and firemen, became the place where John F. Kennedy Jr. dropped in, cap pulled low, for a late-night snack with his then-girlfriend, now wife, Carolyn.

A few blocks away, one of the most dramatic transformations is visible at Teddy's. This was a restaurant I remember my parents occasionally frequented and talked about in almost hushed tones because of rumors that it was a popular Mafia hangout. When new owners took it over in 1985, the ongoing restoration of the Statue of Liberty inspired artist Antonio Miralda to create a huge crown replica for the roof of the one-story restaurant. A few blocks away, the 1930s Tower Cafeteria was transformed into the upscale Odeon Restaurant, with its streamlined, chrome and wood-paneled interior intact.

"In 20 years, it just grew up around me by increments," Mancini says. "One success led to another, but it was always the neighborhood in the lead, not the city. Everywhere you turn, there is something to discover." A young entrepreneur opening a small store. A former water authority building restored for residential use with its terra-cotta façade intact. A one-time liquor store turned restaurant and bar with the old neon sign giving the nightspot its name, the Liquor Store Bar. Industrial overhangs remain now as awnings for new uses. Electrical and plumbing businesses survive, precariously to be sure, and small neighborhood service stores are only beginning to appear.

Mancini's greatest enthusiasm is directed at Washington Market Park, an unplanned leftover of the Independence Plaza urban renewal project that includes middle-income housing, a community college, and a public elementary school across the street. The ethnically and racially integrated population of Independence Plaza, Mancini says, enriched his son, Nick's, classes. Several years after the project was built in 1975, a forgotten corner of the assembled site was claimed by residents and eventually turned into Washington Market Park, designed by landscape architect Lee Weintraub. Small sitting and play areas, a gazebo, and an area of individually planted community gardens all enclose an open lawn, attracting the diversified uses witnessed at Bryant Park, with the balance here weighted toward the families with children that are increasingly populating TriBeCa.

Jon McMillan, former director of planning for the Battery Park City Authority, observed in a *New York Newsday* opinion article (January 23, 1995), titled "Community Development, Tribeca-Style":

> In little more than a decade, the residents of Tribeca have achieved two remarkable feats. One, they have created what many a well-heeled New Yorker finds to be the city's best neighborhood for raising children. This is no mean accomplishment, considering New York's half-century of failure to hold on to middle-class and affluent families. Two, hundreds of new businesses in Tribeca are now producing goods and services tailored for a global market, helping to ensure New York's future economic prominence.

FROM FOOD MARKET TO ENTERTAINMENT HUB

The Washington Market district that was cleared for Independence Plaza was the center of the city's produce business and remained until the city relocated the market in 1967 to Hunts Point in the Bronx. The market district evolved along the West Side's Hudson River piers and railroad, spread throughout the local streets, reusing the area's Federal and Greek Revival houses and warehouses as storage for fruits and vegetables.

As the old cliché states with more than a small kernel of truth, as much as things change, the more they stay the same...if given a chance, that is. The old market district now forms the heart of TriBeCa. The smell of food is everywhere. On a bitter cold December day, as I walked the streets with Mancini, every block, it seemed, had a different food scent. Old food-based businesses remain. They undergo changes to keep up with the times. Some are taken over by a younger generation of a family. And some are moving their wholesale businesses out of TriBeCa and transforming their on-site space to a retail operation to take advantage of city policies aimed at abetting the transformation of old industrial districts.

Vestiges of the old market district stand alongside newer additions.

The last butter-and-egg wholesaler, Harry Wils & Company, for example, operates in five contiguous buildings on the south side of Duane Park, a half-block triangle that has been a city park since the 18th century. Bouley, one of the city's most elegant restaurants, opened facing Duane Park on the north side and later moved around the corner to Hudson Street. Coexistence of a messy wholesaler and elegant restaurant? Can't be. Another stark example of the wrongheaded ideas that elegant and industrial uses must be separate. The city turned a deaf ear to Stephen Wils' quest for assistance in keeping the family business, founded in 1921, in the city, as it outgrew this site, now worth more as loft residences than as a food business.

Bazzini's wholesale nuts business, another example, expanded to include a wide assortment of candy and gift packages. Encouraged by a zoning change that doubled the permissible size of street-level retail and discouraged by constant harassment by city agencies, Bazzini's is moving its wholesale operation to New Jersey and converting its corner space to retail and upstairs lofts. On its face, this move looks benign, even positive. Yet, the doubling of permissible street-level retail size is bound to accelerate the nibbling away of industrial businesses and the blue-collar jobs so critical to a diversified economy.

Is this terrible? Not if you choose to ignore the cumulative impacts of nibbling change, and not if you accept the erroneous but frequent planning rationalization that "those businesses are disappearing anyway." *This is about accelerating cumulative-impact change.* The same loosening of city regulations will permit entry into the neighborhood of the chain store consumer culture, from which people come here to get away.

INVISIBLE POLICIES STIMULATE CHANGE

Subtle and invisible city policies encourage erosion of blue-collar businesses so officials can then turn around and claim that they are "disappearing anyway." On the one hand, businesses like Bazzini's complain about all the hassles involved in doing business in the city, constant harassment by code enforcement officials, constant parking summonses (in New York, like most cities, enforcement of parking rules is infinitely better than enforcement of speed limits), constant hurdles with sanitation service, and other bothersome intrusions that give leaving the city appeal. The same complaint is heard from long-time businesses in other industrial districts for which city officials sought zoning changes to encourage new superstores.

Project Planners have worked hard for years to turn New York, especially Manhattan, into a financial-service and tourist center free of the messy, somewhat anarchistic blend of businesses that actually create things. The politically dominant real estate industry wants manufacturing out of the way for the higher values achievable with high-rise office or residential construction. Some of this transformation is natural. City policies, however, from zoning to code enforcement to tax incentives, accelerate the process that otherwise would be slower, more natural, and less harmful. This is true of many cities and towns. *The invisible "hassle" policy helps drive out long-time uses to create "underused" or "underoccupied" industrial areas that justify to the public either a change in zoning or a big new demolish-and-build project.* Many gritty downtown districts across the country have deteriorated in just such an *unnatural* manner.

When city officials want businesses to stay, however, or if they want to encourage new investors and developers to get interested in a new area, "hassles" have a magical way of diminishing. Clearly, unofficial policy is to discourage the endurance of industrial uses in TriBeCa, as in other sections of the city.

All kinds of commercial activity occurs within the walls of hundreds of anonymous TriBeCa buildings, yet a slew of big-name restaurants shape the district's public persona as the home or hangout of Hollywood stars, namely, Robert DeNiro, Harvey Keitel, and Bette Midler. Hollywood East meets Industrial Chic. DeNiro brought film activity to TriBeCa more than a decade ago, when he purchased a loft building first to live in and then to work in, and then invested in upscale restaurants. Since then, young businesses have been born around TriBeCa to serve the growing film and media industry that is attracting or keeping so much young talent in New York.

Hollywood East meets Industrial Chic.

DeNiro, a downtown person by birth, grew up in Greenwich Village, the son of an artist and a photographer. His mother later moved to SoHo. He moved to TriBeCa strictly on his own urban instinct. Most people told him he was crazy, says Jane Rosenthal, chairman of DeNiro's Tribeca Productions. "People told him he was wasting his money and that the area was desolate," Rosenthal says. "'Who will come there? Who can find it?' people asked," she says. Rosenthal's own Hollywood friends and associates said the same things to her, when she decided to leave Tinseltown for the world of urban grit as DeNiro's executive director. "New York was not a city I grew up in. It was a difficult decision. Friends thought I lost my mind. TriBeCa could have been New Jersey but I just put blinders on and did what I wanted," she recalls. "You have to trust your own instincts. That is what the movie business is about." Rosenthal, who supervised the building renovations for DeNiro, didn't anticipate becoming the construction expert that she did. "Creatively," Rosenthal says, "it is one of the most rewarding experiences in my life, not like a movie that comes and goes." She also did not anticipate responding so positively to the neighborhood. "The fun part of the neighborhood is the mix of factories, the arts and everything else," she says. "That charm made it unique."

SILICON ALLEY

TriBeCa is the southern point of what is now called Silicon Alley, an area stretching north along Manhattan's West Side to the Flatiron District. (The Greenmarket/Union Square District and the Sixth Avenue superstore corridor, mentioned in earlier chapters, border sections of the east and west flanks of Silicon Alley.) In the north, Silicon Alley is anchored by the Flatiron Building, the 1902 landmark designed by Daniel H. Burnham of World Colombian Exposition fame, which derives its three-sided shape from Broadway's crossing the city's street grid at an angle.

(The same condition occurs at Times Square, where the former Times Tower sits.)

The Economist (May 25, 1996) took note of the Silicon Alley phenomenon and reported the findings of a survey by the New York New Media Association (NYNMA) and the consulting firm of Coopers & Lybrand. The survey found that 18,000 people in New York were working full-time for more than 1100 new firms, while fewer than 17,000 still work in radio and television and 13,000 in newspapers. New media include entertainment software, online/Internet services, CD-ROM title development, Web site design, advertising, publishing, video, and film. Of the new media businesses, 700 are in SoHo, 56 percent of all those in Manhattan, a concentration that evolved rapidly over two years. This new industrial district is already affecting the national culture. Microsoft, the giant corporation, long relied on legions of anonymous programmers to add to its product mix. In 1997, however, Microsoft scouts combed Silicon Alley, where individual authorship is highly valued, for new programs.

New York, the *Economist* article notes, has long been "America's traditional media hub." "Tradmed" is what the "new digiterati" (digital literati) call it. But while the big "tradmed powerhouses" like Time Warner and Rupert Murdoch's News Corporation dominate the public and political consciousness, they "are vastly outnumbered by small start-up companies. These small companies—half of the new media firms in the New York area have a turnover of less than $500,000 a year— are mainly responsible for the new media boom in New York."

This new business community, which, in turn, is giving birth to and nurturing a slew of new arts-based and product-based businesses, emerged under the radar screen of traditional city experts. *It is no small coincidence that this economically vibrant assemblage is located in one of the oldest, most traditional, hodgepodge districts, long undervalued by Project Planners and largely protected by historic district designations. The basics of urbanism, the accumulations of years of history, are fundamentally intact.* If this were true only in SoHo, this would be unique to New York. But the process is recognizable everywhere.

OTHER DOWNTOWNS, OTHER SOHOS

In almost every downtown, we have either visited or received reports from young, active, entrepreneurial, retired, adventuresome people, alone and in pairs, are resettling old districts that have survived, like SoHo and TriBeCa. In the process, the spontaneous urban regeneration evident in SoHo is repeating itself, giving hope that the urban process still has room to take root.

In many places across America, what was spontaneous has reached the point of such *acknowledged* success that the SoHo phenomenon is a

St. Louis, Missouri. The SoHo phenomenon has become a marketer's dream.

marketer's dream. "Loft Apartments," "Warehouse District," and "New York-Style Lofts" are the current voguish terms in real estate jargon anywhere old buildings exist. In Chicago, developers are building townhouses on a parking lot and marketing them as "row lofts." (This, of course, is an oxymoron. A loft is a large open space formerly used for a commercial purpose.) This risks diluting the essence of the natural process of urban change. But in downtowns where the spontaneous process has room to take hold, that urbanism has a chance to flourish, occurring differently in each place. SoHo and TriBeCa. Same process. Different places.

ST. LOUIS

The SoHo potential is not so easy to realize in cities such as St. Louis, where so much of the onetime urban fabric is gone. St. Louis, a once grand city, earned its title as Gateway to the West. Today, it is hard to see why. Still a city that believes real progress is defined by demolishing old and building new, St. Louis continues to let much of what is left of its notable older commercial buildings crumble away. Instead, those historic buildings could be the best resource on which to recultivate a genuine urban garden, but that does not seem to be this city's inclination. A once-grand avenue, like Cleveland's Euclid or Chicago's Michigan, no longer even exists. In the 1950s, the Saarinen Arch replaced the heart of its manufacturing district. Two stadiums, a hockey arena, blocks and blocks of surface and tiered parking lots, and a series of little-used green spaces between big projects wiped away much of the building diversity necessary for urbanism to occur. Only remnants of a city with pockets of urbanism are left. Less than 1 percent of the city's 360,000 people live downtown. Considerable emptiness separates the corporate concentration from the budding loft district, making it more difficult for the SoHo syndrome to have a significant impact on downtown St. Louis.

In St. Louis, and other cities as dramatically and purposefully cleared and rebuilt, one asks: What compelling and active areas are there to even draw people? Two stadiums and an arena which outsiders drive to and from without touching the city are not what bring new innovative businesses and young residents and the vibrant urban life they create. Nor do they spur the kind of economic activity that reenergizes a city's economy. *Cities that don't know how to be cities, or don't want to be cities, build downtown stadiums catering to car owners, corporate box owners, and wealthy ticket holders. Tax-draining stadiums serve the very people who deserted the city. To think that stadiums can provide a salvation or even a mild assist to the ills of downtown is pure folly, especially when most games are played at night.* The biggest use around the St. Louis stadiums is parking lots. Even where there are real economic uses, the question remains: Whom do they serve when no game is played?

North of the St. Louis central business district, and between the stadiums, is an emerging Warehouse District. This is made up of the former

St. Louis, Missouri. Gateway to the West, but where are all the people?

shoe and hat districts, and is not far from the remnants of the garment district. St. Louis was once known as the city of "Shoes, Booze, and Blues." The actual distance from the stadiums may be less than a mile, but the disconnection is total. The Warehouse District corridor runs along Washington Avenue, once a major east-west road through the city, the primary commercial avenue, and a popular streetcar route, especially during the 1920s. Twelve-story masonry buildings dominate the streetscape. Extended cornices reach out over the avenue. The buildings date from the first decade or two after the turn of the century. Although austere in their bulk, they display good proportion and are predominantly brick and stone. Occasional bold detailing matches each building's scale. Large display windows and grand entrances are common. Many storefronts are empty, but new uses, restaurants, and art supply stores are beginning to fill in between thrift shops, office suppliers, and discount furniture stores. Just the stirrings are evident, but, as one observer noted, "Midwest cities are 10 years behind" everyone else.

Tim Boyle is a person who has bought and renovated a 10-story 1922 loft building, once filled with printing companies. He named the building Artloft. With windows on the building's four sides, 63 apartment/studio spaces enjoy the natural light that appeals to artists. Boyle has created restaurant and entertainment spaces for the ground and top floors, including a small, blackbox 350-seat theater. Artloft is tenanted with young residents seeking an urban life style, a spacious live-and-work space, and friends nearby with a similar life style. Artists in residence span the cultural spectrum—music, writing, poetry, dance, printmaking, architecture, fashion design, acting, painting, sculpting, photography, and illustration. Slowly, the district around Artloft is waking up from a deep sleep. "Nothing in St. Louis takes off," says Boyle. "Everything takes a long time." That condition is a common characteristic of downtowns.

In the same vein and a stone's throw from Boyle, sculptor and building renovator Bob Cassilly is creating a whimsical children's museum in an abandoned shoe factory. Cassilly has already profited from a warehouse and office building he renovated and rents, but the novelty of his "visionary" museum project caught the attention of *The Wall Street Journal* in "A Renovator Offers One Possible Remedy for St. Louis Blues" (June 17, 1997). Cassilly, who is sculpting his own museum animals, found total resistance from the city's financial community and potential investors and donors who could not envision suburbanites coming downtown for such an attraction. Yet *Journal* reporter Robert L. Rose observed, "nearby, new nightclubs have made pockets of downtown cool again for people in their 20s, and artists have taken up residence in recently renovated lofts."

This pattern is familiar. New restaurants and other entertainment uses favor the ground floors of these buildings. In similar districts elsewhere, the top floors, despite their interior columns, are favorite special event spots for weddings and private parties. They offer great views of the downtowns that have them and hold great appeal to young couples looking for an interesting, unconventional locale for a wedding. Already, in St. Louis, the first of these, Windows on Washington, has appeared.

The lack of a potentially interesting business district in

New York City loft wedding: Chic and loft are synonymous for weddings from New York City to St. Louis. Photo: Miki Duisterhof.

St. Louis makes the emergence of a loft district all the more fascinating. A corporate center exists, for sure, rebuilt, clean, and dull. Business districts, like downtown St. Louis, lack a steady flow of people on the street to give it life. A 9-to-5 location for indoor, car-bound, monolithic activity. Smokers, forced to the street to smoke, are the sidewalks' biggest users. These "redeveloped" areas lack personality and appeal. Instead, the young and innovative migrate to traditional urban areas—the potential SoHos not yet rebuilt and sanitized. These gritty areas are reviving the urban life that the barren, near-lifeless corporate centers have erased. St. Louis' Loft District has become so popular that the 1997 First Night celebration was held there, instead of the Theater District, the traditional site. Where such districts exist, they offer hope of new vitality. St. Louis' Warehouse District could evolve into an island of vibrancy even if the room to spread has been stunted by decades of misguided rebuilding. Time will tell.

In most places, loft or commercial building conversions are occurring in fragmented areas of cities. Decades of "renewal" projects have severed most of the close-grained connections of a functioning urban fabric, leaving cleared, empty areas between urban fragments. Reweaving those fragments is a challenge. Understanding of and sensitivity to the fundamental characteristics of urbanism are imperative.

DETROIT

In Detroit, for example, several such productive areas exist, quite separate from each other and disconnected even from nearby districts. The old Stroh's Brewery and adjacent buildings have been admirably converted to a luxury hotel, apartments, offices, and small nightspots.

Other loft and commercial building conversions are happening in Detroit, far from the Stroh's district and separate from each other. The Harmonie Park district, a triangle of short blocks and assorted commercial buildings, is adjacent to the Detroit Athletic Club and the restored and expanded Detroit Opera. The Harmonie Park district, with apartments, restaurants, work/living spaces, and offices, is a five-minute walk from an assortment of spectacular theaters in one direction and Greektown, one isolated long block of restaurants, in the opposite direction. Greektown used to be a sizable district that, in time, would have spread and flourished. Detroit's propensity for demolition stunted that expansion. But separating Harmonie Park from those and other nearby districts are vast parking lots and difficult-to-cross, highway-width streets. So much of the connective tissue that knits a city together is gone. That tissue has been in a constant state of erosion since highways sliced through the city after World War II, destroying stable neighborhoods and blazing the trail to the suburbs. This condition is more common than not in most downtowns. Wise citizens advocate narrowing the overly wide streets to make them pedestrian-friendly. Official Detroit stubbornly resists, instead focusing on an active demolition program and building new stadiums and gambling casinos.

PHILADELPHIA

In some cities, the process took root with the defeat of a highway similar to SoHo. Old City, near the waterfront in Philadelphia, is, one local observer noted, "SoHo in 1975." But the process started earlier, in the 1960s and 1970s, near South Street, an area of three- and four-story commercial buildings that were condemned for a highway that was never built. Old City is 20 to 25 blocks of mostly loft and small commercial buildings occupied primarily by artists. A smattering of machine shops and assorted industrial uses, along with family-owned and operated kitchen supply businesses, survive as they did in the early stages of SoHo's rebirth.

In the center of Old City is the Arden Theater, an increasingly popular and newly built attraction, that started in a church and now has a citywide following. Restaurants are drawing convention center visitors looking for interesting places away from the sleepy corporate core. Almost two dozen galleries are scattered about, and their "First Friday" events (every gallery has an open house on the first Friday of every month) are quite popular. The population is typically young. Some couples have children. Most are professionals. The Betsy Ross homestead within Old City draws a smattering of tourists, and Independence Hall is a short walk away. Like SoHo, Old City is spreading to other areas, as ten-

Old City, Philadelphia, an emerging SoHo.

ant artists get priced out. Fishtown, the former garment center in the Kensington area of north Philadelphia, and Mannyunk, a commuter rail suburb and still a blue-collar neighborhood, are two of them. Mannyunk, like Carson Street in Pittsburgh, Greenpoint in Brooklyn, and the North Side in Boston, are classic immigrant neighborhoods where the current wave of "immigrants" happens to be young Americans born and raised here.

SAN FRANCISCO

With a slightly different twist, the current rebirth of a San Francisco neighborhood started with the demise of a highway, or a piece of one. It took the 1989 earthquake to bring down the six-block freeway terminus that neighborhood residents could not stop in the 1960s.[6] The 70-foot-high, double-decker structure had long bisected San Francisco's Hayes Valley neighborhood and left it to dangle in a semi-deteriorated state more hospitable to prostitutes and drug dealers than the kind of residents cities have needed to retain for years. Before the earthquake, only two blocks of Hayes Street, west of the elevated highway and closest to the Civic Center, had experienced a modest commercial renaissance. A small number of restaurants and galleries opened in ground-floor spaces and law firms moved into upper floors. After the highway came down, rejuvenation spread naturally.

More than a dozen new businesses have opened in the neighborhood, a short walk from City Hall, the Opera House, and Symphony Hall. Trendy home decor stores, expensive shoe stores, a designer coat store, and others opened east of where the freeway stood. Most, if not all, of the new businesses serve a citywide, even a regional, market, rather than the local community. Upper floors, however, have been upgraded for residential use.

Neighborhood activists fought the rebuilding of the freeway terminus at the same site and have been active in debates over where it should be relocated. The community has coalesced around the issue, having come to fully understand the impact of such a use. While primarily anti-expressway, not anti-automobile, neighborhood merchants and residents understand clearly what they are fighting for. With the freeway, their local streets became arterials, with no curbside parking and one-way traffic speeding through in four to five lanes. Pedestrian and street life suffered. The din of cars was unceasing. Now, residents marvel at their ability to have on-street conversations. They are determined to keep traffic passing through at slower speeds, to maintain the street grid undisturbed, to allow on-street parking, and to plant street trees. They seek new housing to redress damage inflicted by demolishing blocks of Victorian houses for the highway.

These are sensible expectations, simply the basics of urbanism. A neighborhood has been reborn as an innovative economic and social contributor to the city. Reconnecting torn pieces of city fabric is possible. In many places, a highway's construction started the decay. Its removal may jump-start rebirth.

"One of the great public works projects of the next century will be the deconstruction of freeways," Milwaukee Mayor John Norquist told James Auer, arts critic of the *Milwaukee Journal Sentinel*, for an article in *Progressive Architecture* magazine (May 1995). "There's going to be a lot of that happening once economists apply themselves to the economics of transportation." Skeptics will dismiss this possibility. But, as Yogi

Berra loved to say: "If they say it can't be done, it doesn't always work out that way."

Clearly, the piecing back together of the abused and undervalued precincts of downtowns is happening. But the SoHo Syndrome doesn't work if assets are not there. The places where it works have context, urban fabric, and history to make it work. It can't work where demolition is overwhelming. At that point, reproducing the urban fabric may be as alien as an enclosed shopping center. Local people must shape the reconnections. Replication is a trap. The result is form, not substance.

1. Chester Rapkin, "The South Houston Industrial Area" (New York: City of New York City Planning Commission—Department of City Planning, 1963), p. 282.

2. The East Village is at the far eastern side of Greenwich Village, which, until the 1950s and 1960s, was still considered the northern end of the Lower East Side, which went up to 14th Street.

3. As quoted in Robert A. M. Stern, Thomas Mellins, and David Fishman, *New York 1960,* The Monacelli Press, 1995.

4. J. Alex Tarquino of *The Wall Street Journal*, in an article, "Windy City Takes To Loft Conversions" (September 3, 1997), said: "...Five years ago, the greater metropolitan area entered the top five in residential development for the first time in about 20 years, and it's been there ever since. New housing starts in the city soared 40 percent between 1993 and 1996. The boom in residential loft conversions accounts for much of that."

5. Cast-iron façades are assemblages of prefabricated parts, produced in almost every architectural style imaginable and made to look like stone. Parts could be produced quickly and economically, a valuable addition to American building technology at a time of strong demand for rapid construction. "Architecturally they represented one of the most important building innovations of the 19th century and were a giant step toward modern skyscraper construction," notes Gayle in her definitive book on the subject, *Cast-Iron Architecture in New York* (New York: Dover, 1974).

6. We are indebted to San Francisco native Joan Tally, now a New York planner, for on-site research help about Hayes Valley.

BACK FROM THE EDGE

Jane Jacobs lives on a street in a Toronto neighborhood more typical of an American urban street than the Greenwich Village street she left behind more than 25 years ago when she, her husband, and three children moved to this Canadian city. One- and two-family homes line up close to one another, separated by a narrow alley or driveway, some with garages and a small backyard. Small front yards, mature street trees, and a sidewalk of modest width separate the houses from the street. Cars park on both sides and traffic passes slowly. Cars can't speed through the mazelike streets. The neighborhood streets seem to change direction in the middle, make a driver go in circles, and serve drivers only with local destinations. Parking is limited to resident permit holders. At one corner is a major neighborhood commercial thoroughfare, under which the subway runs, and two blocks in the other direction is a small, tranquil park. And within a few blocks in a different direction is another commercial thoroughfare with a streetcar line.

To walk this block with Jacobs is to observe and discuss all the small changes of one street that mirror large urban dynamics. Some of the mostly early-20th-century three-story houses have been converted to two-family dwellings or contain modest apartments. Jacobs points out the newly planted gardens, the creative new landscaping, the latest flowering tree, or the newest decorative edge fencing. She discusses with her neighbor, front porch to front porch, the goings-on of the raccoon family residing on her roof. The block has undergone major changes over the years, remaining as up-to-date and viable as any residential street anywhere. Yet, the overall physical appearance remains the same. *Many small initiatives, over time, do add up to big change without massive development overwhelming and replacing a functional place.* Urban Husbandry, not Project Planning. This block is part of the Annex, one of downtown Toronto's older and most desirable neighborhoods, born during the era of the streetcar like so many of today's popular urban neighborhoods across America. Here, however, the streetcar survives, in sharp contrast to American cities that destroyed theirs. The streetcar is key to the long-term stability of this and many vibrant Toronto neighborhoods. A subway was added in the 1950s, complementing the heavily used streetcars and buses.

A few years have passed since my last visit to this block, and as we walk to a nearby restaurant for lunch, I observe some of the seemingly small changes. A few houses have converted their front yards to parking pads, probably to accommodate the new residents of the apartments created in recent years. Yet, Jacobs notes, the reverse is also true. A variety of landscaped spaces exist where drive-in pavement had been. Near the corner is a relatively new, small apartment house on the site under which the subway was built. At one corner is a popular restaurant with sidewalk tables and a definite cosmopolitan air. And while houses divided into apartments seem to have increased for the moment, the ability to reverse that alteration in the future is undisturbed, assuring small adjustments over time without destabilizing the larger neighborhood.

Jacobs particularly enjoys stopping before the Victorian house on the double lot, probably the first built on the block, where, only a few decades earlier, the owner refused to sell to a developer. This single holdout thwarted a plan to assemble the whole block, demolish all the homes, and replace them with a high-rise building. The owner simply refused to sell, committed to protecting a legacy she had inherited. The developer's plan thus collapsed. The homes survived. A few years ago, the then-current owners hosted a block party in honor of that single woman who saved the neighborhood. The message that one person can save a neighborhood and make a real difference is such an appropriate one to be embodied on the street where Jane Jacobs lives.

Two purposes have brought me to Toronto for this visit: the annual conference of the Congress of the New Urbanism (CNU) and Toronto itself, a model of enduring urbanism that more and more stands in admirable contrast to the majority of American cities.

The New Urbanists, a disparate group of architects, planners, academics, transportation engineers, developers, and assorted anti-sprawl sympathizers, have, in recent years, gained considerable attention for their promotion of a planning, design, and development approach that resoundingly rejects almost every automobile-centered principle on which this country has been building since World War II.[1] They have been both praised and vilified in excess. The excessive believers embrace it as *the answer* to most, if not all, problems, from community disintegration to aesthetic purgatory. This ridiculous assumption threatens to replace an inherently destructive dogma with a better dogma, but a dogma nevertheless. Only in the hands of the excessive believers does the New Urbanism become dogma, however. The excessive skeptics, whose professional practices seem most threatened by this increasingly popular phenomenon, are blind to the positive value of the New

Urbanists' fundamental challenge to the status quo. Critics throw the baby out with the bathwater.

The New Urbanists have helped direct the national spotlight on the automobile-centered development path this country has followed since World War II. They have reshaped public expectations, broken through conventional planning dogma, and shaken up developers' rigid, standardized assumptions...no small task. They cannot and should not be dismissed. The New Urbanists had purposely chosen Toronto as, what Jacobs identifies as "a rather wonderful laboratory...a cautionary and inspiring location for the Congress." In a letter urging them to assemble in Toronto, Jacobs wrote:

> The city's old neighborhoods and streets incorporate many of the principles that the CNU promotes, and so do significant infill projects within the city. By contrast, the postwar fringes of the city and the urban sprawl beyond embody all the idiocies of older small towns which, even as remnants, still have so much to teach. In other words, Toronto is anything but hopeless, yet there is very much work to be done and a growing realization that this must be tackled with adaptations, ameliorations, densifications, major rethinkings of subsidies, and above all, vision.

Since, with Jacobs' help, I had drawn lessons from Toronto for my first book, *The Living City*, a revisit was in order.

THE NEW URBANIST MESSAGE IS NEITHER MONOLITHIC NOR SIMPLE

Almost everybody who knows anything about the New Urbanists has a different understanding of the message. That is appropriate, since the variations are many among adherents and most New Urbanist developments are still under construction or on the drawing boards. The confusion and, in many cases, criticism are based on a few well-publicized developer-built sites. The fundamentals, however, with a few critical exceptions, parallel some of the pre-Auto Age principles illustrated in this book that shaped the most livable, memorable, and enduring communities of this country—the ones that grew in increments over time.

New Urbanists have drawn direct lessons from these "old," traditional districts and translated "old," commonsense principles into "new" development prescriptions: *Pedestrian movement and comfort, not vehicular mobility, form the central and defining standard.* Buildings are scaled to the individual on foot. A front door or building entrance is what it is supposed to be. A garage or underground/overground entry does not replace the entrance. On-street parking is allowed. Tightly spaced housing of different types with small front yards stand close to a sidewalk and on a grid system that diffuses slow-moving traffic. Garages are placed behind houses, accessible by modest driveways. Neighborhood shopping is planned to be within walking distance. Multifamily housing and single-family homes of different price scales exist together. Live/work spaces and flexible spaces convertible to in-law or rental units are encouraged. Parks, squares, sidewalks, and inviting public spaces are designed to foster chance meetings and neighborly familiarity. The multiple components of daily life—workplace, residence, shopping, public space, public institutions—are reintegrated, after 50 years of sorting, separating, and segregating functions and people. Connecting to public transit is advocated with varying enthusiasm and realism, depending on the individual New Urbanist. The zoning, building, fire, and traffic codes that make the above impossible are thrown out and replaced with shorter, simpler ones.

Idealistic? Surely, but one can acknowledge flaws without dismissing the essential value of the message. Developers often pick and choose the principles they accept. Many miss much of the point, build the form without the substance, and apply the New Urbanist label to a poor imitation. The media oversimplifies the issue by spotlighting the same new developments. New Urbanist interest in revitalization of existing neighborhoods, infill development, historic preservation, and citizen participation is less apparent. A single New Urbanist voice does not exist, however, making a single judgment impossible. Inevitably, as well, differences often emerge between articulated principles and accomplished practice. The New Urbanism, most significantly, is an opportunity to look at urban design issues comprehensively. Nothing can be overlooked. Transportation, physical form, heritage, school or government facility placement, and stores. Name it. It can't be ignored. This multidimensional, cross-disciplined approach to place building disappeared with the overprofessionalization of planning, design, and development in postwar America. It cannot come back fast enough. Community, transit, and preservation advocates working to rebuild existing inner-city neighborhoods have been articulating these ideas for years, using these principles to defend surviving urban precincts. Those urban defenders do not command the attention, however, either in the press or the halls of power and finance, that a star-studded group of architects and developers do.

New Urbanists learn from successful places how to encourage, plan, and design for similar success, even if most of the models are almost exclusively high-value places. This is not high-minded theory.

So where are the problems? Much of the criticism is somewhat valid. So far, the most highly publicized, widely photographed expression of New Urbanist principles are new, primarily suburban communities, highly designed, almost too picture-perfect, too architectural, too controlling, and seeming to promote prettified versions of small-town architecture. To make a development a place, people have to make it theirs. Overly constrictive rules can stifle individual expression. Developer-built and controlled, many New Urbanist projects are new communities, mostly on the fringe of existing places and quite separate and isolated from their surroundings, if not actually gated. Many of the in-town projects meant to rebuild cities are too demolition-and-rebuild oriented, giving short shrift to the physical, social, and economic resources that remain everywhere. Too much replacement and not enough repair. Some New Urbanists bemoan the spotlight falling so heavily on the new, the suburban, the small-town look. High-profile people and projects, for better or worse, always shape an image. Differences between articulated principles and accomplished practice are inevitable.

DENSITY IS KEY

In *The Death and Life of Great American Cities*, Jane Jacobs berated orthodox planners for confusing high density and overcrowding, and for assuming they always go together. Her brilliant chapter, "The Need for Concentration," illustrates the fallacy of the confusion, observes the overcrowding frequently found in low-density neighborhoods, and shows how the liveliest and safest city districts are often the densest. She wrote:

> Everyone is aware that tremendous numbers of people concentrate in city downtowns and that, if they did not, there would be no downtown to amount to anything—certainly not one with much downtown diversity.
>
> But this relationship between concentration and diversity is very little considered when it comes to city districts where residence is a chief use. Yet dwellings form a large part of most city districts. The people who live in a district also form a large share, usually, of the people who use the streets, the parks and enterprises of the place. Without help from the concentration of the people who live there, there can be little convenience or diversity where people live, and where they require it.[2]

The "awareness" that downtowns need the concentration of "tremendous numbers of people" to "amount to anything" was surely lost in the years since 1961, when her book was first published. The lack of concentration marks the highly celebrated rebuilt-but-not-reborn downtowns discussed in this book, and it is the distinguishing feature of their failure as urban downtowns.

If anything, Jacobs' second observation that few people realize the similar need for density in residential districts is even more true today than when she wrote it. "The exuberant variety inherent in great numbers of people, tightly concentrated" is still, for the most, part unrecognized.

Thus, suburbanizing residential neighborhoods are following behind the already suburbanized downtown commercial districts. Eventually, the results will be equally deadening. After the newness wears off, problems will set in. The regenerative potential that comes with concentration is absent. The next generation of serious problems will be upon us.

While New Urbanism, in principle, promotes density and public transit, it does not do enough to debunk the myths associated with both. Those myths and prejudices stand in the way of redeveloping the kind of transit systems and neighborhoods that are the true definition of viable urban districts. Across the board, citizen, developer, planner, architect, and elected official all think density is to be blamed for the ills of urban America. This is contradicted everywhere. Mention density, and nightmarish visions of high-rise, crime-infested, minority residences emerge in most people's minds. Primarily the disasters catch the attention of the press. Surely, desolate high-rise projects destroyed the connective physical, social, and institutional fabric of neighborhoods. Ironically, most destroyed more low-rise density than they replaced in the high-rises. Yet, among high-rise public housing projects, one can find well-functioning examples. Good management, a degree of resident control, social support systems, a sense of ownership—these features are present in successful public housing, of which there are numerous examples in New York, Pittsburgh, and St. Louis, to name a few. One of the great social mistakes of urban renewal was that it demolished more than it rebuilt. Unfortunately, this mistake is being repeated in almost every city, tearing down or blowing up failed public housing projects. These mostly federally funded projects are displacing more people than they are providing for. The mostly carefully planned and designed new construction replacements embrace New Urbanist principles but lack the variety and density required for a balanced urban neighborhood. Relocation opportunities for the displaced hardly exist.

High-rise or even low-rise density is not, by definition, bad and, in fact, it is the only thing that makes feasible a cost-effective and efficient urban infrastructure. Cities must have sufficient density to function well. In fact, downtowns are at their most productive when density is high. The form of the density can vary. The high density of low-rise neighborhoods, former streetcar suburbs, contributes significantly to their appeal.

One need only look to the New York borough of Brooklyn, filled with spectacular, functional neighborhoods of varying price, race, and class structure, all with high densities (unless recently rebuilt with low-density, suburbanized housing). If Brooklyn were its own city, it would be the nation's fourth largest, yet the dominant building type does not exceed four- or five-story row houses. Of course, all of Brooklyn's neighborhoods evolved along expansive streetcar and subway lines. The need to constantly "dodge" the streetcars, in fact, is what gave the Brooklyn Dodgers their name, originally the "Trolley Dodgers."

The density of automobile suburbs, even if well-designed in compact, walkable communities, cannot support town centers or neighborhood shopping. Suburban density was never meant to support local business. Shopping centers reached by car were supposed to do that. The corner store and integral commercial streets are urban phenomena. In smaller communities, downtown and neighborhoods were a short walk or trolley ride away. The sprawl New Urbanists decry cannot be contained adequately without redensification of existing and new communities. Mass transit, as well, is a pipe dream without density. Some New Urbanists recognize public transit as critical to functional places. But not enough make it central to their message.

These issues were thoughtfully debated during the three-day New Urbanist conference in Toronto. Every discussion and debate was extremely relevant. But whether advocate or skeptic, participants were examining, questioning, and debating some of the most fundamental redevelopment issues. These are hopeful signs.

Among the New Urbanists, however, the need *to educate the community* is heard often. The value of *being educated by the community* is not. The positive models of traditional urbanism that New Urbanists cite to learn lessons from seem to exclude the most interesting and complex assortment of successful communities, rebuilding themselves from the inside out, from the bottom up, and with a community-based process that will endure long after a developer completes a "new community," sells out its real estate, and moves on. Civic engagement and community process, in fact, are much more important to the long-term success of places than either the architect who designs or the developer who builds them.

An astute and experienced community of advocacy planners and neighborhood rebuilders, against all odds—official policy, financial institutions, and Project Planning agendas—have done the so-called impossible and done it without benefit of real estate developers. The vision of these civic rebuilders emerges from a deep understanding of the diversity they live with and the vitality that comes from that diversity. The community-based rebirth movement is a loose network of very individualized places with common challenges and similar experiences. They are all gardens with different assortments of plants, localized strategies for rebirth, and shaped by the people and history of their place. This is a broad community with a lot to teach. Design and planning precepts are not enough to bring about the New Urbanist vision. An alliance with the racially, ethnically, and economically mixed neighborhoods of existing cities would produce a social and economic substance of broadest value to American society.

TORONTO—AN OLD URBANISM MODEL

Toronto is indeed a good laboratory in which to study urban successes. Toronto never lost its tradition of urbanism. Nor did Toronto experience the redlining of city centers and neighborhoods that fostered U.S. downtown and community decline. The one area where Toronto lost its sense of urbanism is where it imitated Houston and went underground with a network of pedestrian tunnels that pulled life off the street and put it down under. However, above ground, in contrast to many American downtowns, open parking lots and garages do not proliferate between the familiar modern skyscrapers. Filling in vacant land with development in scale with its surroundings has long been Toronto's style. Repairing the old before building new is habit. And, years ago, Toronto rebuilt a cleared section of its city, the St. Lawrence neighborhood, according to commonsense principles. The city street grid was extended. Housing faces the street, varies in scale, with an eight-story maximum height. Mixed-income units controlled by nonprofit cooperatives ensure an interesting mix. The subsidized are indistinguishable from the unsubsidized units. Public spaces of appeal to all age groups are within view of residential and commercial windows. Community facilities include an expandable school. Small and large retail, historic preservation, commercial office space, and good public transit connections are all included. And a vibrant public market of long standing in an historic structure is a community centerpiece. Twenty years after its creation, one can hardly tell that the St. Lawrence neighborhood was created almost from scratch. This is the antithesis of rebuilding the inner city in a suburban form of low density. The commonsense plan emerged from a process in which the city sent planners out to ask people what they wanted, to study nearby streets and the buildings on them, to learn what made them flexible and workable.[3]

Traditional urbanism is part of Toronto's soul. It is what so appealed to Jane Jacobs and her family when they settled there. And it probably explains why this Canadian city so fully embraced Jacobs's urban precepts, took her harsh critiques to heart, and, in many instances, applied her ideas to improving the city. For Toronto, current urban principles are more a continuation than a return to traditional urban development. Toronto builders are more willing than those in the United States to accept a genuine urban, rather than suburban, standard. More New Urbanist projects seem to be advancing faster there than in the United States, gaining wide and enthusiastic acceptance, and exhibiting at least twice or three times the density of their U.S. counterparts. Many connect to public transit.

PUBLIC TRANSIT: A KEY TO TORONTO'S ENDURING URBANISM
Toronto's well-functioning network of trolleys, buses, subways, and bicycle routes is unequaled in North America. Canada's broad political consensus behind mass transit contrasts sharply with the United States' combined adulation of the car and deep disdain for mass transit as an

oversubsidized sop to the poor. Similarly, Toronto's highly diversified and integrated neighborhoods, comfortable absorption of immigrants, and lack of large ghettoes or desperate slums contrasts with the United States' highly separated, segregated, and isolationist patterns shaped by the automobile. The ease with which people travel through, between, and around this open and accessible city is surely attributable to the transit system.

Streetcars are a smoothly functioning mainstay of Toronto's transit, and to take a half-day ride is to understand why. Engineer and transportation consultant Nickolas Poulos points out that trolleys are the matrix of Toronto's transit system, one-third faster than buses in traffic, one-third cheaper to run, and carrying 10,000 passengers an hour. The streetcar passes through a continuous string of thriving commercial streets, and each segment is a reflection of its distinct community. These are urban Main Streets of the best kind. Locally-owned stores dominate. Few vacancies appear. If regional malls have undermined urban retail, little evidence is apparent. Right off the corner of the commercial thoroughfare are compact, residential neighborhoods with great variation in population and price range. No slums are apparent. No significant parking lots interrupt consistent streetfronts. A parking requirement for new retail was removed entirely a few years ago and allowable density along the commercial streets increased.

Four lanes—two for parking, two for traffic—with the trolley down the middle make pedestrian crossing easy and keep traffic slow. When the trolley stops, a stop sign goes out to the side. Cars behind must wait. Drivers appear patient and respectful. Wide streets are not conducive for trolleys, Poulos notes, "because they are difficult for pedestrians to cross," which translates into diminished trolley usage. "Narrow is better," he adds, "because it lends itself to good land use. The wider the lane, the higher the speed cars travel. The narrower, the slower." Clearly, his point is apparent as the mostly two- and three-story streetscape along the route could not be more vibrant and functional. Trolleys run every 8 to 10 minutes and stop every 1500 feet, and within 50 feet of subway and bus transfer points. New residential and commercial development is strongest in close proximity to all transit lines and, in fact, the most valuable real estate is at subway stops.

This is what the United States traded in for the car.

Toronto almost lost its streetcar system to less efficient buses in the early 1980s. A citizen coalition fought to save it. Officials argued that no streetcar manufacturers were left and maintenance costs were prohibitive. The citizen group proved otherwise, went to Switzerland to find the manufacturer, and lobbied to bring five cars home as prototypes. After successful trial runs, the city bought manufacturing rights from the Swiss and set up a manufacturing company in Toronto. Once again, citizen efforts saved the day.

THE LESSONS, THE BASICS

Rebirth is occurring, as we have seen throughout this book, where people have successfully challenged conventional dogma and achieved dramatic course changes. Rebirth, not just rebuilding. Urban Husbandry, not Project Planning. Important lessons thus become clear, from Mansfield to Toronto.

In the 1960s and 1970s, with all the advances in communications and electronic entertainment, prophets of doom declared downtown an anachronism. They were wrong, as lively and popular SoHo districts attest. In the 1990s, with the rise of the Internet, cyberspace, and whatever is yet to come, the message is heard again. Cities will be unnecessary, experts claim again. If anything, contrary to all these "expert" pronouncements, the public's expressed need, attachment, and longing for downtowns is stronger than ever. "People who say downtown is dead and that the computer will keep everyone home are prophesying based on misinformation," says Kennedy Smith, head of the National Main Street Center. "They are not looking at what is actually happening. People are tired of isolation. They want the sense of community renewed. They want reconnection, not isolation."

Smart thinking today recognizes one incontrovertible fact: The way we have been developing for the past 50 years just does not work. Innovation, creativity, a willingness to try something different are key to setting a new direction. In fact, dense, unpredictable, and complex urban districts that developed over time are the future, wherever a downtown is fortunate enough to have them left to build on. Predictions were wrong that cities no longer offer appeal as living sites. Creative, adventuresome entrepreneurs, artists, families, empty nesters, and downtown workers are moving in. Urban rebirth follows them. These settlers are young and old, rich and poor, conventional and offbeat, city-born and suburban transplant, black and white, native and immigrant, the hodgepodge of people that reflects an interesting and stimulating society. They select the surviving traditional pieces of the forgotten city.

Something old is new again, but with a difference. The SoHo Syndrome illustrates how the city remains what *New York Times* architecture critic Herbert Muschamp calls a "dynamic experiment." These revived or enlivened districts are not enclaves rooted in nostalgia, but viable, vibrant neighborhoods rooted instead in urban authenticity. These places reflect principles and serve human needs that are timeless, exhibit a broad culture, interesting history, varied experiences, human interaction, and the character of that particular place, that garden. Newcomers seek them out and add new life to an enduring garden. Downtowns are alive or are coming alive where a garden remains to cultivate.

We spent decades fixing what was not broken. Modest repairs would have done the job at less cost and with fewer mistakes. We were sold a bill of goods about failure and progress. Not coincidentally, that bill of goods always seemed to profit private, and often narrow and short-term, interests. Cities, downtowns, small businesses, manufacturing, old buildings, public transportation, streets, sidewalks, farmers' markets, public squares, and all related elements did not match the image of progress defined for post-World War II America. They were the old way, to be discarded.

We became trapped by that image of failure and got into the habit of looking at the glass as half empty, not half full. Instead of building on the opportunities presented by the half-full glass, we pursued the more expensive, ineffective route. We destroyed the whole glass, disposed of its contents and its potential, and, instead, acquired a new glass. We filled the new glass with a different content. This made matters worse. We replaced the urban garden with a more expensive but less adjustable and resilient one.

Today, failure remains an overpowering focus. But failure compared to what? A student failure rate of 15 percent sounds terrible. But that also means 85 percent succeeded and graduated! New small businesses fail at a high rate. But look how many succeed. Grass-roots efforts don't always take root and grow. But look how many do. Failure in these contexts is Failure With Value. If we focus on what is wrong, nothing looks good. If societal health is analyzed with and measured by statistics, communities all look bad and local assets are ignored or undervalued. If plans are based on macro statistics, local impacts are ignored. In every locality today, the assortment of big new projects reflects only the success that place had in building the fad of the moment and capturing the public funding that came with it. *When downtowns are revamped according to the newest government funding fad/program or trendy style, a price must be paid. Local assets and values are destroyed. Local character is erased. Local place disappears. The national landscape is transformed. The 1950s mindset brought us to this point. Intransigence keeps us there.*

Government alone is really not to be blamed. Blame rests, as well, with the private sector that uses short-term objectives to reap the highest profits, as often as possible with the help of government funding. Short-term bottom lines, not long-term investments. The private sector uses whatever government resources are available, advocates their availability, and uses politicians to manipulate the rules. The private sector, whether corporations, real estate developers, or lending institutions, are what has become known as the "invisible government." This is private money with power and not accountable to the people. Government money answerable to people results in different, and more accountable, outcomes.

Two antithetical directions in city planning are visible across America today. Every community is at the crossroads between them, a fork in the road. A choice must be made.

DIRECTION ONE—THE FAMILIAR APPROACH,
REPLACING THE GARDEN: PROJECT PLANNING

One direction, bankable and safe, is the suburbanization of downtowns, large and small, the path many downtowns have followed for decades, replacing the damaged but repairable place with a sterile one, notable only for its assortment of visitor attractions or Project Plans. Some of these downtowns have invested in some rejuvenation efforts of greatest benefit to the local populace. Usually, however, these advancements gain a fraction of the resources and official interest that the Project Plans do. The priorities are backwards. So many communities feel second-class without some assortment of Project Plans. Even Mansfield, a small city with so many traditional assets in place generating new strength, feels the need for a convention center. Cleveland, St. Louis, Indianapolis, Charlotte, and many others proclaim their cities renewed by attention-getting sports facilities, retail malls, or designer-label museums, all Project Plans that neither solve problems nor revive local places.

This has reached ludicrous proportions. For the past few years, car-dependent stadiums have been the fad of choice. Stadiums wipe out complex districts needing repair, while addressing a problem that never existed. Sometimes they get built on land cleared for an earlier Project Plan vision. They are like urban renewal projects of an earlier time. *If you don't know how to rejuvenate an area or how to recognize and nurture rejuvenation when it begins spontaneously, you build a stadium or some mega-equivalent.* If you are lucky, you'll do it well (Denver, Toronto, Baltimore) and connect it to the existing city, rather than suspend it in its own isolated space in a sea of parking. If you're even luckier (Denver again), other positive things were already going on that are really about city building, not just project building.

But no one should be deceived. Most cities easily give in to the corporate threat of departure with financial incentives of budget-busting scale. Projects that could directly benefit the city and add momentum to genuine city rebuilding are either ignored or given crumbs. Small investments illustrated throughout this book mean real economic development, real entrepreneur generation, real community building, real people building, instead of what Indiana professor Mark Rosentraub (author of *Major League Losers*) calls "this perverse transfer of public money to wealthy players and wealthier owners." Too often, the corporate team owners use government funds to benefit themselves in the name of public policy, instead of government investment in people, in the cultivation of well-seasoned gardens. As *Newsweek* reporter John McCormick wrote:

> Giving welfare to team owners is America's newest civic sport. By one count, 44 major-league pro teams have recently finagled new playpens for themselves or are angling to do so.

Critics call much of this extortion: you help me or I'll take my team to a city that will. Local officials typically cower when the owners play hardball, fearful that the loss of a pro franchise will relegate their city to the status of a ghost town. But the costs in tax breaks, bond issues and other goodies are making all but the blindest fans ask if the stadium game is worth the price...[4]

The new stadiums that owners demand today are an exaggeration of the accelerating trend of privatization of onetime public space. This is, perhaps, the most damaging aspect of their proliferation. Ballparks were, at one time, among the great democratic levelers—where rich and poor, young and old, college grad and high school dropout, black and white cheered, jeered, yelled, and booed together. Fans were fans. They sat in the same seats, ate the same hot dogs, and withstood the same weather. Not, however, in the new stadiums where private boxes do for stadiums what gates do for upscale residential enclaves.

Stadiums (two, of course—one for football, and one for baseball) and casinos have been the most recent of the long line of Project Plans. But just when you think the height of idiocy has been reached, a new one emerges to begin the next ignore-the-problem fad. Financially desperate cities like Buffalo, Utica, Syracuse, and Schenectady, all in upstate New York, are actually seriously debating putting themselves out of existence, merging with a larger entity, eliminating a layer of government and the elected officials that go with it. How simple! A money saver! A bureaucracy eliminator! But not really. Governance and control are thus moved farther away from the people and businesses being governed and controlled. The ability of the small unit—the neighborhood, the block, the commercial street, or the industrial district—to pursue its own initiatives and stimulate its own rebirth is diluted beyond its already limited state. But what does this bureaucratic quick fix repair on the street, in the neighborhood, in a business corporation? The focus here is strictly money, not solutions. How does having more financial resources to fund services for a bigger, more spread out area do more than maintain the status quo? How are centers strengthened in this new structure, as control is shifted farther from them? How are current destructive development or investment patterns altered or repaired? Solutions can be forged within current frameworks, as the stories throughout this book show. Even regional cooperation will work only if beneficial change evolves in small, localized steps.

Such bureaucratic juggling merely reflects the bankruptcy of ideas about solving urban problems. It is such nonsense, in fact, that it is hard to believe this is seriously being discussed. In such places where this is seriously discussed, every possible expensive Project Plan has been tried.

Failure and worsening financial conditions are the common result. Not enough money is left even to build the stadium that will distract attention from real problems and maintain the illusion of improvement. No ability to *assess* enduring assets remains, but assets *do* remain. The vision of how to build on them is absent. The glass is now really more than half empty. We can expect more cities to debate this notion.

Another ludicrous idea has emerged, one that truly epitomizes the transformation of cities into suburban playgrounds and the total disinclination of urban leaders to solve real problems. A nine-hole golf course surrounded by luxury housing, winding lanes, and pastoral lagoons was proposed to go right in the middle of inner-city St. Louis, sold as a way to keep people (read suburbanites) downtown after work. This idea is so preposterous that one has to laugh, despite the serious ramifications. The site includes the almost-forestlike lot of the 1955 former award-winning Pruitt Igoe public housing project that was partially blown up in 1972 because of its failure to achieve its original objective of providing stable affordable housing. An adjacent low-income neighborhood of 209 turn-of-the-century row houses and scattered small businesses would be razed to enlarge the empty site, for a total of 180 acres. St. Louis took the proposal seriously enough to spend $38,000 on the plans, proposed spending $8 million of city funds, and requested $127 million of federal housing money to build it. The federal request was denied and, due to a change in city administration, the proposal is now off the front burner. The area to be demolished is on the edge of a privately rebuilt multifamily, low-rise, mixed-income neighborhood of new and rehabilitated housing. Nearby is an extraordinary inner-city success story where, under the dynamic leadership of resident Bertha Gilkey, public housing tenants took control more than a decade ago of a group of buildings as bad as Pruitt Igoe, repaired and rebuilt them with 1000 apartments, restored historic single-family housing, added new developer-built infill housing, created new businesses, and turned gang members into employed family men. These Urban Husbanders, untrained instinctivists, rebuilt a public housing project that had defeated the experts. They rebuilt the lives of the residents at the same time, with the products of their own effort. This is a local resource, as good as gold, to rebuild on. What better potential could one ask for?

THE SECOND DIRECTION—INNOVATION, CULTIVATING THE GARDEN: URBAN HUSBANDRY

The second direction, visible today, is embodied in the multiple solutions illustrated throughout this book and stands in total contrast to the non-solutions of Project Planners. The SoHo Syndrome. The proliferation of farmers' markets and spontaneous growth that accompanies them. The Urban Husbanding of Main Streets, downtown districts, former streetcar commercial and residential neighborhoods, and empty public spaces. The innovations of mass transit advocates, rails-to-trails creators, traffic calmers, farmland preservers, community-based developers, New Urbanists. The recycling of historic buildings. The retention of downtown essentials. The modest, nurturing assistance of against-the-grain public officials. The commitment of local residents, business owners, and hometown corporations. The Urban Husbanding paths followed by a small but growing group of developers, lenders, and investors. The entrepreneurship emerging across the small business and manufacturing landscape. Intuitive rebuilders, untrained instinctivists, community defenders, alternative planners, creative risk takers—yes, "do-gooders," evident wherever vitality of place is reemerging. Highway resisters, stadium fighters, sprawl busters, Project Plan opponents. All of the above are elements of a new direction. Together they add up to an extraordinary reawakening with great problem-solving potential, modest efforts leading to major change. These solutions replenish existing gardens without bankrupting public treasuries.

No simple formula for success exists. Period. As H. L. Mencken said, "For every problem there is a simple solution and it is wrong." Complex places with complex problems require many separate but interrelated efforts. The key measure of each success is the answer to the question: Does the effort generate the seeds for continued organic and community growth? The endless need for the next Project Plan fad and big public investment is a sure sign of failure. *Urban Husbandry requires modest nurturing, not major underwriting. It is cost-effective and generous, liberating and empowering, liberal and conservative all at the same time.*

PUBLIC PROCESS, NOT PRIVATE OWNERSHIP

All the successes identified in these pages, from farmers' markets to SoHo districts, reflect and contain many privately owned and initiated pieces within a deeply and profoundly public context not totally controlled by either a private or a governmental entity. This defines a true democratic community, a genuine public realm. An unevenness, unpredictability, spontaneity, and individuality characterize these often-managed but never-controlled efforts. These qualities are essential to a real place. They define authenticity. A government process in which the public is substantively involved and local stakeholders feel ownership must be the controlling framework, not private ownership. Authentic places and successful renewing efforts cannot be rigidly controlled and privately owned, like malls. Malls can only simulate public places.

The malling of America has malled the culture and homogenized taste. A mall mindset is penetrating the public consciousness in insidious ways, often in the name of good design, improved style, and a perceived need for order. It contributes to the loss of local character. Standardization, a spreading sameness, is overwhelming individualism, artistic quirkiness, the marks that distinguish one thing or one place from another.

Take the newsstands of New York. A newsstand, like the pushcart food vendor or flower stand, is an urban phenomenon, found only where people actually walk. Like cruising taxis, newsstands are unique to cities with a rich street life. For years, newsstands acted as unofficial watchdogs for their streets. "Newsies,"[5] as the vendors are called, were unofficial block captains, warning systems, security guards, message or package conveyors, unofficial gossip and news bearers. In misguided improvement efforts, many neighborhoods lost newsstands. Others went out of business on streets where new buildings included interior lobby stands. Newsstands have always been a bootstrap industry. They historically have drawn new entrepreneurs, usually immigrants. Surely, many newsstands are in deplorable condition, patched together with dented metal, and covered with graffiti. Unsightly, to say the least. The need to clean them up or replace some of them is the problem. Design guidelines that allow for individuality and artistry could accomplish that. Controls without discouraging enterprise. Wholesale replacement is not a solution.

Recently, however, the city promulgated new rules to govern newsstands that will replace them and put most current "newsies" out of business. Replacement, not solution. The annual fee charged the city's 330 vendors would be increased from $538 to as much as $5000, depending on the location. Individualized, personality-rich stands will be either eliminated or replaced with a new streamlined (read uniform) version, built by the same corporation that wins a citywide contract to provide bus shelters and public toilets laden with advertising. Newsstands, too, will have advertising. The advertising is now the city's bottom line. "A blizzard of advertising on look-alike stands," former newsstand builder and operator Steven Stollman told *New York Times* columnist David Gonzalez (May 17, 1997). Like David against Goliath, Stollman rallied newsies in opposition. "This is mall furniture," Stollman told Gonzalez. "New York should strive to maintain its uniqueness. We shouldn't accept these things that are the same like Des Moines or even Paris." Of course, Stollman is right. New York is a leading workplace for great design talent. As Stollman noted: "We're Fort Knox when it comes to design...We could do it in a New York kind of way. We have so many artists and designers who can render objects in our common spaces. Each could be unique and it could be the result of what each community decides is best in its judgment." Sadly, this way of looking at things is like an endangered species. The budget, the cost of services, the corporate bottom line, the rush to designed uniformity win out. The city will benefit financially but could, as well, if done with individuality. The winning company will benefit financially. City streets, however, will be less interesting places. The public realm will be diminished. More formula-thinking. Another nibble.

SUBURBAN CHALLENGE, NOT SUBURBAN SOLUTION

A fad today is the selective recreation of appealing urban elements, a kind of editing of the urban environment that results in a stage-set version of a city. History is sanitized. Form without substance. Pristine and perfect but dull and lifeless. Place is reduced to a commodity that emerges from a kit of parts, not the result of culture, history, folklore, topography, intuition, entrepreneurship, the spontaneity of people, the mystical forces that shape our places. Problems are kept offstage. Spontaneity is controlled. Efficiency is the goal. The stage-set version permanently remains a stage set, always needing to be produced and directed, never improvised and spontaneous, never quite real. *Vitality, however, can't be produced; it happens.*

A fundamental loss of understanding of authentic urbanism is already a consequence of the long-standing dominance of Project Planning. Too many young people think urban places with sidewalks, cafés, streets filled with people exist only in movies, foreign cities, or vacation sites. Authentic urbanism, however, time-tested and traditional, is not a lost art. The real thing exists. Knowing how to respect it, nurture it, and build on it is also rare. Thus, some observers erroneously believe that a hybrid suburban urbanism is possible. Suburbs are urbanizing. Cities are suburbanizing. While suburbs can gain from new or stronger centers, they cannot replace cities and they cannot shake their irrevocable dependency on cities. Cities, on the other hand, can only lose through suburbanization. The suburban city is an oxymoron. A thinning of a city erodes the very qualities needed for regeneration and stabilization. A distinction exists, and must continue to exist, between a city and a suburb.

Many urban dwellers resist this reality. They advocate or applaud suburbanizing influences, striving for the best of two contradictory worlds, the unachievable hybrid. Many are former suburbanites who moved for the alternative life a city offers. Some are onetime city residents who left for the suburbs to raise children and now have returned. Still others are long-time urban dwellers who yearn for a few suburban perks. The suburban influence grows. They bring a car-oriented life style. They thumb their noses at public transit, look down on those who have to ride with "them," the larger public. They drive within the city, want parking to stay cheap, and think highway tolls are excessive. They want a car life style in the city. They want society's less fortunate out of sight and out of mind. They want order, predictability, armed camp security, extreme cleanliness. They want neighborhood convenience and individualized shops, but want to be able to get in their cars to stock up on household goods at superstores. Many miss the irony of how easily they, not the poor, can take advantage of the sometimes lower prices, of how they use their expensive cars to save a few dollars and are able to store the bargains in their spare closets, row house attics, or apartment house basement storage rooms. *These are residents* of *the city, not city residents. They must make a choice.* They can't have both city and suburb.

At the same time, the urban impulse is bursting through even the most contrived suburban enclaves. This underscores the observation that the urban impulse has not died, but has just been suppressed. But that urban impulse should be cultivated in its rightful place, not transferred. The suburb is still a sub-urb, a dependent offshoot of a more complex urban center.

Sooner or later, the problems of the dense, intimidating city spread to the suburbs, sometimes in different guises. Parking lot crime grows, but is kept under wraps or minimized. Death by vehicular accident strikes 120 people each day around the country. Road rage is making headlines. Car crashes are the largest killers of Americans under age 35. Angry protests organize around less dramatic death statistics than that. Prime office tenants move out of specially-designed suburban complexes, leaving a job void and tax burden that parallel an earlier urban experience. Suburban malls lose retail anchors to mega-mergers and new-style retailing, much like urban department stores of an earlier generation. Gangs invade malls. Discomfiting racial and ethnic changes encroach on suburban monocultures, made more difficult by the unfamiliarity with different people. Traffic congestion, security measures, and distance from markets increase business costs. Car dependency robs family life in more ways than suburbanites anticipated.

Does it always have to come back to the automobile? It certainly does seem that way. Vincent Scully writes: "The automobile was, and remains, the agent of chaos, the breaker of the city...Whatever other factors have been involved in this disintegration of community, it is still the automobile—and how much we all love it—which has done the job." But eliminating the car is neither an option nor desirable. It is one of the modern era's most useful inventions. Even appropriately taming the car is not enough to repair the torn urban fabric. Most important is understanding and respecting the complexities that define and distinguish a city. To repair it, one must understand how it works. As Jane Jacobs noted in *The Death and Life of Great American Cities*:

> Automobiles are often conveniently tagged as the villains responsible for the ills of cities and the disappointments and futilities of city planning. But the destructive effects of automobiles are much less a cause than a symptom of our incompetence at city building. The simple needs of automobiles are more easily understood and satisfied than the complex needs of cities, and a growing number of planners and designers have come to believe that if they can only solve the problems

of traffic, they will thereby have solved the major problems of cities. Cities have much more intricate economic and social concerns than automobile traffic. How can you know what to try with traffic until you know how the city itself works, and what else it needs to do with its streets? You can't.

KEEP THE FOCUS ON SPRAWL AND UNDERSTAND THE VALUE OF DENSITY

Sprawl clearly undermines the rebirth potential for cities and makes it difficult for small towns and suburbs to maintain a stable center and gain strength from it. Changing direction is likely to hurt the pocketbooks of many who have profited handsomely from our misguided growth and whose influence and power are formidable. This creates a politically difficult impediment to healthy change.

The critical antidote to sprawl is density, concentration, and the rebuilding of centers. In essence, forging reconnections. Sprawl-related problems should be discussed, strategized, and coordinated within broad contexts and logical geographic sectors. Problems will, however, be solved with local solutions. This is how it is happening. Jurisdictions of every size are developing individualized transit programs to make welfare to workfare work in the many poor communities ill-served by meager transit. Corporations and small businesses establish day care programs to prevent the loss of valuable employees. General Motors is providing buses to bring suburban employees to its new downtown Detroit headquarters to minimize parking costs. Individualized, innovative farmland protection programs are emerging, community by community, each voted on and requiring taxpayer expense. Localities are developing their own innovative recycling and environmental programs to save money and improve the quality of their community. They are also revising zoning, building, and fire codes and passing landmark preservation ordinances to protect and build on the traditional elements that remain. Each solution is crafted to local idiosyncrasies, but offers ideas and inspiration for other communities to fashion parallel solutions. Standards and guideposts may be coming from a national or state agency, sometimes governmental, sometimes a private organization. Small towns and big cities, for example, fight to keep their post offices or resist conventional highway policies. Eventually, in Washington or in the state houses, if anyone is smart enough to recognize deficiencies, national and state policies will be forced to change. Proliferation of local solutions gather momentum from the bottom up to change policy. All the small-scale initiatives reported in this book address regional and national, even global, problems. "Think globally, act locally," the bumper sticker wisely instructs us. An increased coordination of infrastructure development and operation is definitely called for. What form that coordination takes is not the substance of the solution. Modification is possible. Local differences survive. Public process is key. And, at the heart of it all, are what Jane Jacobs called "adaptations, ameliorations, densifications, major rethinkings of subsidies, and above all, vision."

The process within which small initiatives are encouraged has variations. If one looks closely at what is really happening, observes change on the ground, listens and talks to people, questions official policies, gives more weight to the observable than to the statistical, and studies what works and what doesn't, one reaches the obvious conclusion that *deep trouble and serious problems still get fixed, piece by piece. Think big, devise a broad strategy, but develop the foundation on small actions and small components. Thinking globally and acting locally really works.*

Fix the worst house on a block, and others will invest on their own. Convert the first few warehouses or 1920s office buildings, and a momentum will build. Revive an historic theater and open the first restaurant, and an entertainment district may emerge. Reopen the corner store, the neighborhood café, the community center, and a community of neighbors will reconnect. Install speed humps and widen sidewalks, and pedestrian life will renew itself in unpredictable ways. Take down one piece of highway or remove the entrance/exit ramp, and a neighborhood can come back to life. Close a highway after an earthquake, and traffic disappears. Open a public market, and new businesses are born to fill nearby vacancies. Design a public space to be inviting to all instead of intimidating to most. Unlikely combinations of people will share that space in a secure atmosphere. None of this is guaranteed. But this book is filled with examples of such occurrences.

Skeptics insist that such successes are unique, "non-replicable." To replicate is not the point. To encourage a similar, but different, version, a local variation of a common theme, should be the goal. This works. Grandiose visions, utopian dreams, high-minded abstractions don't. Cities, towns, neighborhoods, commercial districts should be as unpredictable, diverse, idiosyncratic, shaped by the unexpected and colorful, as interesting as life itself.

One of Robert Moses' most memorable quotes was: "When you're working in an overbuilt metropolis, you have to hack your way through with a meat axe." We have been "hacking" away at our downtowns, once productively filled with buildings of all sizes, styles, and age, many adaptable for new uses over and over again and many replaceable with new ones. We have been similarly "hacking" away at our productive countryside, piling up unnecessary debt upon unnecessary debt to duplicate and triplicate expensive infrastructure, while letting publicly developed downtown infrastructure fall apart to the point of needing expensive public reinvestment. This is so ludicrous it boggles the mind.

"Hacking" today most often occurs in small, nibbling bites. An eight-story, solid 19th-century warehouse with SoHo-style potential is replaced by a one-story retail-only mall. A row of Main Street buildings with upper-story residential potential loses out to a single-story, one-store windowless box. Buildings go down, parking goes up. Neighborhood shopping streets are lost, along with the dense, mixed scale of housing that once supported them. In their place come rows upon rows of poor-quality, suburban-style single-family homes without the density to support either local shopping or mass transit. Car suburbs in the city are no approximation of the trolley-car neighborhoods they replace.

The SoHo Syndrome struggles to take root in car-dependent, suburbanized downtowns, separated, segregated, and isolated by overscaled mega-projects. Local economies and the tradition of free competition will continue to be undermined, as long as national superstores and global corporations with short-term appeal are indirectly subsidized on the urban and rural landscape with publicly financed infrastructure. These corporations, along with the vast transportation lobby existing around the automobile and oil industries, have become the real professional planners of the country. Where they choose to locate, what form they demand to build in, the destruction they argue is necessary to create jobs—all these boardroom decisions shape everything around them. *Corporations shape the landscape and life style for everybody.* Ironically, some of the fiercest property rights defenders oppose zoning and building code changes to contain sprawl, but show no resistance to corporate planners who have taken the public destiny into their own hands. *The anger and resistance to superstores and national retailers on a local level is as much about the expanding corporate control of American life on the national level. Big corporate interests elbow out small private interests and in the name of "job creation" preclude "entrepreneur creation."*

Urbanism must be understood as more than urbane amenities scattered between and within self-contained projects, more than cultural institutions, public parks, sports stadiums, attractive street furnishings, clean streets, and public art. Those are critical urbane embellishments, not the urban essence. The basics run deeper and are more complex than such surface attractions. Diverse economic functions evolve naturally in proximity to each other, giving strength to a whole that would not survive if distance separated the parts. Infrastructure costs are contained, lessening the unacceptable strains on public budgets of the smallest town and largest city. Cultural and leisure time amenities draw local and distant audiences sufficient to support them and add immeasurably to the locale's importance and quality of life. The public realm is fostered in a manner consistent with the democratic principles to which so much lip service is paid.

Traditional urban districts illustrate, above all, that genuine economic development, healthy growth, dramatic change—in short, dynamic and regenerative transformation—are all possible without a wholesale replacement of built places. Respect for existing buildings does not mean some can't be replaced or added onto. It does mean that new buildings are not necessary to foster creative and positive change. For too long, Project Planners have dismissed defenders of traditional urban districts as opponents of change, growth, progress—NIMBY (Not In My Back Yard). Nonsense! *Such defenders of the authentic, functional place are the true promoters of economic development and positive change.* Such defenders need to take the offensive. Where necessary, they should cease compromises that only change the scale but not the nature of change. Opposition to Project Plans should get stronger.

Architect John Belle, then-president of the American Institute of Architects (AIA), noted in his presidential address to the 1996 national AIA convention, "Preservation and the reuse of older buildings has long been synonymous in the United States with fringe groups, saving a building to which they have an emotional attachment. It is time that the true value of renovation, restoration, and reuse take center stage, for they are the front line of sustainable design." The same can be said of mass transit advocates, community developers, farmland preservationists, open-space advocates, small business promoters, Main Street rebuilders, and manufacturing promoters. Reality requires such civic defenders to be more, not less, aggressive. Despite the proven value of the traditional basics, despite the illustrated longing of the public for alternatives to car-dependent living, despite the unending exposure of past mistakes and continuous successes of rule-defying efforts, we continue to tear down instead of value. Stadiums proliferate where centers could be reborn. Project Planning precepts are shamelessly repeated as gospel. Lessons are unceasingly ignored or misinterpreted. We are in more trouble than we recognize.

NEW LIFE DOWNTOWN

There is good news, however. A different planning mindset has been taking root, growing out of the renewal battles of the 1960s, 1970s, and 1980s, infused with varying degrees of genuine respect for traditional urbanism where it exists, sensitized by the sterility of post-war planning and development, and influenced by the environmental movement. This new, forward-thinking planning mindset has been a minority influence for years but is increasingly visible. This can't be measured. If one gets around enough, observes enough places, and talks to enough involved participants, one senses a new groundswell. It has taken root, but not yet taken over. Young city planners, community advocates, neighborhood and small private developers, innovative architects, historic preservationists, transportation planners, and environmentalists are working in agencies and development organizations, bringing a fresh perspective not burdened by the orthodoxies of the Project Planners. Graduating students come to the professions with a different experience and more environmental awareness than ever. A small but growing number of mayors, governors, legislators, and other public officials recognize the fiscal wisdom of husbanding existing places, infrastructure, and resources. Amazingly, they sound like Urban Husbanders. The citizen army opposing the excessive and advocating the modest is increasing. The number and membership of the advocacy groups swells daily. An increasing number of developers and banks are discovering that following an Urban Husbandry course can be profitable. The signs bode well for increasing positive change.

As Norman Mailer's words indicated on the first page, "I feel the hints, the clues, the whisper of a new time coming." Activists at the most local level are sowing the seeds of change. Nibble by nibble, they are reversing the mistakes of the past, dispelling myths, repairing the "hacked"-up landscape, reweaving torn districts, reconnecting people and places, rebuilding the public realm, and repairing democracy itself. Citizen leaders will show the way. Smart government officials will follow and, in the process, become great leaders. With all of them rests the hope of a brighter future.

---

1. The term "the New Urbanism" wasn't coined until 1992 or 1993. Design and market consultant Peter Katz and Judith A. Corbett, executive director of the Sacramento-based Local Government Commission, were both looking for terms to describe what they were separately promoting. Corbett chose Livable Communities for the Commission's work and Katz and a group of like-minded architects decided on the New Urbanism. These architects were independently doing similar work, among them Peter Calthorpe, Andres Duany, Elizabeth Plater-Zyberk, Elizabeth Moule, Stefanos Polyzoides, and were included in Peter Katz's 1994 book, *The New Urbanism* (New York: McGraw-Hill Inc.). Two documents, the Ahwahnee Principles of the Local Government Commission and the Charter of the Congress for the New Urbanism, articulate the core principles of New Urbanists.
2. Modern Library Edition, 1963, p. 262.
3. See *The Living City*, pp. 164–67, for this success story.
4. June 30, 1997.
5. The term "newsie" was first applied to newsboys selling papers on the street. Over time, it has shifted to newsstands.

INDEX

Index

Index

Index

Index